Ways of Knowing

The First-Year Seminar Anthology

Belmont University
FIFTH EDITION
2019

Editor: Daniel Schafer
Introduction: Noel Boyle

Editorial Board: Noel Boyle, Ann Coble,
Nathan Griffith, Charmion Gustke, Mona Ivey-Soto,
Peter Kuryla, Daniel Schafer

Acknowledgments:

pp. 1-2: From "Statement on Liberal Learning" by Association of American Colleges & Universities. Reprinted by permission.

pp. 23–29, 90–111: From *Plato: Complete Works* edited by John M. Cooper, Translated by G. M. A. Grube. Copyright © 1997 by Hackett Publishing Company, Inc. Reprinted by permission.

pp. 30–40: From *Why Teach? In Defense of Real Education* by Mark Edmundson. Copyright © 2013 by Mark Edmundson. Reprinted by permission fo Bloomsbury USA.

pp. 41–61: From *Love Your Enemies: How Decent People Can Save America from the Culture of Contempt* by Arthur C. Brooks. Copyright © 2019 by Broadside Books. Reprinted by permission of the publisher.

pp. 62–79: As appeared in *The Atlantic Monthly*, September, 2015. Copyright © 2015 by The Atlantic Media, Inc. Reprinted by permission of the publisher.

pp. 80–89: From *Life's Too Short to Pretend You're Not Religious* by David Dark. Copyright © 2016 by InterVarsity Press. Reprinted by permission of the publisher.

pp. 120–128: From *Discourse on Method and Meditations on First Philosophy*, Fourth Edition, by René Descartes, translated by Donald A. Cress. Copyright © 1998 by Hackett Publishing Company, Inc. Reprinted by permission.

pp. 129–142: From: *UFOs, Chemtrails, and Aliens: What Science Says* by Donald R. Prothero and Timothy D. Callahan. Copyright © 2017 by Indiana University Press. Reprinted by permission of the publisher.

4750 Venture Drive, Suite 400
Ann Arbor, MI 48108
800-562-2147
www.xanedu.com

Contents

Statement on Liberal Education
Association of American Colleges & Universities

"Statement on Liberal Education," adopted by the Board of Directors of the Association of American Colleges & Universities October 1, 1998. Available from https://www.aacu.org/about/statements/liberal-education

The Association of American Colleges & Universities *is a national organization headquartered in Washington, D.C. that focuses on advancing liberal education and improving the quality of undergraduate teaching.*

Why we are reading this: *This statement, adopted by the Board of Directors in October 1998, lays out a concise description of the ideals and goals of liberal education in the United States.*

A truly liberal education is one that prepares us to live responsible, productive, and creative lives in a dramatically changing world. It is an education that fosters a well-grounded intellectual resilience, a disposition toward lifelong learning, and an acceptance of responsibility for the ethical consequences of our ideas and actions. Liberal education requires that we understand the foundations of knowledge and inquiry about nature, culture and society; that we master core skills of perception, analysis, and expression; that we cultivate a respect for truth; that we recognize the importance of historical and cultural context; and that we explore connections among formal learning, citizenship, and service to our communities.

We experience the benefits of liberal learning by pursuing intellectual work that is honest, challenging, and significant, and by preparing ourselves to use knowledge and power in responsible ways. Liberal learning is not confined to particular fields of study. What matters in liberal education is substantial content, rigorous methodology and an active engagement with the societal, ethical, and practical implications of our learning. The spirit and value of liberal learning are equally relevant to all forms of higher education and to all students.

Because liberal learning aims to free us from the constraints of ignorance, sectarianism, and myopia, it prizes curiosity and seeks to expand the boundaries of human knowledge. By its nature, therefore, liberal learning is global and pluralistic. It embraces the diversity of ideas and experiences that characterize the social, natural, and intellectual

1

world. To acknowledge such diversity in all its forms is both an intellectual commitment and a social responsibility, for nothing less will equip us to understand our world and to pursue fruitful lives.

The ability to think, to learn, and to express oneself both rigorously and creatively, the capacity to understand ideas and issues in context, the commitment to live in society, and the yearning for truth are fundamental features of our humanity. In centering education upon these qualities, liberal learning is society's best investment in our shared future.

Introduction: Liberal Education, Knowledge, and Belmont's First-Year Seminar
Noel Boyle

Noel Boyle (b. 1973) is a professor in Belmont's Philosophy Department, where he specializes in philosophy of mind and philosophy of science. In addition to teaching introductory and upper-level philosophy courses, he regularly teaches First-Year Seminar. In his scholarly work, he examines consciousness through physical and phenomenological approaches. In 2017, he was named Director of the BELL Core, Belmont's distinctive general education program.

Why we are reading this: Dr. Boyle draws upon major thinkers both ancient and modern to outline a more detailed description and defense of liberal learning than the AAC&U statement above. He also lays out how the First-Year Seminar and other courses in the BELL Core are designed to advance students' liberal education.

Shortly before becoming my undergraduate advisor, Stephen Rowe wrote of a paradox in acquiring a liberal education.[1] As college attendance rates soar, our cultural understanding of the nature of a college education diminishes. More students than ever have access to liberal education, but students can't take full advantage of that access because they don't genuinely understand what a liberal education is. Nearly thirty years on, the trend continues. Ever larger numbers of students are going to wonderful institutions that carefully preserve the tradition of liberal education, but that has almost nothing to do with why the students choose to go there. Not understanding the fullness of the opportunity available to them, students graduate less impacted by their education than they ought to have been.

First-Year Seminar exists to help you (incoming Belmont freshmen) unlock these paradoxes and make the most of your Belmont education. My goal in this introduction is to summarize an intellectual terrain in which you can place Belmont's general education program, the First-Year Seminar course, and this anthology.

---

[1] Stephen Rowe, "Access to a Vision: Claiming a Liberal Education," introduction to *Claiming a Liberal Education*, ed. by Stephen Rowe (Course Book for Introduction to Liberal Education at GVSU in Allendale, MI), 1991.

The Socratic Spirit

The underlying spirit of liberal education is perhaps best conveyed through the life and outlook of an ancient Athenian named Socrates (470-399 BCE). Most of what we know about Socrates we infer from the writings of his student, Plato. Socrates was eminently literate, but he refused to write anything of philosophical significance, preferring oral discourse. After Socrates' eventual execution on spurious charges, the aristocratic young Plato dedicated the rest of his life to preserving the Socratic legacy.

The *Apology* is Plato's account of Socrates' defense while on trial. In it, Socrates relates the story of when his friend, Chaerephon, asked the oracle at Delphi and was told that there is no one in Athens wiser than Socrates.[2] I suspect Chaerephon found nothing surprising in the oracle's response, but Socrates did. After all, Socrates was painfully aware that he did not possess substantive wisdom. He was in pursuit of wisdom. He was a philosopher, literally a "friend or lover of wisdom." The oracle's response left Socrates in a bind. Lacking wisdom, he could not accept the oracle's declaration. Deeply and sincerely religious, he could not fail to accept it.

He went in search of someone with wisdom, intending to bring this person before the oracle to seek clarification. He consistently found that those who were thought to be wise, or who claimed to be wise, did not actually possess the wisdom alleged. Socrates eventually concluded that he was wiser than them because, though neither he nor his interlocutors had knowledge of, say, the nature of justice, Socrates knew that he did not know. The people that Socrates talked to did not even know that they didn't know. So, Socrates knew something they didn't. Socrates eventually concluded that the oracle meant that the highest wisdom possible for human beings is knowledge of the limits of their knowledge. Only the gods actually possess wisdom. He further concluded that the gods intended him to spend his life showing his fellow Athenians that they do not know many of the things they think they know, imploring them to turn their attention to seeking knowledge and wisdom.

In an iconic quote, Socrates said, "the unexamined life is not worth living."[3] We all enter adult life with various beliefs that we have never questioned, that we simply assume to be true. We may think everyone

---

[2] For details about Socrates' biography I'm drawing from: Plato, *Apology* in *Plato Complete Works*, ed. John Cooper (Hackett Publishing: Indianapolis, 1997).

[3] Plato, *Apology* in *Plato Complete Works*, ed. John Cooper (Indianapolis: Hackett Publishing, 1997), 38a.

4

shares the belief, or even find it too obvious to think of it as a belief. Many people live unexamined lives, in which they never identify and test such beliefs to see if they are worth holding. Shielding themselves from such examination, many people will only discuss fundamental questions of religion, morality, and politics with those they know will agree with them. Or, looking to avoid a lack of certainty, people will latch onto some ideological framework for seeing the world and refuse to entertain the possibility that the basic framework is misguided. When such ideologies take hold, new information cannot reshape people's system of ideas; the system of ideas reshapes their new information. The foundational principles of the ideology are outside the bounds of discussion. And anyone who sees the world differently is a fool, a puppet, a crony, or a villain. As a result of these and similar strategies, most people go through life rarely even wondering if their beliefs are actually true, never growing in their basic understanding of the world, never changing actions and dispositions, never improving as human beings.

They are, we are, like the prisoners in Plato's famous "The Allegory of the Cave." In the allegory, Socrates asks us to imagine a group of men who are imprisoned in a cave, able to only look forward. They see only a series of images on the wall of the cave. They become quite absorbed in predicting what image will come next, and other such games. Suddenly, one among them is freed from the chains. He turns around to see that the images on the wall are nothing more than shadows cast by various little statues of things like horses and trees, with light from the fire inside the cave. Ascending out of the cave, he comes to see actual horses and trees and such. Feeling called to help, he returns to the cave to free the others. They think he is a pesky dreamer, a weaver of fantasy, an irritant. After all, he doesn't even know or care what image might appear next on the wall of the cave. Some in the cave think he has lost his mind. They even threaten him with violence.

Like the prisoners in Plato's cave, our basic understanding of the world is largely framed by factors entirely outside of our control or choice. Where and when humans are born almost entirely determines how we will frame and attempt to resolve questions about morality, religion, politics, even art. Yet, like the prisoners in the cave, the overwhelming majority of human beings go through life considering their understanding of such questions to be the final word on the truth of the matter. No one entirely escapes conflating their own prejudices with objective reality. Like the prisoners in the cave, our lives largely proceed on an unquestioned assumption that our viewpoint on the world is the world as it actually is. We assume that appearance (how it seems to me) and reality (what it actually is) are aligned. But things are not what they seem.

5

Plato's image of ascending out of a cave of ignorance is an ideal metaphor for liberal education. At first it is disorienting and sometimes trudging. But then, like Plato said of philosophy generally, "like a blaze kindled from a leaping spark, it is generated in the soul and - at once - becomes self-sustaining."[4] Liberal education is map and fuel for an attempted escape from Plato's cave.

A Socratic disposition toward one's own beliefs offers inoculation against the ideological and dogmatic life of cave dwellers. While most people seem to be in love with their opinions, Socrates preferred being proven wrong to being proven right. He had no interest in scoring rhetorical points for some ideology. He treated his ethical, political, and theological inclinations as suspicious sources of probable falsehood, not as absolute principles of uncompromising conscience. If he was mistaken on some topic, he would rather lose an argument and change his belief than win the argument by some luck or trickery. He refused to believe anything merely because it was conventional wisdom, or because he had been told to believe it.

In conversations, he skillfully rooted out the unquestioned beliefs of others and subjected them to almost ruthless logical examination. He actively sought out those whose views differed from his own, seeking a different perspective from which to look upon his own view. Through the process of seeking out productive intellectual conflict, by putting divergent views into critical interchange, Socrates repeatedly showed people that their worldview was far too simplistic to be true. He left them with the suggestion that they could hope to gain wisdom and virtue only through hard intellectual work.

Ultimately, in 399 BCE, Socrates was tried and convicted on charges of corrupting the youth and being an atheist. He was executed. Though he was no atheist, I suppose there was something to the charge of corrupting the youth. He taught young people to think for themselves, to question what they had been told by teachers, parents, priests, or any other authority figure. He taught them to put the pursuit of wisdom and virtue in the center of their lives, and to ignore the attractions of money and power. He taught them to have the courage and discipline to live according to their convictions. He taught them to speak truth to the face of tyranny, and do so without fear for their lives, because suffering injustice is not as bad as doing injustice. Some people still consider it a form of corruption to teach young people to think like that. They are wrong. It is the best advice that a young person could possibly get.

---

[4] Plato, *Seventh Letter* in *Plato Complete Works*, ed. John Cooper (Indianapolis: Hackett Publishing, 1997).

On one of multiple levels of possible interpretation, the hero in Plato's allegory, the cave dweller who was freed from his chains and ascended to see things as they truly are, was Socrates himself. Having a deeper wisdom than others, a wisdom that left him in pursuit of wisdom, Socrates made himself into an exemplary human being by cultivating *arete*, virtue or excellence, in his soul. Analogous to the petty cave squabbles over prizes given for correctly predicting the next image on the cave wall, in the *Apology* Socrates asserts that Athenians show the greatest concern for the least important things and the least concern for the most important things. They dedicate their lives to pursuing power, wealth, and honors while giving no consideration to the goodness of their own souls.

John Stuart Mill said that, "no intelligent human being would consent to be a fool, no instructed person would be an ignoramus."[5] Plato suggests the same notion when Socrates points out, almost in passing, that no one who has left the cave could fail to pity those who are still in it. The freed former prisoner knows what the still imprisoned do not; he knows that what is useful inside the cave counts for nothing against the importance of getting out of the cave. At the end of the *Apology*, having been sentenced to death, speaking directly to the Athenian people, he foretold that others, younger and more numerous, would continue to question both themselves and others in the way Socrates had been doing. He declared that it is neither possible nor good to escape such examination.

Plato wrote the *Apology* and the "Allegory of the Cave" a generation after Socrates' death, when he was likely already running a thriving school of Socratic philosophy called the Academy.[6] Plato putting such a "foretelling" in Socrates' mouth was probably intended to be partially tongue-in-cheek. But the story hardly ends there. With some interruptions, Plato's school would remain open for nearly a thousand years. Its name would enter our language, in multiple forms general enough to cover nearly anything related to the pursuit of knowledge. In fact, it is now common to refer to the entire system of universities and colleges as "the academy."

The Nature and Purpose of Liberal Education

Today's academy is the descendant of Plato's Academy; the spirit of Socratic enquiry is what lies behind and unites the core mission of these schools as institutions dedicated to the pursuit of truth and knowledge. The

---

[5] John Stuart Mill, *Utilitarianism* (Indianapolis: Hackett Publishing, 2002).
[6] The exact date of composition for all of Plato's writings is unknown and is, in fact, a point of contentious scholarly debate.

name for this historical core of the university mission is "liberal education," and the various subject matters studied that are relevant to that core mission are called "liberal arts."

At Belmont, like nearly all universities, there is a general education program that constitutes the core liberal arts education shared by all the students. The First-Year Seminar (FYS) is the first and foundational step in that program. In order to do well in the course, and to get the most out of your Belmont education, it is crucial that you understand something of the nature, value, and purpose of liberal education. You've indicated an intention to get a liberal education; you ought to know what one is.

Liberal education can be described in terms of its *content*: it is a broad-based education in which students have at least a cursory familiarity with the most important discoveries, ideas, and contributions of the academic disciplines. It can also be described in terms of its underlying *value* system: it cherishes integrity, sincerity, diversity, rigor, and, above all, truth. Liberal education can also be described in terms of the *impact* it has on the student: a liberally educated person is curious, well-informed, deliberative, open-minded, and rational.

Even where this general picture is broadly understood, there are several misconceptions about the liberal arts to overcome. Primary among them is that the liberal arts cannot be meaningfully distinguished from other arts. Though other distinctions can be made, it is most crucial to distinguish between the liberal, professional, and fine arts. The professional arts, such as medicine or accounting, are pursued for their usefulness to society and for the profit that comes to those who have mastered them. The fine arts, such as musical performance, theater, or painting are pursued for their beauty and capacity to enrich human experience. The liberal arts are pursued for their own sake; their pursuit and possession is the manifestation and fulfillment of human curiosity.

Traditionally conceived, there were seven liberal arts, in two groups. The *trivium* consisted of grammar, rhetoric, and logic. Through the study of these arts, students learned how to construct linguistic expressions properly, with beauty and persuasive appeal, and in accord with reason. The *quadrivium* consisted of arithmetic, geometry, music (by which they meant music theory), and astronomy. The relation between these four arts is fascinating. Arithmetic is the study of number; geometry is the study of number in space; music is the study of number in time; astronomy, considered the crowning gem, is the study of number in time and space simultaneously. Considering all seven arts together, a liberal education is an education in words and numbers. Though no liberal arts education is still structured around the *trivium* and the *quadrivium*, no understanding of the contemporary liberal arts is complete without an awareness of these historical roots.[7]

Such historical understanding evades another all too common misconception: that the natural sciences (such as physics, chemistry, biology) are not among the liberal arts. Many mistakenly think the liberal arts include only the humanities (such as philosophy, literature, and religion), or that the liberal arts are the humanities along with the social sciences (such as history, sociology, political science). There is an important distinction, even a misguided rivalry, between the natural sciences and the humanities, but that is a distinction within the liberal arts, one roughly akin to the older distinction between the *trivium* and the *quadrivium*. Further confusing things, some now mistakenly think the liberal arts are a contrasting term to the very newly constructed group called STEM (science, technology, engineering, mathematics). STEM is largely a political and economic construct, originating only a couple decades ago, with a focus on advancing certain economic sectors perceived as both lucrative for students and aligned with the national interest. While science and math are among the liberal arts, technology and engineering are among the professional arts. Though discoveries and innovations of the natural sciences are often valuable commercially, science itself is uninterested in profit and is motivated by curiosity. In short, there is a distinction between science and technology, between science and the marketable application of science.

Any variety of misconceptions about the nature of liberal education arise from the meaning of "liberal." The use of "liberal" in "liberal education" has nothing at all to do with the liberal-conservative distinction that is the obsession of our media and the poison of our politics. "Liberal" is from the Latin *liber*, meaning "to free." If you understand the relationship between a broad-based education and freedom then you have come very far in grasping the purpose of a liberal education.

Though it does not resonate well with contemporary values or economics, a liberal education was long understood as proper for persons free from want and labor. It existed for a wealthy class who could afford to study without thought of profit or professional credential but were nevertheless expected to have a certain breadth of understanding and a cultured disposition. There were things that people of a certain class were

---

[7] For a clear exposition of the *trivium* and *quadrivium*, as well as a defense of their continued importance, see Mark Van Doren, *Liberal Education* (New York: Henry Holt and Company, 1943). For a recent account of the history of liberal education in America, including a defense of its underlying values, see Michael S. Roth, *Beyond the University: Why Liberal Education Matters* (New Haven, CT: Yale UP, 2014).

expected to know and understand. While this vision rightly strikes us as elitist, that is because we think wealth ought to be earned and that all people should be free. Nevertheless, I think we should agree that free people, possessed of the dignity of self-determination, ought to know certain things, possess certain skills, and display certain virtues. Free people ought to be educated people, and there are certain things that educated people know.

While there is no definitive or uncontested list of the contents of an educated mind, one can paint a mosaic that indicates the general essence. Educated people have a sound familiarity with the broad outlines of contemporary science. They can intelligently discuss something of genetics, neuroscience, geological timeframes, and astronomical distances. Educated people know the broad outline of civilization's historical arc and the varieties of human societies. They can intelligently discuss something of ancient Greek family structure, Hindu religious beliefs, or the cause and effect of the emergence of modern Israel. Educated people have read a broad range of literature. They can intelligently participate in a discussion ranging over James Joyce, Jane Austen, Shakespeare, Gabriel Garcia Marquez, and Toni Morrison. Educated people have at least encountered those landmark figures through whom human beings have confronted and addressed the most fundamental questions about the nature of existence, the limits of knowledge, and the meaning of human life. They can at least say something of Plato, Aristotle, St. Thomas Aquinas, Rene Descartes, Friedrich Nietzsche, Karl Marx, and maybe even Ludwig Wittgenstein. As I mentioned, no such list could be definitive, and mine certainly is shaped by my own intellectual background and interests. The point is that the world is a complex place that humans have tried, over all of human history, to explain and understand through science, literature, philosophy, mathematics, cultural studies, etc. Becoming educated involves a substantive encounter with the basic scaffolding of the full range of those efforts.

The purpose of such knowledge for free people has, of course, nothing to with appearing impressive at a cocktail party. The reason that free people ought to be educated was best expressed by Aristotle. In another way of understanding the connection between liberal education and freedom, Aristotle held that a liberal education provides the freedom to express our nature and live properly as human beings. Aristotle famously noted that "man is a rational animal."[8] Distinguishing us from all other

---

[8] Aristotle, *Politics* in *The Complete Works of Aristotle*, ed. Johnathan Barnes (New Jersey: Princeton UP, 1984), 1253a. The traditional translation of this passage as "man is a rational animal" is disputable. A precise translation might

kinds of things, human beings engage in "activity of the soul in accord with reason."[9] In short, we think, use our minds, explore, puzzle things out, and try to understand. Engaging in such activities is proper to us in the sense that it is the most definitive way in which a human being can be human. Just as the best acorn is the one that most expresses its nature by becoming a majestic oak, the best human being is the one who grows over the span of a lifetime to become the most flourishing exemplar of rational activities of the soul. A human life that is good and happy has a central role for thought, reason, and knowledge, using such understanding to guide action. Life lived otherwise is still biologically human, but it does not fully manifest what is uniquely human. Aristotle would say it is a warped and degraded form of human existence. His position shouldn't be interpreted as degrading people denied the opportunity to be educated (by poverty, tyranny, or disease). On the contrary, it upholds their dignity by demanding that the existential nature of what they have been denied be acknowledged.

Under ideal conditions, a healthy acorn will become a magnificent oak as a matter of natural course. No other oak will have to teach it how to make new branches. To get it to live against its nature, you would have to intervene to steer it away from what is proper to it. Human beings seem just the opposite. We need to be educated in order to fully express our nature. It is when we are left to our own devices that we tend to become warped, distorted by the pursuit of pleasure, wealth, or power.[10]

As an expression of our rational nature, human beings seek out what Cardinal John Newman described as knowledge worth having "for its own sake."[11] Some things we want to know for their *instrumental value*; we want to know because it will be useful in getting some further thing. I might want to know where there is a good auto mechanic because I need to get my car fixed. I'm not just curious; I have a reason for learning about local mechanics. The kind of knowledge that Newman describes is prized for its *intrinsic value*; we want to know just for the sake of knowing. There

---

be, "the human alone of the animals possesses speech." Nevertheless, the idea that rationality distinguishes human beings from other animals is infused throughout the Aristotelian corpus, especially *De Anima, Nicomachean Ethics, Physics,* and *Metaphysics*.

[9] Aristotle, *Nicomachean Ethics* in *The Complete Works of Aristotle*, ed. Johnathan Barnes (New Jersey: Princeton UP, 1984), 1098a.

[10] My parable of the acorn and oak is adapted from Aristotle, *Physics* in *The Complete Works of Aristotle*, ed. Johnathan Barnes (New Jersey: Princeton UP, 1984), 192b.

[11] Cardinal John Henry Newman, *The Idea of a University* (Notre Dame UP), 1982. Originally published in 1854.

is something inherently fascinating about the inner happenings of black holes, the structure of a Bach symphony, the politics of ancient Athens, or the social life of elephant tribes. Satisfying such curiosities is not a matter of idle cocktail party chatter. Deep yet wandering curiosity is a basic feature of human nature. The world is an interesting place and it is in the nature of a human being to be interested in it.

Besides making us free to express our true nature, Aristotle might also point out that a liberal education frees us from ignorance about the causes of things. The idea is a simple one. As children, we don't know how the world works and we therefore don't know what we ought to behave. We are lead to superstitions and tempted by ideologies, both for the easy explanations they seem to offer. By learning how the world actually works, there is a greatly undervalued opportunity to overcome superstition and be armed against ideology.

To say that liberal knowledge is pursued as an expression of our nature, and that it is a kind of knowledge pursued for its own sake, is not to imply that there is no effect or consequence of being liberally educated. That it does not have career preparation as its purpose does not mean that it does not prepare you for anything. Another way in which the "liberal" in "liberal education" has been understood is that liberal learning provides the knowledge required to effectively exercise the rights of free citizens. A liberal education helps you approach the scientific, cultural, and historical facts relevant to exercising your right to self-determination in a way that is informed and effective. It molds an intellectual disposition that lets you make the most of your freedom and construct your own path toward the flourishing of yourself, your community, and your world.

We say democracy is good, but rarely ask why. "Democracy" is Greek and it means, roughly, "rule by the people." Presumably, it is only good for the people to rule if the people are both capable and willing. Otherwise, the society will not be fertile ground for human flourishing. Plato opposed democracy, thinking it a fatally flawed form of government. In Plato's *Gorgias*, Socrates explains that ignorant people are easy prey for those who would manipulate the masses, shaping public opinion and exploiting the people's ignorance in the pursuit of power, wealth, or fame.[12] In modern democracies, universal public education is not just a social service. It is the bedrock institution that ensures the next generation of citizens will have the knowledge, skills, and temperament necessary to

---

[12] Plato, *Gorgias* in *Plato Complete Works*, ed. John Cooper (Hackett Publishing: Indianapolis, 1997), 464d/ 490a.

govern themselves prudently and effectively.[13] As I mentioned earlier, free people need to be educated people.

Consider the freedoms enshrined in the American constitution. Does the constitution guarantee that Americans are free? Yes, in one sense. Americans have, for instance, freedom of speech. If you want to say that President Trump is a Nazi trying to control every aspect of daily life, then go ahead. Say what you want. No one can tell you that your speech is prohibited (though they can refuse to listen). John Dewey calls this *external* freedom, freedom from external constraint.[14] Properly understood, privately considered, external freedom is a tool and not an end in itself. Consider the case of Larry Flynt, publisher of Hustler magazine. He wrapped himself in the American flag and proclaimed that his pornographic publication is the highest expression of the freedom of speech. He was wrong. I don't have a position on whether pornography is inherently immoral, but I do assert that it is among the lowest possible expressions of the freedoms of speech and press. There are vastly better, more valuable, and more important things to print and say.

Dewey cherishes *internal* freedom, which requires not merely the absence of external constraint, but also the presence of an internal capacity to deliberatively form and act upon a purpose of one's own construction. The constitution has enshrined your right to say more or less whatever you wish. Now it is incumbent on you to form in yourself something worth saying and listening to, something worthy of your unique presence in the world. You have to decide what you will do with your freedoms, and whether you will make the most of them on behalf of yourself and others. The most available and reliable path for developing the capacity to deploy your freedoms in ways that bring meaning and significance to your life is a traditional liberal education, with its broad base of factual knowledge about the world combined with certain skills of reasoning, communication, and reflection.

---

[13] Some will point out that we have a constitutional republic, in which the citizens vote to determine which few among us will engage in political action, not a democracy in which the citizens directly move the levers of power. But it amounts to the same thing for this point. We have built a civilization on the principle self-determination, of the fundamental freedom of each individual. In our constitutional republic, it may be the case that only a few "rule" in the sense of engaging directly in political action. Nevertheless, each individual is left to rule him or herself.

[14] John Dewey, *Experience and Education* (Free Press: New York, 1997). Originally published in 1938.

It is sometimes said that this kind of liberal education is "useless." Brand Blanshard best explained the flaw in this comment.[15] He started with the familiar distinction between means and ends. Some things, appropriately called "useful," are desired for the sake of other things. A hammer is useful because it is used to drive in a nail. Knowledge of how to fix cars is useful for making a living fixing people's cars.

Some things, however, are not desired because they are useful; they are not means used for pursuing some further end; they are those desired ends that the useful things aim toward. Happiness, security, and love are, strictly speaking, useless. You cannot use true love or happiness to get ahead in the world. But we don't desire love because it useful. We desire love directly. Blanshard refers to "the transcendent usefulness of useless things." Useless things like love and happiness have a value that transcends usefulness and thus they become useful in a different, and higher sense. They are not the tools used to achieve human flourishing; they partly constitute human flourishing.

Knowledge of the world and our place in it is one such transcendently useful thing. It need not prove its effectiveness in helping us attain worthwhile things in order to display its value. The worth of such an education is not reducible to its tangible value in the market. Knowledge of the how and why of things is worthwhile as a source of direct and genuine satisfaction in human life. Education is best treasured not as the means of making of a living, but as the end to which those are directed. It seems our society's way of thinking is backward: we value education as a way to make money; we've lost sight of the fact that money should be valued as a means and education should be valued as an end.

As Blanchard summarized at the end of his essay,

> The educators of the West were those restlessly active people, the Greeks. But not one ship or bridge, not one palace or fortress or temple that their impatient activity erects has come down to us except as a ruin... Does anything of them remain? Yes, the Greek spirit remains, the thought of Plato remains, the art of Sophocles, the logic and ethics of Aristotle... No doubt there were hardheaded practical men in Athens who stopped before the door of Plato's Academy and asked what was the use of it all. They and their names have vanished; the little Academy became a thousand academies among nations then

---

[15] Brand Blanshard, "The Uses of a Liberal Education," in *The Uses of a Liberal Education: and Other Talks to Students* (Chicago: Open Court Publishing, 1977), 27-43.

unborn. There is a moral, I think, in this history. It is the usefulness, the transcendent usefulness, of useless things.[16]

Belmont and the BELL Core

Today, there are many kinds of higher education; "the Academy" has grown quite diverse. After all, much education today is in arts other than the liberal arts.

An education in a professional art characteristically consists of courses leading to recognized professional credentials such as an RN, MSW, OT and so on. Also in the category of professional education is the pursuit of equally practical but not formally recognized credentials in marketing, finance, public relations, and so on. I think it fair to say that this is the type of education that is most in demand. Parents think such education is prudent and politicians think it drives economic growth. Plenty of evidence suggests they are both right.

Parents and politicians are far more reticent to support fine arts education. Tragically, we have come to see expression through music, painting, theatre, etc. as mere entertainment, something secondary in priority to money making activities. We are an enormously wealthy society, but we are not a particularly accomplished artistic society. We have forgotten that markets serve to make life possible, but art makes life worthwhile. Count me among those who firmly believe that our culture needs more, not less, fine and performing arts education.

Belmont University is a hybrid institution, with strong programs in the professional, fine (especially performing), and liberal arts. As the Mission Statement says, Belmont is committed to "bringing together the best of liberal arts and professional education in a Christian community of learning and service." Belmont has formalized its commitment to this ideal as a member of The New American Colleges & Universities, an association self-described as being "dedicated to the purposeful integration of liberal education, professional studies, and civic engagement."[17]

As a professor in Belmont's Philosophy Department, I'm keen to point out that Belmont is a wonderful place to major in a broad range of the liberal arts. As is typical of Belmont's liberal arts programs, our philosophy majors and minors form a vibrant intellectual community doing excellent work. Every year, Belmont philosophy graduates head off

---

[16] Blanshard, "Uses of a Liberal Education," 43.
[17] See the Association of New American Colleges & Universities website at, www.anac.org, accessed May 5, 2015.

to philosophy graduate school, law school, and a wide range of other destinations. Graduates from our department are teachers, attorneys, ministers, and university professors. One is a former director of Amnesty International in North America. Another was a researcher on the Mars Rover project at NASA. The other liberal arts departments at Belmont all have similar stories.

Though we have some excellent liberal arts programs, the vast majority of Belmont students major in one of the professional or performing arts, especially Belmont's nationally recognized programs in music, business, health care, and the music industry. As a result, for the vast majority of students, a Belmont education consists of two more or less distinct parts: a major offering training in a performing or professional art and the BELL Core, the general education program, offering a foundation in the liberal arts.

A quick summary of the BELL Core indicates the program is in three broad parts (for a detailed guide, go online or speak with your advisor). Reflecting the centrality of intellectual skills, both as a part of a liberal education and as tools in accessing a liberal education, you get to take courses in math, writing, speech, and wellness. Reflecting the broad-based content of a liberal education, you get to take courses in the natural sciences, social sciences, humanities, and religion. Reflecting the integrated nature of liberal education, you also get to experience a series of Belmont signature courses that organize and bring coherence to the whole journey. "BELL," by the way, stands for "Belmont Education Learning for Life." For most Belmont students, the BELL Core adds up a greater number of credit hours than the courses leading to their professional credential. Make no mistake about it: *general education is the core of your Belmont education; study in your major is secondary.*

Like students everywhere, Belmont students too often do not get a satisfactory answer to a natural and reasonable question: "why do I have to take all these classes that have nothing to do with my major?" Behind the question, of course, lie some of those paradoxes in accessing a liberal education that Rowe noted. In a hundred ways, students have been told that higher education is about their professional future. They hear that message from the culture at large, their parents, their high school teachers and guidance counselor, even – most sadly – from university admissions offices. They arrive at the university with their professional aspirations coming into view. When told that most of their courses do not directly relate to that future, nor exist purely in order to prepare them for that future, they are rightly perplexed. They deserve an answer.

The most authentic answer is, of course, outlined above: *you have to take such courses because they will lead you toward wisdom and truth, bequeath you your cultural heritage, free you from ignorance and ideology, and make you both worthy and capable of self-determination.*

But the question comes from a place of practical, hard-headed, and career-focused deliberation. The summary expression of an abstract ideal will not satisfy the questioner. There is a more concrete answer, one that is both true and good enough to be getting along while the deeper answer comes into view.

Good classes that have nothing to do with your major will still help you in your career. You will be a better nurse if you have studied theology and understand the ways in which human beings have responded spiritually to suffering and death. You will be a better pharmacist if you have studied political science and understand how public policy decisions lead to differential access to health care. You will be a better music industry executive if you study a foreign language, take courses in cross cultural psychology, and become adept at working and thinking across cultural divides.

Admittedly, the likelihood of such direct application varies across professions, and might be rare for some professions. Health care and teaching seem particularly clear examples of professions in which you would be most hindered by a narrow professional training, and most benefit from a broad and robust general education. To thrive as nurse or teacher, you need to be able to reach a wide variety of people who are going through a wide variety of often tumultuous experiences and emotions. If a pediatric nurse cannot gain the parents' trust because of an inability and unwillingness to comprehend their culture, care standards could be impaired.

More important than such direct application, however, is the development of what are sometimes called transfer skills, skills developed in one context but able to be transferred and applied in multiple other contexts. I hope it is obvious that an education in the liberal arts greatly improves your skills of written and oral communication, critical thinking, abstract reasoning, integrating new information, avoiding rush to judgment, working with others, disagreeing productively, staying on track to meet long-term goals, and organization. Those are core skills no matter what profession you pursue. Studying the liberal arts is not the only way to acquire such skills, but it the best, surest, and most efficient way.[18]

Liberal education is sometimes summarized by saying that students "learn how to learn." For example, reading Immanuel Kant is not easy. In

---

[18] The practical case for the economic benefit of a liberal education has been made many times. For a particularly strong and recent example, see Fareed Zakaria, *In Defense of a Liberal Education* (New York: W.W. Norton and Company, 2015).

order to get through one of his treatises, you will have to learn how to navigate a technical vocabulary and see how seemingly disparate ideas fit together into a larger implied whole. The content of Kant's treatise won't directly help you in a professional setting, but the intellectual skills you acquired by reading the treatise will transfer to any context in which there is technical language and a complex whole. My college roommate and fellow philosophy major now works for a Washington D.C. tech firm as the manager of a team of network security something or other. Honestly, I don't know what he does; I don't know nearly enough about computers to understand. I do know that he has no formal university training in computers or in management. There is no overlap whatsoever between the *content* of his professional work and the *content* of his college coursework. Yet, he denies any claim that he is not "using" his philosophy degree, suggesting that anyone who knows how to read Kant can figure out a programming manual.

The concrete and practical defense of liberal education is not limited to being more prepared for a dynamic marketplace. Thanks to those same transfer skills, the BELL Core can teach you useful skills and life habits that will make you a better neighbor, spouse, citizen, parent, consumer, and all around human being. For instance, if you know how to disagree civilly, giving reasons for your claims and changing your mind on the basis of what others say, then your romantic relations will benefit tremendously. In other words, one reason you need to take classes that don't directly relate to your professional ambitions is that your Belmont education should prepare you for the whole of your life, not just your career. I hope that, after graduation, you go on to have a successful and meaningful professional career. But I hope so much more for you than that. After all, life is so much more than a career. If you graduate from Belmont with nothing but the credentials to get a great first job and the tools to succeed in that job, then you did not make the most of your time here. You should leave Belmont better prepared for your career, yes, but you should also leave better prepared for life in all of its manifestations.

Knowledge and First-Year Seminar

The first step in your journey through the BELL Core is First-Year Seminar (FYS), which is required for all incoming freshmen at Belmont. Though faculty members choose their own individual subtitles and themes for the course, the overall topic of every section of FYS is the same: "ways of knowing." The shared focus of all FYS sections is an interrogation of the role of knowledge in human life.

People often mistakenly presume that knowledge is one of those abstract concepts that evade definition. On the contrary, there is broad consensus among philosophers that Plato was basically on the right track when defining knowledge as "justified true belief."[19] The definition means that there are three parts to knowledge. For a person to know statement or assertion *x*, 1) the person must believe *x* is true, 2) *x* must indeed be true, and 3) the person must be justified in believing *x*.

The first criterion is so obvious that it seems simplistic. In order to know some certain statement, you have to believe that statement. The second is also logically straightforward. Believing false stuff is never knowledge, no matter how good your reasons for believing it. For thousands of years humans had excellent reason for believing that the sun moves around the Earth. Nevertheless, they were wrong. They *thought that they knew* the sun moves, but it is clearly incorrect to say that they *actually knew* the sun moved. A false belief can never be knowledge.

The third criterion, justification, is an intellectual gold mine. A bit of reflection can show that even a true belief is not necessarily knowledge. Imagine a hypochondriac who always thinks he has some disease or another. This week, he irrationally believes that he has cancer (there are no symptoms); last week it was congestive heart failure. Imagine that it turns out he actually does have a nearly undetectable tumor. Though his belief that he has cancer is true, it gives him far too much credit to say that he *knows* that he has cancer. He correctly believes that he has cancer but he is not *justified* in having the belief.

To have knowledge, you need not only believe what is true (hard enough in itself), but you also have to believe for rational and legitimate reasons.[20] You have to have evidence, hopefully strong evidence. It is easy to choose to believe this or that thing about any given subject matter. Inevitably, some of those beliefs are going to turn out to be true. But the difference between the person who is actually knowledgeable and the

---

[19] Plato, *Theaetetuts* in *Plato Complete Works*, ed. John Cooper (Hackett Publishing: Indianapolis,, 1997), 201d. Plato's definition is "true judgment with an account." Nevertheless, the equivalent expression "justified true belief" is most commonly used and cited.

[20] There are some counter-examples to the claim that justified true belief is knowledge. For example, consider the person who believes it to be a certain time of day, justifying that belief by appeal to a generally reliable public clock that happened to have broken exactly twelve hours earlier. For widely discussed, if rather technical, examples see: Edmund Gettier, "Is Knowledge Justified True Belief?," *Analysis* 23 (1966): 121-123. Nevertheless, all of these counter-examples deal with degree of justification and do not undermine the general claim that knowledge involves belief, truth, and justification.

person who is going off guesses, vague intuitions, or the implications of some ideology is that the person with knowledge has formed beliefs around a genuine understanding of the subject matter. Knowledge isn't simply firmly holding a belief. It isn't even merely about being right. Knowledge is having true beliefs that grow from rational reflections, reflections that are themselves grounded in substantive and accurate comprehension of the subject matter at hand.

The relevant branch of study here is called epistemology, the sub-branch of philosophy focused on the study of knowledge. Some of the broadest and deepest questions epistemologists study relate directly to this third criterion. What does it take to be sufficiently justified in holding a certain belief? How strong does that justification have to be before meeting the minimal standard for knowledge? What is the relationship between knowledge and certainty? What is good reason to believe something? In slightly technical language, what warrants epistemic license?

Mercifully, First-Year Seminar is not at all like the course in epistemology I offer. Though broad philosophical questions may arise in First-Year Seminar, other kinds of issues about knowledge are typically more central to the course.

Questions about the varieties of knowledge are commonly explored in FYS. How do biologists construct knowledge claims? How do theologians construct knowledge claims? How do historians construct them? What about philosophers, political scientists, or mathematicians? What about music critics, medical doctors, or cultural commentators? How do these knowledge claims relate to, even compete with, one another?

Questions about the means of establishing knowledge are also common questions in FYS. Is intuition or a gut feeling a way of knowing? Is faith? Can scripture provide us with knowledge? If so, what kind? Does knowledge always ultimately rely on observation? Can we gain knowledge by reading fiction or poetry? What kind of knowledge?

Questions about the scope and limits of knowledge are some of the most interesting that are often explored in FYS. Can beliefs about morality, religion, or politics be considered knowledge? Can I know that something is immoral, or beautiful? What are the limits of scientific knowledge? Are there facts that can be known, but cannot be explored scientifically? What should be done when competing claims to knowledge collide?

Questions about the preservation and transmission of knowledge are critical in many sections of FYS. How do technological societies preserve knowledge? What various methods did traditional societies use to pass knowledge from one generation to the next? How is the internet transforming libraries and research? What role have universities historically played in building and disseminating knowledge? How is that role changing? How widely should knowledge be disseminated? When, if ever, is it appropriate to consider knowledge to be private property?

The goal of First-Year Seminar is for students to launch their general education program by interrogating the role of knowledge in human life. Through reading the core of the anthology, readings related to the instructor's sub-theme, and selections from the supplemental material in the anthology, certain course learning objectives are met. First of all, students learn some of the traditional and contemporary claims about the nature, value, and purpose of liberal education. They are exposed to academic values about what it is to be educated, and what it is value knowledge and truth. Secondly, students encounter representative examples of knowledge claims constructed and evaluated from a variety of disciplinary perspectives. Likely, through the instructor's sub-theme, they explore one academic discipline or issue in particular. Also, students consider the role of knowledge in human life generally, outside of academic contexts. They read literature and watch films that poignantly raise questions about how human beings claim to know the things they know, the pitfalls of living in the absence of knowledge, the tragedies that tend to emerge when people feel certain despite being wrong. Finally, students get an introduction to the cultural and intellectual life of the university community beyond the classroom through invited speakers, stage productions, academic lectures, and musical performances.

Conclusion: Some Unsolicited Advice

I've passed along to you some rather grand claims about liberal education, the BELL Core, and First-Year Seminar. I've even, once you put all the dots together, suggested that FYS can make you a better person. Like Socrates, you should be open enough to consider that my claims might be true, while also being skeptical enough to subject them to critical examination. Don't prejudge the question one way or the other.

Too many students at Belmont and everywhere else treat the general education program as nothing but a series of obstacles to overcome on the way to graduation. The more quickly and effortlessly they can be "gotten out of the way," the better. As a result, many students arrive at graduation little altered by most of their BELL Core courses, having never sought from them anything other than another checked box.

I advise you to take a different approach. Take the BELL Core seriously and test for yourself whether the grandiose claims about a liberal education are true. Treat general education courses like the core of your education that they are intended to be. Consider a major or minor in one

21

of the liberal arts. Come and see me at graduation and tell me the early results of your experiment.

I'll be delighted to hear it, but I already know what you'll say in some version or another; I've heard it too many times to be in suspense. If you take general education seriously, the world we inhabit together will be more interesting to you, and you will be both more interesting and useful to it. You will be better equipped to flourish as a free human being. So, answer for yourself the same questions my old advisor Stephen Rowe still asks incoming students: do you seek only to be informed, or are you also open to being transformed? Are you here just to get a degree, or do you also want an education?

The Allegory of the Cave
Plato

From *The Republic*, Book VII. In *Plato: Complete Works*. Trans. G. M. A. Grube and ed. John M. Cooper. Indianapolis: Hackett Publishing Company, 1997.

Plato (429-347 BCE) is a foundational figure in Western intellectual history. Born into a prominent Athenian family during a time when Athens was the center of Greek cultural and political life, Plato became a student and follower of the great philosopher Socrates. After Socrates' death in 399 BC, Plato founded the Academy, a school that endured several centuries and served as the source of the word "academic." He was also teacher of the influential thinker Aristotle. Plato's works are often written as imagined dialogues between Socrates and his followers.

Why we are reading this: Plato describes the nature of education through an extended metaphor that has become one of the most enduring images of Western civilization. He suggests that humans often work from false assumptions of which they are entirely unaware, assumptions that may draw them toward complacency, smugness, and dogmatism about the way things are. His allegory spotlights the difficulties that may come when one tries to see the world as it actually is and the great opportunities that emerge when one commits to moving beyond one's limited worldview to pursue truth and reality.

SOCRATES: Next, I said, compare the effect of education and of the lack of it on our nature to an experience like this: Imagine human beings living in an underground, cavelike dwelling, with an entrance a long way up, which is both open to the light and as wide as the cave itself. They've been there since childhood, fixed in the same place, with their necks and legs fettered, able to see only in front of them, because their bonds prevent them from turning their heads around. Light is provided by a fire burning far above and behind them. Also behind them, but on higher ground, there is a path stretching between them and the fire. Imagine that along this path a low wall has been built, like the screen in front of puppeteers above which they show their puppets.

GLAUCON: I'm imagining it.

SOCRATES: Then also imagine that there are people along the wall, carrying all kinds of artifacts that project above it – statues of people and other animals, made out of stone, wood, and every material. And, as you'd expect, some of the carriers are talking, and some are silent.

GLAUCON: It's a strange image you're describing, and strange prisoners.

SOCRATES: They're like us. Do you suppose, first of all, that these prisoners see anything of themselves and one another besides the shadows that the fire casts on the wall in front of them?

GLAUCON: How could they, if they have to keep their heads motionless throughout life?

SOCRATES: What about the things being carried along the wall? Isn't the same true of them?

GLAUCON: Of course.

SOCRATES: And if they could talk to one another, don't you think they'd suppose that the names they used applied to the thing they see passing before them?

GLAUCON: They'd have to.

SOCRATES: And what if their prison also had an echo from the wall facing them? Don't you think they'd believe that the shadows passing in front of them were talking whenever one of the carriers passing along the wall was doing so?

GLAUCON: I certainly do.

SOCRATES: Then the prisoners would in every way believe that the truth is nothing other than the shadows of those artifacts.

GLAUCON: They must surely believe that.

SOCRATES: Consider, then, what being released from their bonds and cured of their ignorance would naturally be like, if something like this came to pass. When one of them was freed and suddenly compelled to stand up, turn his head, walk, and look up toward the light, he'd be pained and dazzled and unable to see the things whose shadows he'd seen before. What do you think he'd say, if we told him that what he'd seen before was inconsequential but that now – because he is a bit closer to the things that are and is turned towards things that are more – he sees more correctly? Or, to put it another way, if we pointed to each of the things passing by, asked him what each of them is, and compelled him to answer, don't you think he'd be at a loss and that he'd believe that the things he saw earlier were truer than the ones he was now being shown?

GLAUCON: Much truer.

SOCRATES: And if someone compelled him to look at the light itself, wouldn't his eyes hurt, and wouldn't he turn around and flee towards the things he's able to see, believing that they're really clearer than the ones he's being shown?

GLAUCON: He would.

SOCRATES: And if someone dragged him away from there by force, up the rough, steep path, and didn't let him go until he had dragged him into the sunlight, would he be pained and irritated at being treated that way? And when he came into the light, with the sun filling his eyes, would he be unable to see a single one of the things now said to be true?

GLAUCON: He would be unable to see them, at least at first.

SOCRATES: I suppose, then, that he'd need time to get adjusted before he could see things in the world above. At first, he'd see shadows most easily, then images of men and other things in water, then the things themselves. Of these, he'd be able to study the things in the sky and the sky itself more easily at night, looking at the light of the stars and the moon, than during the day, looking at the sun and the light of the sun.

GLAUCON: Of course.

SOCRATES: Finally, I suppose, he'd be able to see the sun, not images of it in water or some alien place, but the sun itself, in its own place, and be able to study it.

GLAUCON: Necessarily so.

SOCRATES: And at this point he would infer and conclude that the sun provides the seasons and the years, governs everything in the visible world, and is in some way the cause of all the things that he used to see.

GLAUCON: It's clear that would be his next step.

SOCRATES: What about when he reminds himself of his first dwelling place, his fellow prisoners, and what passed for wisdom there? Don't you think that he'd count himself happy for the change and pity the others?

GLAUCON: Certainly.

SOCRATES: And if there had been any honors, praises, or prizes among them for the one who was sharpest at identifying the shadows as they passed by and who remembered which usually came earlier, which later, and which simultaneously, and who could thus best divine the future, do you think that our man would desire these rewards or envy those among the prisoners who were honored and held power? Instead, wouldn't he feel, with Homer, that he'd much prefer to "work the earth as a serf to another, one without possessions," and go through any sufferings, rather than share their opinions and live as they do?

GLAUCON: I suppose he would rather suffer anything than live like that.

SOCRATES: Consider this too. If this man went down into the cave again and sat down in his same seat, wouldn't his eyes – coming suddenly out of the sun like that – be filled with darkness.

GLAUCON: They certainly would.

SOCRATES: And before his eyes had recovered – and the adjustment would not be quick – while his vision was still dim, if he had to compete again with the perpetual prisoners in recognizing the shadows, would he invite ridicule? Wouldn't it be said of him that he'd returned from his upward journey with his eyesight ruined and that it isn't worthwhile even to try to travel upward? And, as for anyone who tried to free them and lead them upward, if they could somehow get their hands on him, would they kill him?

GLAUCON: They certainly would.

SOCRATES: This whole image, Glaucon, must be fitted together with what we said before. The visible realm should be linked to the prison dwelling, and the light of the fire inside it to the power of the sun. And if you interpret the upward journey and the study of things above as the upward journey of the soul to the intelligible realm, you'll grasp what I hope to convey, since that is what you wanted to hear about. Whether it's true or not, only the god knows. But this is how I see it: In the knowable realm, the form of the good is the last thing to be seen, and it is reached only with difficulty. Once one has seen it, however, one must conclude that it is the cause of all that is correct and beautiful in anything, that it produces both light and its source in the visible realm, and that in the intelligible realm it controls and provides truth and understanding, so that anyone who is to act sensibly in private or public must see it.

GLAUCON: I have the same thought, at least as far as I'm able.

SOCRATES: Come, then, share with me this thought also: It isn't surprising that the ones who get to this point are unwilling to occupy themselves with human affairs and that their souls are always pressing upwards, eager to spend their time above, for, after all, this is surely what we'd expect, if indeed things fit the image I described before.

GLAUCON: It is.

SOCRATES: What about what happens when someone turns from divine study to the evils of human life? Do you think it's surprising, since his sight is still dim, and he hasn't yet become accustomed to the darkness around him, compelled, either in the courts or elsewhere, to contend about the shadows of justice or the statutes of which they are the shadows and to dispute about the way these things are understood by people who have never seen justice itself?

GLAUCON: That's not surprising at all.

SOCRATES: No it isn't. But anyone with any understanding would remember that the eyes may be confused in two ways and from two causes, namely, when they've come from the light into the darkness *and* when they've come from the darkness into the light. Realizing that the same applies to the soul, when someone sees a soul disturbed and unable to see something, he won't laugh mindlessly, but he'll take into consideration whether it has come from a brighter life and is dimmed through not having yet become accustomed to the dark or whether it has come from greater ignorance into greater light and is dazzled by the increased brilliance. Then he'll declare the first soul happy in its experience and life, and he'll pity the latter – but even if he chose to make fun of it, at least he'd be less ridiculous than if he laughed at a soul that has come from the light above.

GLAUCON: What you say is very reasonable.

SOCRATES: If that's true, then here's what we must think about these matters: Education isn't what some people declare it to be, namely, putting knowledge into souls that lack it, like putting sight into blind eyes.

GLAUCON: They do say that.

SOCRATES: But our present discussion, on the other hand, shows that the power to learn is present in everyone's soul and that the instrument with which each learns is like an eye that cannot be turned around from darkness to light without turning the whole body. This instrument cannot be turned around from that which is coming into being without turning the whole soul until it is able to study that which is and the brightest thing that is, namely, the one we call the good. Isn't that right?

GLAUCON: Yes.

SOCRATES: Then education is the craft concerned with doing this very thing, this turning around, and with how the soul can most easily and effectively be made to do it. It isn't the craft of putting sight into the soul. Education takes for granted that sight is there but that it isn't turned the right way or looking where it ought to look, and it tries to redirect it appropriately.

GLAUCON: So it seems.

SOCRATES: Now, it looks as though the other so-called virtues of the soul are akin to those of the body, for they really aren't there beforehand but are added later by habit and practice. However, the virtue of reason seems to belong above all to something more divine, which never loses it power but is either useful and beneficial or useless and harmful, depending on the way it is turned. Or have you never noticed this about people who are said to be vicious but clever, how keen the vision of their little soul is and how sharply it distinguishes the things it is turned towards? This shows that its sight isn't inferior but rather is forced to serve evil ends, so that the sharper it sees, the more evil it accomplishes.

GLAUCON: Absolutely.

SOCRATES: However, if a nature of this sort had been hammered at from childhood and freed from the bonds of kinship with becoming, which have been fastened to it by feasting, greed, and other such pleasures and which, like leaden weights, pull its vision downwards – if, being rid of these, it turned to look at true things, then I say that the same soul of the same person would see these most sharply, just as it now does the things it is presently turned towards.

GLAUCON: Probably so.

SOCRATES: And what about the uneducated who have no experience of truth? Isn't it likely – indeed, doesn't it follow necessarily from what was said before – that they will never adequately govern a city? But neither would those who've been allowed to spend their whole lives being educated. The former would fail because they don't have a single goal at which all their actions, public and private, inevitably aim; the latter would fail because they'd refuse to act, thinking that they had settled while still alive in the faraway Isled of the Blessed.

GLAUCON: That's true.

SOCRATES: It is our task as founders, then, to compel the best natures to reach the study we said before is the most important, namely, to make the ascent and see the good. But when they've make it and looked sufficiently, we mustn't allow them to do what they're allowed to do today.

GLAUCON: What's that?

SOCRATES: To stay there and refuse to go down again to the prisoners in the cave and share their labors and honors, whether they are of less worth or of greater.

GLAUCON: Then are we to do them an injustice by making them live a worse life when they could live a better one?

SOCRATES: You are forgetting again that it isn't the law's concern to make any one class in the city outstandingly happy but to contrive to spread happiness throughout the city by bringing the citizens into harmony with each other through persuasion or compulsion and by making them share with each other the benefits that each class can confer on the community. The law produces such people in the city, not in order to allow them to turn in whatever direction they want, but to make use of them to bind the city together.

GLAUCON: That's true, I had forgotten.

SOCRATES: Observe, then, Glaucon, that we won't be doing an injustice to those who've become philosophers in our city and that what we'll say to them, when we compel them to guard and care for the others, will be just. We'll say: "When people like you come to be in other cities, they're justified in not sharing in their city's labors, for they've grown there spontaneously, against the will of the constitution. And what grows of its own accord and owes no debt for its upbringing has justice on its side when it isn't keen to pay anyone for that upbringing. But we've made you kings in our city and leaders of the swarm, as it were, both for yourselves and for the rest of the city. You're better and more completely educated than the others and grow accustomed to seeing in the dark. When you are used to it, you'll see vastly better than the people there. And because you've seen the truth about fine, just, and good things, you'll know each image for what it is and also that of which it is the image. Thus, for you and for us, the city will be governed, not like the majority of cities nowadays, by people who fight over shadows and struggle against one another in order to rule – as if that were a great good – but by people who are awake rather than dreaming, for the truth is surely this: A City whose prospective rulers are least eager to rule must of necessity be most free from civil war, whereas a city with the opposite kind of rulers is governed in the opposite way."

GLAUCON: Absolutely.

SOCRATES: Then do you think that those we've nurtured will disobey us and refuse to share the labors of the city, each in turn, while living the greater part of their time with one another in the pure realm?

GLAUCON: It isn't possible, for we'll be giving just orders to just people. Each of them will certainly go to rule as to something compulsory, however, which is exactly the opposite of what's done by those who now rule in each city.

SOCRATES: This is how it is. If you can find a way of life that's better than ruling for the prospective rulers, your well-governed city will become a possibility, for only in it will the truly rich rule – not those who are rich in gold but those who are rich in the wealth that the happy must have, namely, a good and rational life. But if beggars hungry for private good go into public life, thinking that the good is there for the seizing, then the well-governed city is impossible, for then ruling is something fought over, and this civil and domestic war destroys these people and the rest of the city as well.

GLAUCON: That's very true.

SOCRATES: Can you name any life that despise political rule besides that of the true philosopher?

GLAUCON: No, by god, I can't.

SOCRATES: But surely it is those who are not lovers of ruling who must rule, for if they don't, the lovers of it, who are rivals, will fight over it.

GLAUCON: Of course.

SOCRATES: Then who will you compel to become guardians of the city, if not those who have the best understanding of what matters for good government and who have other honors than political ones, and a better life as well?

GLAUCON: No one.

Who Are You and What Are You Doing Here? A Word to the Incoming Class
Mark Edmundson

In *Why Teach? In Defense of Real Education*. New York: Bloomsbury, 2013, pp. 51-67.

Mark Edmundson (b. 1952) currently serves as University Professor at the University of Virginia. With a specialty in nineteenth-century British and American poetry, he earned a Ph.D. in English from Yale University in 1985. He is the author of books on diverse topics: Freud, the relationship between literature and philosophy, Gothic culture, rock & roll, and American football. His best-known works and presentations articulate and defend the value of traditional liberal learning in American higher education, and the contemporary relevance of that vision. The following essay was first published in 2011 in the literary magazine Oxford American *and was anthologized in* The Best American Essays of 2012.

Why we are reading this: Edmundson frames his defense of liberal learning in a more personal way than our other authors, as a letter to incoming university students. He reflects on the challenges of pursuing a liberal education from the students' point of view, urging them to take responsibility for their own education.

WELCOME AND CONGRATULATIONS: Getting to the first day of college is a major achievement. You're to be commended, and not just you, but the parents, grandparents, uncles, and aunts who helped get you here.

It's been said that raising a child effectively takes a village: Well, as you may have noticed, our American village is not in very good shape. We've got guns, drugs, wars, fanatical religions, a slime-based popular culture, and some politicians who – a little restraint here – aren't what they might be. Merely to survive in this American village and to win a place in the entering class has taken a lot of grit on your part. So, yes, congratulations to all.

You now may think that you've about got it made. Amid the impressive college buildings, in company with a high-powered faculty, surrounded by the best of your generation, all you need is to keep doing what you've done before: Work hard, get good grades, listen to your teachers, get along with the people around you, and you'll emerge in four years as an educated young man or woman. Ready for life.

Do not believe it. It is not true. If you want to get a real education in America, you're going to have to fight – and I don't mean just fight against the drugs and the violence and against the slime-based culture that is still going to surround you. I mean something a little more disturbing. To get an education, you're probably going to have to fight against the institution that you find yourself in – no matter how prestigious it may be. (In fact, the more prestigious the school, the more you'll probably have to push.) You can get a terrific education in America now – there are astonishing opportunities at almost every college – but the education will not be presented to you wrapped and bowed. To get it, you'll need to struggle and strive, to be strong, and occasionally even to piss off some admirable people.

I came to college with few resources, but one of them was an understanding, however crude, of how I might use my opportunities there. This I began to develop because of my father, who had never been to college – in fact, he'd barely gotten out of high school. One night after dinner, he and I were sitting in our kitchen at 58 Clewley Road in Medford, Massachusetts, hatching plans about the rest of my life. I was about to go off to college, a feat no one in my family had accomplished in living memory. "I think I might want to be prelaw," I told my father. I had no idea what being prelaw was. My father compressed his brow and blew twin streams of smoke, dragonlike, from his magnificent nose. "Do you want to be a lawyer?" he asked. My father had some experience with lawyers, and with policemen, too; he was not well disposed toward either. "I'm not really sure," I told him, "but lawyers make pretty good money, right?"

My father detonated. (That was not uncommon. He detonated a lot.) He told me that I was going to go to college only once, and that while I was there I had better study what I wanted. He said that when rich kids went to school, they majored in the subjects that interested them, and that my younger brother Philip and I were as good as any rich kids. (We were rich kids minus the money.) Wasn't I interested in literature? I confessed that I was. Then I had better study literature, unless I had inside information to the effect that reincarnation wasn't just hype, and I'd be able to attend college thirty or forty times. If I had such info, prelaw would be fine, and maybe even a tour through invertebrate biology could also be tossed in. But until I had the reincarnation stuff from a solid source, I better get to work and pick out some English classes from the course catalog.

"How about the science requirements?" I asked.

"Take 'em later," he said. "You never know."

My father, Wright Aukenhead Edmundson, Malden High School class of 1948 (by a hair), knew the score. What he told me that evening at the Clewley Road kitchen table was true in itself, and it also contains the germ of an idea about what a university education should be. But apparently almost everyone else – students, teachers, trustees, and parents – see the matter much differently. They have it wrong.

Education has one salient enemy in present-day America, and that enemy is education – university education in particular. To almost everyone, university education is a means to an end. For students, that end is a good job. Students want the credentials that will help them get ahead. They want the certificate that will grant them access to Wall Street, or entrance into law or medical or business school. And how can we blame them? America values power and money, big players with big bucks. When we raise our children, we tell them in multiple ways that what we want most for them is success – material success. To be poor in America is to be a failure. It's to be without decent health care, without basic necessities, often without dignity. Then there are those backbreaking student loans: People leave school as servants, indentured to pay massive bills, so that first job better be a good one. Students come to college with the goal of a diploma in mind – what happens to them in between, especially in classrooms, is often of no deep and determining interest to them.

In college, life is elsewhere. Life is at parties, at clubs, in music, with friends, in sports. Life is what celebrities have. The idea that the courses you take should be the primary objective of going to college is tacitly considered absurd. In terms of their work, students live in the future and not the present; they live with their prospects for success. If universities stopped issuing credentials, half of the clients would be gone by tomorrow morning, with the remainder following fast behind.

The faculty, too, is often absent: Their real lives are also elsewhere. Like most of their students, they aim to get on. The work they are compelled to do to advance – get tenure, promotion, raises, outside offers – is, broadly speaking, scholarly work. No matter what anyone says, this work has precious little to do with the fundamentals of teaching. The proof is that virtually no undergraduate students can read and understand their professors' scholarly publications. The public senses this disparity and so thinks of the professors' work as being silly or beside the point. Some of it is. But the public also senses that because professors don't pay full-bore attention to teaching, they don't have to work very hard – they've created a massive feather bed for themselves and called it a university.

This is radically false. Ambitious professors, the ones who, like their students, want to get ahead in America, work furiously. Scholarship, even if pretentious and almost unreadable, is nonetheless labor-intense. One can slave for a year or two on a single article for publication in this or that refereed journal. These essays are honest: Their footnotes reflect real reading, real assimilation, and real dedication. Shoddy work – in which the author cheats, cuts corners, copies from others – is quickly detected. The people who do the work have highly developed intellectual powers, and they push themselves hard to reach a certain standard. That the results have almost no practical relevance for students, the public, or even, frequently, other scholars is a central element in the tragicomedy that is often academia.

The students and the professors have made a deal: Neither of them has to throw himself heart and soul into what happens in the classroom. The students write their abstract, overintellectualized essays; the professors grade the students for their capacity to be abstract and overintellectual – and often genuinely smart. For their essays can be brilliant, in a chilly way; they can also be clipped from the Internet, and often are. Whatever the case, no one wants to invest too much in them – for life is elsewhere. The professor saves his energies for the profession, while the student saves his for friends, social life, volunteer work, making connections, and getting in position to clasp hands on the true grail, the first job.

No one in this picture is evil; no one is criminally irresponsible. It's just that smart people are prone to look into matters to see how they might go about buttering their toast. Then they butter their toast.

As for the administrators, their relation to the students often seems based not on love but fear. Administrators fear bad publicity, scandal, and dissatisfaction on the part of their customers. More than anything else, though, they fear lawsuits. Throwing a student out of college for this or that piece of bad behavior is very difficult, almost impossible. The student will sue your eyes out. One kid I knew (and rather liked) threatened on his blog to mince his dear and esteemed professor (me) with a samurai sword for the crime of having taught a boring class. (The class was a little boring – I had a damn cold – but the punishment seemed a bit severe.) The dean of students laughed lightly when I suggested that this behavior might be grounds for sending the student on a brief vacation. I was, you might say, discomfited, and showed up to class for a while with my cell phone jiggered to dial 911 with one touch.

Still, this was small potatoes. Colleges are even leery of disciplining guys who have committed sexual assault, or assault plain and simple. Instead of being punished, these guys frequently stay around, strolling the quad and swilling the libations, an affront (and sometimes a terror) to their victims.

You'll find that cheating is common as well. As far as I can discern, the student ethos goes like this: If the professor is so lazy that he gives the same test every year, it's okay to go ahead and take advantage – you've got better things to do. The Internet is amok with services selling term papers, and those services exist, capitalism being what it is, because people purchase the papers – lots of them. Fraternity files bulge with old tests from a variety of courses. Periodically, the public gets exercised about this situation and there are articles in the national news. But then interest dwindles and matters go back to normal.

One of the reasons professors sometimes look the other way when they sense cheating is that it sends them into a world of sorrow. A friend of mine had the temerity to detect cheating on the part of a kid who was the nephew of a well-placed official in an Arab government complexly aligned with the U.S. Black limousines pulled up in front of his office and disgorged decorously suited negotiators. Did my pal fold? No, he's not the type. But he did not enjoy the process.

What colleges generally want are well-rounded students, civic leaders, people who know what the system demands, how to keep matters light and not push too hard for an education or anything else; people who get their credentials and leave professors alone to do their brilliant work so they may rise and enhance the rankings of the university. Such students leave and become donors and so, in their own turn, contribute immeasurably to the university's standing. They've done a fine job skating on surfaces in high school – the best way to get an across-the-board outstanding record – and now they're on campus to cut a few more figure eights.

In a culture where the major and determining values are monetary, what else could you do? How else would you live if not by getting all you can, succeeding all you can, making all you can?

The idea that a university education really should have no substantial content, should not be about what John Keats was disposed to call "Soul-making," is one that you might think professors and university presidents would be discreet about. Not so. This view informed an address that Richard Brodhead gave to the senior class at Yale before he departed to become president of Duke. Brodhead, an impressive, articulate man, seems to take as his educational touchstone the Duke of Wellington's precept that the Battle of Waterloo was won on the playing fields of Eton. Brodhead suggests that the content of the course isn't really what matters. In five years (or five months, or minutes), the student is likely to have forgotten how to do the problem sets and will only hazily recollect what happens in the ninth book of *Paradise Lost*. The legacy of their college years will be a legacy of difficulties overcome. When they face equally arduous tasks later in life, students will tap their old resources of determination, and they'll win.

All right, there's nothing wrong with this as far as it goes – after all, the student who writes a brilliant forty-page thesis in a hard week has learned more than a little about her inner resources. Maybe it will give her needed confidence in the future. But doesn't the content of the courses matter at all?

On the evidence of this talk, no. Trying to figure out whether the stuff you're reading is true or false and being open to having your life changed is a fraught, controversial activity. Doing so requires energy from the professor – which is better spent on other matters. This kind of perspective-altering teaching and learning can cause the things that administrators fear above all else: trouble, arguments, bad press, et cetera. After the kid-samurai episode, the chair of my department not unsympathetically suggested that this was the sort of incident that could happen when you brought a certain intensity to teaching. At the time I found this remark a tad detached, but maybe he was right.

So if you want an education, the odds aren't with you: The professors are off doing what they call their own work; the other students, who've doped out the way the place runs, are busy leaving their professors alone and getting themselves in position for bright and shining futures; the student-services people are trying to keep everyone content, offering plenty of entertainment and building another state-of-the-art workout facility every few months. The development office is already scanning you for future donations.

So why make trouble? Why not just go along? Let the profs roam free in the realms of pure thought, let yourselves party in the realms of impure pleasure, and let the student-services gang assert fewer prohibitions and newer delights for you. You'll get a good job, you'll have plenty of friends, you'll have a driveway of your own.

You'll also, if my father and I are right, be truly and righteously screwed. The reason for this is simple. The quest at the center of a liberal arts education is not a luxury quest; it's a necessity quest. If you do not undertake it, you risk leading a life of desperation – maybe quiet; maybe, in time, very loud – and I am not exaggerating. For you risk trying to be someone other than who you are, which, in the long run, is killing.

By the time you come to college, you will have been told who you are numberless times. Your parents and friends, your teachers, your counselors, your priests and rabbis and ministers and imams have all had their say. They've let you know how they size you up, and they've let you know what they think you should value. They've given you a sharp and protracted taste of what they feel is good and bad, right and wrong. Much

35

is on their side. They have confronted you with scriptures – holy books that, whatever their actual provenance, have given people what they feel to be wisdom for thousands of years. They've given you family traditions – you've learned the ways of your tribe and community. And, too, you've been tested, probed, looked at up and down and through. The coach knows what your athletic prospects are, the guidance office has a sheaf of test scores that relegate you to this or that ability quadrant, and your teachers have got you pegged. You are, as Foucault might say, the intersection of many evaluative and potentially determining discourses: You, boy, you, girl, have been made.

And – contra Foucault – that's not so bad. Embedded in all of the major religions are profound truths. Schopenhauer, who despised belief in transcendent things, nonetheless taught Christianity to be of inexpressible worth. He couldn't believe in the divinity of Jesus or in the afterlife, but to Schopenhauer, a deep pessimist, a religion that had as its central emblem the figure of a man being tortured on a cross couldn't be entirely misleading. To the Christian, Schopenhauer said, pain was at the center of the understanding of life, and that was just as it should be.

One does not need to be as harsh as Schopenhauer to understand the use of religion, even if one does not believe in an otherworldly God. And all those teachers and counselors and friends – and the prognosticating uncles, the dithering aunts, the fathers and mothers with their hopes for your fulfillment, or their fulfillment in you – should not necessarily be cast aside or ignored. Families have their wisdom. The question "Who do they think you are at home?" is never an idle one.

The major conservative thinkers have always been very serious about what goes by the name of common sense. Edmund Burke saw common sense as a loosely made but often profound collective work in which humanity deposited its hard-earned wisdom – the precipitate of joy and tears – over time. You have been raised in proximity to common sense, if you've been raised at all, and common sense is something to respect, though not quite – peace unto the formidable Burke – to revere.

You may be all that the good people who raised you say you are; you may want all they have shown you is worth wanting; you may be someone who is truly your father's son or your mother's daughter. But then again, you may not be.

For the power that is in you, as Emerson suggested, may be new in nature. You may not be the person that your parents take you to be. And – this thought is both more exciting and more dangerous – you may not be the person that you take yourself to be, either. You may not have read yourself aright, and college is the place where you can find out whether you have or not. The reason to read Blake and Dickinson and Freud and

Dickens is not to become more cultivated or more articulate or to be someone who, at a cocktail party, is never embarrassed (or can embarrass others). The best reason to read them is to see if they know you better than you know yourself. You may find your own suppressed and rejected thoughts following back to you with an "alienated majesty." Reading the great writers, you may have the experience Longinus associated with the sublime: You feel that you have actually created the text yourself. For somehow your predecessors are more yourself than you are.

This was my own experience reading the two writers who have influenced me the most, Sigmund Freud and Ralph Waldo Emerson. They gave words to thoughts and feelings that I had never been able to render myself. They shone a light onto the world, and what they saw, suddenly I saw, too. From Emerson I learned to trust my own thoughts, to trust them even when every voice seems to be on the other side. I need the wherewithal, as Emerson did, to say what's on my mind and to take the inevitable hits. Much more I learned from the sage – about character, about loss, about joy, about writing and its secret sources, but Emerson most centrally preaches the gospel of self-reliance, and that is what I have tried most to take from him. I continue to hold in mind one of Emerson's most memorable passages: "Society is a joint-stock company, in which the members agree, for the better securing of his bread to each shareholder, to surrender the liberty and culture of the eater. The virtue in most request is conformity. Self-reliance is its aversion. It loves not realities and creators, but names and customs."

Emerson's greatness lies not only in showing you how powerful names and customs can be, but also in demonstrating how exhilarating it is to buck them. When he came to Harvard to talk about religion, he shocked the professors and students by challenging the divinity of Jesus and the truth of his miracles. He wasn't invited back for decades.

From Freud I found a great deal to ponder as well. I don't mean Freud the aspiring scientist, but the Freud who was a speculative essayist and interpreter of the human condition like Emerson. Freud challenges nearly every significant human ideal. He goes after religion. He says that it comes down to the longing for the father. He goes after love. He calls it "the overestimation of the erotic object." He attacks our desire for charismatic popular leaders. We're drawn to them because we hunger for absolute authority. He declares that dreams don't predict the future and that there's nothing benevolent about them. They're disguised fulfillments of repressed wishes.

Freud has something challenging and provoking to say about virtually every human aspiration. I learned that if I wanted to affirm any consequential ideal, I had to talk my way past Freud. He was – and is – a perpetual challenge and goad.

Never has there been a more shrewd and imaginative cartographer of the psyche. His separation of the self into three parts, and his sense of the fraught, anxious, but often negotiable relations among them (negotiable when you come to the game with a Freudian knowledge), does a great deal to help one navigate experience. (Though sometimes – and I owe this to Emerson – it seems right to let the psyche fall into civil war, accepting barrages of anxiety and grief for this or that good reason.)

The battle is to make such writers one's own, to winnow them out and to find their essential truths. We need to see where they fall short and where they exceed the mark, and then to develop them a little, as the ideas themselves, one comes to see, actually developed others. (Both Emerson and Freud live out of Shakespeare – but only a giant can be truly influenced by Shakespeare.) In reading, I continue to look for one thing – to be influenced, to learn something new, to be thrown off my course and onto another, better way.

My father knew that he was dissatisfied with life. He knew that none of the descriptions people had for him quite fit. He understood that he was always out of joint with life as it was. He had talent: My brother and I each got about half the raw ability he possessed, and that's taken us through life well enough. But what to do with that talent – there was the rub for my father. He used to stroll through the house intoning his favorite line from Groucho Marx's ditty "Whatever It Is, I'm Against It." (I recently asked my son, now twenty-one, if he thought I was mistaken in teaching him this particular song when he was six years old. "No!" he said, filling the air with an invisible forest of exclamation points.) But what my father never managed to get was a sense of who he might become. He never had a world of possibilities spread before him, never made sustained contact with the best that has been thought and said. He didn't get to revise his understanding of himself, figure out what he'd do best that might give the world some profit.

My father was a gruff man but also a generous one, so that night at the kitchen table at 58 Clewley Road he made an effort to let me have the chance that had been denied to him by both fate and character. He gave me the chance to see what I was all about, and if it proved to be different from him, proved even to be something he didn't like or entirely comprehend, then he'd deal with it.

Right now, if you're going to get a real education, you may have to be aggressive and assertive.

Your professors will give you some fine books to read, and they'll probably help you understand them. What they won't do, for reasons that perplex me, is ask you if the books contain truths you could live your life by. When you read Plato, you'll probably learn about his metaphysics and his politics and his way of conceiving the soul. But no one will ask you if his ideas are good enough to believe in. No one will ask you, in the words of Emerson's disciple William James, what their "cash value" might be. No one will suggest that you might use Plato as your bible for a week or a year or longer. No one, in short, will ask you to use Plato to help you change your life.

That will be up to you. You must put the question of Plato to yourself. You must ask whether reason should always rule the passions, philosophers should always rule the state, and poets should inevitably be banished from a just commonwealth. You have to ask yourself if wildly expressive music (rock and rap and the rest) deranges the soul in ways that are destructive to its health. You must inquire of yourself if balanced calm is the most desirable human state.

Occasionally – for you will need some help in fleshing out the answers – you may have to prod your professors to see if they will take the text at hand – in this case the divine and disturbing Plato – to be true. And you will have to be tough if the professor mocks you for uttering a sincere question instead of keeping matters easy for all concerned by staying detached and analytical. (Detached analysis has a place, but in the end you've got to speak from the heart and pose the question of truth.) You'll be the one who pesters your teachers. You'll ask your history teacher about whether there is a design to our history, whether we're progressing or declining, or whether, in the words of a fine recent play, *The History Boys*, history's "just one fuckin' thing after another." You'll be the one who challenges your biology teacher about the intellectual conflict between evolutionist and creationist thinking. You'll not only question the statistics teacher about what numbers can explain but what they can't.

Because every subject you study is a language, and since you may adopt one of these languages as your own, you'll want to know how to speak it expertly and also how it fails to deal with those concerns for which it has no adequate words. You'll be looking into the reach of every metaphor that every discipline offers, and you'll be trying to see around their corners.

The whole business is scary, of course. What if you arrive at college devoted to premed, sure that nothing will make you and your family happier than life as a physician, only to discover that elementary schoolteaching is where your heart is?

You might learn that you're not meant to be a doctor at all. Of course, given your intellect and discipline, you can still probably be one. You can pound your round peg through the very square hole of medical school, then go off into the profession. And society will help you. Society has a cornucopia of resources to encourage you in doing what society needs done but that you don't much like doing and are not cut out to do. To ease your grief, society offers alcohol, television, drugs, divorce, and buying, buying, buying what you don't need. But all those, too, have their costs.

Education is about finding out what form of work for you is close to being play – work you do so easily that it restores you as you go. Randall Jarrell once said that if he were a rich man, he would pay money to teach poetry to students. (I would, too, for what it's worth.) In saying that, he (like my father) hinted in the direction of a profound and true theory of learning.

Having found what's best for you to do, you may be surprised by how far you rise, how prosperous, even against your own projections, you become. The student who eschews medical school to follow his gift for teaching small children spends his twenties in low-paying but pleasurable and soul-rewarding toil. He's always behind on his student-loan payments; he still lives in a house with four other guys, not all of whom got proper instructions on how to clean a bathroom. He buys shirts from the Salvation Army, has intermittent Internet, and vacations where he can. But lo – he has a gift for teaching. He writes an essay about how to teach, then a book – which no one buys. But he writes another – in part out of a feeling of injured merit, perhaps – and that one they do buy.

Money is still a problem, but in a new sense. The world wants him to write more, lecture, travel more, and will pay him for his efforts, and he likes this a good deal. But he also likes staying around and showing up at school and figuring out how to get this or that little runny-nosed specimen to begin learning how to read. These are the kinds of problems that are worth having, and if you advance, as Thoreau asked us to do, in the general direction of your dreams, you may have them. If you advance in the direction of someone else's dreams – if you want to live someone else's dreams rather than yours – then get a TV for every room, buy yourself a lifetime supply of your favorite quaff, crank up the porn channel, and groove away. But when we expend our energies in rightful ways, Robert Frost observed, we stay whole and vigorous and we don't get weary. "Strongly spent," the poet says, "is synonymous with kept."

The Culture of Contempt
Arthur C. Brooks

Chapter 1 in *Love Your Enemies: How Decent People Can Save America from the Culture of Contempt*. New York: Broadside Books, 2019, pp. 19-43. Slightly edited for length and clarity.

Arthur C. Brooks (b. 1964) is an American economist and political commentator. After high school he pursued a decade-long career as a professional French hornist before earning his bachelor's and master's degrees in economics and a Ph.D. in policy analysis. He has taught at Syracuse University and Georgia State University, and is currently the head of the American Enterprise Institute. He is the author of several books on charitable giving, free enterprise, and economic policy.

Why we are reading this: This work is the first of three in the anthology that provide thought-provoking critiques of contemporary intellectual and cultural life. Brooks addresses the frequently toxic atmosphere of today's politics and social media. He suggests that our problem is a pervasive "culture of contempt," which he argues is more corrosive of social relations than anger or other such emotions. Brooks suggests some ways to break out of this culture of contempt so we can have more fulfilling and productive conversations and relationships with people with whom we disagree.

The year was 2006. I was a professor at Syracuse University, and I had just released my first commercial book, *Who Really Cares*. It was about charitable giving – about the people in America who give the most to charity, broken down by categories such as politics and religion.

Sounds like a real page-turner, doesn't it? Frankly, I didn't expect it to get much attention. I would have been happy if it had sold a couple thousand copies. Why? My past work had consisted mostly of dense academic journal articles with blood-pumping titles like "Genetic Algorithms and Public Economics" and "Contingent Valuation and the Winner's Curse in Internet Art Auctions." *Who Really Cares* was a little more interesting, but not much. I published the book, and waited for the phone to not ring.

Instead, it rang. And rang. As sometimes happens with academic books, it hit the popular zeitgeist in just the right way. For whatever reason, it was a hot news story that some people gave a lot to charity and some didn't, and my book appeared to explain why. A few famous people talked about the book, and before I knew it, I was on TV and the book started selling hundreds of copies a day.

Weirdest of all for me, total strangers began to reach out. I quickly got used to e-mails from people I had never met, pouring out intimate details of their lives, because, I learned, when people read a whole book by you, they feel that they know you. Moreover, if they don't like the book, they don't like *you*.

One afternoon a couple of weeks after the book came out, I got an e-mail from a man in Texas that began "Dear Professor Brooks: You are a fraud." Tough start. But my Texan correspondent didn't stop there. His e-mail was about five thousand words long, criticizing in vitriolic detail every chapter in the book and informing me of my numerous inadequacies as a researcher and person. It took me twenty minutes just to get through his screed.

OK now, put yourself in my position. What would you do at this point? Here are three options:

Option 1. Ignore him. He's just some random guy, right? Why waste *my* time, even if he wasted *his* lambasting my book, chapter and verse?

Option 2. Insult him. Say, "Get a life, man. Don't you have something better to do than reach out and bother a stranger?"

Option3. Destroy him. Pick out three or four of his most glaring, idiotic errors and throw them in his face, adding, "Hey, blockhead, if you don't know economics, best not to embarrass yourself in front of a professional economist."

More and more, these three alternatives (or a combination of them) are the only ones we feel are available to us in modern ideological conflicts. Few other options come to mind when we're confronted with disagreement. Notice that they all grow from the same root: contempt. They all express the view that my interlocutor is unworthy of my consideration.

Each option will provoke a different response, but what they all have in common is that they foreclose the possibility of a productive discussion. They basically guarantee permanent enmity. You might note that *he started it*. True – although you could probably say I started it by writing the book. Either way, just as the rejoinder "he started it" never cut any ice for me when my kids were little and fighting in the back seat of the car, it has no moral weight here, where our goal is to undercut the culture of contempt.

Later, I'll tell you which of the three options – ignore, insult, or destroy – I chose in responding to my Texan correspondent. But before I do so, we have a trip to make through the science and philosophy of contempt.

In 2014, researchers at Northwestern University, Boston College, and the University of Melbourne published an article in the *Proceedings of the National Academy of Sciences,* a prestigious academic journal.[1] The subject was human conflict due to "motive attribution asymmetry" – the phenomenon of assuming that your ideology is based in love, while your opponent's ideology is based in hate.

The researchers found that a majority of Republicans and Democrats today suffer from a level of motive attribution asymmetry that is comparable to that of Palestinians and Israelis. In both cases, the two sides think that they are driven by benevolence, while the other side is evil and motivated by hate. Therefore neither side is willing to negotiate or compromise. As a result, the authors found, "political conflict between American Democrats and Republicans and ethnoreligious conflict between Israelis and Palestinians seem intractable, despite the availability of reasonable compromise solutions in both cases."

Think about what this means: We are headed to the point where achieving bipartisan compromise, on issues from immigration to guns to confirming a Supreme Court justice, is as difficult as achieving Middle East peace. We may not be engaging in daily violence against each other, but we can't make progress as a society when both sides believe that they are motivated by love while the other side is motivated by hate.

People often characterize the current moment as being "angry." I wish this were true, because anger tends to be self-limiting. It is an emotion that occurs when we want to change someone's behavior and believe we can do so. While anger is often perceived as a negative emotion, research shows that its social purpose is not actually to drive others away but rather to remove problematic elements of a relationship and bring people back

---

[1] Adam Waytz, Liane L. Young, and Jeremy Ginges, "Motive Attribution Asymmetry for Love vs. Hate Drives Intractable Conflict," *Proceedings of the National Academy of Sciences of the United States of America* 111, no. 44 (Nov. 2014): 15687-92, doi: 10.1073/pnas.1414146111.

together.[2] Believe it or not, there is little evidence that anger in marriage is correlated with separation or divorce.[3]

Think about a fight you've had with a close friend, sibling, or spouse. If you were upset and got angry, was your goal to push her out of your life entirely? Did you suppose that the person was motivated by her *hatred* for you? Of course not. Whether anger is the right strategy or not, we get angry because we recognize that things are not as they should be, we want to set them right, and we think we can.

Motive attribution asymmetry doesn't lead to anger, because it doesn't make you want to repair the relationship. Believing your foe is motivated by hate leads to something far worse: contempt. While anger seeks to bring someone back into the fold, contempt seeks to exile. It attempts to mock, shame, and permanently exclude from relationships by belittling, humiliating, and ignoring. So while anger says, "I care about this," contempt says, "You disgust me. You are beneath caring about."

Once I asked a psychologist friend about the root of violent conflict. He told me it was "contempt that is poorly hidden." What makes you violent is the perception that you are being held in contempt. This rips families, communities, and whole nations apart. If you want to make a lifelong enemy, show him contempt.

The destructive power of contempt is well documented in the work of the famous social psychologist and relationship expert John Gottman. He is a longtime professor at the University of Washington in Seattle and cofounder with his wife, Julie Schwartz Gottman, of the Gottman Institute, which is dedicated to improving relationships. In his work, Gottman has studied thousands of married couples. He'll ask each couple to tell their story – how they met and courted, their highs and lows as a couple, and how their marriage has changed over the years – before having them discuss contentious issues.

After watching a couple interact for just one hour, he can predict with *94 percent accuracy* whether that couple will divorce within three years.[4] How can he tell? It's not from the anger that the couples express. Gottman

---

[2] Agneta H. Fischer and Ira J. Roseman, "Beat Them or Ban Them: The Characteristics and Social Functions of Anger and Contempt," *Journal of Personality and Social Psychology* 93, no. 1 (July 2007): 103-15, doi: 10.1037/0022-3514.93.1.103.

[3] John M. Gottman, "A Theory of Marital Dissolution and Stability," *Journal of Family Psychology* 7, no. 2 (June 1993): 57-75, doi: 10.1037/0893-3200.7.1.57.

[4] Kim T. Buehlman, John M. Gottman, and Lynn F. Katz, "How a Couple Views Their Past Predicts Their Future: Predicting Divorce from an Oral History Interview," *Journal of Family Psychology* 5, nos. 3-4 (Mar.-June 1992): 295-318, doi: 10.1037/0893-3200.5.3-4.295.

confirms that anger doesn't predict separation or divorce.[5] The biggest warning signs, he explains, are indicators of *contempt*. These include sarcasm, sneering, hostile humor, and – worst of all – eye-rolling. These little acts effectively say "You are worthless" to the one person you should love more than any other. Want to see if a couple will end up in divorce court? Watch them discuss a contentious topic, and see if either partner rolls his or her eyes.

What does all this have to do with American politics? I asked him that. At this question, Gottman – an ebullient, happy person – becomes somber.

There's been a denigration of respect in the dialogue in this country. It's always us versus them.... We see Republicans thinking they're better than Democrats, Democrats thinking they're better than Republicans, people from the coast thinking they're better than people inland. It goes on and on, and I think it's very harmful. This "us versus them" is what gets our medial prefrontal cortex – that's the part of the brain between our eyes – to not respond with understanding and compassion. And that's not what our country's about.

The pandemic of contempt in political matters makes it impossible for people of opposing views to work together. Go to YouTube and watch the 2016 presidential debates: they are masterpieces of eye-rolling, sarcasm, and sneering derision. For that matter, listen as politicians at all levels talk about their election opponents, or members of the other party. Increasingly, they describe people unworthy of any kind of consideration, with no legitimate ideas or views. And social media? On any contentious subject, these platforms are contempt machines.

Of course this is self-defeating in a nation in which political competitors must also be collaborators. How likely are you to want to work with someone who has told an audience that you are a fool or a criminal? Would you make a deal with someone who publicly said you are corrupt? How about becoming friends with someone who says your opinions are idiotic? Why would you be willing to compromise politically with such a person? You can resolve problems with someone with whom you disagree, even if you disagree angrily, but you can't come to a solution with someone who holds you in contempt or for whom you have contempt.

Contempt is impractical and bad for a country dependent on people working together in politics, communities, and the economy. Unless we

---

[5] John M. Gottman, "A Theory of Marital Dissolution and Stability," *Journal of Family Psychology* 7, no. 2 (June 1993): 57-75, doi: 10.1037/0893-3200.7. 1.57.

hope to become a one-party state, we cannot afford contempt for our fellow Americans who simply disagree with us.

Nor is contempt morally justified. The vast majority of Americans on the other side of the ideological divide are not terrorists or criminals. They are people like us who happen to see certain contentious issues differently. When we treat our fellow Americans as enemies, we lose friendships, and thus, love and happiness. That's exactly what's happening. One poll shows that a sixth of Americans have stopped talking to a family member or close friend because of the 2016 election. People have ended close relationships, the most important source of happiness, because of politics.

In one particularly sad example of this in the run-up to the 2018 midterm election, *six siblings* of an incumbent congressman made a television advertisement for his opponent.[6] One sister called him a racist. A brother said, "He just doesn't appear to be well." Another brother impugned his motives for his policies, saying his views on regulation must be motivated by money from industry. The congressman's public response? His siblings "are related by blood to me but like leftists everywhere, they put political ideology before family. Stalin would be proud."[7]

In 1960, only 5 percent of Americans said they would be displeased if their child married someone from the other political party. By 2010, that number was 40 percent, and no doubt has risen from there.[8] We have become far removed indeed from Thomas Jefferson's admonition that a "difference in politics should never be permitted to enter into social intercourse, or to disturb its friendships, its charities or justice."[9]

Gottman calls contempt "sulfuric acid for love." However, it doesn't just destabilize our relationships and our politics. Gottman tells me that it

---

[6] Joseph Flaherty, "Arizona Congressman Paul Gosar's Siblings Endorse Rival in New Campaign Ads," *Phoenix New Times,* Sept. 21, 2018, https://www.phoenixnewtimes.com/news/arizona-congressman-paul-gosars-siblings-endorse-opponent-10849863.

[7] Paul Gosar (@DrPaulGosar), "My siblings who chose to film ads against me are all liberal Democrats who hate President Trump. These disgruntled Hillary supporters are related by blood to me but like leftists everywhere, they put political ideology before family. Stalin would be proud. #Azo4 #MAGA2018," Twitter, Sept. 22, 2018, 11:24 a.m.

[8] David A. Graham, "Really, Would You Let Your Daughter Marry a Democrat?" *Atlantic,* Sept. 27, 2012, https://www.theatlantic.com/politics/archive/2012/09/really-would-you-let-your-daughter-marry-a-democrat/262959/.

[9] Thomas Jefferson, "From Thomas Jefferson to Henry Lee, 10 August 1824," Rotunda, http://rotunda.upress.virginia.edu/founders/default.xqy?keys=FOEA-print-04-02-02-4451.

also causes a comprehensive degradation of our immune systems. It damages self-esteem, alters behavior, and even impairs cognitive processing.[10] According to the American Psychological Association, the feeling of rejection, so often experienced after being treated with contempt, increases "anxiety, depression, jealousy, and sadness" and "reduces performance on difficult intellectual tasks."[11] Being treated with contempt takes a measurable physical toll. Those who routinely feel excluded "have poorer sleep quality, and their immune systems don't function as well" as those of people who don't suffer contemptuous treatment.[12]

As important, contempt isn't just harmful for the person being treated poorly. It is also harmful for the contemptuous person, because treating others with contempt causes us to secrete two stress hormones, cortisol and adrenaline. The consequence of constantly secreting these hormones – the equivalent of living under significant consistent stress – is staggering. Gottman points out that people in couples who are constantly battling die *twenty years earlier,* on average, than those who consistently seek mutual understanding. Our contempt is inarguably disastrous for *us,* let alone the people we are holding in contempt.

In truth, contempt is *not* what we really want. How do I know this? To begin with, that's what I hear all day, every day. I travel constantly, and for my job I talk about policy and politics. Not a day goes by when someone doesn't bemoan the fact that we are coming apart as a country, unable to have a respectful airing of political views like civilized adults. People are exhausted.

That's exactly what Tim Dixon, cofounder of the organization More in Common, calls the "exhausted majority": Americans who are tired of the constant conflict and worried about the future of the country. In a groundbreaking study on political attitudes in the US, he finds that 93 percent of Americans say that they are tired of how divided we have become as a country; 71 percent believe this "strongly." Large majorities say privately that they believe in the importance of compromise, reject the

---

[10] Agneta H. Fischer and Ira J. Roseman, "Beat Them or Ban Them: The Characteristics and Social Functions of Anger and Contempt."

[11] Kirsten Weir, "The Pain of Social Rejection," American Psychological Association, *Monitor on Psychology* 43, no. 4 (Apr. 2012), 50, http://www.apa.org/monitor/2012/04/rejection.aspx.

[12] Weir, "Pain of Social Rejection."

absolutism of the extreme wings of both parties, and are not motivated by partisan loyalty.[13]

A lot of other evidence backs up Dixon's claim that a majority of Americans dislike the culture of contempt. A 2017 *Washington Post*-University of Maryland poll asked, "Do you think problems in America's politics right now are similar to most periods of partisan disagreement, or do you think problems have reached a dangerous low point?" Seventy-one percent of respondents chose the latter.[14] Almost two-thirds of Americans say that the future of the country is a very or somewhat significant source of stress, more than the percentage who say they are stressed by money concerns or work.[15] Even more disconcerting, 60 percent of Americans consider our current political moment the lowest point in U.S. history that they can remember – a figure, the American Psychological Association points out, that spans "every generation, including those who lived through World War II and Vietnam, the Cuban missile crisis and the September 11 terrorist attacks."[16] More than 70 percent of Americans believe that the country will be greatly hurt if opposing parties don't work together.[17]

This defies the idea that America is split between two big groups of hyperpartisans intent on vanquishing the other side. On the contrary, most are quite nuanced in their views and don't fit into a neat ideological camp. As just one illustrative example, Dixon's exhausted majority is significantly more likely than the highly partisan minority to believe that hate speech in America is a problem, but that political correctness is *also* a problem. In other words, this majority wants our country to address the former, but not by embracing the latter.

---

[13] Stephen Hawkins, et al., "Hidden Tribes: A Study of America's Polarized Landscape," More in Common, 2018, https://static1.squarespace.com/static/5a70a7c3010027736a2274of/t/5bbcea6b7817f7bf7342b718/1539107467397/hidden_tribes_report-2.pdf.

[14] John Wagner and Scott Clement, "'It's Just Messed Up': Most Think Political Divisions as Bad as Vietnam Era, New Poll Shows," *Washington Post,* Oct. 28, 2017, https://www.washingtonpost.com/graphics/2017/national/democracy-poll/?utm_term=.c6b95de49f42.

[15] "APA Stress in America Survey: US at 'Lowest Point We Can Remember'; Future of Nation Most Commonly Reported Source of Stress," American Psychological Association, Nov. 1, 2017, http://www.apa.org/news/press/releases/2017/11/lowest-point.aspx.

[16] "APA Stress in America Survey."

[17] "Many See Potential Harm from Future Gridlock, for the Nation and Personally," Pew Research Center, Dec. 11, 2014, http://www.people-press.org/2014/12/11/few-see-quick-cure-for-nations-political-divisions/12-11-2014_02.

You might be thinking I have some explaining to do here. On the one hand, I am asserting that our culture, especially our political culture, is overrun with contempt. On the other hand, I'm saying it's not what a pretty big majority of us want. But don't we get what we want in democracies and free markets?

Yes and no. There are lots of cases in which people demand something they hate. Have you ever met a problem drinker? Every morning, he berates himself for his lack of self-discipline and resolves not to drink that night. When night rolls around, filled with anxiety and cravings, he says, "Eh, I'll quit tomorrow." Similarly, most smokers say they wish they didn't smoke, yet they voluntarily continue, spending their money and wrecking their health in the process.

What's going on here? The answer is addiction, of course. Addiction clouds our ability to make long-run choices in our own interest. Personally, I have a terrible sweet tooth. I know perfectly well that I should cut refined sugar out of my diet. I *want* to get off the sweet stuff. But I just know that tonight, around eight p.m., I'll lose my resolve and hit the Oreos. (It's my wife's fault for buying them.) You probably have your own weakness, out of which you demand something in the short run that you don't really want in the long run. Maybe it's a bad relationship you just can't quit, or gambling, or buying clothes you can't afford.

Economists carve out a special sort of demand for addictive things. They note that we make decisions that are deeply suboptimal in the long run because the pain of breaking the habit is so high in the short run. Therefore, we really wish we didn't drink, but we put off the discomfort of quitting, day after day.

America is addicted to political contempt. While most of us hate what it is doing to our country and worry about how contempt coarsens our culture over the long term, many of us still compulsively consume the ideological equivalent of meth from elected officials, academics, entertainers, and some of the news media. Millions actively indulge their habit by participating in the cycle of contempt in the way they treat others, especially on social media. We wish our national debates were nutritious and substantive, but we have an insatiable craving for insults to the other side. As much as we know we should ignore the nasty columnist, turn off the TV loudmouth, and stop checking our Twitter feeds, we indulge our guilty urge to listen as our biases are confirmed that the other guys are not just wrong, but stupid and evil.

We are responsible for our contempt addiction, of course, just as meth addicts are ultimately accountable for their addiction. But there are also our pushers – the political meth dealers. Knowing our weakness, dividing leaders on both the left and right seek power and fame by setting American against American, brother against brother, compatriot against compatriot. These leaders assert that we must choose sides, then argue that the other side is wicked – not worthy of any consideration – rather than challenging them to listen to others with kindness and respect. They foster a culture of contempt.

There is an "outrage industrial complex" in American media today, which profits handsomely from our contempt addiction. This starts by catering to just one ideological side. Leaders and media on the left and right then keep their audiences hooked on contempt by telling audiences what they want to hear, selling a narrative of conflict and painting gross caricatures of the other side. They make us feel justified in our own beliefs while affirming our worst assumptions about those who disagree with us – namely that they are, in fact, stupid, evil, and not worth giving the time of day.

In a battle for public attention, elite opinion makers on both the right and left increasingly describe our political disagreements as an apocalyptic struggle between good and evil, comparing the other side to animals and using metaphors of terrorism. Open your favorite newspaper or browse the prime-time cable lineup and you will find example after example. The result of hyperbolic rhetoric becoming commonplace? A deepening culture of contempt, a growing threat of actual violence, and – of course – record profits. (Hey, you saw *Breaking Bad,* right? Meth is very profitable, too.)

Social media intensifies our addiction by allowing us to filter out the news and opinions we disagree with, thus purifying the contempt drug. According to the Brookings Institution, the average Facebook user has five politically like-minded friends for every friend on the other side of the political spectrum.[18] Researchers from the University of Georgia have shown that Twitter users are unlikely to be exposed to cross-ideological content because the users they follow are politically homogeneous.[19] Even in the world of dating apps, scholars have found that people sort themselves based on political affiliation.[20] These companies give us

---

[18] Joshua Bleiberg and Darrell M. West, "Political Polarization on Facebook," May 13, 2015, https://www.brookings.edu/blog/techtank/2015/05/13/political-polarization-on-facebook.

[19] Itai Himelboim, Stephen McCreery, and Marc Smith, "Birds of a Feather Tweet Together: Integrating Network and Content Analysis to Examine Cross-Ideology Exposure on Twitter," *Journal of Computer-Mediated Communication* 18, no. 2 (Jan. 2013): 40-60, doi: 10.1111/jcc4.12001.

[20] Neil Malhotra and Gregory Huber, "Dimensions of Political Homophily: Isolating Choice Homophily along Political Characteristics," Stanford Graduate School of Business Working Paper No. 3108 (Oct. 2013), https://www.gsb

platforms to create feedback loops where we are exposed only to those who think similarly, and where people can hide behind a cloak of anonymity and spew hateful, vitriolic commentary.

"Ideological siloing" means we stop interacting entirely with those who hold opposing views. Polls show that a majority of both Republicans and Democrats have "just a few" or no friends who are members of the other party.[21] By contrast, just 14 percent of Republicans and 9 percent of Democrats have "a lot" of close friends from the opposing party.[22] The results of not knowing people of opposing viewpoints and seeing them only through the lens of hostile media is predictable. Today, 55 percent of Democrats have a "very unfavorable" view of Republicans, and 58 percent of Republicans hold that view of Democrats. This represents a threefold increase since 1994.[23]

There is evidence that as we become less exposed to opposing viewpoints, we become less logically competent as people. Author David Blankenhorn has noted a rise in several modes of weak political thinking in the past decade.[24] Notable among these modes are: extreme binary opinions ("I am completely right, so you are completely wrong"); seeing any uncertainty as a mark of weakness; motivated reasoning (looking only for evidence that supports your own opinion – which is easier when one can curate one's news and social media); *argumentum ad hominem* ("You have selfish and immoral reasons for your opinion"); and a refusal to agree on any basic facts ("Your news is fake news").

The structure of party politics is also driving the culture of contempt. Every two years, 435 seats in the House of Representatives are up for election. In the last three national elections, more and more of those seats have become noncompetitive, with incumbents winning reelection at rates of 90 percent, 95 percent, and 97 percent.[25] Both political parties draw up

---

.stanford.edu/faculty-research/working-papers/dimensions-political-homophily-isolating-choice-homophily-along.

[21] "Partisan Animosity, Personal Politics, Views of Trump," Pew Research Center, Oct. 5, 2017, http://www.people-press.org/2017/10/05/8-partisan-animosity -personal-politics-views-of-trump.

[22] "Partisan Animosity."

[23] "Partisanship and Political Animosity in 2016," Pew Research Center, June 22, 2016, http://www.people-press.org/2016/06/22/partisanship-and- political-animosity-in-2016.

[24] David Blankenhorn, "The Top 14 Causes of Political Polarization," *American Interest,* May 16, 2018, https://www.the-american-interest.com/2018/05/16/the-top-14-causes-of-political-polarization.

[25] "Reelection Rates over the Years," Open Secrets, Center for Responsive Politics, https://www.opensecrets.org/overview/reelect.php. Election results are

gerrymandered districts that are filled with true believers, dividing theirs into many districts and lumping opponents into few so as to decrease their legislative representation. As a result, politicians increasingly have to appeal only to members of their own party for votes. Primaries often devolve into a competition to see who can take the most extreme positions in order to prove party fealty and turn out the hard-core base. The inevitable result is the demonization of the other side.

Members of Congress often say that a big change over the past decade is that they no longer spend much social time with members of the opposing party. Not only do they disagree about politics; they hardly know one another as people. You have probably heard many times that in decades past, Democrats and Republicans would argue vigorously on the floor by day, and then go out to dinner together by night. This was part of how they ultimately got business done. By sharing life together outside of work, they developed the trust and goodwill necessary to make difficult choices for the good of all, including those beyond their own political camps.

Politicians often tell me they have felt the need to avoid these friendships for self-preservation; they worry about being seen as too chummy with the other side. In an environment of gerrymandered ideological purity and extreme political contempt, a primary challenger's dream is finding an incumbent fraternizing with the "enemy."

This isn't bad for just our politics; it's bad for politicians as people. Of course, some politicians on both sides like the polarized status quo – it has made their careers possible. Perhaps I would have believed this is the norm before I moved to Washington, DC, ten years ago, but today I know that's not the case at all. I have gotten to know many members of Congress as friends, and – as surprising as it might seem to some readers – my admiration for politicians has grown enormously. They are some of the most patriotic, hardworking people I have ever met. They love America and hate our culture of contempt as much as you and I. They tell me they regret how polarized things have become and wish they knew how to fight the trend. Like us, they are victims of America's political contempt addiction.

One of their biggest regrets is that important issues that require cooperation become a political Ping-Pong match. One side gains power and imposes its vision on strict party-line voting, and then the other side

---

for 2012, 2014, and 2016; at the time of writing, final results for the 2018 midterms are not available, but the incumbent reelection rate will likely be similar to recent reelection rates of at least 90 percent.

gains power and tries to impose its vision in the same way. The people caught in the middle are those with the least power.

Take health care in America. The Affordable Care Act of 2010 – aka Obamacare – changed how health care was purchased and delivered for millions of low-income Americans. It was passed on party-line Democratic votes in the House and Senate, with no Republican support at all. This, of course, set it up to be rolled back the minute the Republicans took over both houses and the White House, which they did in 2016. While getting rid of Obamacare proved harder than Republicans planned, they did succeed in dismantling large parts of it, once again changing how poorer Americans got their health care, and doing so on strict party-line terms. No one doubts that when (not *if*) the Democrats take full control once again, the political Ping-Pong match will continue, wherein low-income Americans' health care is the ball.

As an old African proverb has it, "When elephants fight, it's the grass that suffers." The weak get hurt in conflicts between the powerful. Americans at the bottom of the income scale are always the ones who lose when contempt crowds out cooperation at the top. The politics of contempt never hurts the rich very much. It hurts people in poverty. We should all be able to agree that that's bad.

Contempt is driving us apart and making us miserable. It is holding us hostage. What exactly do we want instead?

For the answer to this, let me start by turning back to my opening story – about my correspondent in Texas who hated my book and let me know in vivid terms. My response options seemed to be (1) ignore, (2) insult, or (3) destroy.

Instead, I accidentally picked a fourth option, and it created a huge epiphany for me. Here's what happened: As I read his e-mail, I was insulted and felt attacked. But I also kept thinking, *He read my book!* I was filled with gratitude. As an academic, I was used to writing things that almost no one would read. I had put my whole heart into that project for two years, and this guy had taken the time to read the whole thing. That amazed me. I became conscious of that particular sentiment, and for whatever reason, I decided to tell him that. I wrote back and said I realized he really hated my book, but that it had taken me a lot of work to write, and I deeply appreciated his time and attention to every detail.

Fifteen minutes later, a second message from the guy popped up in my in-box. I opened the e-mail and braced myself. But instead of another salvo, he said he was shocked that I'd read his note and the next time I was in Dallas we should grab some dinner. This message was completely friendly. From enemy to friend in a matter of minutes! Did he suddenly like my book? Of course not. He simply learned that he liked *me* because I had taken the time to read his e-mail and was nice in the way I responded.

Don't get the wrong impression here. I'm not some saint who always reacts that way when personally attacked. Perhaps our unexpected rapprochement that day was just dumb luck. But here's what I learned from that lucky interaction: contempt is no match for love. The cycle of contempt depended on me, and I broke it with just a few words of gratitude. Doing so felt great for me, and it changed another person's heart.

I saw firsthand that contempt transmuted into friendliness when it was met with an overt expression of kindness and respect. From this, I saw for myself that kindness, reconciliation, and connection – not contempt, division, and isolation – are what our hearts really desire. I have since sought to understand the science behind this, reading all the scholarship I could find, and getting to know scholars on this topic.

One of the leading experts is Matthew Lieberman, a social psychologist at the University of California-Los Angeles. Lieberman has spent decades exploring the neuroscience of human relationships. He contends that we have an innate desire for positive social connections with one another, and that our brains experience deep pleasure when we achieve these connections.

You can think about this in dollars and cents. In his book, *Social: Why Our Brains Are Wired to Connect,* Lieberman observes that simply having a friend you see on most days gives the equivalent happiness boost of earning an additional $100,000 of income each year.[26] Seeing your neighbors on a regular basis gives as much happiness as an extra $60,000. Meanwhile, the experience of breaking a critical social tie, such as with a family member, is like experiencing a large income decline.[27] I suppose the congressman I mentioned before (who was denounced by his six siblings) effectively suffered bankruptcy.

In a similar study, psychologists from Brigham Young University examined the habits and social connections of more than three hundred thousand participants, and found that a lack of strong relationships increases the risk of premature death from all causes by 50 percent.[28] A Harvard University publication notes that this lack of communion through

---

[26] Matthew D. Lieberman, *Social: Why Our Brains Are Wired to Connect* (New York: Crown, 2013), 247.

[27] Lieberman, *Social*, 247.

[28] Julianne Holt-Lunstad, Timothy B. Smith, and J. Bradley Layton, "Social Relationships and Mortality Risk: A Meta-analytic Review," *PLOS Medicine* 7, no. 7 (July 2010): doi: 10.1371/journal.pmed.1000316.

social connections is roughly equivalent in health effects to that of smoking fifteen cigarettes a day.[29]

Here's what these facts and figures mean to you and me. We all want to earn a lot more, and no one wants a big loss in income. We can't always control that, but we can affect something just as valuable for our well-being: our connections with others. Would you trade away $100,000 of your salary, or years of healthy life, over a political disagreement? Probably not. So don't sacrifice a friendship or family relationship over one either, and don't pass up a possible new friendship just because of politics.

A number of recent studies have asked why we crave connection and have found physiological answers. As neuroscientists from Emory University have discovered, social cooperation activates the parts of our brain that are linked to reward processing.[30] Using brain scans, they demonstrate that when we experience the pleasure of connection, these reward circuits are activated, proving that "social cooperation is intrinsically rewarding to the human brain."[31] By contrast, when we experience exclusion or rejection, the brain's pain centers are activated. In fact, the brain processes relational rejection the same way it processes physical pain. As Lieberman has found in his research, a broken heart can in many ways feel like a broken leg.[32]

Once again, ask yourself: Would I be willing to break a bone to be "right," politically?

We probably shouldn't need brain scans to tell us that building relationships is far preferable to the consequences of contempt and division. After all, the great thinkers and religions of the world have been counseling the wisdom of unity for millennia.

In Plato's *Republic,* the great philosopher writes, "Can there be any greater evil than discord and distraction and plurality where unity ought to reign? Or any greater good than the bond of unity? There cannot."[33] Aristotle believed the same thing. If separated from the unifying bonds of

---

[29] "The Health Benefits of Strong Relationships," *Harvard Women's Health Watch*, Dec. 2010, https://www.health.harvard.edu/newsletter _article/the-health-benefits-of-strong-relationships.

[30] "Emory Brain Imaging Studies Reveal Biological Basis for Human Cooperation," Emory Health Sciences Press Release, July 19, 2002, http://whsc.emory.edu/_releases/2002july/altruism.html.

[31] "Emory Brain Imaging Studies."

[32] Matthew D. Lieberman, *Social: Why Our Brains Are Wired to Connect* (New York: Crown Publishers, 2013).

[33] Plato, *The Republic*, trans. Benjamin Jowett (Los Angeles: Madison Park, 2010), 75.

friendship, he wrote in his *Nicomachean Ethics,* "no one would choose to live, though he had all other goods."[34]

This theme is consistent throughout the sacred texts of the world's religions, too. Psalm 133 proclaims, "How good and pleasant it is when God's people live together in unity!"[35] In Matthew's Gospel, Jesus warns, "Every kingdom divided against itself will be ruined, and every city or household divided against itself will not stand."[36] And the Bhagavad Gita, one of the ancient holy books of Hinduism, teaches that knowledge that "sees in all things a single, imperishable being, undivided among the divided" is *sattvic* – meaning pure, good, and virtuous.[37]

The Founding Fathers knew that social harmony would form the backbone of America. In his celebrated pamphlet *Common Sense,* Thomas Paine held that "it is not in numbers, but in unity, that our great strength lies."[38] James Madison, in the fourteenth Federalist Paper, warned that the "most alarming of all novelties, the most wild of all projects, the most rash of all attempts, is that of rendering us in pieces, in order to preserve our liberties and promote our happiness."[39] John Adams believed that the cancer of faction in America was to be "dreaded as the greatest political Evil, under our Constitution."[40] In his farewell address, George Washington famously warned against "the baneful effects" of political enmity.[41]

We try to have it both ways, of course – love for our friends and contempt for our enemies. Indeed, sometimes we even try to build unity around the common bonds of contempt for "the other." But it doesn't work, any more than an alcoholic can have "just a little drink" to take the edge off. Drunkenness crowds out sobriety. Contempt crowds out love

---

[34] Aristotle, *Nicomachean Ethics*, trans. W. D. Ross (Stilwell: Digireads.com, 2005), 8.1.

[35] Psalms 133:1 (New International Version).

[36] Matthew 12:25 (New International Version).

[37] Bhagavad Gita, trans. Stephen Mitchell (New York: Harmony Books, 2000), 186.

[38] Thomas Paine, *Common Sense,* Project Gutenberg, June 9, 2008, https://www.gutenberg.org/files/147/147-h/147-h.htm.

[39] James Madison, *The Federalist Papers*, No. 14, Avalon Project, Lillian Goldman Law Library, Yale University, 2008, http://avalon.law.yale.edu/18th_century/fed14.asp.

[40] John Adams, "From John Adams to Jonathan Jackson, 2 October 1780," Founders Online, National Archives, last modified June 13, 2018, https://founders.archives.gov/documents/Adams/06-10-02-0113.

[41] George Washington, "Washington's Farewell Address," Avalon Project, Lillian Goldman Law Library, Yale University, 2008, http://avalon.law.yale.edu/18th_century/washing. asp.

because it becomes our focus. If you have contempt for "them," more and more people will become "them." Monty Python made this point hilariously in the movie *Life of Brian,* where the bitterest of enemies are two rival Jewish dissident groups: the Judean People's Front and the People's Front of Judea.

From the philosophers of ancient Greece to the world's great religions to our own Founding Fathers to the psychology research of the modern era, we are exhorted to choose our heart's true desire: love and kindness. All warn unambiguously that division, if allowed to take permanent root, will be our misery and downfall.

Two caveats are in order here. First, unity does not necessarily mean agreement. I will devote a whole chapter later in this book to the importance of respectful *dis*agreement. Second, unity is always an aspiration; we will never be 100 percent unified. Even in times of war, our nation has not been unanimously behind the effort. Nevertheless, though not perfectly attainable, the goal to be *more* unified is still the right one to give us more of what we want as people.

We want love. How do we get it? We have to start by saying that it *is* what we really want. That is easier said than done. A famous Bible story makes this point:

> As Jesus and his disciples, together with a large crowd, were leaving the city, a blind man, Bartimaeus, was sitting by the roadside begging. When he heard that it was Jesus of Nazareth, he began to shout, "Jesus, Son of David, have mercy on me!"... "What do you want me to do for you?" Jesus asked him. The blind man said, "Rabbi, I want to see."[42]

At first, it seems kind of silly. A blind man, Bartimaeus, wants a miracle from Jesus. Jesus asks, "What do you want?" As my kids might say, "Duh – he wants to see." And, in fact, that is pretty much what the blind man answers.

This story is profound because, while people *do* know what they really want, they often *don't* ask for it. Think about the last time you had a real conflict with someone you love. You badly wanted the conflict to end and affection to return, but you kept fighting anyway. I have a friend who didn't talk to his daughter for twenty years and didn't even know his grandchildren's names. He badly wanted to reconcile but couldn't bring himself to do it. Maybe you have never done anything this extreme, but at

---

[42] Mark 10:46-51 (New International Version).

one time or another, we have all experienced the pain of a relational fracture that our pride prevents us from fixing.

Once again, there's the addiction. Addicts *all* want to be free from addiction, and there is a lot of help out there to set them free. All they have to do is let go of the thing they hate, and ask for what they truly want. But they don't, sometimes even until death. Why not? Most say the short-term agony of quitting is just too great, or that booze or other drugs, as terrible as they are, are the only thing that give real satisfaction in an empty life.

We have a cultural addiction to contempt – an addiction abetted by the outrage industrial complex for profit and power – and it's tearing us apart. Most of us don't want that, though. We want love, kindness, and respect. *But* we have to ask for it, choose it. It's hard; we are prideful, and contempt can give a sense of short-term purpose and satisfaction, like one more drink. No one ever said that breaking an addiction was easy. But make no mistake: Like Bartimaeus, we *can* choose what we truly want, as individuals and as a nation.

How? It's not good enough to leave it up to chance, hoping we accidentally react as I did to my Texan e-mailer. What can we do starting today to reject contempt and embrace love?

For an answer, I asked two experts.

The first is Dr. John Gottman, whom we met earlier in this chapter. I asked him how he thought we could use his ideas on marital harmony to improve our national discourse. If you want a more unified America based on bonds of love, how should you treat others with whom you disagree politically?

Gottman paused when I asked him this, because he had never answered this question before. Professors are always reluctant to go outside the range of their data and specific expertise. Nevertheless, he told me that he loved America, was brokenhearted by the contempt spreading across the country, and wanted to bring us back together. So he gave me four rules:

1. Focus on other people's distress, and focus on it empathetically. When others are upset about politics, listen to them respectfully. Try to understand their point of view before offering your own. Never listen only to rebut.
2. In your interactions with others, particularly in areas of disagreement, adopt the "five-to-one rule," which he gives couples. Make sure you offer five positive comments for every criticism. On social media, that means five positive messages for every one others might see as negative.

3. No contempt is *ever* justified, even if, in the heat of the moment, you think someone deserves it. It is unjustified more often than you know, it is always bad for you, and it will never convince anyone that she is wrong.
4. Go where people disagree with you and learn from them. That means making new friends and seeking out opinions you know you don't agree with. How to act when you get there? See rules 1 to 3!

The second person I consulted about how to fight contempt is the wisest man I know, who also happens to be one of the world's experts on bringing people together through bonds of compassion and love: His Holiness the Dalai Lama.

The Dalai Lama is the spiritual leader of the Tibetan Buddhist people and one of the most respected leaders in the world today. We have had a collaboration for a number of years, and although I am a Catholic and not a Buddhist, for me he is a mentor and guide. I was visiting him at his monastery in Dharamshala, India, in the Himalayan foothills, when I was starting to work on this book. "Your Holiness," I asked him, "what do I do when I feel contempt?" He responded, "Practice warm-heartedness."

To be honest, at first I thought, *You got anything else?* It sounded more like an aphorism than useful counsel. But when I thought about it, I saw it was actually tough and practical advice. He was not advocating surrender to the views of those with whom we disagree. If I believe I am right, I have a duty to stick to my views. But my duty is also to be kind, fair, and friendly to all, even those with whom I have great differences.

Difficult? Sure. The Dalai Lama would be the first to note that warm-heartedness is for strong people, not weak people. It is advice he has taken himself. At the age of just fifteen, he became the leader of the Tibetan Buddhist people after China's invasion of Tibet in 1950.[43] Following brutal suppression of his people, the Dalai Lama escaped into exile in 1959, and has since led a poor and dispossessed Tibetan community from his home in Dharamshala. The Dalai Lama and his people have been treated with contempt worse than most of us will ever experience in our lives – driven from their homes and barely recognized as people.

How has he responded? The Dalai Lama begins each day by offering up prayers for China, its leaders, and its people.[44] He practices warm-

---

[43] "Brief Biography," Office of His Holiness the Dalai Lama, https://www.dalailama.com/the-dalai-lama/biography-and-daily-life/brief-biography.
[44] Pico Iyer, *The Open Road: The Global Journey of the Fourteenth Dalai Lama* (New York: Borzoi Books, 2008).

heartedness toward the very regime that drove him and his followers into exile and continues to oppress the people of Tibet. That is strong, not weak. Warm-heartedness is not for the faint-hearted.

My next question to him was: How do I do that? Give me some practical tips, Your Holiness. He told me: Think back to a time in your life when you answered contempt with warm-heartedness. Remember how it made you feel, and then do it again. It was at that moment that I realized that warm-heartedness is exactly what transformed my e-mail exchange at the beginning of this chapter. I accidentally answered contempt with warm-heartedness and watched the contempt melt away in an instant.

Kindness and warm-heartedness are the antivenom for the poisonous contempt coursing through the veins of our political discourse. Contempt is what we saw when Tommy Hodges and Hawk Newsome – the Trump rally organizer and the Black Lives Matter activist – arrived on the National Mall. By inviting Hawk up onstage, Tommy did more than give Hawk a platform to speak. He acknowledged his dignity as a fellow American. He effectively said, *I may not agree with you, but what you have to say matters.* That simple demonstration of respect broke through the wall of mutual contempt that had separated them and completely transformed their interaction.

Hawk then responded in kind, by engaging his audience in a positive, warm-hearted way. He expressed moral common cause with his listeners – declaring that he was an American who loves his country and who wants to make America great – while challenging them to think differently about the plight of African Americans. His approach was deeply unifying. He made a moral case for compassion and fairness, and appealed to something that everyone had written on their hearts.

That doesn't mean that everyone in the audience agreed with what he said; they didn't. Something more profound happened than mere political agreement: a human connection that led to a respectful, productive competition of ideas.

This is exactly what America needs. It is what our hearts desire. And it does not have to be a flash in the pan. It's actually something that we can engineer and replicate all over America if we have the courage and will to do so.

How? Start with your own interactions. When you are treated with contempt, don't see it as a threat but as an opportunity. In the Dhammapada, one of the primary collections of the teachings of the Buddha, the master says:

> Conquer anger through gentleness,
> unkindness through kindness,

greed through generosity,
and falsehood by truth.[45]

When I first read that, I thought it was strange that the Buddha would instruct us to turn loving-kindness into an instrumentality to conquer others, but that was the wrong way of reading it. On reflection, I realized that *I* am the angry one, the ill-tempered one, the miser, and the liar. My job is to conquer *me*. My tool for doing so is to show warm-heartedness to others, especially when they are not showing it to me.

Your opportunity when treated with contempt is to change at least one heart – yours. You may not be able to control the actions of others, but you can absolutely control your reaction. *You* can break the cycle of contempt. You have the power to do that.

Your opportunity will come sooner than you think, whether on the left or right. Feel that you've been unfairly attacked on social media? Respond with warm-heartedness. Overhear someone make a snide remark about people who vote like you? Respond with kindness. Want to say something insulting about people who disagree with you? Take a breath, and show love instead.

That sounds great, you may be saying, but what if l don't feel it? *It doesn't matter.* It is what we *do* that most often determines how we *feel,* not the other way around. If you wait to feel warm-hearted toward your ideological foes, you may as well have WAITING TO FEEL WARM-HEARTED chiseled on your tombstone. Action doesn't follow attitude except in the rarest of circumstances. Rather, attitude follows action. Don't feel it? Fake it. Soon enough you'll start to feel it.

If we learn how to answer contempt with warm-heartedness, how to choose kindness over contempt, we can be leaders who fight contempt in society and bring more people – no matter how they vote or see the world – to the joy of loving one another.

---

[45] Eknath Easwaran, *Essence of the Dhammapada: The Buddha's Call to Nirvana* (Tomales, CA: Nilgiri Press, 2013), 263.

The Coddling of the American Mind
Greg Lukianoff and Jonathan Haidt

In *The Atlantic*, September 2015.

*Greg Lukianoff (b. 1974) is president of the Foundation for Individual Rights in Education, and a frequent commentator on higher education while **Jonathan Haidt** (b. 1963) is a social psychologist and business professor at New York University. Both have written extensively about how people talk to each other in today's America.*

Why we are reading this: Growing calls for trigger warnings and protection from microaggressions have become part of campus life at many universities. In this controversial article, Lukianoff and Haidt contend that the desire to protect students from ideas they deem offensive has had troubling consequences, including a possible threat to free speech. Students who would like to go deeper might read some of the responses to this essay, including Aaron R. Hanlon's "The Trigger Warning Myth," published in The New Republic *on Aug. 14, 2015, and available at https://newrepublic.com/article/122543/trigger-warning-myth.*

Something strange is happening at America's colleges and universities. A movement is arising, undirected and driven largely by students, to scrub campuses clean of words, ideas, and subjects that might cause discomfort or give offense. Last December, Jeannie Suk wrote in an online article for *The New Yorker* about law students asking her fellow professors at Harvard not to teach rape law – or, in one case, even use the word *violate* (as in "that violates the law") lest it cause students distress. In February [2015], Laura Kipnis, a professor at Northwestern University, wrote an essay in *The Chronicle of Higher Education* describing a new campus politics of sexual paranoia – and was then subjected to a long investigation after students who were offended by the article and by a tweet she'd sent filed Title IX complaints against her. In June, a professor protecting himself with a pseudonym wrote an essay for Vox describing how gingerly he now has to teach. "I'm a Liberal Professor, and My Liberal Students Terrify Me," the headline said. A number of popular comedians, including Chris Rock, have stopped performing on college campuses. Jerry Seinfeld and Bill Maher have publicly condemned the oversensitivity of college students, saying too many of them can't take a joke.

Two terms have risen quickly from obscurity into common campus parlance. *Microaggressions* are small actions or word choices that seem on their face to have no malicious intent but that are thought of as a kind of violence nonetheless. For example, by some campus guidelines, it is a microaggression to ask an Asian American or Latino American "Where were you born?," because this implies that he or she is not a real American. *Trigger warnings* are alerts that professors are expected to issue if something in a course might cause a strong emotional response. For example, some students have called for warnings that Chinua Achebe's *Things Fall Apart* describes racial violence and that F. Scott Fitzgerald's *The Great Gatsby* portrays misogyny and physical abuse, so that students who have been previously victimized by racism or domestic violence can choose to avoid these works, which they believe might "trigger" a recurrence of past trauma.

Some recent campus actions border on the surreal. In April, at Brandeis University, the Asian American student association sought to raise awareness of microaggressions against Asians through an installation on the steps of an academic hall. The installation gave examples of microaggressions such as "Aren't you supposed to be good at math?" and "I'm colorblind! I don't see race." But a backlash arose among other Asian American students, who felt that the display itself was a microaggression. The association removed the installation, and its president wrote an e-mail to the entire student body apologizing to anyone who was "triggered or hurt by the content of the microaggressions."

This new climate is slowly being institutionalized, and is affecting what can be said in the classroom, even as a basis for discussion. During the 2014–15 school year, for instance, the deans and department chairs at the 10 University of California system schools were presented by administrators at faculty leader-training sessions with examples of microaggressions. The list of offensive statements included: "America is the land of opportunity" and "I believe the most qualified person should get the job."

The press has typically described these developments as a resurgence of political correctness. That's partly right, although there are important differences between what's happening now and what happened in the 1980s and '90s. That movement sought to restrict speech (specifically hate speech aimed at marginalized groups), but it also challenged the literary, philosophical, and historical canon, seeking to widen it by including more diverse perspectives. The current movement is largely about emotional well-being. More than the last, it presumes an extraordinary fragility of the collegiate psyche, and therefore elevates the goal of protecting students from psychological harm. The ultimate aim, it seems, is to turn campuses into "safe spaces" where young adults are shielded from words and ideas that make some uncomfortable. And more than the last, this movement

63

seeks to punish anyone who interferes with that aim, even accidentally. You might call this impulse *vindictive protectiveness*. It is creating a culture in which everyone must think twice before speaking up, lest they face charges of insensitivity, aggression, or worse.

We have been studying this development for a while now, with rising alarm. (Greg Lukianoff is a constitutional lawyer and the president and CEO of the Foundation for Individual Rights in Education, which defends free speech and academic freedom on campus, and has advocated for students and faculty involved in many of the incidents this article describes; Jonathan Haidt is a social psychologist who studies the American culture wars.) The dangers that these trends pose to scholarship and to the quality of American universities are significant; we could write a whole essay detailing them. But in this essay we focus on a different question: What are the effects of this new protectiveness *on the students themselves*? Does it benefit the people it is supposed to help? What exactly are students learning when they spend four years or more in a community that polices unintentional slights, places warning labels on works of classic literature, and in many other ways conveys the sense that words can be forms of violence that require strict control by campus authorities, who are expected to act as both protectors and prosecutors?

There's a saying common in education circles: Don't teach students *what* to think; teach them *how* to think. The idea goes back at least as far as Socrates. Today, what we call the Socratic method is a way of teaching that fosters critical thinking, in part by encouraging students to question their own unexamined beliefs, as well as the received wisdom of those around them. Such questioning sometimes leads to discomfort, and even to anger, on the way to understanding.

But vindictive protectiveness teaches students to think in a very different way. It prepares them poorly for professional life, which often demands intellectual engagement with people and ideas one might find uncongenial or wrong. The harm may be more immediate, too. A campus culture devoted to policing speech and punishing speakers is likely to engender patterns of thought that are surprisingly similar to those long identified by cognitive behavioral therapists as causes of depression and anxiety. The new protectiveness may be teaching students to think pathologically.

How Did We Get Here?

It's difficult to know exactly why vindictive protectiveness has burst forth so powerfully in the past few years. The phenomenon may be related to recent changes in the interpretation of federal antidiscrimination statutes (about which more later). But the answer probably involves generational shifts as well. Childhood itself has changed greatly during the past generation. Many Baby Boomers and Gen Xers can remember riding their bicycles around their hometowns, unchaperoned by adults, by the time they were 8 or 9 years old. In the hours after school, kids were expected to occupy themselves, getting into minor scrapes and learning from their experiences. But "free range" childhood became less common in the 1980s. The surge in crime from the '60s through the early '90s made Baby Boomer parents more protective than their own parents had been. Stories of abducted children appeared more frequently in the news, and in 1984, images of them began showing up on milk cartons. In response, many parents pulled in the reins and worked harder to keep their children safe.

The flight to safety also happened at school. Dangerous play structures were removed from playgrounds; peanut butter was banned from student lunches. After the 1999 Columbine massacre in Colorado, many schools cracked down on bullying, implementing "zero tolerance" policies. In a variety of ways, children born after 1980 – the Millennials – got a consistent message from adults: life is dangerous, but adults will do everything in their power to protect you from harm, not just from strangers but from one another as well.

These same children grew up in a culture that was (and still is) becoming more politically polarized. Republicans and Democrats have never particularly liked each other, but survey data going back to the 1970s show that on average, their mutual dislike used to be surprisingly mild. Negative feelings have grown steadily stronger, however, particularly since the early 2000s. Political scientists call this process "affective partisan polarization," and it is a very serious problem for any democracy. As each side increasingly demonizes the other, compromise becomes more difficult. A recent study shows that implicit or unconscious biases are now at least as strong across political parties as they are across races.

So it's not hard to imagine why students arriving on campus today might be more desirous of protection and more hostile toward ideological opponents than in generations past. This hostility, and the self-righteousness fueled by strong partisan emotions, can be expected to add force to any moral crusade. A principle of moral psychology is that "morality binds and blinds." Part of what we do when we make moral judgments is express allegiance to a team. But that can interfere with our ability to think critically. Acknowledging that the other side's viewpoint has any merit is risky – your teammates may see you as a traitor.

Social media makes it extraordinarily easy to join crusades, express solidarity and outrage, and shun traitors. Facebook was founded in 2004, and since 2006 it has allowed children as young as 13 to join. This means that the first wave of students who spent all their teen years using Facebook reached college in 2011, and graduated from college only this year.

These first true "social-media natives" may be different from members of previous generations in how they go about sharing their moral judgments and supporting one another in moral campaigns and conflicts. We find much to like about these trends; young people today are engaged with one another, with news stories, and with prosocial endeavors to a greater degree than when the dominant technology was television. But social media has also fundamentally shifted the balance of power in relationships between students and faculty; the latter increasingly fear what students might do to their reputations and careers by stirring up online mobs against them.

We do not mean to imply simple causation, but rates of mental illness in young adults have been rising, both on campus and off, in recent decades. Some portion of the increase is surely due to better diagnosis and greater willingness to seek help, but most experts seem to agree that some portion of the trend is real. Nearly all of the campus mental-health directors surveyed in 2013 by the American College Counseling Association reported that the number of students with severe psychological problems was rising at their schools. The rate of emotional distress reported by students themselves is also high, and rising. In a 2014 survey by the American College Health Association, 54 percent of college students surveyed said that they had "felt overwhelming anxiety" in the past 12 months, up from 49 percent in the same survey just five years earlier. Students seem to be reporting more emotional crises; many seem fragile, and this has surely changed the way university faculty and administrators interact with them. The question is whether some of those changes might be doing more harm than good.

The Thinking Cure

For millennia, philosophers have understood that we don't see life as it is; we see a version distorted by our hopes, fears, and other attachments. The Buddha said, "Our life is the creation of our mind." Marcus Aurelius said, "Life itself is but what you deem it." The quest for wisdom in many traditions begins with this insight. Early Buddhists and the Stoics, for example, developed practices for reducing attachments, thinking more clearly, and finding release from the emotional torments of normal mental life.

Cognitive behavioral therapy is a modern embodiment of this ancient wisdom. It is the most extensively studied nonpharmaceutical treatment of mental illness, and is used widely to treat depression, anxiety disorders, eating disorders, and addiction. It can even be of help to schizophrenics. No other form of psychotherapy has been shown to work for a broader range of problems. Studies have generally found that it is as effective as antidepressant drugs (such as Prozac) in the treatment of anxiety and depression. The therapy is relatively quick and easy to learn; after a few months of training, many patients can do it on their own. Unlike drugs, cognitive behavioral therapy keeps working long after treatment is stopped, because it teaches thinking skills that people can continue to use.

The goal is to minimize distorted thinking and see the world more accurately. You start by learning the names of the dozen or so most common cognitive distortions (such as overgeneralizing, discounting positives, and emotional reasoning; see the list at the bottom of this article). Each time you notice yourself falling prey to one of them, you name it, describe the facts of the situation, consider alternative interpretations, and then choose an interpretation of events more in line with those facts. Your emotions follow your new interpretation. In time, this process becomes automatic. When people improve their mental hygiene in this way – when they free themselves from the repetitive irrational thoughts that had previously filled so much of their consciousness – they become less depressed, anxious, and angry.

The parallel to formal education is clear: cognitive behavioral therapy teaches good critical-thinking skills, the sort that educators have striven for so long to impart. By almost any definition, critical thinking requires grounding one's beliefs in evidence rather than in emotion or desire, and learning how to search for and evaluate evidence that might contradict one's initial hypothesis. But does campus life today foster critical thinking? Or does it coax students to think in more-distorted ways?

Let's look at recent trends in higher education in light of the distortions that cognitive behavioral therapy identifies. We will draw the names and descriptions of these distortions from David D. Burns's popular book *Feeling Good*, as well as from the second edition of *Treatment Plans and Interventions for Depression and Anxiety Disorders*, by Robert L. Leahy, Stephen J. F. Holland, and Lata K. McGinn.

Higher Education's Embrace of "Emotional Reasoning"

Burns defines *emotional reasoning* as assuming "that your negative emotions necessarily reflect the way things really are: 'I feel it, therefore it must be true.'" Leahy, Holland, and McGinn define it as letting "your feelings guide your interpretation of reality." But, of course, subjective feelings are not always trustworthy guides; unrestrained, they can cause people to lash out at others who have done nothing wrong. Therapy often involves talking yourself down from the idea that each of your emotional responses represents something true or important.

Emotional reasoning dominates many campus debates and discussions. A claim that someone's words are "offensive" is not just an expression of one's own subjective feeling of offendedness. It is, rather, a public charge that the speaker has done something objectively wrong. It is a demand that the speaker apologize or be punished by some authority for committing an offense.

There have always been some people who believe they have a right not to be offended. Yet throughout American history – from the Victorian era to the free-speech activism of the 1960s and '70s – radicals have pushed boundaries and mocked prevailing sensibilities. Sometime in the 1980s, however, college campuses began to focus on preventing offensive speech, especially speech that might be hurtful to women or minority groups. The sentiment underpinning this goal was laudable, but it quickly produced some absurd results.

Among the most famous early examples was the so-called water-buffalo incident at the University of Pennsylvania. In 1993, the university charged an Israeli-born student with racial harassment after he yelled "Shut up, you water buffalo!" to a crowd of black sorority women that was making noise at night outside his dorm-room window. Many scholars and pundits at the time could not see how the term *water buffalo* (a rough translation of a Hebrew insult for a thoughtless or rowdy person) was a racial slur against African Americans, and as a result, the case became international news.

Claims of a right not to be offended have continued to arise since then, and universities have continued to privilege them. In a particularly egregious 2008 case, for instance, Indiana University–Purdue University at Indianapolis found a white student guilty of racial harassment for reading a book titled *Notre Dame vs. the Klan*. The book honored student opposition to the Ku Klux Klan when it marched on Notre Dame in 1924. Nonetheless, the picture of a Klan rally on the book's cover offended at least one of the student's co-workers (he was a janitor as well as a student), and that was enough for a guilty finding by the university's Affirmative Action Office.

These examples may seem extreme, but the reasoning behind them has become more commonplace on campus in recent years. Last year, at the University of St. Thomas, in Minnesota, an event called Hump Day, which would have allowed people to pet a camel, was abruptly canceled. Students had created a Facebook group where they protested the event for animal cruelty, for being a waste of money, and for being insensitive to people from the Middle East. The inspiration for the camel had almost certainly come from a popular TV commercial in which a camel saunters around an office on a Wednesday, celebrating "hump day"; it was devoid of any reference to Middle Eastern peoples. Nevertheless, the group organizing the event announced on its Facebook page that the event would be canceled because the "program [was] dividing people and would make for an uncomfortable and possibly unsafe environment."

Because there is a broad ban in academic circles on "blaming the victim," it is generally considered unacceptable to question the reasonableness (let alone the sincerity) of someone's emotional state, particularly if those emotions are linked to one's group identity. The thin argument "I'm offended" becomes an unbeatable trump card. This leads to what Jonathan Rauch, a contributing editor at this magazine, calls the "offendedness sweepstakes," in which opposing parties use claims of offense as cudgels. In the process, the bar for what we consider unacceptable speech is lowered further and further.

Since 2013, new pressure from the federal government has reinforced this trend. Federal antidiscrimination statutes regulate on-campus harassment and unequal treatment based on sex, race, religion, and national origin. Until recently, the Department of Education's Office for Civil Rights acknowledged that speech must be "objectively offensive" before it could be deemed actionable as sexual harassment – it would have to pass the "reasonable person" test. To be prohibited, the office wrote in 2003, allegedly harassing speech would have to go "beyond the mere expression of views, words, symbols or thoughts that some person finds offensive."

But in 2013, the Departments of Justice and Education greatly broadened the definition of sexual harassment to include verbal conduct that is simply "unwelcome." Out of fear of federal investigations, universities are now applying that standard – defining unwelcome speech as harassment – not just to sex, but to race, religion, and veteran status as well. Everyone is supposed to rely upon his or her own subjective feelings to decide whether a comment by a professor or a fellow student is unwelcome, and therefore grounds for a harassment claim. Emotional reasoning is now accepted as evidence.

If our universities are teaching students that their emotions can be used effectively as weapons – or at least as evidence in administrative proceedings – then they are teaching students to nurture a kind of hypersensitivity that will lead them into countless drawn-out conflicts in college and beyond. Schools may be training students in thinking styles that will damage their careers and friendships, along with their mental health.

Fortune-telling and Trigger Warnings

Burns defines *fortune-telling* as "anticipat[ing] that things will turn out badly" and feeling "convinced that your prediction is an already-established fact." Leahy, Holland, and McGinn define it as "predict[ing] the future negatively" or seeing potential danger in an everyday situation. The recent spread of demands for trigger warnings on reading assignments with provocative content is an example of fortune-telling.

The idea that words (or smells or any sensory input) can trigger searing memories of past trauma – and intense fear that it may be repeated – has been around at least since World War I, when psychiatrists began treating soldiers for what is now called post-traumatic stress disorder. But explicit trigger warnings are believed to have originated much more recently, on message boards in the early days of the Internet. Trigger warnings became particularly prevalent in self-help and feminist forums, where they allowed readers who had suffered from traumatic events like sexual assault to avoid graphic content that might trigger flashbacks or panic attacks. Search-engine trends indicate that the phrase broke into mainstream use online around 2011, spiked in 2014, and reached an all-time high in 2015. The use of trigger warnings on campus appears to have followed a similar trajectory; seemingly overnight, students at universities across the country have begun demanding that their professors issue warnings before covering material that might evoke a negative emotional response.

In 2013, a task force composed of administrators, students, recent alumni, and one faculty member at Oberlin College, in Ohio, released an online resource guide for faculty (subsequently retracted in the face of faculty pushback) that included a list of topics warranting trigger warnings. These topics included classism and privilege, among many others. The task force recommended that materials that might trigger negative reactions among students be avoided altogether unless they

70

"contribute directly" to course goals, and suggested that works that were "too important to avoid" be made optional.

It's hard to imagine how novels illustrating classism and privilege could provoke or reactivate the kind of terror that is typically implicated in PTSD. Rather, trigger warnings are sometimes demanded for a long list of ideas and attitudes that some students find politically offensive, in the name of preventing other students from being harmed. This is an example of what psychologists call "motivated reasoning" – we spontaneously generate arguments for conclusions we want to support. Once *you* find something hateful, it is easy to argue that exposure to the hateful thing could traumatize some *other* people. You believe that you know how others will react, and that their reaction could be devastating. Preventing that devastation becomes a moral obligation for the whole community. Books for which students have called publicly for trigger warnings within the past couple of years include Virginia Woolf's *Mrs. Dalloway* (at Rutgers, for "suicidal inclinations") and Ovid's *Metamorphoses* (at Columbia, for sexual assault).

Jeannie Suk's *New Yorker* essay described the difficulties of teaching rape law in the age of trigger warnings. Some students, she wrote, have pressured their professors to avoid teaching the subject in order to protect themselves and their classmates from potential distress. Suk compares this to trying to teach "a medical student who is training to be a surgeon but who fears that he'll become distressed if he sees or handles blood."

However, there is a deeper problem with trigger warnings. According to the most basic tenets of psychology, the very idea of helping people with anxiety disorders avoid the things they fear is misguided. A person who is trapped in an elevator during a power outage may panic and think she is going to die. That frightening experience can change neural connections in her amygdala, leading to an elevator phobia. If you want this woman to retain her fear for life, you should help her avoid elevators.

But if you want to help her return to normalcy, you should take your cues from Ivan Pavlov and guide her through a process known as exposure therapy. You might start by asking the woman to merely look at an elevator from a distance – standing in a building lobby, perhaps – until her apprehension begins to subside. If nothing bad happens while she's standing in the lobby – if the fear is not "reinforced" – then she will begin to learn a new association: elevators are not dangerous. (This reduction in fear during exposure is called habituation.) Then, on subsequent days, you might ask her to get closer, and on later days to push the call button, and eventually to step in and go up one floor. This is how the amygdala can get rewired again to associate a previously feared situation with safety or normalcy.

Students who call for trigger warnings may be correct that some of their peers are harboring memories of trauma that could be reactivated by course readings. But they are wrong to try to prevent such reactivations. Students with PTSD should of course get treatment, but they should not try to avoid normal life, with its many opportunities for habituation. Classroom discussions are safe places to be exposed to incidental reminders of trauma (such as the word *violate*). A discussion of violence is unlikely to be followed by actual violence, so it is a good way to help students change the associations that are causing them discomfort. And they'd better get their habituation done in college, because the world beyond college will be far less willing to accommodate requests for trigger warnings and opt-outs.

The expansive use of trigger warnings may also foster unhealthy mental habits in the vastly larger group of students who do not suffer from PTSD or other anxiety disorders. People acquire their fears not just from their own past experiences, but from social learning as well. If everyone around you acts as though something is dangerous – elevators, certain neighborhoods, novels depicting racism – then you are at risk of acquiring that fear too. The psychiatrist Sarah Roff pointed this out last year in an online article for *The Chronicle of Higher Education*. "One of my biggest concerns about trigger warnings," Roff wrote, "is that they will apply not just to those who have experienced trauma, but to all students, creating an atmosphere in which they are encouraged to believe that there is something dangerous or damaging about discussing difficult aspects of our history."

In an article published last year by *Inside Higher Ed*, seven humanities professors wrote that the trigger-warning movement was "already having a chilling effect on [their] teaching and pedagogy." They reported their colleagues' receiving "phone calls from deans and other administrators investigating student complaints that they have included 'triggering' material in their courses, with or without warnings." A trigger warning, they wrote, "serves as a guarantee that students will not experience unexpected discomfort and implies that if they do, a contract has been broken." When students come to *expect* trigger warnings for any material that makes them uncomfortable, the easiest way for faculty to stay out of trouble is to avoid material that might upset the most sensitive student in the class.

Magnification, Labeling, and Microaggressions

Burns defines *magnification* as "exaggerat[ing] the importance of things," and Leahy, Holland, and McGinn define *labeling* as "assign[ing] global negative traits to yourself and others." The recent collegiate trend of

72

uncovering allegedly racist, sexist, classist, or otherwise discriminatory microaggressions doesn't *incidentally* teach students to focus on small or accidental slights. Its *purpose* is to get students to focus on them and then relabel the people who have made such remarks as aggressors.

The term *microaggression* originated in the 1970s and referred to subtle, often unconscious racist affronts. The definition has expanded in recent years to include anything that can be perceived as discriminatory on virtually any basis. For example, in 2013, a student group at UCLA staged a sit-in during a class taught by Val Rust, an education professor. The group read a letter aloud expressing their concerns about the campus's hostility toward students of color. Although Rust was not explicitly named, the group quite clearly criticized his teaching as microaggressive. In the course of correcting his students' grammar and spelling, Rust had noted that a student had wrongly capitalized the first letter of the word *indigenous*. Lowercasing the capital *I* was an insult to the student and her ideology, the group claimed.

Even joking about microaggressions can be seen as an aggression, warranting punishment. Last fall, Omar Mahmood, a student at the University of Michigan, wrote a satirical column for a conservative student publication, *The Michigan Review*, poking fun at what he saw as a campus tendency to perceive microaggressions in just about anything. Mahmood was also employed at the campus newspaper, *The Michigan Daily*. *The Daily*'s editors said that the way Mahmood had "satirically mocked the experiences of fellow Daily contributors and minority communities on campus … created a conflict of interest." *The Daily* terminated Mahmood after he described the incident to two Web sites, The College Fix and The Daily Caller. A group of women later vandalized Mahmood's doorway with eggs, hot dogs, gum, and notes with messages such as "Everyone hates you, you violent prick." When speech comes to be seen as a form of violence, vindictive protectiveness can justify a hostile, and perhaps even violent, response.

In March, the student government at Ithaca College, in upstate New York, went so far as to propose the creation of an anonymous microaggression-reporting system. Student sponsors envisioned some form of disciplinary action against "oppressors" engaged in belittling speech. One of the sponsors of the program said that while "not … every instance will require trial or some kind of harsh punishment," she wanted the program to be "record-keeping but with impact."

Surely people make subtle or thinly veiled racist or sexist remarks on college campuses, and it is right for students to raise questions and initiate discussions about such cases. But the increased focus on microaggressions coupled with the endorsement of emotional reasoning is a formula for a constant state of outrage, even toward well-meaning speakers trying to engage in genuine discussion.

What are we doing to our students if we encourage them to develop extra-thin skin in the years just before they leave the cocoon of adult protection and enter the workforce? Would they not be better prepared to flourish if we taught them to question their own emotional reactions, and to give people the benefit of the doubt?

Teaching Students to Catastrophize and Have Zero Tolerance

Burns defines *catastrophizing* as a kind of magnification that turns "commonplace negative events into nightmarish monsters." Leahy, Holland, and McGinn define it as believing "that what has happened or will happen" is "so awful and unbearable that you won't be able to stand it." Requests for trigger warnings involve catastrophizing, but this way of thinking colors other areas of campus thought as well.

Catastrophizing rhetoric about physical danger is employed by campus administrators more commonly than you might think – sometimes, it seems, with cynical ends in mind. For instance, last year administrators at Bergen Community College, in New Jersey, suspended Francis Schmidt, a professor, after he posted a picture of his daughter on his Google+ account. The photo showed her in a yoga pose, wearing a T-shirt that read I WILL TAKE WHAT IS MINE WITH FIRE & BLOOD, a quote from the HBO show *Game of Thrones*. Schmidt had filed a grievance against the school about two months earlier after being passed over for a sabbatical. The quote was interpreted as a threat by a campus administrator, who received a notification after Schmidt posted the picture; it had been sent, automatically, to a whole group of contacts. According to Schmidt, a Bergen security official present at a subsequent meeting between administrators and Schmidt thought the word *fire* could refer to AK-47s.

Then there is the eight-year legal saga at Valdosta State University, in Georgia, where a student was expelled for protesting the construction of a parking garage by posting an allegedly "threatening" collage on Facebook. The collage described the proposed structure as a "memorial" parking garage – a joke referring to a claim by the university president that the garage would be part of his legacy. The president interpreted the collage as a threat against his life.

It should be no surprise that students are exhibiting similar sensitivity. At the University of Central Florida in 2013, for example, Hyung-il Jung, an accounting instructor, was suspended after a student reported that Jung had made a threatening comment during a review session. Jung explained to the *Orlando Sentinel* that the material he was reviewing was difficult, and he'd noticed the pained look on students' faces, so he made a joke. "It looks like you guys are being slowly suffocated by these questions," he recalled saying. "Am I on a killing spree or what?"

After the student reported Jung's comment, a group of nearly 20 others e-mailed the UCF administration explaining that the comment had clearly been made in jest. Nevertheless, UCF suspended Jung from all university duties and demanded that he obtain written certification from a mental-health professional that he was "not a threat to [himself] or to the university community" before he would be allowed to return to campus.

All of these actions teach a common lesson: smart people do, in fact, overreact to innocuous speech, make mountains out of molehills, and seek punishment for anyone whose words make anyone else feel uncomfortable.

Mental Filtering and Disinvitation Season

As Burns defines it, *mental filtering* is "pick[ing] out a negative detail in any situation and dwell[ing] on it exclusively, thus perceiving that the whole situation is negative." Leahy, Holland, and McGinn refer to this as "negative filtering," which they define as "focus[ing] almost exclusively on the negatives and seldom notic[ing] the positives." When applied to campus life, mental filtering allows for simpleminded demonization.

Students and faculty members in large numbers modeled this cognitive distortion during 2014's "disinvitation season." That's the time of year – usually early spring – when commencement speakers are announced and when students and professors demand that some of those speakers be disinvited because of things they have said or done. According to data compiled by the Foundation for Individual Rights in Education, since 2000, at least 240 campaigns have been launched at U.S. universities to prevent public figures from appearing at campus events; most of them have occurred since 2009.

Consider two of the most prominent disinvitation targets of 2014: former U.S. Secretary of State Condoleezza Rice and the International Monetary Fund's managing director, Christine Lagarde. Rice was the first black female secretary of state; Lagarde was the first woman to become finance minister of a G8 country and the first female head of the IMF. Both speakers could have been seen as highly successful role models for female students, and Rice for minority students as well. But the critics, in effect, discounted any possibility of something positive coming from those speeches.

Members of an academic community should of course be free to raise questions about Rice's role in the Iraq War or to look skeptically at the IMF's policies. But should dislike of *part* of a person's record disqualify her altogether from sharing her perspectives?

If campus culture conveys the idea that visitors must be pure, with résumés that never offend generally left-leaning campus sensibilities, then higher education will have taken a further step toward intellectual homogeneity and the creation of an environment in which students rarely encounter diverse viewpoints. And universities will have reinforced the belief that it's okay to filter out the positive. If students graduate believing that they can learn nothing from people they dislike or from those with whom they disagree, we will have done them a great intellectual disservice.

What Can We Do Now?

Attempts to shield students from words, ideas, and people that might cause them emotional discomfort are bad for the students. They are bad for the workplace, which will be mired in unending litigation if student expectations of safety are carried forward. And they are bad for American democracy, which is already paralyzed by worsening partisanship. When the ideas, values, and speech of the other side are seen not just as wrong but as willfully aggressive toward innocent victims, it is hard to imagine the kind of mutual respect, negotiation, and compromise that are needed to make politics a positive-sum game.

Rather than trying to protect students from words and ideas that they will inevitably encounter, colleges should do all they can to equip students to thrive in a world full of words and ideas that they cannot control. One of the great truths taught by Buddhism (and Stoicism, Hinduism, and many other traditions) is that you can never achieve happiness by making the world conform to your desires. But you can master your desires and habits of thought. This, of course, is the goal of cognitive behavioral therapy. With this in mind, here are some steps that might help reverse the tide of bad thinking on campus.

The biggest single step in the right direction does not involve faculty or university administrators, but rather the federal government, which should release universities from their fear of unreasonable investigation and sanctions by the Department of Education. Congress should define peer-on-peer harassment according to the Supreme Court's definition in the 1999 case *Davis v. Monroe County Board of Education*. The *Davis* standard holds that a single comment or thoughtless remark by a student does not equal harassment; harassment requires a pattern of objectively offensive behavior by one student that interferes with another student's access to education. Establishing the *Davis* standard would help eliminate universities' impulse to police their students' speech so carefully.

Universities themselves should try to raise consciousness about the need to balance freedom of speech with the need to make all students feel welcome. Talking openly about such conflicting but important values is just the sort of challenging exercise that any diverse but tolerant community must learn to do. Restrictive speech codes should be abandoned.

Universities should also officially and strongly discourage trigger warnings. They should endorse the American Association of University Professors' report on these warnings, which notes, "The presumption that students need to be protected rather than challenged in a classroom is at once infantilizing and anti-intellectual." Professors should be free to use trigger warnings if they choose to do so, but by explicitly discouraging the practice, universities would help fortify the faculty against student requests for such warnings.

Finally, universities should rethink the skills and values they most want to impart to their incoming students. At present, many freshman-orientation programs try to raise student sensitivity to a nearly impossible level. Teaching students to avoid giving unintentional offense is a worthy goal, especially when the students come from many different cultural backgrounds. But students should also be taught how to live in a world full of potential offenses. Why not teach incoming students how to practice cognitive behavioral therapy? Given high and rising rates of mental illness, this simple step would be among the most humane and supportive things a university could do. The cost and time commitment could be kept low: a few group training sessions could be supplemented by Web sites or apps. But the outcome could pay dividends in many ways. For example, a shared vocabulary about reasoning, common distortions, and the appropriate use of evidence to draw conclusions would facilitate critical thinking and real debate. It would also tone down the perpetual state of outrage that seems to engulf some colleges these days, allowing students' minds to open more widely to new ideas and new people. A greater commitment to formal, public debate on campus – and to the assembly of a more politically diverse faculty – would further serve that goal.

Thomas Jefferson, upon founding the University of Virginia, said:

> This institution will be based on the illimitable freedom of the human mind. For here we are not afraid to follow truth wherever it may lead, nor to tolerate any error so long as reason is left free to combat it.

We believe that this is still – and will always be – the best attitude for American universities. Faculty, administrators, students, and the federal government all have a role to play in restoring universities to their historic mission

Common Cognitive Distortions

A partial list from Robert L. Leahy, Stephen J. F. Holland, and Lata K. McGinn's *Treatment Plans and Interventions for Depression and Anxiety Disorders* (2012).

1. Mind reading. You assume that you know what people think without having sufficient evidence of their thoughts. "He thinks I'm a loser."

2. Fortune-telling. You predict the future negatively: things will get worse, or there is danger ahead. "I'll fail that exam," or "I won't get the job."

3. Catastrophizing. You believe that what has happened or will happen will be so awful and unbearable that you won't be able to stand it. "It would be terrible if I failed."

4. Labeling. You assign global negative traits to yourself and others. "I'm undesirable," or "He's a rotten person."

5. Discounting positives. You claim that the positive things you or others do are trivial. "That's what wives are supposed to do – so it doesn't count when she's nice to me," or "Those successes were easy, so they don't matter."

6. Negative filtering. You focus almost exclusively on the negatives and seldom notice the positives. "Look at all of the people who don't like me."

7. Overgeneralizing. You perceive a global pattern of negatives on the basis of a single incident. "This generally happens to me. I seem to fail at a lot of things."

8. Dichotomous thinking. You view events or people in all-or-nothing terms. "I get rejected by everyone," or "It was a complete waste of time."

9. Blaming. You focus on the other person as the source of your negative feelings, and you refuse to take responsibility for changing yourself. "She's to blame for the way I feel now," or "My parents caused all my problems."

10. What if? You keep asking a series of questions about "what if" something happens, and you fail to be satisfied with any of the answers. "Yeah, but what if I get anxious?," or "What if I can't catch my breath?"

11. Emotional reasoning. You let your feelings guide your interpretation of reality. "I feel depressed; therefore, my marriage is not working out."

12. Inability to disconfirm. You reject any evidence or arguments that might contradict your negative thoughts. For example, when you have the thought *I'm unlovable,* you reject as irrelevant any evidence that people like you. Consequently, your thought cannot be refuted. "That's not the real issue. There are deeper problems. There are other factors."

Religion Happens
David Dark

Introduction to *Life's Too Short to Pretend You're Not Religious*. Downers Grove, IL: InterVarsity Press, 2016.

***David Dark** (b. 1969) is the critically acclaimed author of* The Sacredness of Questioning Everything, Everyday Apocalypse, *and* The Gospel According to America. *He began his teaching career as a high school English teacher; his fascination with story stayed with him through his doctoral work in religion at Vanderbilt University. Now a professor of religion at Belmont University, and he also teaches at the Tennessee Prison for Women. He has published in* Pitchfork, Killing the Buddha, Books and Culture, *and* Christian Century. *A frequent speaker, Dark has also appeared on C-SPAN's Book-TV and in the documentaries* Marketing the Message *and* American Jesus. *Dark views popular culture as a vibrant contemporary means of exploring humankind's biggest questions.*

***Why we are reading this:** In this last of three articles that critique and comment on contemporary intellectual and cultural life, Dark takes on the question of religion. He tries to move beyond the application of abusive and derogatory labels in discussions of religion in part by redefining the term "religion" itself. In Dark's approach, "religion" can serve as one's controlling story, as way of entering a relationship, as the way we organize our lives, or as a witness. Ultimately, for Dark, even someone's "obsession with* Game of Thrones*" is "religious." As the title of the book from which this reading comes suggests, Dark thinks that everyone is religious, even people who don't consider themselves religious. What do you think? Can this be true? Is it useful to broaden a commonly-used term like "religion" beyond its traditional definition? How so?*

It wasn't their fault, it wasn't her fault. It wasn't even a matter of fault.
Elmore Leonard, The Switch

"No one doesn't believe in God as much as I do," a slightly intoxicated friend assured me as we huddled together in a busy restaurant one Saturday evening. I knew we were in for an extraordinary conversation. Sometimes this kind of thing comes up when I'm asked what I do.

When I could honestly call myself a high school English teacher, my responses generated less heat. Someone might recite Shelley's "Ozymandias," recall a beloved teacher or ask for a reading recommendation, but it rarely took a turn for the intensely personal. Now that I work with undergraduates, they want to know what it is I teach, exactly.

Religion.

But what classes?

Bible. World religions.

And now we're awash in the prickliest of questions – the existence of God. The moment my friend asserted his superlative disbelief in God did not come out of the blue. We'd been at it a while on the subject of weird religious backgrounds (his and mine), life after death, music, science and all the different things people say *the Bible says*. I suspect I surprised him a little when I noted that we read it badly until we learn to read it as a collection and that, wherever one lands on the question of the existence of God, the Bible's likely as good as it gets when it comes to challenging everyday injustice.

He wanted to know if I believed it, and I assured him that I did. But I described my love for the Bible with so many seemingly diverse points of entry that he seemed a little taken aback: Kurt Vonnegut's devotion to the Sermon on the Mount, the ethical momentum set in motion within human societies by the prophets, the vision of beloved community in the civil rights movement and my own dependence on the wisdom of my incarcerated students. Before we knew it, we were talking about the power of love, the joys and difficulties of true neighborliness and the long-haul work of human hopefulness. Who would want to be a hater when it comes to these things? Why not pay this busy little book club a visit from time to time?

It was right about then that he felt understandably compelled to drop a clarifying word amid our escalating love fest: "Nobody doesn't believe in God as much as I do." Boom. Was it something I said? Can we still be friends?

I was pleasantly stumped and strangely excited. Why the rush to disassociate? Was there a problem? Did he think I was trying to sell him on something? I wasn't looking to keep him on any kind of hook or ask him to sign a statement of belief, but I so didn't want our commonality to end. I wanted him to know – and said so – that he was kin to many a psalmist, poet and pilgrim *within* the Bible who shared his disbelief. I wanted him to believe that there was still *so much* we could have a good time talking about. Was there a way I might playfully overcome this defensiveness? How might I keep the frequency open?

Here's what I'm up to. I come to you as one bummed out by the way people talk about religion. Be it an online rant, a headline, a news report or a conversation overheard, I feel a jolt of sympathy pain whenever someone characterizes someone else as religious. It's as if a door just got slammed. A person has been somehow shrink-wrapped. Some sweet and perfectly interesting somebody gets left out. And in a subtle, hard-to-get-a-handle-on kind of way, it's kind of like someone's been told to shut up.

This is the way it goes with our words. When I label people, I no longer have to deal with them thoughtfully. I no longer have to feel overwhelmed by their complexity, the lives they live, the dreams they have. I know exactly where they are inside – or forever outside – my field of care, because they've been *taken care of*. The mystery of their existence has been solved and led away before I've had a chance to be moved by them or even begun to catch a glimpse of who they might be. They've been neutralized. There's hardly any action quite so undemanding, so utterly unimaginative, as the affixing of a label. It's the costliest of mental shortcuts.

Of course we get to call it like we see it. What else can we do? But when we do so with undue haste, when we're neither remotely inquisitive nor especially curious in our regard for other people, we may find that a casual demonization comes to pepper our conversations. This is why it often seems to me that calling someone liberal, conservative, fundamentalist, atheist or extremist is to largely deal in curse words. It puts a person in what we take to be their place, but it only speaks in shorthand. When I go no further in my consideration of my fellow human, I betray my preference for caricature over perception, a shrug as opposed to a vision of the lived fact of somebody in a body. In the face of a perhaps beautifully complicated life, I've opted for oversimplification.

And so it goes with the application of that impossibly broad brush called religion. It's as if we can't even speak the word without walking into the mine field of someone else's wounds. Guards go up immediately and with good reason. It's the ultimate conversation-stopper, an association to end all associations. Who would want to get caught anywhere near it? And in our day, could calling someone religious ever function as a compliment? It's one more label we use as a placeholder of persons and populations, as if we've somehow gotten to the bottom of who they are with an adjective.

I want very much to take this attitude aside and punch it lovingly in the stomach. I want good humor and candor and more truth between us than a label could ever afford. And if it's the case that mention of religion mostly shuts conversation down, I want very badly to somehow crack it open again. If we're open to it, the word need not always signal a dead end; it might even be a means to a breakthrough, a way of fessing up to the facts of what we're all up to.

Religion as Controlling Story

Let's talk about religion. In its root meaning, religion (from the Latin *religare*, to bind again, to bind back) is simply a tying together, a question of how we see fit to organize ourselves and our resources, a question, we might say, of how things have been tied together so far *and* of how they might be tied together differently, a binding, an unbinding and a binding again. As has always been the case, the organizing of selves and societies can go beautifully or badly or both, but the development of bonds – like the dissolution of bonds – is inescapable. With this in mind, I find it most helpful to define religion as follows: a religion is a controlling story, and there are at least as many as there are people. Stories change but the fact of story doesn't. When we escape a bad story – or see through one into the shock, the awe or the absurdity of what's *really* going on – we haven't escaped stories; we've simply awakened our way into better and truer ones, and we've probably only managed that feat with the considerate assistance of others, whether living or dead. No one awakens all by themselves. Conversions occur all the time. For better *and* worse, we drink the Kool-Aid. Religion happens.

We're often admonished to keep religion out of politics (or vice versa), and civil exchange does require that no one be allowed to hog the microphone while decreeing that the God in his head trumps the reasoning power in everyone else's. But human life won't divide itself up quite so neatly. Given the overwhelming complications of trying to negotiate a just, joyful and more-helpful-than-not existence in a world of raw data with which we often have no idea what to do, we can perhaps be forgiven for wanting to rope off one issue from the other. ("That's political. That's religious. That's a private matter. This is worship. That's a guilty pleasure. And this one over here is just… it's just business. It is what it is. It's nothing personal. Sorry about that.") But these divisions can obscure the living fact of certain connections and often leave us estranged from our own sense of ourselves, insulated from the possibility of undivided living.

If we're willing to apply religion to the whole of our own lives as readily as we level it at others, it can wonderfully disrupt whatever it was we thought we were talking about, whatever we thought we had in mind and hand. Like culture, it cuts to the core of what we're really doing and believing, of what values – we all have them – lurk behind our words and actions. Yes, we can use it to disavow and detract. ("I *used* to be religious." "I'm spiritual but not religious." "Let's keep religion out of it.") But I believe there's something dishonest and deluded at work when we speak as if it's only other people who are guided by unreasoning rage or strange notions about the way the world works, only others who, as the saying goes, have an agenda. In this view, *religion* is only a word for the way intellectually underdeveloped people get carried away, a snob's word, and it strikes me as a strange disowning of one's own vulnerability and, if you like, gullibility; it's a rude denial of the fact of our common creatureliness.

My fellow creatures, I propose that we not play that way. If what we believe is what we see is what we do is who we are, there's no getting away from religion. We all want to know who we are, where and how we fit in, and what our lives might yet mean. And in this sense, *religion* might be the best word we have for seeing, naming, confessing and really waking up to what we're after in all we do, of becoming aware of what's going on in our minds. Putting religion on the table in this way, if we're open to doing so, might be the most pressing, interesting and wide-ranging conversation we can have. We might even find ourselves amused.

How's that? Because religion can radically name the specific ways we've put our lives together and, perhaps more urgently, the ways we've allowed other people to put our lives together for us. To be clear, I'm not trying to encourage anyone to begin self-identifying *as* religious. That's as futile and redundant a move as calling yourself political or cultural. But I *am* arguing that we should cease and desist from referring to others as religious as if they're participants in games we ourselves aren't playing, as if they're somehow weirdly and hopelessly enmeshed in cultures of which we're always only detached observers. On the one hand, this is a distancing move that keeps us detached from the fact of our own enthusiasms, our own rituals, our own enmeshments and our own loves. But it also holds another person – the ostensibly religious person – under a scrutiny I have yet to apply to myself. Calling someone else religious doesn't answer the question of my own.

Religion as Relationship

To be attentive to the question of religion is to see relationally, to examine the stories we inherit and hand down to others without too much thought as well as those we cobble together to work a crowd, fund a campaign, target a market or convince ourselves to get out of bed in the morning. Sociology invites us to form the words *belief systems* around these phenomena. Doing so is profoundly helpful in the work of achieving a degree of critical distance when it comes to our perceived have-tos. ("Our belief systems may differ here and there, but we both want better public schools, right? *Right*.") And in the age-old task of listening sympathetically to our fellow creatures, of imagining them well, we need all the help we can get. Thank you, social science.

But I'm not sure anyone's ever experienced enlightenment, been born again, been called to repentance or decided to sell their belongings on account of a system. The voice, the tale, the image, the parable that gets through to you – that *wins your heart* – religiously is the one that makes it past your defenses. You've been won over, and you probably didn't see it coming. You've been enlisted into a drama, whether positively or negatively, and it shouldn't be controversial to note that it happens all the time. When you really think about it, there's one waiting around every corner. It's as near as the story, song or image you can't get out of your head.

Religion happens when we get pulled in, moved, called out or compelled by something outside ourselves. It could be a car commercial, a lyric, a painting, a theatrical performance or the magnetic pull of an Apple store. The calls to worship are everywhere. And when we see as much, we begin to understand why Marx would insist that "the critique of religion is the prerequisite of every critique." It is that with which we have to do (or the way we do everything we do or think we do). It is certainly often an opiate for the masses, but it can also function as the poetry of the people. Whether we spy it in ritual, symbol or ceremony, religion isn't something one can be coherently for or against or decide to somehow suddenly engage, because it's always already there. Or as the old Palmolive commercial once put it, we're *soaking* in it. Whatever the content of the script we're sticking to for dear life – that would be our religion – it binds us for worse or for better till we begin to critique it religiously and relentlessly, in view of the possibility of conversion to better boundedness, different and more redeeming orientations or, to put it a little strangely, *less bad* religion. And a person's religiosity is never not in play. It names the patterns, shifting or consistent, avowed or not, of all our interactions. Religion is the question of how we dispose our energies, how we see fit to organize our own lives and, in many cases, the lives of others.

This need be neither buzzkill nor bummer. On the contrary, it's an invitation to be more present to my own life, to access and examine more deeply what I'm up to. It also levels the playing field more than a little, because suddenly a Muslim going to prayers isn't more or less religious than a grown man with a big piece of pretend cheese on his head going to watch a Green Bay Packers game. Is it good religion? Bad religion? True? False? Idolatrous? Righteous? Opinions will vary. But to hit Pause long enough to consider *the content* of our devotion, our lives and our investments is to begin to see the question clearly. What are my controlling stories? Do I like the stories my one life tells? Do I need to see about changing them?

In this sense, we're never *not* speaking and acting upon our religion. We're never *not* involved in everyday worship. We're always in the thick of it, this living fact of what our human hands have wrought under the dictation of what's actually going on in our human hearts and minds. Our real sense of what's really sacred is regularly on display. David Byrne of the Talking Heads bears witness to the religious situation when he invites us to consider the cities. Having made a regular habit of biking through as many as he can as often as he can, he describes his ongoing realization that cities are nothing less than "physical manifestations of our deepest beliefs and our often unconscious thoughts." It's merely a matter of recognition: "A cognitive scientist need only look at what we have made – the hives we have created – to know what we think and what we believe to be important… It's all there, in plain view, right out in the open." We evade. We compartmentalize. We say *this* doesn't have anything to do with *that*. But what we're up to isn't, as it turns out, a secret: "You don't need CAT scans and cultural anthropologists to show you what's going on inside the human mind; its inner workings are manifested in three dimensions." Our religion, practically speaking, is, after all, alarmingly self-evident if we're open to taking a hard look around: "Our values and hopes are sometimes awfully embarrassingly easy to read. They're right there – in the storefronts, museums, temples, shops, and office buildings… They say, in their unique visual language, 'This is what we think matters, this is how we live and how we play.'"[1]

No Communion without Nuance

Like God and the devil, religion is in the details. Like any artist, Byrne would have us begin to think about them, to lean into the fact of certain connections we're in the weird habit of denying, to move through the world with our antennae out, saying – or singing – what we see. To do so artfully is to engage in the kind of poetic thinking we associate with Byrne or any creative personality determined to be awake and alive to the myths in which we otherwise swim unknowingly, myths in which we've been immersed so long that they've become second nature to us, myths by and through which we've measured our lives so unconsciously that we've forgotten how arbitrary they are, myths from which we're perfectly free to withdraw our consent when we begin to ask ourselves, "Well, how did we get here?"

To genuinely ask this kind of question is to be a practitioner of simple self-awareness, a way of wondering at ourselves and all the strange things

---

[1] David Byrne, *Bicycle Diaries* (New York: Viking Penguin, 2009), 2.

we put up with, sustain and perpetuate, a way of bringing it all to consciousness. What task could be more urgent for a person? For my money, religion is the farthest-reaching readily available concept for looking hard and honestly at our own lives, for *really* leveling with ourselves and for abandoning our dysfunctional ideas for better ones, truer, livelier, more sustainable ways of negotiating our existence. Life's too short to pretend we're not religious.

Why do I insist on framing the conversation this way? I'm in it for beauty. As someone who has dared to try to teach people for most of my adult life, I often suspect that what I'm up to is, in large part, an effort to try to stop people from becoming bored and giving up too soon, to help them find their own lives and the lives of others powerfully interesting, weird and somehow beautiful. Look again, *re*-spect, stay with me and consider the possibility that there might be more going on in a neighbor, a novel, an image or an issue than your mind grasped the first time around, something worthy of your time, something beautiful. In this, I share Elaine Scarry's conviction that the "willingness continually to revise one's own location in order to place oneself in the path of beauty is the basic impulse underlying education."[2] This is to define education as a journey, certainly, but it is also to envision education as a creative task that involves finding and seeing beauty in the very places where we've grown accustomed to only sensing and feeling conflict.

Which brings us back to religion as a divider. I want very badly to challenge the ease with which we succumb to the false divide of labels, that moment in which our empathy gives out and we refuse to respond openhandedly or even curiously to people with whom we differ. As I see it, to refuse the possibility of finding another person interesting, complex and as complicated as oneself is a form of violence. At bottom, this is a refusal of nuance, and I wish to posit that nuance is sacred. To call it sacred is to value it so much and esteem it so highly that we find it fitting to somehow set it apart as something to which we're forever committed. Nuance refuses to envision others degradingly, denying them the content of their own experience, and talks us down tenderly from the false ledges we've put ourselves on. When we take it on as a sacred obligation, nuance also delivers us out of the deadly habit of cutting people out of our own imaginations. This opens us up to the possibility of at least occasionally finding one another beautiful, the possibility of communion. I happen to live for these openings, and I suspect I write "NUANCE" in the margins

---

[2] Elaine Scarry, *On Beauty and Being Just* (Princeton, NJ: Princeton University Press, 1999), 7.

of research papers more than any other word. It could be that there's no communion without it.

I hasten to add that the communion I'm hoping for isn't a retreat from the everyday or the realistic but a more profound engagement with it. This brings to mind Iris Murdoch's definition of love: "Love is the extremely difficult realisation that something other than oneself is real. Love, and so art and morals, is the discovery of reality."[3]

The work of consciousness, we begin to understand, is never done.

Religion is Witness

In this vein, I offer my vision of religion as central to all human experience as a way of getting unstuck from our failures of imagination in the way we see ourselves and others, those mean mental habits with which we casually but all too definitively deny commitment, connection and kinship to neighbors, strangers and family when they disturb our defensive sense of our own identities. By letting religion name all our own ultimate concerns and the ways we pursue them, we open our lives to an ever-renewed perception and recognition of our profoundly interdependent relationship to the rest of the world. I view this as a summons to see ourselves anew *and* to discover reality as it is – not *making* connections exactly, because the truth is they're already there, preceding us as the very facts on the ground, whether we recognize them or not. To begin to respond to such a summons is to enter the kind of accountability – the deep awareness – that occurs when we see and think poetically, because poetry is the work of recognition, the work of seeing beautifully.

It would have been a mouthful, and good conversations know no definitive ending, but what I hoped to convey – and still do – to my disbelieving friend is that we lose no ground when we note that there are myriad ways to be a true believer and that we might even gain something in the way of candor, ownership, transparency and substance if we can fess up to our own devotions. What manner of devotee art thou? What's the what, the how and the why of your day-to-day? Let's hold our devotions out with open hands. Or as Leonard Cohen so memorably puts it, let us compare mythologies.

It's a life's work for sure, but with humor and compassion we can try to own what we're up to; we can try to be true in all we do. Your obsession with *Game of Thrones*? Religious. Your determination to hold on to that

---

[3] Iris Murdoch, "The Sublime and the Good," in Peter Conradi, ed., *Existentialists and Mystics: Writings on Philosophy and Literature* (New York: Penguin, 1997), 215. With thanks to Sallie McFague for the tip.

plastic bottle till you've found a recycling receptacle? Religious. The song you sing when you're alone? Religious. Your response to your fellow pilgrim who just cut you off in traffic? Religious. The bad ideas you're leaving behind *and* the new ones you're trying on: Religious.

You're always telling your controlling story. Or to borrow a phrase from Jesus of Nazareth, we'll be known by our fruit. The operative term – the excruciatingly helpful word I have in mind here – is witness. As much as I'd often prefer otherwise, there is no on-and-off switch when it comes to my witness. It's simply the evidence of my output. My witness is the sum of everything I do and leave undone. The words are there, but the actions speak louder.

Our witness isn't what we say we believe or even what we think we believe. Neither is it the image, pose or posture we try to present to others. It's what we do, what we give, what we take and what we actually bring to our little worlds. Witness knows no division. In some sense, the future will know what our witness was better than we can, the ways we rang true (or didn't). Time's the revelator when it comes to what your witness is or what your religion, as it turns out, was. Your religion is your witness is the shape your love takes. In all things.

But I'm getting ahead of myself. Before I go too far asking anyone to consider the ups and downs of their weird religious background, I'd like to devote some space to describing, as best as I can, my own. For every hero or villain, there's always an origin story. Here's hoping that our neuroses might also be, in some deep sense, our wisdom. I'll go first.

The Apology
Plato

In *Plato: Complete Works*. Trans. G. M. A. Grube and ed. John M. Cooper. Indianapolis: Hackett Publishing Company, 1997.

We have already met **Plato** *(429-347 BCE) as the author of the* Allegory of the Cave. *This work, the* Apology *is perhaps Plato's most widely read piece of writing, in which he provides his own account of what his mentor Socrates had said when on trial in 399 BCE.*

Why we are reading this: *The* Apology *is the first of several readings that focus on the techniques humans have developed over the centuries to create and evaluate knowledge. Here Socrates (or is it really Plato?) outlines the critical importance of inquisitive skepticism and questioning as a path towards knowledge. Socrates was fueled by the conviction that there is always more to understand, that one must begin by admitting one's own ignorance, and that wisdom consists in not pretending to know what one does not know. For Socrates, nothing in human life is more important than the pursuit of wisdom and truth. As he notes in his famous dictum: "the unexamined life is not worth living."*

SOCRATES: I do not know, men of Athens, how my accusers affected you; as for me, I was almost carried away in spite of myself, so persuasively did they speak. And yet, hardly anything of what they said is true. Of the many lies they told, one in particular surprised me, namely that you should be careful not to be deceived by an accomplished speaker like me. That they were not ashamed to be immediately proved wrong by the facts, when I show myself not to be an accomplished speaker at all, that I thought was most shameless on their part – unless indeed they call an accomplished speaker the man who speaks the truth. If they mean that, I would agree that I am an orator, but not after their manner, for indeed, as I say, practically nothing they said was true. From me you will hear the whole truth, though not, by Zeus, gentlemen, expressed in embroidered and stylized phrases like theirs, but things spoken at random and expressed in the first words that come to mind, for I put my trust in the justice of what I say, and let none of you expect anything else. It would not be fitting at my age, as it might be for a young man, to toy with words when I appear before you.

One thing I do ask and beg of you, gentlemen: if you hear me making my defense in the same kind of language as I am accustomed to use in the market place by the bankers' tables, where many of you have heard me, and elsewhere, do not be surprised or create a disturbance on that account. The position is this: this is my first appearance in a lawcourt, at the age of seventy; I am therefore simply a stranger to the manner of speaking here. Just as if I were really a stranger, you would certainly excuse me if I spoke in that dialect and manner in which I had been brought up, so too my present request seems a just one, for you to pay no attention to my manner of speech – be it better or worse – but to concentrate your attention on whether what I say is just or not, for the excellence of a judge lies in this, as that of a speaker lies in telling the truth.

It is right for me, gentlemen, to defend myself first against the first lying accusations made against me and my first accusers, and then against the later accusations and the later accusers. There have been many who have accused me to you for many years now, and none of their accusations are true. These I fear much more than I fear Anytus and his friends, though they too are formidable. These earlier ones, however, are more so, gentlemen; they got hold of most of you from childhood, persuaded you and accused me quite falsely, saying that there is a man called Socrates, a wise man, a student of all things in the sky and below the earth, who makes the worse argument the stronger. Those who spread that rumor, gentlemen, are my dangerous accusers, for their hearers believe that those who study these things do not even believe in the gods. Moreover, these accusers are numerous, and have been at it a long time; also, they spoke to you at an age when you would most readily believe them, some of you being children and adolescents, and they won their case by default, as there was no defense.

What is most absurd in all this is that one cannot even know or mention their names unless one of them is a writer of comedies.[1] Those who maliciously and slanderously persuaded you – who also, when persuaded themselves then persuaded others – all those are most difficult to deal with: one cannot bring one of them into court or refute him; one must simply fight with shadows, as it were, in making one's defense, and cross-examine when no one answers. I want you to realize too that my accusers are of two kinds: those who have accused me recently, and the old ones I mention; and to think that I must first defend myself against the latter, for you have also heard their accusations first, and to a much greater extent than the more recent.

Very well then, men of Athens. I must surely defend myself and attempt to uproot from your minds in so short a time the slander that has resided there so long. I wish this may happen, if it is in any way better for

---

[1] This is Aristophanes. Socrates refers later to his character in his *Clouds*, first produced in 423 BC. [note by John M. Cooper, JMC]

you and me, and that my defense may be successful, but I think this is very difficult and I am fully aware of how difficult it is. Even so, let the matter proceed as the god may wish, but I must obey the law and make my defense.

Let us then take up the case from its beginning. What is the accusation from which arose the slander in which Meletus trusted when he wrote out the charge against me? What did they say when they slandered me? I must, as if they were my actual prosecutors, read the affidavit they would have sworn. It goes something like this: Socrates is guilty of wrongdoing in that he busies himself studying things in the sky and below the earth; he makes the worse into the stronger argument, and he teaches these same things to others. You have seen this yourself in the comedy of Aristophanes, a Socrates swinging about there, saying he was walking on air and talking a lot of other nonsense about things of which I know nothing at all. I do not speak in contempt of such knowledge, if someone is wise in these things – lest Meletus bring more cases against me – but, gentlemen, I have no part in it, and on this point I call upon the majority of you as witnesses. I think it right that all those of you who have heard me conversing, and many of you have, should tell each other if anyone of you has ever heard me discussing such subjects to any extent at all. From this you will learn that the other things said about me by the majority are of the same kind.

Not one of them is true. And if you have heard from anyone that I undertake to teach people and charge a fee for it, that is not true either. Yet I think it a fine thing to be able to teach people as Gorgias of Leontini does, and Prodicus of Ceos, and Hippias of Elis.[2] Each of these men can go to any city and persuade the young, who can keep company with anyone of their own fellow citizens they want without paying, to leave the company of these, to join with themselves, pay them a fee, and be grateful to them besides. Indeed, I learned that there is another wise man from Paros who is visiting us, for I met a man who has spent more money on Sophists than everybody else put together, Callias, the son of Hipponicus. So I asked him – he has two sons – "Callias," I said, "if your sons were colts or calves, we could find and engage a supervisor for them who would make them excel in their proper qualities, some horse breeder or farmer. Now since they are men, whom do you have in mind to supervise them? Who is an expert in this kind of excellence, the human and social kind? I think you must have given thought to this since you have sons. Is there such a person," I asked, "or is there not?" "Certainly there is," he said. "Who is

---

[2] These were all well-known Sophists. For Gorgias and Hippias see Plato's dialogues named after them; both Hippias and Prodicus appear in *Protagoras*. [JMC]

he?" I asked, "What is his name, where is he from? and what is his fee?" "His name, Socrates, is Evenus, he comes from Paros, and his fee is five minas." I thought Evenus a happy man, if he really possesses this art, and teaches for so moderate a fee. Certainly I would pride and preen myself if I had this knowledge, but I do not have it, gentlemen.

One of you might perhaps interrupt me and say: "But Socrates, what is your occupation? From where have these slanders come? For surely if you did not busy yourself with something out of the common, all these rumors and talk would not have arisen unless you did something other than most people. Tell us what it is, that we may not speak inadvisedly about you." Anyone who says that seems to be right, and I will try to show you what has caused this reputation and slander. Listen then. Perhaps some of you will think I am jesting, but be sure that all that I shall say is true. What has caused my reputation is none other than a certain kind of wisdom. What kind of wisdom? Human wisdom, perhaps. It may be that I really possess this, while those whom I mentioned just now are wise with a wisdom more than human; else I cannot explain it, for I certainly do not possess it, and whoever says I do is lying and speaks to slander me. Do not create a disturbance, gentlemen, even if you think I am boasting, for the story I shall tell does not originate with me, but I will refer you to a trustworthy source. I shall call upon the god at Delphi as witness to the existence and nature of my wisdom, if it be such. You know Chaerephon. He was my friend from youth, and the friend of most of you, as he shared your exile and your return. You surely know the kind of man he was, how impulsive in any course of action. He went to Delphi at one time and ventured to ask the oracle – as I say, gentlemen, do not create a disturbance – he asked if any man was wiser than I, and the Pythian replied that no one was wiser. Chaerephon is dead, but his brother will testify to you about this.

Consider that I tell you this because I would inform you about the origin of the slander. When I heard of this reply I asked myself: "Whatever does the god mean? What is his riddle? I am very conscious that I am not wise at all; what then does he mean by saying that I am the wisest? For surely he does not lie; it is not legitimate for him to do so." For a long time I was at a loss as to his meaning; then I very reluctantly turned to some such investigation as this: I went to one of those reputed wise, thinking that there, if anywhere, I could refute the oracle and say to it: "This man is wiser than I, but you said I was." Then, when I examined this man – there is no need for me to tell you his name, he was one of our public men – my experience was something like this: I thought that he appeared wise to many people and especially to himself, but he was not. I then tried to show him that he thought himself wise, but that he was not. As a result he came to dislike me, and so did many of the bystanders. So I withdrew and thought to myself: "I am wiser than this man; it is likely that neither of us knows anything worthwhile, but he thinks he knows something when he does not, whereas when I do not know, neither do I think I know; so I am likely to be wiser than he to this small extent, that I do not think I know what I do not know." After this I approached another man, one of those thought to be wiser than he, and I thought the same thing, and so I came to be disliked both by him and by many others.

After that I proceeded systematically. I realized, to my sorrow and alarm, that I was getting unpopular, but I thought that I must attach the greatest importance to the god's oracle, so I must go to all those who had any reputation for knowledge to examine its meaning. And by the dog, gentlemen of the jury – for I must tell you the truth – I experienced something like this: in my investigation in the service of the god I found that those who had the highest reputation were nearly the most deficient, while those who were thought to be inferior were more knowledgeable. I must give you an account of my journeyings as if they were labors I had undertaken to prove the oracle irrefutable. After the politicians, I went to the poets, the writers of tragedies and dithyrambs and the others, intending in their case to catch myself being more ignorant then they. So I took up those poems with which they seemed to have taken most trouble and asked them what they meant, in order that I might at the same time learn something from them. I am ashamed to tell you the truth, gentlemen, but I must. Almost all the bystanders might have explained the poems better than their authors could. I soon realized that poets do not compose their poems with knowledge, but by some inborn talent and by inspiration, like seers and prophets who also say many fine things without any understanding of what they say. The poets seemed to me to have had a similar experience. At the same time I saw that, because of their poetry, they thought themselves very wise men in other respects, which they were not. So there again I withdrew, thinking that I had the same advantage over them as I had over the politicians.

Finally I went to the craftsmen, for I was conscious of knowing practically nothing, and I knew that I would find that they had knowledge of many fine things. In this I was not mistaken; they knew things I did not know, and to that extent they were wiser than I. But, gentlemen of the jury, the good craftsmen seemed to me to have the same fault as the poets: each of them, because of his success at his craft, thought himself very wise in other most important pursuits, and this error of theirs overshadowed the wisdom they had, so that I asked myself, on behalf of the oracle, whether I should prefer to be as I am, with neither their wisdom nor their ignorance, or to have both. The answer I gave myself and the oracle was that it was to my advantage to be as I am.

As a result of this investigation, gentlemen of the jury, I acquired much unpopularity, of a kind that is hard to deal with and is a heavy burden; many slanders came from these people and a reputation for wisdom, for in each case the bystanders thought that I myself possessed the wisdom that I proved that my interlocutor did not have. What is probable, gentlemen, is that in fact the god is wise and that his oracular response meant that human wisdom is worth little or nothing, and that when he says this man, Socrates, he is using my name as an example, as if he said: "This man among you, mortals, is wisest who, like Socrates, understands that his wisdom is worthless." So even now I continue this investigation as the god bade me – and I go around seeking out anyone, citizen or stranger, whom I think wise. Then if I do not think he is, I come to the assistance of the god and show him that he is not wise. Because of this occupation, I do not have the leisure to engage in public affairs to any extent, nor indeed to look after my own, but I live in great poverty because of my service to the god.

Furthermore, the young men who follow me around of their own free will, those who have most leisure, the sons of the very rich, take pleasure in hearing people questioned; they themselves often imitate me and try to question others. I think they find an abundance of men who believe they have some knowledge but know little or nothing. The result is that those whom they question are angry, not with themselves but with me. They say: "That man Socrates is a pestilential fellow who corrupts the young." If one asks them what he does and what he teaches to corrupt them, they are silent, as they do not know, but, so as not to appear at a loss, they mention those accusations that are available against all philosophers, about "things in the sky and things below the earth," about "not believing in the gods" and "making the worse the stronger argument;" they would not want to tell the truth, I'm sure, that they have been proved to lay claim to knowledge when they know nothing. These people are ambitious, violent and numerous; they are continually and convincingly talking about me; they have been filling your ears for a long time with vehement slanders against me. From them Meletus attacked me, and Anytus and Lycon, Meletus being vexed on behalf of the poets, Anytus on behalf of the craftsmen and the politicians, Lycon on behalf of the orators, so that, as I started out by saying, I should be surprised if I could rid you of so much slander in so short a time. That, gentlemen of the jury, is the truth for you. I have hidden or disguised nothing. I know well enough that this very conduct makes me unpopular, and this is proof that what I say is true, that such is the slander against me, and that such are its causes. If you look into this either now or later, this is what you will find.

Let this suffice as a defense against the charges of my earlier accusers. After this I shall try to defend myself against Meletus, that good and patriotic man, as he says he is, and my later accusers. As these are a different lot of accusers, let us again take up their sworn deposition. It goes something like this: Socrates is guilty of corrupting the young and of not believing in the gods in whom the city believes, but in other new spiritual things. Such is their charge. Let us examine it point by point.

He says that I am guilty of corrupting the young, but I say that Meletus is guilty of dealing frivolously with serious matters, of irresponsibly bringing people into court, and of professing to be seriously concerned with things about none of which he has ever cared, and I shall try to prove that this is so. Come here and tell me, Meletus. Surely you consider it of the greatest importance that our young men be as good as possible? – Indeed I do.

Come then, tell the jury who improves them. You obviously know, in view of your concern. You say you have discovered the one who corrupts them, namely me, and you bring me here and accuse me to the jury. Come, inform the jury and tell them who it is. You see, Meletus, that you are silent and know not what to say. Does this not seem shameful to you and a sufficient proof of what I say, that you have not been concerned with any of this? Tell me, my good sir, who improves our young men?

MELETUS: The laws.

SOCRATES: That is not what I am asking, but what person who has knowledge of the laws to begin with?

MELETUS: These jurymen, Socrates.

SOCRATES: How do you mean, Meletus? Are these able to educate the young and improve them?

MELETUS: Certainly.

SOCRATES: All of them, or some but not others?

MELETUS: All of them.

SOCRATES: Very good, by Hera. You mention a great abundance of benefactors. But what about the audience? Do they improve the young or not?

MELETUS: They do, too.

SOCRATES: What about the members of Council?

MELETUS: The Councillors, also.

SOCRATES: But, Meletus, what about the assembly? Do members of the assembly corrupt the young, or do they all improve them?

MELETUS: They improve them.

SOCRATES: All the Athenians, it seems, make the young into fine good men, except me, and I alone corrupt them. Is that what you mean?

MELETUS: That is most definitely what I mean.

SOCRATES: You condemn me to a great misfortune. Tell me: does this also apply to horses do you think? That all men improve them and one individual corrupts them? Or is quite the contrary true, one individual is able to improve them, or very few, namely the horse breeders, whereas the majority, if they have horses and use them, corrupt them? Is that not the case, Meletus, both with horses and all other animals? Of course it is, whether you and Anytus say so or not. It would be a very happy state of affairs if only one person corrupted our youth, while the others improved them.

You have made it sufficiently obvious, Meletus, that you have never had any concern for our youth; you show your indifference clearly; that you have given no thought to the subjects about which you bring me to trial.

And by Zeus, Meletus, tell us also whether it is better for a man to live among good or wicked fellow-citizens. Answer, my good man, for I am not asking a difficult question. Do not the wicked do some harm to those who are ever closest to them, whereas good people benefit them?

MELETUS: Certainly.

SOCRATES: And does the man exist who would rather be harmed than benefited by his associates? Answer, my good sir, for the law orders you to answer. Is there any man who wants to be harmed?

MELETUS: Of course not.

SOCRATES: Come now, do you accuse me here of corrupting the young and making them worse deliberately or unwillingly?

MELETUS: Deliberately.

SOCRATES: What follows, Meletus? Are you so much wiser at your age than I am at mine that you understand that wicked people always do some harm to their closest neighbors while good people do them good, but I have reached such a pitch of ignorance that I do not realize this, namely that if I make one of my associates wicked I run the risk of being harmed by him so that I do such a great evil deliberately, as you say? I do not believe you, Meletus, and I do not think anyone else will. Either I do not corrupt the young or, if I do, it is unwillingly, and you are lying in either case. Now if I corrupt them unwillingly, the law does not require you to bring people to court for such unwilling wrongdoings, but to get hold of them privately, to instruct them and exhort them; for clearly, if I learn better, I shall cease to do what I am doing unwillingly. You, however, have avoided my company and were unwilling to instruct me, but you bring me

97

here, where the law requires one to bring those who are in need of punishment, not of instruction.

And so, gentlemen of the jury, what I said is clearly true: Meletus has never been at all concerned with these matters. Nonetheless tell us, Meletus, how you say that I corrupt the young; or is it obvious from your deposition that it is by teaching them not to believe in the gods in whom the city believes but in other new spiritual things? Is this not what you say I teach and so corrupt them?

MELETUS: That is most certainly what I do say.

SOCRATES: Then by those very gods about whom we are talking, Meletus, make this clearer to me and to the jury: I cannot be sure whether you mean that I teach the belief that there are some gods – and therefore I myself believe that there are gods and am not altogether an atheist, nor am I guilty of that – not, however, the gods in whom the city believes, but others, and that this is the charge against me, that they are others. Or whether you mean that I do not believe in gods at all, and that this is what I teach to others.

MELETUS: This is what I mean, that you do not believe in gods at all.

SOCRATES: You are a strange fellow, Meletus. Why do you say this? Do I not believe, as other men do, that the sun and the moon are gods?

MELETUS: No, by Zeus, gentlemen of the jury, for he says that the sun is stone, and the moon earth.

SOCRATES: My dear Meletus, do you think you are prosecuting Anaxagoras?[3] Are you so contemptuous of the jury and think them so ignorant of letters as not to know that the books of Anaxagoras of Clazomenae are full of those theories, and further, that the young men learn from me what they can buy from time to time for a drachma, at most, in the bookshops, and ridicule Socrates if he pretends that these theories are his own, especially as they are so absurd? Is that, by Zeus, what you think of me, Meletus, that I do not believe that there are any gods?

MELETUS: That is what I say, that you do not believe in the gods at all.

SOCRATES: You cannot be believed, Meletus, even, I think, by yourself. The man appears to me, gentlemen of the jury, highly insolent and uncontrolled. He seems to have made this deposition out of insolence, violence and youthful zeal. He is like one who composed a riddle and is trying it out: "Will the wise Socrates realize that I am jesting and contradicting myself, or shall I deceive him and others?" I think he

---

[3] Anaxagoras of Clazomenae (c. 510-c. 428) had theorized that heavenly objects like the sun, moon, and stars were not gods but physical objects made of stone or metal. By this point he had been dead almost thirty years. [Ed.]

contradicts himself in the affidavit, as if he said: "Socrates is guilty of not believing in gods but believing in gods," and surely that is the part of a jester!

Examine with me, gentlemen, how he appears to contradict himself, and you, Meletus, answer us. Remember, gentlemen, what I asked you when I began, not to create a disturbance if I proceed in my usual manner.

Does any man, Meletus, believe in human activities who does not believe in humans? Make him answer, and not again and again create a disturbance. Does any man who does not believe in horses believe in horsemen's activities? Or in flute-playing activities but not in flute-players? No, my good sir, no man could. If you are not willing to answer, I will tell you and the jury. Answer the next question, however. Does any man believe in spiritual activities who does not believe in spirits?

MELETUS: No one.

SOCRATES: Thank you for answering, if reluctantly, when these gentlemen made you. Now you say that I believe in spiritual things and teach about them, whether new or old, but at any rate spiritual things according to what you say, and to this you have sworn in your deposition. But if I believe in spiritual things I must quite inevitably believe in spirits. Is that not so? It is indeed. I shall assume that you agree, as you do not answer. Do we not believe spirits to be either gods or the children of gods? Yes or no?

MELETUS: Of course.

SOCRATES: Then since I do believe in spirits, as you admit, if spirits are gods, this is what I mean when I say you speak in riddles and in jest, as you state that I do not believe in gods and then again that I do, since I do believe in spirits. If on the other hand the spirits are children of the gods, bastard children of the gods by nymphs or some other mothers, as they are said to be, what man would believe children of the gods to exist, but not gods? That would be just as absurd as to believe the young of horses and asses, namely mules, to exist, but not to believe in the existence of horses and asses. You must have made this deposition, Meletus, either to test us or because you were at a loss to find any true wrongdoing of which to accuse me. There is no way in which you could persuade anyone of even small intelligence that it is possible for one and the same man to believe in spiritual but not also in divine things, and then again for that same man to believe neither in spirits nor in gods nor in heroes.

I do not think, men of Athens, that it requires a prolonged defense to prove that I am not guilty of the charges in Meletus' deposition, but this is sufficient. On the other hand, you know that what I said earlier is true, that I am very unpopular with many people. This will be my undoing, if I am undone, not Meletus or Anytus but the slanders and envy of many people.

This has destroyed many other good men and will, I think, continue to do so. There is no danger that it will stop at me.

Someone might say: "Are you not ashamed, Socrates, to have followed the kind of occupation that has led to your being now in danger of death?" However, I should be right to reply to him: "You are wrong, sir, if you think that a man who is any good at all should take into account the risk of life or death; he should look to this only in his actions, whether what he does is right or wrong, whether he is acting like a good or a bad man." According to your view, all the heroes who died at Troy were inferior people, especially the son of Thetis[4] who was so contemptuous of danger compared with disgrace. When he was eager to kill Hector, his goddess mother warned him, as I believe, in some such words as these: "My child, if you avenge the death of your comrade, Patroclus, and you kill Hector, you will die yourself, for your death is to follow immediately after Hector's." Hearing this, he despised death and danger and was much more afraid to live a coward who did not avenge his friends. "Let me die at once," he said, "when once I have given the wrongdoer his deserts, rather than remain here, a laughing-stock by the curved ships, a burden upon the earth." Do you think he gave thought to death and danger?

This is the truth of the matter, men of Athens: wherever a man has taken a position that he believes to be best, or has been placed by his commander, there he must I think remain and face danger, without a thought for death or anything else, rather than disgrace. It would have been a dreadful way to behave, gentlemen of the jury, if, at Potidaea, Amphipolis and Delium,[5] I had, at the risk of death, like anyone else, remained at my post where those you had elected to command had ordered me, and then, when the god ordered me, as I thought and believed, to live the life of a philosopher, to examine myself and others, I had abandoned my post for fear of death or anything else. That would have been a dreadful thing, and then I might truly have justly been brought here for not believing that there are gods, disobeying the oracle, fearing death, and thinking I was wise when I was not. To fear death, gentlemen, is no other than to think oneself wise when one is not, to think one knows what one does not know. No one knows whether death may not be the greatest of all blessings for a man, yet men fear it as if they knew that it is the greatest of evils. And surely it is the most blameworthy ignorance to believe that one knows what one does not know. It is perhaps on this point and in this respect, gentlemen, that I differ from the majority of men, and if I were to

---

[4] See *Iliad* xviii.94 ff. [JMC]. The "son of Thetis" refers to the hero Achilles. [Ed.]
[5] Socrates was a veteran of the Peloponnesian War and had fought at the battles of Potidaea (432 BCE), Amphipolis (422 BCE), and Delium (424 BCE). [Ed.].

claim that I am wiser than anyone in anything, it would be in this that as I have no adequate knowledge of things in the underworld, so I do not think I have. I do know, however, that it is wicked and shameful to do wrong, to disobey one's superior, be he god or man. I shall never fear or avoid things of which I do not know, whether they may not be good rather than things that I know to be bad. Even if you acquitted me now and did not believe Anytus, who said to you that either I should not have been brought here in the first place, or that now I am here, you cannot avoid executing me, for if I should be acquitted, your sons would practice the teachings of Socrates and all be thoroughly corrupted; if you said to me in this regard: "Socrates, we do not believe Anytus now; we acquit you, but only on condition that you spend no more time on this investigation and do not practice philosophy, and if you are caught doing so you will die;" if, as I say, you were to acquit me on those terms, I would say to you: "Men of Athens, I am grateful and I am your friend, but I will obey the god rather than you, and as long as I draw breath and am able, I shall not cease to practice philosophy, to exhort you and in my usual way to point out to anyone of you whom I happen to meet: Good Sir, you are an Athenian, a citizen of the greatest city with the greatest reputation for both wisdom and power; are you not ashamed of your eagerness to possess as much wealth, reputation and honors as possible, while you do not care for nor give thought to wisdom or truth or the best possible state of your soul?" Then, if one of you disputes this and says he does care, I shall not let him go at once or leave him, but I shall question him, examine him and test him, and if I do not think he has attained the goodness that he says he has, I shall reproach him because he attaches little importance to the most important things and greater importance to inferior things. I shall treat in this way anyone I happen to meet, young and old, citizen and stranger, and more so the citizens because you are more kindred to me. Be sure that this is what the god orders me to do, and I think there is no greater blessing for the city than my service to the god. For I go around doing nothing but persuading both young and old among you not to care for your body or your wealth in preference to or as strongly as for the best possible state of your soul, as I say to you: "Wealth does not bring about excellence, but excellence makes wealth and everything else good for men, both individually and collectively."[6]

Now if by saying this I corrupt the young, this advice must be harmful, but if anyone says that I give different advice, he is talking nonsense. On

---

[6] Alternatively, this sentence could be translated: "Wealth does not bring about excellence, but excellence brings about wealth and all other public and private blessings for men." [JMC]

this point I would say to you, gentlemen of the jury: "Whether you believe Anytus or not, whether you acquit me or not, do so on the understanding that this is my course of action, even if I am to face death many times." Do not create a disturbance, gentlemen, but abide by my request not to cry out at what I say but to listen, for I think it will be to your advantage to listen, and I am about to say other things at which you will perhaps cry out. By no means do this. Be sure that if you kill the sort of man I say I am, you will not harm me more than yourselves. Neither Meletus nor Anytus can harm me in any way; he could not harm me, for I do not think it is permitted that a better man be harmed by a worse; certainly he might kill me, or perhaps banish or disfranchise me, which he and maybe others think to be great harm, but I do not think so. I think he is doing himself much greater harm doing what he is doing now, attempting to have a man executed unjustly. Indeed, gentlemen of the jury, I am far from making a defense now on my own behalf, as might be thought, but on yours, to prevent you from wrongdoing by mistreating the god's gift to you by condemning me; for if you kill me you will not easily find another like me. I was attached to this city by the god – though it seems a ridiculous thing to say – as upon a great and noble horse which was somewhat sluggish because of its size and needed to be stirred up by a kind of gadfly. It is to fulfill some such function that I believe the god has placed me in the city. I never cease to rouse each and every one of you, to persuade and reproach you all day long and everywhere I find myself in your company.

Another such man will not easily come to be among you, gentlemen, and if you believe me you will spare me. You might easily be annoyed with me as people are when they are aroused from a doze, and strike out at me; if convinced by Anytus you could easily kill me, and then you could sleep on for the rest of your days, unless the god, in his care for you, sent you someone else. That I am the kind of person to be a gift of the god to the city you might realize from the fact that it does not seem like human nature for me to have neglected all my own affairs and to have tolerated this neglect now for so many years while I was always concerned with you, approaching each one of you like a father or an elder brother to persuade you to care for virtue. Now if I profited from this by charging a fee for my advice, there would be some sense to it, but you can see for yourselves that, for all their shameless accusations, my accusers have not been able in their impudence to bring forward a witness to say that I have ever received a fee or ever asked for one. I, on the other hand, have a convincing witness that I speak the truth, my poverty.

It may seem strange that while I go around and give this advice privately and interfere in private affairs, I do not venture to go to the assembly and there advise the city. You have heard me give the reason for this in many places. I have a divine or spiritual sign which Meletus has ridiculed in his deposition. This began when I was a child. It is a voice, and whenever it speaks it turns me away from something I am about to do, but it never encourages me to do anything. This is what has prevented me from taking part in public affairs, and I think it was quite right to prevent me. Be sure, gentlemen of the jury, that if I had long ago attempted to take part in politics, I should have died long ago, and benefited neither you nor myself. Do not be angry with me for speaking the truth; no man will survive who genuinely opposes you or any other crowd and prevents the occurrence of many unjust and illegal happenings in the city. A man who really fights for justice must lead a private, not a public, life if he is to survive for even a short time.

I shall give you great proofs of this, not words but what you esteem, deeds. Listen to what happened to me, that you may know that I will not yield to any man contrary to what is right, for fear of death, even if I should die at once for not yielding. The things I shall tell you are commonplace and smack of the lawcourts, but they are true. I have never held any other office in the city, but I served as a member of the Council, and our tribe Antiochis was presiding at the time when you wanted to try as a body the ten generals who had failed to pick up the survivors of the naval battle[7]. This was illegal, as you all recognized later. I was the only member of the presiding committee to oppose your doing something contrary to the laws, and I voted against it. The orators were ready to prosecute me and take me away; and your shouts were egging them on, but I thought I should run any risk on the side of law and justice rather than join you, for fear of prison or death, when you were engaged in an unjust course.

This happened when the city was still a democracy. When the oligarchy was established, the Thirty[8] summoned me to the Hall, along with four others, and ordered us to bring Leon from Salamis, that he might be executed. They gave many such orders to many people, in order to implicate as many as possible in their guilt. Then I showed again, not in words but in action, that, if it were not rather vulgar to say so, death is something I couldn't care less about, but that my whole concern is not to do anything unjust or impious. That government, powerful as it was, did not frighten me into any wrongdoing. When we left the Hall, the other four went to Salamis and brought in Leon, but I went home. I might have been

---

[7] This was the battle of Arginusae (south of Lesbos) in 406 BC, the last Athenian victory of the Peloponnesian war. A violent storm prevented the Athenians from rescuing the survivors. [JMC]

[8] This was the harsh oligarchy that was set up after the final defeat of Athens in 404 BC, and that ruled Athens for some nine months in 404-3 before the democracy was restored. [JMC]

put to death for this, had not the government fallen shortly afterwards. There are many who will witness to these events.

Do you think I would have survived all these years if I were engaged in public affairs and, acting as a good man must, came to the help of justice and considered this the most important thing? Far from it, gentlemen of the jury, nor would any other man. Throughout my life, in any public activity I may have engaged in, I am the same man as I am in private life. I have never come to an agreement with anyone to act unjustly, neither with anyone else nor with anyone of those who they slanderously say are my pupils. I have never been anyone's teacher. If anyone, young or old, desires to listen to me when I am talking and dealing with my own concerns, I have never begrudged this to anyone, but I do not converse when I receive a fee and not when I do not. I am equally ready to question the rich and the poor if anyone is willing to answer my questions and listen to what I say. And I cannot justly be held responsible for the good or bad conduct of these people, as I never promised to teach them anything and have not done so. If anyone says that he has learned anything from me, or that he heard anything privately that the others did not hear, be assured that he is not telling the truth.

Why then do some people enjoy spending considerable time in my company? You have heard why, men of Athens, I have told you the whole truth. They enjoy hearing those being questioned who think they are wise, but are not. And this is not unpleasant. To do this has, as I say, been enjoined upon me by the god, by means of oracles and dreams, and in every other way that a divine manifestation has ever ordered a man to do anything. This is true, gentlemen, and can easily be established.

If I corrupt some young men and have corrupted others, then surely some of them who have grown older and realized that I gave them bad advice when they were young should now themselves come up here to accuse me and avenge themselves. If they were unwilling to do so themselves, then some of their kindred, their fathers or brothers or other relations should recall it now if their family had been harmed by me. I see many of these present here, first Crito, my contemporary and fellow demesman,[9] the father of Critobulus here; next Lysanias of Sphettus, the father of Aeschines here; also Antiphon the Cephisian, the father of Epigenes; and others whose brothers spent their time in this way; Nicostratus, the son of Theozotides, brother of Theodotus, and Theodotus has died so he could not influence him; Paralius here, son of Demodocus, whose brother was Theages; there is Adeimantus, son of Ariston, brother of Plato here; Aeantodorus, brother of Apollodorus here.

---

[9] Member of the same *deme* or township in ancient Greece. [Ed.]

I could mention many others, some one of whom surely Meletus should have brought in as witness in his own speech. If he forgot to do so, then let him do it now; I will yield time if he has anything of the kind to say. You will find quite the contrary, gentlemen. These men are all ready to come to the help of the corruptor, the man who has harmed their kindred, as Meletus and Anytus say. Now those who were corrupted might well have reason to help me, but the uncorrupted, their kindred who are older men, have no reason to help me except the right and proper one, that they know that Meletus is lying and that I am telling the truth.

Very well, gentlemen. This, and maybe other similar things, is what I have to say in my defense. Perhaps one of you might be angry as he recalls that when he himself stood trial on a less dangerous charge, he begged and implored the jury with many tears, that he brought his children and many of his friends and family into court to arouse as much pity as he could, but that I do none of these things, even though I may seem to be running the ultimate risk. Thinking of this, he might feel resentful toward me and, angry about this, cast his vote in anger. If there is such a one among you – I do not deem there is, but if there is – I think it would be right to say in reply: My good sir, I too have a household and, in Homer's phrase, I am not born "from oak or rock" but from men, so that I have a family, indeed three sons, men of Athens, of whom one is an adolescent while two are children. Nevertheless, I will not beg you to acquit me by bringing them here. Why do I do none of these things? Not through arrogance, gentlemen, nor through lack of respect for you. Whether I am brave in the face of death is another matter, but with regard to my reputation and yours and that of the whole city, it does not seem right to me to do these things, especially at my age and with my reputation. For it is generally believed, whether it be true or false, that in certain respects Socrates is superior to the majority of men. Now if those of you who are considered superior, be it in wisdom or courage or whatever other virtue makes them so, are seen behaving like that, it would be a disgrace. Yet I have often seen them do this sort of thing when standing trial, men who are thought to be somebody, doing amazing things as if they thought it a terrible thing to die, and as if they were to be immortal if you did not execute them. I think these men bring shame upon the city so that a stranger, too, would assume that those who are outstanding in virtue among the Athenians, whom they themselves select from themselves to fill offices of state and receive other honors, are in no way better than women. You should not act like that, gentlemen of the jury, those of you who have any reputation at all, and if we do, you should not allow it. You should make it very clear that you will more readily convict a man who performs these pitiful dramatics in court and so makes the city a laughingstock, than a man who keeps quiet.

Quite apart from the question of reputation, gentlemen, I do not think it right to supplicate the jury and to be acquitted because of this but to teach and persuade them. It is not the purpose of a juryman's office to give justice as a favor to whoever seems good to him, but to judge according to law, and this he has sworn to do. We should not accustom you to perjure yourselves, nor should you make a habit of it. This is irreverent conduct for either of us.

Do not deem it right for me, gentlemen of the jury, that I should act towards you in a way that I do not consider to be good or just or pious, especially, by Zeus, as I am being prosecuted by Meletus here for impiety; clearly, if I convinced you by my supplication to do violence to your oath of office, I would be teaching you not to believe that there are gods, and my defense would convict me of not believing in them. This is far from being the case, gentlemen, for I do believe in them as none of my accusers do. I leave it to you and the god to judge me in the way that will be best for me and for you.

[*The jury now gives its verdict of guilty, and Meletus asks for the penalty of death.*]

SOCRATES: There are many other reasons for my not being angry with you for convicting me, men of Athens, and what happened was not unexpected. I am much more surprised at the number of votes cast on each side, for I did not think the decision would be by so few votes but by a great many. As it is, a switch of only thirty votes would have acquitted me. I think myself that I have been cleared on Meletus' charges, and not only this, but it is clear to all that, if Anytus and Lycon had not joined him in accusing me, he would have been fined a thousand drachmas for not receiving a fifth of the votes.

He assesses the penalty at death. So be it. What counter-assessment should I propose to you, men of Athens? Clearly it should be a penalty I deserve, and what do I deserve to suffer or to pay because I have deliberately not led a quiet life but have neglected what occupies most people: wealth, household affairs, the position of general or public orator or the other offices, the political clubs and factions that exist in the city? I thought myself too honest to survive if I occupied myself with those things. I did not follow that path that would have made me of no use either to you or to myself, but I went to each of you privately and conferred upon him what I say is the greatest benefit, by trying to persuade him not to care for any of his belongings before caring that he himself should be as good and as wise as possible, not to care for the city's possessions more than for the city itself, and to care for other things in the same way. What do I deserve for being such a man? Some good, gentlemen of the jury, if I must truly make an assessment according to my deserts, and something suitable. What is suitable for a poor benefactor who needs leisure to exhort you? Nothing is more suitable, gentlemen, than for such a man to be fed in the Prytaneum,[10] much more suitable for him than for anyone of you who has won a victory at Olympia with a pair or a team of horses. The Olympian victor makes you think yourself happy; I make you be happy. Besides, he does not need food, but I do. So if I must make a just assessment of what I deserve, I assess it at this: free meals in the Prytaneum.

When I say this you may think, as when I spoke of appeals to pity and entreaties, that I speak arrogantly, but that is not the case, men of Athens; rather it is like this: I am convinced that I never willingly wrong anyone, but I am not convincing you of this, for we have talked together but a short time. If it were the law with us, as it is elsewhere, that a trial for life should not last one but many days, you would be convinced, but now it is not easy to dispel great slanders in a short time. Since I am convinced that I wrong no one, I am not likely to wrong myself, to say that I deserve some evil and to make some such assessment against myself. What should I fear? That I should suffer the penalty Meletus has assessed against me, of which I say I do not know whether it is good or bad? Am I then to choose in preference to this something that I know very well to be an evil and assess the penalty at that? Imprisonment? Why should I live in prison, always subjected to the ruling magistrates, the Eleven? A fine, and imprisonment until I pay it? That would be the same thing for me, as I have no money. Exile? for perhaps you might accept that assessment.

I should have to be inordinately fond of life, gentlemen of the jury, to be so unreasonable as to suppose that other men will easily tolerate my company and conversation when you, my fellow citizens, have been unable to endure them, but found them a burden and resented them so that you are now seeking to get rid of them. Far from it, gentlemen. It would be a fine life at my age to be driven out of one city after another, for I know very well that wherever I go the young men will listen to my talk as they do here. If I drive them away, they will themselves persuade their elders to drive me out; if I do not drive them away, their fathers and relations will drive me out on their behalf.

Perhaps someone might say: But Socrates, if you leave us will you not be able to live quietly, without talking? Now this is the most difficult point on which to convince some of you. If I say that it is impossible for me to

---

[10] The Prytaneum was the magistrates' hall or town hall of Athens, in which public entertainments were given, particularly to Olympian victors on their return home. [JMC]

keep quiet because that means disobeying the god, you will not believe me and will think I am being ironical. On the other hand, if I say that it is the greatest good for a man to discuss virtue every day and those other things about which you hear me conversing and testing myself and others, for the unexamined life is not worth living for men, you will believe me even less.

What I say is true, gentlemen, but it is not easy to convince you. At the same time, I am not accustomed to think that I deserve any penalty. If I had money, I would assess the penalty at the amount I could pay, for that would not hurt me, but I have none, unless you are willing to set the penalty at the amount I can pay, and perhaps I could pay you one mina of silver.[11] So that is my assessment.

Plato here, gentlemen of the jury, and Crito and Critobulus and Apollodorus bid me put the penalty at thirty minae, and they will stand surety for the money. Well then, that is my assessment, and they will be sufficient guarantee of payment.

[The jury now votes again and sentences Socrates to death.]

SOCRATES: It is for the sake of a short time, gentlemen of the jury, that you will acquire the reputation and the guilt, in the eyes of those who want to denigrate the city, of having killed Socrates, a wise man, for they who want to revile you will say that I am wise even if I am not. If you had waited but a little while, this would have happened of its own accord. You see my age, that I am already advanced in years and close to death. I am saying this not to all of you but to those who condemned me to death, and to these same jurors I say: Perhaps you think that I was convicted for lack of such words as might have convinced you, if I thought I should say or do all I could to avoid my sentence. Far from it. I was convicted because I lacked not words but boldness and shamelessness and the willingness to say to you what you would most gladly have heard from me, lamentations and tears and my saying and doing many things that I say are unworthy of me but that you are accustomed to hear from others. I did not think then that the danger I ran should make me do anything mean, nor do I now regret the nature of my defense. I would much rather die after this kind of defense than live after making the other kind. Neither I nor any other man should, on trial or in war, contrive to avoid death at any cost. Indeed it is often obvious in battle that one could escape death by throwing away one's weapons and by turning to supplicate one's pursuers, and there are many

---

[11]One mina was the equivalent of 100 drachmas. In the late fifth century, one drachma was the standard daily wage of a laborer. A mina, then, was a considerable sum. [JMC]

ways to avoid death in every kind of danger if one will venture to do or say anything to avoid it. It is not difficult to avoid death, gentlemen; it is much more difficult to avoid wickedness, for it runs faster than death. Slow and elderly as I am, I have been caught by the slower pursuer, whereas my accusers, being clever and sharp, have been caught by the quicker, wickedness. I leave you now, condemned to death by you, but they are condemned by truth to wickedness and injustice. So I maintain my assessment, and they maintain theirs. This perhaps had to happen, and I think it is as it should be.

Now I want to prophesy to those who convicted me, for I am at the point when men prophesy most, when they are about to die. I say gentlemen, to those who voted to kill me, that vengeance will come upon you immediately after my death, a vengeance much harder to bear than that which you took in killing me. You did this in the belief that you would avoid giving an account of your life, but I maintain that quite the opposite will happen to you. There will be more people to test you, whom I now held back, but you did not notice it. They will be more difficult to deal with as they will be younger and you will resent them more. You are wrong if you believe that by killing people you will prevent anyone from reproaching you for not living in the right way. To escape such tests is neither possible nor good, but it is best and easiest not to discredit others but to prepare oneself to be as good as possible. With this prophecy to you who convicted me, I part from you.

I should be glad to discuss what has happened with those who voted for my acquittal during the time that the officers of the court are busy and I do not yet have to depart to my death. So, gentlemen, stay with me awhile, for nothing prevents us from talking to each other while it is allowed. To you, as being my friends, I want to show the meaning of what has occurred. A surprising thing has happened to me, jurymen – you I would rightly call jurymen. At all previous times my familiar prophetic power, my spiritual manifestation, frequently opposed me, even in small matters, when I was about to do something wrong, but now that, as you can see for yourselves, I was faced with what one might think, and what is generally thought to be, the worst of evils, my divine sign has not opposed me, either when I left home at dawn, or when I came into court, or at any time that I was about to say something during my speech. Yet in other talks it often held me back in the middle of my speaking, but now it has opposed no word or deed of mine. What do I think is the reason for this? I will tell you. What has happened to me may well be a good thing, and those of us who believe death to be an evil are certainly mistaken. I have convincing proof of this, for it is impossible that my familiar sign did not oppose me if I was not about to do what was right.

Let us reflect in this way, too, that there is good hope that death is a blessing, for it is one of two things: either the dead are nothing and have no perception of anything, or it is, as we are told, a change and a relocating for the soul from here to another place. If it is complete lack of perception, like a dreamless sleep, then death would be a great advantage. For I think that if one had to pick out that night during which a man slept soundly and did not dream, put beside it the other nights and days of his life, and then see how many days and nights had been better and more pleasant than that night, not only a private person but the great king would find them easy to count compared with the other days and nights. If death is like this I say it is an advantage, for all eternity would then seem to be no more than a single night. If, on the other hand, death is a change from here to another place, and what we are told is true and all who have died are there, what greater blessing could there be, gentlemen of the jury? If anyone arriving in Hades will have escaped from those who call themselves jurymen here, and will find those true jurymen who are said to sit in judgement there, Minos and Radamanthus and Aeacus and Triptolemus and the other demi-gods who have been upright in their own life, would that be a poor kind of change? Again, what would one of you give to keep company with Orpheus and Musaeus, Hesiod and Homer? I am willing to die many times if that is true. It would be a wonderful way for me to spend my time whenever I met Palamedes and Ajax, the son of Telamon, and any other of the men of old who died through an unjust conviction, to compare my experience with theirs. I think it would be pleasant. Most important, I could spend my time testing and examining people there, as I do here, as to who among them is wise, and who thinks he is, but is not.

What would one not give, gentlemen of the jury, for the opportunity to examine the man who led the great expedition against Troy, or Odysseus, or Sisyphus, and innumerable other men and women one could mention. It would be an extraordinary happiness to talk with them, to keep company with them and examine them. In any case, they would certainly not put one to death for doing so. They are happier there than we are here in other respects, and for the rest of time they are deathless, if indeed what we are told is true.

You too must be of good hope as regards death, gentlemen of the jury, and keep this one truth in mind, that a good man cannot be harmed either in life or in death, and that his affairs are not neglected by the gods. What has happened to me now has not happened of itself, but it is clear to me that it was better for me to die now and to escape from trouble. That is why my divine sign did not oppose me at any point. So I am certainly not angry with those who convicted me, or with my accusers. Of course that was not their purpose when they accused and convicted me, but they thought they were hurting me, and for this they deserve blame. This much I ask from them: when my sons grow up, avenge yourselves by causing them the same kind of grief that I caused you, if you think they care for money or anything else more than they care for virtue, or if they think they are somebody when they are nobody. Reproach them as I reproach you, that they do not care for the right things and think they are worthy when they are not worthy of anything. If you do this, I shall have been justly treated by you, and my sons also.

Now the hour to part has come. I go to die, you go to live. Which of us goes to the better lot is known to no one, except the god.

Concerning Whether God Exists
St. Thomas Aquinas

From *Summa Theologica, Part I*. Trans. Fathers of the English Dominican Province, 1947.

St. Thomas Aquinas (1225-1274) was a Catholic philosopher and theologian who has been widely influential among Christians for centuries. Philosophically, he is best known for trying to bring Aristotle's philosophy into line with Christian theology, and vice versa. In doing so he helped establish a conception of the relationship between faith and reason that would dominate Western thought until the scientific revolution of the 1500s-1600s. This reading is a tiny extract from Aquinas comprehensive study of Christian theology, the Summa Theologica, *a massive multivolume work that runs to around 3500 pages.*

Why we are reading this: Can it be known that God does or does not exist? If it can be known, is it possible to demonstrate this rationally on the basis of reason and logic alone? Resting in part upon arguments made many centuries earlier by Aristotle and elaborated by the Muslim philosopher Avicenna (Ibn Sina), Aquinas presents five arguments for the existence of God. For Aquinas, such arguments could prove only the barest fact of God's existence – further knowledge of God's attributes or purposes would require revelation through scripture and prayer. Aquinas' "Five Ways" to prove God's existence have been debated ever since. Many thinkers, both Christian and non-Christian, argue that Aquinas' arguments rest on unjustified premises or debatable inferences, while others find them sound. Plotting the structure of his argument and discovering where one might object to his premises is an excellent lesson in logic and critical thinking. As a heads up, please note that Aquinas follows the form of medieval scholastic disputation – in each article below, Aquinas raises a question, presents two or three "objections" (with which he actually disagrees), presents what he thinks is the correct answer ("on the contrary" and "I answer that"), and then answers each objection.

QUESTION 2: THE EXISTENCE OF GOD

Concerning whether God exists, there are three points of inquiry:
    (1) Whether the proposition "God exists" is self-evident?
    (2) Whether it is demonstrable?
    (3) Whether God exists?

Article 1: Whether the proposition "God exists" is self-evident

Objection 1: It seems that the existence of God is self-evident. Now those things are said to be self-evident to us the knowledge of which is naturally implanted in us, as we can see in regard to first principles. But as Damascene says, "the knowledge of God is naturally implanted in all."[1] Therefore the existence of God is self-evident.

Objection 2: Further, those things are said to be self-evident which are known as soon as the terms are known, which the Philosopher says is true of the first principles of demonstration.[2] Thus, when the nature of a whole and of a part is known, it is at once recognized that every whole is greater than its part. But as soon as the signification of the word "God" is understood, it is at once seen that God exists. For by this word is signified that thing than which nothing greater can be conceived. But that which exists actually and mentally is greater than that which exists only mentally. Therefore, since as soon as the word "God" is understood it exists mentally, it also follows that it exists actually. Therefore the proposition "God exists" is self-evident.[3]

Objection 3: Further, the existence of truth is self-evident. For whoever denies the existence of truth grants that truth does not exist: and, if truth does not exist, then the proposition "Truth does not exist" is true: and if there is anything true, there must be truth. But God is truth itself: "I am the way, the truth, and the life" (John 14:6) Therefore "God exists" is self-evident.

On the contrary: No one can mentally admit the opposite of what is self-evident; as the Philosopher states concerning the first principles of demonstration.[4] But the opposite of the proposition "God is" can be mentally admitted: "The fool said in his heart, There is no God" (Psalm 52:1). Therefore, that God exists is not self-evident.

I answer that: A thing can be self-evident in either of two ways: on the one hand, self-evident in itself, though not to us; on the other, self-evident in itself, and to us. A proposition is self-evident because the predicate is included in the essence of the subject, as "Man is an animal," for animal is contained in the essence of man. If, therefore the essence of the predicate and subject be known to all, the proposition will be self-

---

[1] Here Aquinas cites John of Damascus (676-749) and his work *De Fide Orthodoxa* (The Orthodox Faith), i, 1,3.

[2] Aristotle, *Posterior Analytics*, 1, 3.

[3] In this paragraph Aquinas summarizes the famous ontological proof for the existence of God devised by St. Anselm of Canterbury (c. 1033-1109).

[4] Aristotle, *Metaphysics*, iv, lect. vi.

evident to all; as is clear with regard to the first principles of demonstration, the terms of which are common things that no one is ignorant of, such as being and non-being, whole and part, and such like. If, however, there are some to whom the essence of the predicate and subject is unknown, the proposition will be self-evident in itself, but not to those who do not know the meaning of the predicate and subject of the proposition. Therefore, it happens, as Boethius says, "that there are some mental concepts self-evident only to the learned, as that incorporeal substances are not in space."[5] Therefore I say that this proposition, "God exists," of itself is self-evident, for the predicate is the same as the subject, because God is His own existence as will be hereafter shown.[6] Now because we do not know the essence of God, the proposition is not self-evident to us; but needs to be demonstrated by things that are more known to us, though less known in their nature – namely, by effects.

Reply to Objection 1: To know that God exists in a general and confused way is implanted in us by nature, inasmuch as God is man's beatitude.[7] For man naturally desires happiness, and what is naturally desired by man must be naturally known to him. This, however, is not to know absolutely that God exists; just as to know that someone is approaching is not the same as to know that Peter is approaching, even though it is Peter who is approaching; for many there are who imagine that man's perfect good which is happiness, consists in riches, and others in pleasures, and others in something else.

Reply to Objection 2: Perhaps not everyone who hears this word "God" understands it to signify something than which nothing greater can be thought, seeing that some have believed God to be a body. Yet, granted that everyone understands that by this word "God" is signified something than which nothing greater can be thought, nevertheless, it does not therefore follow that he understands that what the word signifies exists actually, but only that it exists mentally. Nor can it be argued that it actually exists, unless it be admitted that there actually exists something than which nothing greater can be thought; and this precisely is not admitted by those who hold that God does not exist.[8]

Reply to Objection 3: The existence of truth in general is self-evident but the existence of a Primal Truth is not self-evident to us.

---

[5] Reference to the theological treatise *De hebdomadibus* by Boethius (480-524).

[6] In Q. 3, Art. 4, not part of this excerpt.

[7] Beatitude is supreme happiness or a state of blessedness.

[8] Here Aquinas seeks to refute Anselm's ontological argument. See Objection 2 above.

Article 2: Whether it can be demonstrated that God exists

Objection 1: It seems that the existence of God cannot be demonstrated. For it is an article of faith that God exists. But what is of faith cannot be demonstrated, because a demonstration produces scientific knowledge; whereas faith is of the unseen (Hebrews 11:1). Therefore it cannot be demonstrated that God exists.

Objection 2: Further, the essence is the middle term of demonstration. But we cannot know in what God's essence consists, but solely in what it does not consist; as Damascene says.[9] Therefore we cannot demonstrate that God exists.

Objection 3: Further, if the existence of God were demonstrated, this could only be from His effects. But His effects are not proportionate to Him, since He is infinite and His effects are finite; and between the finite and infinite there is no proportion. Therefore, since a cause cannot be demonstrated by an effect not proportionate to it, it seems that the existence of God cannot be demonstrated.

On the contrary: The Apostle says: "The invisible things of Him are clearly seen, being understood by the things that are made" (Romans 1:20). But this would not be unless the existence of God could be demonstrated through the things that are made; for the first thing we must know of anything is whether it exists.

I answer that: Demonstration can be made in two ways: One is through the cause, and is called *a priori,* and this is to argue from what is prior absolutely. The other is through the effect, and is called a demonstration *a posteriori*; this is to argue from what is prior relatively only to us. When an effect is better known to us than its cause, from the effect we proceed to the knowledge of the cause. And from every effect the existence of its proper cause can be demonstrated, so long as its effects are better known to us; because since every effect depends upon its cause, if the effect exists, the cause must pre-exist. Hence the existence of God, in so far as it is not self-evident to us, can be demonstrated from those of His effects which are known to us.

Reply to Objection 1: The existence of God and other like truths about God, which can be known by natural reason, are not articles of faith, but are preambles to the articles; for faith presupposes natural knowledge, even as grace presupposes nature, and perfection supposes something that can be perfected. Nevertheless, there is nothing to prevent a man, who cannot grasp a proof, accepting, as a matter of faith, something which in itself is capable of being scientifically known and demonstrated.

---

[9] John of Damascus, *De Fide Orthodoxa*, i, 4.

Reply to Objection 2: When the existence of a cause is demonstrated from an effect, this effect takes the place of the definition of the cause in proof of the cause's existence. This is especially the case in regard to God, because, in order to prove the existence of anything, it is necessary to accept as a middle term the meaning of the word, and not its essence, for the question of its essence follows on the question of its existence. Now the names given to God are derived from His effects; consequently, in demonstrating the existence of God from His effects, we may take for the middle term the meaning of the word "God."

Reply to Objection 3: From effects not proportionate to the cause no perfect knowledge of that cause can be obtained. Yet from every effect the existence of the cause can be clearly demonstrated, and so we can demonstrate the existence of God from His effects; though from them we cannot perfectly know God as He is in His essence.

Article 3: Whether God exists?

Objection 1: It seems that God does not exist; because if one of two contraries be infinite, the other would be altogether destroyed. But the word "God" means that He is infinite goodness. If, therefore, God existed, there would be no evil discoverable; but there is evil in the world. Therefore God does not exist.

Objection 2: Further, it is superfluous to suppose that what can be accounted for by a few principles has been produced by many. But it seems that everything we see in the world can be accounted for by other principles, supposing God did not exist. For all natural things can be reduced to one principle which is nature; and all voluntary things can be reduced to one principle which is human reason, or will. Therefore there is no need to suppose God's existence.[10]

On the contrary: It is said in the person of God: "I am Who am." (Exodus 3:14)

I answer that: The existence of God can be proved in five ways.

The first and more manifest way is the argument from motion. It is certain, and evident to our senses, that in the world some things are in motion. Now whatever is in motion is put in motion by another, for nothing can be in motion except it is in potentiality to that towards which it is in motion; whereas a thing moves inasmuch as it is in act. For motion is

---

[10] This paragraph applies Ockham's Razor (described in the Prothero/Callahan reading on "Science and the Paranormal" below) to argue that the phenomena we see in the word can be fully explained without any need to assume the existence of a God.

nothing else than the reduction of something from potentiality to actuality. But nothing can be reduced from potentiality to actuality, except by something in a state of actuality. Thus that which is actually hot, as fire, makes wood, which is potentially hot, to be actually hot, and thereby moves and changes it. Now it is not possible that the same thing should be at once in actuality and potentiality in the same respect, but only in different respects. For what is actually hot cannot simultaneously be potentially hot; but it is simultaneously potentially cold. It is therefore impossible that in the same respect and in the same way a thing should be both mover and moved, i.e. that it should move itself. Therefore, whatever is in motion must be put in motion by another. If that by which it is put in motion be itself put in motion, then this also must needs be put in motion by another, and that by another again. But this cannot go on to infinity, because then there would be no first mover, and, consequently, no other mover; seeing that subsequent movers move only inasmuch as they are put in motion by the first mover; as the staff moves only because it is put in motion by the hand. Therefore it is necessary to arrive at a first mover, put in motion by no other; and this everyone understands to be God.

The second way is from the nature of the efficient cause. In the world of sense we find there is an order of efficient causes. There is no case known (neither is it, indeed, possible) in which a thing is found to be the efficient cause of itself; for so it would be prior to itself, which is impossible. Now in efficient causes it is not possible to go on to infinity, because in all efficient causes following in order, the first is the cause of the intermediate cause, and the intermediate is the cause of the ultimate cause, whether the intermediate cause be several, or only one. Now to take away the cause is to take away the effect. Therefore, if there be no first cause among efficient causes, there will be no ultimate, nor any intermediate cause. But if in efficient causes it is possible to go on to infinity, there will be no first efficient cause, neither will there be an ultimate effect, nor any intermediate efficient causes; all of which is plainly false. Therefore it is necessary to admit a first efficient cause, to which everyone gives the name of God.

The third way is taken from possibility and necessity, and runs thus. We find in nature things that are possible to be and not to be, since they are found to be generated, and to corrupt, and consequently, they are possible to be and not to be. But it is impossible for these always to exist, for that which is possible not to be at some time is not. Therefore, if everything is possible not to be, then at one time there could have been nothing in existence. Now if this were true, even now there would be nothing in existence, because that which does not exist only begins to exist by something already existing. Therefore, if at one time nothing was in existence, it would have been impossible for anything to have begun to exist; and thus even now nothing would be in existence – which is absurd. Therefore, not all beings are merely possible, but there must exist something the existence of which is necessary. But every necessary thing either has its necessity caused by another, or not. Now it is impossible to go on to infinity in necessary things which have their necessity caused by another, as has been already proved in regard to efficient causes. Therefore we cannot but postulate the existence of some being having of itself its own necessity, and not receiving it from another, but rather causing in others their necessity. This all men speak of as God.

The fourth way is taken from the gradation to be found in things. Among beings there are some more and some less good, true, noble and the like. But *more* and *less* are predicated of different things, according as they resemble in their different ways something which is the maximum, as a thing is said to be hotter according as it more nearly resembles that which is hottest; so that there is something which is truest, something best, something noblest and, consequently, something which is uttermost being; for those things that are greatest in truth are greatest in being, as it is written in *Metaphysics,* ii.[11] Now the maximum in any genus is the cause of all in that genus; as fire, which is the maximum heat, is the cause of all hot things. Therefore there must also be something which is to all beings the cause of their being, goodness, and every other perfection; and this we call God.

The fifth way is taken from the governance of the world. We see that things which lack intelligence, such as natural bodies, act for an end, and this is evident from their acting always, or nearly always, in the same way, so as to obtain the best result. Hence it is plain that not fortuitously, but designedly, do they achieve their end. Now whatever lacks intelligence cannot move towards an end, unless it be directed by some being endowed with knowledge and intelligence; as the arrow is shot to its mark by the archer. Therefore some intelligent being exists by whom all natural things are directed to their end; and this being we call God.

Reply to Objection 1: As Augustine says: "Since God is the highest good, He would not allow any evil to exist in His works, unless His omnipotence and goodness were such as to bring good even out of evil."[12] This is part of the infinite goodness of God, that He should allow evil to exist, and out of it produce good.

Reply to Objection 2: Since nature works for a determinate end under the direction of a higher agent, whatever is done by nature must

---

[11] Aristotle.
[12] St. Augustine of Hippo (354-430), *Enchiridion* xi.

needs be traced back to God, as to its first cause. So also whatever is done voluntarily must also be traced back to some higher cause other than human reason or will, since these can change or fail; for all things that are changeable and capable of defect must be traced back to an immovable and self-necessary first principle, as was shown in the body of the Article.

Excerpt from Meditations on First Philosophy
René Descartes

From *Discourse on Method and Meditations on First Philosophy*. 4th ed. Trans. Donald A. Cress. Indianapolis: Hackett Publishing Company, 1998, pp. 59-66.

René Descartes (1596-1650) was a Jesuit-educated French philosopher, mathematician, and scientist. He developed a technique for geometric display of algebraic relations that is now known as Cartesian coordinates. He also made important, often lasting, contributions to meteorology and optics. He is most well-known, however, for his ideas about the method for establishing knowledge and avoiding error that can be found in these two meditations.

Why we are reading this: *This reading recounts Descartes' famous thought experiment in which he doubts the existence of everything around him, knowing that his senses may be deceiving him or that everything he thinks is real may all be a hoax or a dream. In the end he cannot deny that he is doubting and therefore he himself must exist, at the very least ("I think, therefore I am"). This is a classic example of the deployment of radical doubt and* a priori *reasoning.*

MEDITATION ONE: Concerning Those Things That Can Be Called into Doubt

Several years have now passed since I first realized how numerous were false opinions that in my youth I had taken to be true, and thus how doubtful were all those that I had subsequently built upon them. And thus I realized that once in my life I had to raze everything to the ground and begin again from the original foundations, if I wanted to establish anything firm and lasting in the sciences. But the task seemed enormous, and I was waiting until I reached a point in my life that was so timely that no more suitable time for undertaking these plans of action would come to pass. For this reason, I procrastinated for so long that I would henceforth be at fault if I were to waste the time that remains for carrying out the project by brooding over it. Accordingly, I have today suitably freed my mind of all cares, secured for myself a period of leisurely tranquility, and am withdrawing into solitude. At last I will apply myself earnestly and unreservedly to this general demolition of my opinions.

Yet to bring this about I will not need to show that all my opinions are false, which is perhaps something I could never accomplish. But reason persuades me that I should withhold my assent no less carefully from opinions that are not completely certain and indubitable than I would those that are patently false. For this reason, it will suffice for the rejection of all of these opinions, if I find in each of them some reason for doubt. Nor therefore need I survey each opinion individually, a task that would be endless. Rather, because undermining the foundations will cause whatever has been built upon them to crumble of its own accord, I will attack straightaway those principles which supported everything I once believed.

Surely whatever I had admitted until now as most true I received either from the senses or through the senses. However, I have noticed that the senses are sometimes deceptive; and it is a mark of prudence never to place our complete trust in those who have deceived us even once.

But perhaps, even though the senses do sometimes deceive us when it is a question of very small and distant things, still there are many other matters concerning which one simply cannot doubt, even though they are derived from the very same senses: for example, that I am sitting here next to the fire, wearing my winter dressing gown, that I am holding this sheet of paper in my hands, and the like. But on what grounds could one deny that these hands and this entire body are mine? Unless perhaps I were to liken myself to the insane, whose brains are impaired by such an unrelenting vapor of black bile that they steadfastly insist that they are kings when they are utter paupers, or that they are arrayed in purple robes when they are naked, or that they have heads made of clay, or that they are gourds, or that they are made of glass. But such people are mad, and I would appear no less mad, were I to take their behavior as an example for myself.

This would all be well and good, were I not a man who is accustomed to sleeping at night, and to experiencing in my dreams the very same things, or now and then even less plausible ones, as these insane people do when they are awake. How often does my evening slumber persuade me of such ordinary things as these: that I am here, clothed in my dressing gown, seated next to the fireplace – when in fact I am lying undressed in bed! But right now my eyes are certainly wide awake when I gaze upon this sheet of paper. This head which I am shaking is not heavy with sleep. I extend this hand consciously and deliberately, and I feel it. Such things would not be so distinct for someone who is asleep. As if I did not recall having been deceived on other occasions even by similar thoughts in my dreams! As I consider these matters more carefully, I see so plainly that

121

there are no definitive signs by which to distinguish being awake from being asleep. As a result, I am becoming quite dizzy, and this dizziness nearly convinces me that I am asleep.

Let us assume then, for the sake of argument, that we are dreaming and that such particulars as these are not true: that we are opening our eyes, moving our head, and extending our hands. Perhaps we do not even have such hands, or any such body at all. Nevertheless, it surely must be admitted that the things seen during slumber are, as it were, like painted images, which could only have been produced in the likeness of true things, and that therefore at least these general things – eyes, head, hands, and the whole body – are not imaginary things, but are true and exist. For indeed when painters themselves wish to represent sirens and satyrs by means of especially bizarre forms, they surely cannot assign to them utterly new natures. Rather, they simply fuse together the members of various animals. Or if perhaps they concoct something so utterly novel that nothing like it has ever been seen before (and thus is something utterly fictitious and false), yet certainly at the very least the colors from which they fashion it ought to be true. And by the same token, although even these general things – eyes, head, hands and the like – could be imaginary, still one has to admit that at least certain other things that are even more simple and universal are true. It is from these components, as if from true colors, that all those images of things that are in our thought are fashioned, be they true or false.

This class of things appears to include corporeal nature in general, together with its extension; the shape of extended things; their quantity, that is, their size and number; as well as the place where they exist; the time through which they endure, and the like.

Thus it is not improper to conclude from this that physics, astronomy, medicine, and all the other disciplines that are dependent upon the consideration of composite things are doubtful, and that, on the other hand, arithmetic, geometry, and other such disciplines, which treat of nothing but the simplest and most general things and which are indifferent as to whether these things do or do not in fact exist, contain something certain and indubitable. For whether I am awake or asleep, 2 plus 3 make 5, and a square does not have more than 4 sides. It does not seem possible that such obvious truths should be subject to the suspicion of being false.

Be that as it may, there is fixed in my mind a certain opinion of long standing, namely that there exists a God who is able to do anything and by whom I, such as I am, have been created. How do I know that he did not bring it about that there is no earth at all, no heavens, no extended thing, no shape, no size, no place, and yet bringing it about that all these things appear to me to exist precisely as they do now? Moreover, since I judge that others sometimes make mistakes in matters that they believe they know most perfectly, may I not, in like fashion, be deceived every time I add 2 and 3 or count the sides of a square, or perform an even simpler operation, if that can be imagined? But perhaps God has not willed that I be deceived in this way, for he is said to be supremely good. Nonetheless, if it were repugnant to his goodness to have created me such that I be deceived all the time, it would also seem foreign to that same goodness to permit me to be deceived even occasionally. But we cannot make this last assertion.

Perhaps there are some who would rather deny so powerful a God, than believe that everything else is uncertain. Let us not oppose them; rather, let us grant that everything said here about God is fictitious. Now they suppose that I came to be what I am either by fate, or by chance, or by a connected chain of events, or by some other way. But because deceived and being mistaken appear to be a certain imperfection, the less powerful they take the author of my origin to be, the more probable it will be that I am so imperfect that I am always deceived. I have nothing to say in response to these arguments. But eventually I am forced to admit that there is nothing among the things I once believed to be true which it is not permissible to doubt – and not out of frivolity or lack of forethought, but for valid and considered arguments. Thus I must be no less careful to withhold assent henceforth even from these beliefs than I would from those that are patently false, if I wish to find anything certain.

But it is not enough simply to have realized these things; I must take steps to keep myself mindful of them. For long-standing opinions keep returning, and, almost against my will, they take advantage of my credulity, as if it were bound over to them by long use and the claims of intimacy. Nor will I ever get out of the habit of assenting to them and believing in them, so long as I take them to be exactly what they are, namely, in some respects doubtful, as has just now been shown, but nevertheless highly probable, so that it is much more consonant with reason to believe them than to deny them. Hence, it seems to me I would do well to deceive myself by turning my will in completely the opposite direction and pretend for a time that these opinions are wholly false and imaginary, until finally, as if with prejudices weighing down each side equally, no bad habit should turn my judgment any further from the correct perception of things. For indeed I know that meanwhile there is no danger or error in following this procedure, and that it is impossible for me to indulge in too much distrust, since I am now concentrating only on knowledge, not on action.

Accordingly, I will suppose not a supremely good God, the source of truth, but rather an evil genius, supremely powerful and clever, who has directed his entire effort at deceiving me. I will regard the heavens, the air, the earth, colors, shapes, sounds, and all external things as nothing but the bedeviling hoaxes of my dreams, with which he lays snares for my credulity.

I will regard myself as not having hands, or eyes, or flesh, or blood, or any senses, but as nevertheless falsely believing that I possess all these things. I will remain resolute and steadfast in this meditation, and even if it is not within my power to know anything true, it certainly is within my power to take care resolutely to withhold my assent to what is false, lest this deceiver, however powerful, however clever he may be, have any effect on me. But this undertaking is arduous, and a certain laziness brings me back to my customary way of living. I am not unlike a prisoner who enjoyed an imaginary freedom during his sleep, but, when he later begins to suspect that he is dreaming, fears being awakened and nonchalantly conspires with these pleasant illusions. In just the same way, I fall back of my own accord into my old opinions, and dread being awakened, lest the toilsome wakefulness which follows upon a peaceful rest must be spent thenceforward not in the light but among the inextricable shadows of the difficulties now brought forward.

MEDITATION TWO: Concerning the Nature of the Human Mind: That it is Better Known than the Body *(excerpt)*

Yesterday's meditation has thrown me into such doubts that I can no longer ignore them, yet I fail to see how they are to be resolved. It is as if I had suddenly fallen into a deep whirlpool; I am so tossed about that I can neither touch bottom with my foot, nor swim up to the top. Nevertheless I will work my way up and will once again attempt the same path I entered upon yesterday. I will accomplish this by putting aside everything that admits of the least doubt, as if I had discovered it to be completely false. I will stay on this course until I know something certain, or, if nothing else, until I at least know for certain that nothing is certain. Archimedes sought but one firm and immovable point in order to move the entire earth from one place to another. Just so, great things are also to be hoped for if I succeed in finding just one thing, however slight, that is certain and unshaken.

Therefore I suppose that everything I see is false. I believe that none of what my deceitful memory represents ever existed. I have no senses whatever. Body, shape, extension, movement, and place are all chimeras. What then will be true? Perhaps just the single fact that nothing is certain.

But how do I know there is not something else, over and above all those things that I have just reviewed, concerning which there is not even the slightest occasion for doubt? Is there not some God, or by whatever name I might call him, who instills these very thoughts in me? But why would I think that, since I myself could perhaps be the author of these thoughts? Am I not then at least something? But I have already denied that I have any senses and any body. Still I hesitate; for what follows from this? Am I so tied to a body and to the senses that I cannot exist without them? But I have persuaded myself that there is absolutely nothing in the world: no sky, no earth, no minds, no bodies. Is it then the case that I too do not exist? But doubtless I did exist, if I persuaded myself of something. But there is some deceiver or other who is supremely powerful and supremely sly and who is always deliberately deceiving me. Then too there is no doubt that I exist, if he is deceiving me. And let him do his best at deception, he will never bring it about that I am nothing so long as I shall think that I am something. Thus, after everything has been most carefully weighed, it must finally be established that this pronouncement "I am, I exist" is necessarily true every time I utter it or conceive it in my mind.

But I do not yet understand sufficiently what I am – I, who now necessarily exist. And so from this point on, I must be careful lest I unwittingly mistake something else for myself, and thus err in that very item of knowledge that I claim to be the most certain and evident of all. Thus, I will meditate once more on what I once believed myself to be, prior to embarking upon these thoughts. For this reason, then, I will set aside whatever can be weakened even to the slightest degree by the arguments brought forward, so that eventually all that remains is precisely nothing but what is certain and unshaken.

What then did I formerly think I was? A man, of course. But what is a man? Might I not say a "rational animal"? No, because then I would have to inquire what "animal" and "rational" mean. And thus from one question I would slide into many more difficult ones. Nor do I not have enough free time that I want to waste it on subtleties of this sort. Instead, permit me here to focus here on what came spontaneously and naturally into my thinking whenever I pondered what I was. Now it occurred to me first that I had a face, hands, arms, and this entire mechanism of bodily members: the very same as are discerned in a corpse, and which I referred to by the name "body." It next occurred to me that I took in food, that I walked about, and that I sensed and thought various things; these actions I used to attribute to the soul. But as to what this soul might be, I either did not think about it or else I imagined it a rarefied I-know-not-what, like a wind, or a fire, or ether, which had been infused into my coarser parts. But as to the body I was not in any doubt. On the contrary, I was under the impression that I knew its nature distinctly. Were I perhaps tempted to describe this nature such as I conceived in my mind, I would have described it thus: by "body," I understand all that is capable of being bounded by some shape, of being enclosed in a place, and of filling up a space in such a way as to exclude any other body from it; of being perceived by touch, sight, hearing, taste, or smell; of being moved in several ways, not, of course, by itself, but by whatever else impinges upon it. For it was my view that the power of self-motion and likewise of sensing or of thinking, in no way belonged to the nature of the body. Indeed I used rather to marvel that such faculties were to be found in certain bodies.

But now what am I, when I suppose that there is some supremely powerful and, if I may be permitted to say so, malicious deceiver who deliberately tries to fool me in any way he can? Can I not affirm that I possess at least a small measure of all those things which I have already said belong to the nature of the body? I focus my attention on them, I think about them, I review them again, but nothing comes to mind. I am tired of repeating this to no purpose. But what about those things I ascribed to the soul? What about being nourished or moving about? Since I now do not have a body, these are surely nothing but fictions. What about sensing? Surely this too does not take place without a body; and I seemed to have sensed in my dreams many things that I later realized I did not sense. What about thinking? Here I make my discovery: thought exists; it alone cannot be separated from me. I am; I exist – this is certain. But for how long? For as long as I am thinking; for perhaps it could also come to pass that if I were to cease all thinking I would then utterly cease to exist. At this time I admit nothing that is not necessarily true. I am therefore precisely nothing but a thinking thing; that is, a mind, or intellect, or understanding, or reason – words of whose meaning I was previously ignorant. Yet I am a true thing and am truly existing; but what kind of thing? I have said it already: a thinking thing.

What else am I? I will set my imagination in motion. I am not that concatenation of members we call the human body. Neither am I even some subtle air infused into these members, nor a wind, nor a fire, nor a vapor, nor a breath, nor anything I devise for myself. For I have supposed these things to be nothing. The assumption still stands; yet nevertheless I am something. But is it perhaps the case that these very things which I take to be nothing, because they are unknown to me, nevertheless are in fact no different from that me that I know? This I do not know, and I will not quarrel about it now. I can make a judgment only about things that are known to me. I know that I exist; I ask now who is this "I" whom I know? Most certainly, in the strict sense the knowledge of this "I" does not depend upon things whose existence I do not yet know. Therefore it is not dependent upon any of those things that I simulate in my imagination. But this word "simulate" warns me of my error. For I would indeed be simulating were I to "imagine" that I was something, because imagining is merely the contemplating of the shape or image of a corporeal thing. But I now know with certainty that I am and also that all these images – and, generally, everything belonging to the nature of the body – could turn out to be nothing but dreams. Once I have realized this, I would seem to be speaking no less foolishly were I to say: "I will use my imagination in order to recognize more distinctly who I am," than were I to say: "Now I surely am awake and I see something true; but since I do not yet see it clearly enough, I will deliberately fall asleep so that my dreams might represent it to me more truly and more clearly." Thus I realize that none of what I can grasp by means of the imagination pertains to this knowledge that I have of myself. Moreover, I realize that I must be most diligent about withdrawing my mind from these things so that it can perceive its nature as distinctly as possible.

But what then am I? A thing that thinks. What is that? A thing that doubts, understands, affirms, denies, wills, refuses, and that also imagines and senses.

Indeed, it is no small matter if all of these things belong to me. But why should they not belong to me? Is it not the very same "I" who now doubts almost everything, who nevertheless understands something, who affirms that this one thing is true, who denies other things, who desires to know more, who wishes not to be deceived, who imagines many things even against my will, who also notices many things which appear to come from the senses? What is there in all of this that is not every bit as true as the fact that I exist – even if I am always asleep or even if my creator makes every effort to mislead me? Which of these things is distinct from my thought? Which of them can be said to be separate from myself? For it is so obvious that it is I who doubt, I who understand, and I who will, that there is nothing by which it could be explained more clearly. But indeed it is also the same "I" who imagines; for although perhaps, as I supposed before, absolutely nothing that I imagined is true, still the very power of imagining really does exist, and constitutes a part of my thought. Finally, it is this same "I" who senses or who is cognizant of bodily things as if through the senses. For example, I now see a light, I hear a noise, I feel heat. These things are false, since I am asleep. Yet I certainly do seem to see, hear, and feel warmth. This cannot be false. Properly speaking, this is what in me is called "sensing." But this, precisely so taken, is nothing other than thinking.

Science and the Paranormal
Donald R. Prothero and Timothy D. Callahan

Chapter 1 in *UFOs, Chemtrails, and Aliens: What Science Says.*
Bloomington: Indiana University Press, 2017, pp. 1-15.

Donald R. Prothero *(b. 1954) is an American geologist and paleontologist who has authored numerous scientific papers and several geology textbooks. He also writes about science and culture for a general audience, including his recent book* Reality Check: How Science Deniers Threaten Our Future *(2013). His collaborator* ***Timothy D. Callahan*** *is trained as an artist but also writes about science, mythology, and religion.*

Why we are reading this: *This selection serves as the introduction to the authors' recent book on UFOs and aliens. It explains how scientists approach extraordinary and paranormal claims and decide what is most likely to be true. It also lays out the basic principles of scientific method and critical thinking, shows how to distinguish science from pseudoscience, and introduces important concepts such as double-blind testing, peer review, burden of proof, special pleading, and Ockham's razor.*

UFO?

> Science is nothing but developed perception, interpreted intent, common sense rounded out and minutely articulated.
>
> – *George Santayana, philosopher*

September 3, 2013: It's the sixth inning of a minor-league baseball game between the Vancouver Canadians and the Everett AquaSox. The game is being played at ScotiaBank Field's Nat Bailey Stadium in Vancouver. A fan is videotaping the game (available on *YouTube*[1]), and you can hear the crowd cheering and clapping and urging the team on the field to play well. The video clip pans from right to left over a mere 26 seconds, and it zooms in on something in the distance, beyond the trees outside the stadium. For those few brief seconds, it appears that there is some sort of flying saucer,

---

[1] "Did UFO Visit Vancouver Canadians Baseball Game?" *Huffington Post*, September 9, 2013, http://www.huffingtonpost.com/2013/09/09/ufo-canadian-baseball-game-photo-video_n_3895294.html.

complete with a ring of bright lights flashing in all directions, flying off in the distance. Strangely, however, the videographer doesn't hold the zoom on the mysterious UFO but returns to a wide-angle view of the game, then pans farther to the right. Whatever the videographer sees when he or she zooms in on the UFO, it isn't impressive or startling enough to keep him or her focused on it, because he or she goes right back to filming the game.

Nevertheless, this few seconds of footage is soon all over the Internet, mentioned in the news in Vancouver and elsewhere. The *Vancouver Sun* newspaper jokingly calls the object "divine intervention" that helped the local team win the game.[2] Everyone else seems to think that this startling image is proof that UFOs are alien spacecraft, even though few people in Vancouver seem to have noticed it. The other fans in the stands with the videographer who might have reacted much more strongly if it seemed like an alien spacecraft instead were tweeting as if it were nothing unusual. One tweet mentioned[3] that "it hovered for a while, going up and down then gone... weird, but lucky, C's have tacked on 4 runs since it made appearance." The British Columbia news site *The Province* suggested[4] that the "levitating... shiny blue something" may have been a kite or a remote-controlled helicopter.

But this is not enough to stop the huge community of UFO believers from trumpeting the few seconds of footage as "proof" that UFOs are real- without doing any investigation or digging about what was happening in Vancouver that night. They don't even think about the fact that the videographer didn't find the image startling enough to keep filming it and instead went back to the minor-league baseball game. Marc Dantonio, the chief video analyst for the Mutual UFO Network (MUFON), looks at the footage and testifies[5] that the image is not a camera trick or a computer-generated fake inserted into the video after it was filmed. Still, he finds it suspicious that "there was no reaction at all from anyone, nor the videographer." Rather, he says, "I suspect much more strongly, based on the way it was sideslipping to our right a bit while leaning slightly to that side, that this was likely either a lit up kite or a small drone-type object like we created for a National Geographic show. This object's behavior matches either one of those possibilities in the short video snip of it here that we can see. The stability makes this more likely a flying small hobby-type drone."

---

[2] Ibid.
[3] Ibid.
[4] Ibid.
[5] Ibid.

After the story has spread around the world through the internet, the culprit finally confesses.[6] The "UFO" was indeed a drone. It is eventually revealed that the H. R. MacMillan Space Centre built the drone, shaped like its new planetarium, as a form of gonzo advertising. Working with a local advertising agent, the drone is part of an "extreme tease campaign" to generate excitement and mystery-and lots of free publicity and increased attendance at its new planetarium.

After the hoax is revealed, it continues circulating on the internet as a legitimate UFO with no explanation, even though the fakery has been exposed. Even sadder, an internet poll on *Huffington Post*[7] shows that almost 34% of the people who clicked on the polling buttons *still* believe it is proof of a Canadian UFO sighting!

As we shall discuss in later chapters, this story is typical of most UFO sightings: something is spotted that the observer can't identify, so it becomes an "unidentified flying object," or "UFO." Then the account snowballs into a more exaggerated version as people immediately jump to the conclusion that it is an alien craft. The "unidentified" flying object is then exposed as a hoax or as some other more prosaic natural phenomenon. But even after a satisfactory explanation is given (and even when the hoaxer confesses), people *still* refuse to believe the truth and insist that the object was an alien spacecraft.

We will look at all these elements of typical UFO stories in later chapters. But first: how does a scientist examine the claims about UFOs and aliens?

Science and Pseudoscience

There are many hypotheses in science which are wrong. That's perfectly all right; they're the aperture to finding out what's right. Science is a self-correcting process. To be accepted, new ideas must survive the most rigorous standards of evidence and scrutiny.

– *Carl Sagan*

Stories such as this one raise important questions: How do we evaluate the claims? How do we decide whether they're credible? As we shall see in this book, there have been a huge number of hoaxes whenever the topic of

---

[6] Lee Speigel, "UFO Hoax at Canada Baseball Game Exposed; H.R. MacMillan Space Centre Admits Bizarre Stunt," *Huffington Post*, last updated September 14, 2013, http://www.huffingtonpost.com/2013/09/12/ canada-baseball-game-ufo-hoax_n 3908612.html.

[7] "Did UFO Visit Vancouver Canadians Baseball Game?"

UFOs and aliens is involved. How can we tell whether we're being conned and fooled?

In our modern society, critical thinking and science have proven to be the most consistent and effective methods of distinguishing reality from illusion. As Carl Sagan put it, "skeptical scrutiny is the means, in both science and religion, by which deep thoughts can be winnowed from deep nonsense." Even though many of us like to imagine that we can have a "lucky streak," and though we might adhere to superstitions such as avoiding walking on sidewalk cracks, when important issues such as money are involved, we all try to be skeptics. As mature adults, we have learned not to be naive about the world. By hard experience, we are all equipped with a certain degree of healthy skepticism. We have learned that politicians and salesmen are often dishonest, deceptive, and untruthful. We see exaggerated advertising claims everywhere, but deep inside we are experienced enough to recognize that they are often false or misleading. We try not to buy products based on a whim but rather look for the best price and the best quality. We try to live by the famous Latin motto *Caveat emptor:* "Let the buyer beware." When we are dealing with important matters, science and critical thinking are the only techniques we can rely on to avoid being fooled. But what are the principles of science and critical thinking? What do they tell us about UFOs and aliens?

A big problem with our conception of science is that it is based on the classic "mad scientist" stereotypes that are so prevalent in the movies, on television, and in other media. Indeed, there are almost no depictions of scientists in the media that don't include the stereotypical white lab coats and bubbling beakers and sparking Van de Graaff generators – and the "scientist" is usually a nerdy old white guy with glasses and wild hair. But that's strictly Hollywood stereotyping, not reality. Unless a scientist is a chemist or biologist working on material that might spill on your clothes, there is no reason to wear a white lab coat. Even though one of us (Prothero) is a professional scientist, I *never* use a lab coat. I haven't needed one since my days in college chemistry class. Most scientists don't need the fancy glassware or sparking apparatuses-or even have a lab!

What makes someone a scientist is not a white lab coat or lab equipment but rather *how he or she asks questions about nature* and what thought processes he or she employs to solve problems. Science is about suggesting an explanation (a hypothesis) to understand some phenomenon, then *testing* that explanation by examining evidence that might show us whether the hypothesis is right or wrong. Contrary to popular myth, most scientists don't try to prove their hypotheses right. As British philosopher of science Karl Popper pointed out long ago, it's almost impossible to prove statements true, but it's much easier to prove them false. For example, you could hypothesize that "all swans are white," but no matter how many white swans you find, you'll never prove that statement true. But if you find just one nonwhite swan (such as the Australian black swan), you've shot down the hypothesis. It's finished – over – kaput! Time to toss it on the scrap heap and create a new hypothesis) then try to falsify it as well.

Thus science is not about proving things true – it's about proving them false! This is the exact opposite of the popular myths that scientists are looking for "final truth" or that we can prove something "absolutely true." Scientific ideas must *always* remain open to testing, tentative, and capable of being rejected. If they are held up as "truth" and no longer subject to testing or scrutiny, then they are no longer science – they are dogma. This is the feature that distinguishes science from many other beliefs) such as religion or Marxism or any widely accepted belief system. In dogma, you are told what is true, and you must accept it on faith. In science, no one has the right to dictate what is true, and scientists are constantly testing and checking and reexamining ideas to weed out the ones that don't stand up to scrutiny.

Since Popper's time, not all philosophers of science have agreed with the strict criterion of falsifiability, because there are good ideas in science that don't fit this criterion yet that are clearly scientific. Pigliucci[8] proposed a broader definition of science that encompasses scientific topics that might not fit the strict criterion of falsifiability. All science is characterized by the following: (1) *Naturalism:* We can examine only phenomena that happen in the natural world, because we cannot test supernatural hypotheses scientifically. We might want to say about something that "God did it," but there is no way to test that hypothesis. (2) *Empiricism:* Science studies only things that can be observed by our senses – things that are objectively real to not only ourselves but also any other observer. Science does not deal with internal feelings, mystic experiences, or anything else that is in the mind of one person and that no one else can experience. (3) *Theory:* Science works with a set of theories that are well established ideas about the universe and that have survived many tests.

What is a theory? Some ideas in science have been tested over and over again, and instead of being falsified, they are corroborated by more and more evidence. These hypotheses then reach the status of some idea that is well supported and thus widely accepted. In science, that is what is meant by the word *theory*. Sadly, the word *theory* has completely different meanings in general usage. In the pop culture world, a theory is a wild

---

[8] Massimo Pigliucci, *Nonsense on Stilts: How to Tell Science from Bunk* (Chicago: University of Chicago Press, 2010).

guess, such as the "theories" about why JFK was assassinated. But as we just explained, in science, the word *theory* means something completely different: an extremely well supported and highly tested idea that scientists accept as provisionally true. For example, gravity is "just a theory," and we still don't understand every aspect of how it works – but even so, objects don't float up to the ceiling. The germ theory of disease was controversial about 100 years ago, when doctors tried to cure people by bleeding them with leeches – but now people who get sick due to a virus or bacterium will follow modern medical practices if they want to get well. Nevertheless, there are people who don't like what science tells them (such as creationists who reject evolution), and they will deliberately confuse these two different uses of the word *theory* to convey the idea that somehow evolution is not one of the best-tested explanations of the world that we have. Yet these same people do not reject the theory of gravity or the germ theory of disease.

Scientists aren't inherently sourpusses or killjoys who want to rain on everyone else's parades. They are just cautious about and skeptical of any idea until it has survived the gauntlet of repeated testing and possible falsification, then risen to the level of something that is established or acceptable. They have good reason to be skeptical. As discussed herein, humans are capable of all sorts of mistakes and false ideas and self-deception. Scientists cannot afford to blindly accept the ideas of one person, or even a group of people, making a significant claim. They are obligated to criticize and carefully evaluate and test it before accepting it as a scientific idea.

But scientists are human, and we are subject to the same foibles as all mortals. We love to see our ideas confirmed and to believe that we are right. And there are all sorts of ways we can misinterpret or overinterpret data to fit our biases. As the Nobel Prize-winning physicist Richard Feynman put it, "the first principle is that you must not fool yourself and you are the easiest person to fool." That is why many scientific experiments are run by the double-blind method: not only do the subjects of the experiments not know what is in sample A or sample B, but neither do the investigators. Samples are coded so that no one knows what is in each, and only after the experiment is run do they open the key to the code to find out whether the results agree with their expectations.

So if scientists are human and can make mistakes, then why does science work so well? The answer is testability and *peer review.* Individuals might be blinded by their own biases, but once they put their ideas forth in a presentation or publications, their work is subject to intense scrutiny by the scientific community. If the results cannot be replicated by another group of scientists, then they have failed the test. As Feynman put it, "It doesn't matter how beautiful your theory is, it doesn't matter how smart you are. If it doesn't agree with experiment it's wrong."

The mad scientist stereotype that prevails in nearly all media is completely wrong not only because of the stereotypical dress and behavior and apparatuses that are shown but also because the "mad scientist" is not testing hypotheses about nature or experimenting to find out what is really true. In a famous cartoon widely circulated on the internet, someone interrogating a "mad scientist" asks, "Why did you build a death ray?" The mad scientist says, "To take over the world." "No, I mean what hypothesis are you testing? Are you just making mad observations?" The "mad scientist" responds, "Look, I'm just trying to take over the world. That's all." The interrogator continues, "You at least are going to have some of the world as a mad control group, right?" As the cartoon says, he's really not a scientist at all – he's just a "mad engineer." (Although engineers might understand some science, their goal is not to discover truths about nature but rather to apply science to make inventions or practical devices.)

Sham Science

The public is happy to admire science as long as they don't have to understand it deeply. Sham inquiry plays to the admiration of science by the public. A lack of familiarity with how science is supposed to work is a major reason why the public has trouble recognizing counterfeit science. Add an '-ology' to the end of whatever you study and it acts like a toupee of credibility – to hide the lack of substance. The public is vulnerable to pseudoscience that resembles real inquiry and genuine knowledge.

– *Sharon Hill*

Because of the prestige and trust that we attach to science, there are lots of con men and zealots out there who try to peddle stuff that looks and even sounds like science but that doesn't actually pass muster through testing) falsification, experimentation, and peer review. Yet it often sounds "science" to most people or imitates the trappings of science, becoming what geologist and skeptic Sharon Hill called "sham science" or "sham inquiry."

A classic case of mistaking the trappings for the real thing are the famous "cargo cults" of the South Pacific islands. During World War II, many of these islands hosted U.S. military bases, and their native peoples came in contact with the advantages of western civilization for the first time. Then the war ended, and the military left. But the natives wanted the airplanes to return and bring their goodies, so they used local materials to build wooden "radio masts," "control towers," and "airplanes" and other replicas of the real things, hoping that they could summon the planes.

A good example of "sham science" is the many paranormal television shows about "ghost hunters" who poke around dark houses with fancy equipment pretending to be "scientific." In other television shows about Bigfoot or other mythical creatures) we see amateur "Bigfoot hunters" blundering around in the bushes in the night with military-style night-vision goggles, completely mystified by each animal noise they hear (which just shows that they are not trained biologists). They set out "camera traps" and other expensive pieces of equipment – which never photograph anything but the common animals of the area. Sure, they are using the trappings of science (expensive machines that look and sound impressive), but are they following the scientific method? No! In these cases, they are violating one of the most important principles that separates science from pseudoscience: *the unexplained is not necessarily unexplainable.* There are many phenomena in nature for which science doesn't yet have an explanation. But scientists know that eventually we'll probably find one. In the meantime, an unexplained mystery is just that: not *yet* explained. Scientists don't jump to the conclusion that it's a ghost or Bigfoot or some other paranormal idea that has never been established to be real by scientific evidence. A UFO is just "unidentified" until further research is done to rule out simple natural causes; it does not automatically become an alien craft.

One common ploy of UFO believers is to bring up a UFO incident that has yet to be explained, assuming that anything not yet explained utterly confounds both science and any possible explanation of the given incident other than its being the work of extraterrestrial aliens. However, just because something hasn't been explained does not mean that we must invoke paranormal causes as a solution for the mystery. In fact, sometimes the most rational approach to a mystery is to accept that it isn't yet, and might never be, solved. A case in point is that of the *Mary Celeste,* an American merchant brigantine that was found adrift and deserted in the Atlantic Ocean, off the Azores Islands, on December 4, 1872, by the Canadian brigantine *Dei Gratia.* She was in a disheveled but seaworthy condition, under partial sail, with no one on board and her lifeboat missing. The last log entry was dated 10 days earlier. She had left New York City for Genoa on November 7 and on discovery was still amply provisioned. Her cargo of denatured alcohol was intact, and the captain and crew's personal belongings were undisturbed. None of those who had been on board – the captain and his wife, their two-year-old daughter, the crew of seven – was ever seen or heard from again. Although there are several theories about what happened to the crew, a number of them quite viable, the simple fact is that we will probably never know what happened to the crew of the *Mary Celeste*. For all that, we needn't invoke either space aliens or the paranormal as the cause of their disappearance. It's quite all right to let a mystery be a mystery. In any case, evidence of extraterrestrial visitation must be positive and testable to be of any worth. The unexplained remains simply the unexplained.

Accordingly, when investigating paranormal claims, we cannot just practice sham science with expensive toys and claim that we're using the "scientific method." No, the first step is to *think* like a scientist, which means testing hypotheses about what the currently mysterious phenomenon might be, then ruling out explanations one by one. If we hear a strange noise on a "ghost hunt" or a "Bigfoot hunt," instead of jumping to the conclusion that it is a ghost or a Bigfoot, first we should rule out the idea that the noise is some common phenomenon, such as the wind blowing through the boards of the "haunted house" or some animal call that we don't happen to recognize. Even if we rule out *every* possible natural explanation for a strange phenomenon, it *still* doesn't give us the right to jump to the conclusion that it must be a paranormal entity. We must still follow the principle that *the unexplained is not necessarily unexplainable*. As scientists, we put the unexplained phenomenon on the back burner, withholding judgment about whether the phenomenon is real until we actually have firm evidence one way or the other. It is not acceptable to jump to a paranormal conclusion without giving science the time to rule out all the normal explanations. Some day we might find out what is really happening, so the paranormal "solution" just gets in the way of doing science properly and distinguishing reality from baloney.

Baloney Detection

Extraordinary claims require extraordinary evidence.

– *Carl Sagan*

So what are the general principles of science and critical thinking that we need to follow if we wish to separate fact from fiction? How can "deep thoughts... be winnowed from deep nonsense"? Many of these were outlined in Carl Sagan's 1996 book *The Demon-Haunted World* and Michael Shermer's 1997 book *Why People Believe Weird Things*. Some of the most important principles we must use if we are to decipher fact from fiction in UFO claims include the following.

137

Extraordinary claims require extraordinary evidence: This famous statement by Carl Sagan (or the similar "Extraordinary claims require extraordinary proof" by Marcello Truzzi) is highly relevant to separating garbage from truth in claims about UFOs. As Sagan pointed out, there are hundreds of routine claims and discoveries made by scientists nearly every day, but most are just small extensions of what was already known and don't require extensive testing by the scientific community. By contrast, crackpots, fringe scientists, and pseudoscientists make revolutionary claims about the world and argue strenuously that they are right. For such claims, it is not sufficient to have just one· or two suggestive pieces of evidence, such as blurry photographs or ambiguous eyewitness accounts, when most of the evidence goes against their cherished hypothesis. In these cases, we need extraordinary evidence, such as the actual remains of the alien craft or an alien corpse, to overcome the high probability that these things do not exist.

Burden of proof: In a criminal court, the prosecution has the burden of proof. It must prove its case beyond a reasonable doubt, and the defense need do nothing if the prosecution fails to prove its case. In a civil case, the plaintiff needs to prove his or her case based on a preponderance of the evidence, and the respondent need do nothing. In science, extraordinary claims have a higher burden of proof than do routine scientific advances, because they are claiming to overthrow a larger body of knowledge. When evolution by natural selection was first proposed almost 160 years ago, it had the burden of proof, because it overturned the established body of creationist biology. Since then, so much evidence has accumulated to show that evolution has occurred that the burden of proof is now on the shoulders of the creationists who would seek to overthrow evolutionary biology. Similarly, there is so much evidence to show that the Holocaust occurred (not only the accounts of survivors and eyewitnesses but also detailed records kept by the Nazis themselves) that the burden of proof is on the Holocaust deniers to refute this immense body of evidence. Similarly, most of the extraordinary claims about UFOs and aliens discussed in this book require a much higher degree of proof, because so much of what is claimed about them goes against everything we know from biology, astronomy, geology, and other sciences.

Authority, credentials, and expertise: One of the main strategies of pseudoscientists is to cite the authority and credentials of their leading proponents as proof that their claims are credible. But a PhD degree or advanced training is not enough: a true expert has advanced training *in the relevant field.* It's common for people trying to push an argument to point to their advanced degree (usually a PhD) as they make their case. This is a slick strategy to intimidate the audience into believing that the expert's having a PhD makes him or her smarter than the members of the audience-and an expert in everything. But those of us who have earned a PhD know that it qualifies you to talk only about the field of your training-and, moreover, that during the long, hard slog to get your dissertation project finished and written up, you might· actually *lose* some of your breadth of training in other subjects. Most scientists know that anyone who is flaunting his or her PhD in making arguments is "credentialmongering." If a book says "PhD" on the cover, be wary-the arguments between the covers might not be able to stand on their own merits.

Here's a good way to approach it: if you run into someone who flaunts his or her PhD, make sure he or she has some training in a relevant field. Not only did my own training include extensive background in biology and geology (which are relevant to claims about life on other planets), but I have also taught astronomy, meteorology, planetary science, and geophysics at the college level-so I'm familiar with the astronomical issues bearing on the likelihood that life is on other planets (discussed later in this book). As we shall see, most of the "experts" on aliens and UFOs have no training in biology or astronomy, so their "expert opinions" should be taken with a grain of salt. They have no more advanced training in the relevant field than you or I, so their PhD makes no real difference. You wouldn't trust an astronomer to know how to fix your car or write a symphony simply by virtue of his or her having a PhD in astronomy. So why would you trust his or her opinion on biology or some other field in which he or she has no advanced training?

Special pleading and *ad hoc* hypotheses: One of the marks of pseudoscientists is that when the evidence is strongly against them, they do not abandon their cherished hypothesis. Instead, they resort to special pleading to salvage their original idea rather than admitting that it is wrong. These attempts to salvage an idea are known as *ad hoc* (Latin, "for this purpose") hypotheses and are universally regarded as signs of a failed idea. When a psychic conducts a séance and fails to contact the dead, he or she might plead that the skeptic "just didn't believe hard enough" or that the "room wasn't dark enough" or that the "spirits didn't feel like coming out this time." When you demonstrate to a creationist that Noah's ark couldn't possibly have

139

contained the tens of millions of species of animals known, he or she uses evasions such as "only the created kinds were on board" or "fish and insects don't count" or "it was a miracle." If you show a UFO believer the scientific implausibility of his or her claims, he or she usually retreats to some claim that effectively makes the aliens supernatural beings, incapable of being evaluated by any laws of nature or science.

Any time you encounter such special pleading, it is a sure sign that the hypothesis has failed and that the person doing the pleading has abandoned the scientific method and is trying to salvage a favored idea despite the evidence. As the great Victorian naturalist Thomas Henry Huxley said, it is "the great tragedy of science – the slaying of a beautiful hypothesis by an ugly fact."

Ockham's Razor: There is a well-known principle in the philosophy of science known as Ockham's (also spelled "Occam's") Razor, or the Principle of Parsimony. Named after· a famous medieval scholar, William of Ockham (1287-1347) who discussed it many times, it basically says that when there are two or more explanations for something that equally explain the facts, the simplest explanation is likely to be the best. In another formulation, it says that we don't need to create overly complex explanations when simpler ones might do. The metaphorical "razor" shaves away the unnecessarily complicated ideas until only the simplest ones are left. Scientists use this as a basic guide when choosing among hypotheses, although we all know that in the real world, once in a while, the complicated explanation is indeed the real one.

Nonetheless, Ockham's Razor is highly relevant when evaluating two versions or explanations of an event. For example, which seems more likely? Is it more likely that aliens traveled many hundreds of light-years just to make a few crop circles in a farmer's cornfield (and do nothing else, including reveal themselves) or that some prankster made the crop circle in the middle of the night using simple tools such as a long board on a rope staked to the ground? As we shall discuss in later chapters, all the difficulties of imagining aliens traveling all that distance just to do something stupid seem positively ridiculous when it's much easier to imagine that it's a prank or a hoax.

In statistics, there is a similar principal: the Null Hypothesis, or the Hypothesis of No Significant Differences. If we want to statistically evaluate whether two things are truly different, we start with the simplifying assumption that there are *no significant differences* ("Null Hypothesis"). Then we must demonstrate that there is a statistically significant difference between the two things before we can make the assertion that they are truly not the same. We can apply this to many other fields in which scientific reasoning is needed. For example, our Null Hypothesis might be that the strange noise in the room is the wind moving the shutters. To prove that it is not something simple and natural such as this but rather a supernatural ghost requires enough evidence to show that the wind could not possibly have caused the noise. Likewise, crop circles or strange lines drawn in the sand can be evaluated this way as well. Our Null Hypothesis is that some simple common phenomenon, such as ordinary pranksters drawing lines in the sand, or dragging a board across the grain field, explains these features. We must prove that these explanations *cannot* explain the feature before we are allowed to embrace the much less parsimonious explanation that aliens came all the way to this planet just to draw lines in the sand or create flattened crops.

Summary

If we wish to scientifically evaluate the claims that UFOs are flying through our skies or aliens landing on this planet, we need to follow the rules of science. In short, we must follow these principles:

- Do not assume that just because we don't have an explanation right now, it cannot be explained by science eventually. The unexplained is not necessarily unexplainable!
- Don't give credence to people who do not have the proper expert training in a field relevant to the claim being examined.
- Don't fall back on special pleading or ad hoc explanations when your favorite explanation falls apart.
- Don't assume a more complicated scenario when a simpler one will do.
- Recognize that for extraordinary claims, the burden of proof lies with the person making that claim to give extraordinary evidence that will overthrow the mountain of evidence against it – not just blurry photos of supposed UFOs or footage of "aliens" that could be hoaxed or just another "eyewitness account" (which are problematic, as we shall discuss in the next chapter).
- No scientific explanation can veer into the paranormal or the supernatural. If you start talking about aliens and spacecraft that violate the laws of science, you're no longer doing science.

- Most important, be prepared to subject your ideas to critical scrutiny and peer review. If you scorn or ignore the criticisms and corrections of others but persist in your beliefs because they are important to you – despite their rejection by science – then you are no longer acting as a scientist but rather are acting like a true believer or a zealot.

The problem boils down to evidence: how good is it? A with the "evidence" for Bigfoot or the Loch Ness monster or other cryptids, photos and video and footprints and eyewitness accounts are not enough, because all these are easily faked, altered, or hoaxed. A scientist tells the cryptozoologist to "show me the body" (or at least its bones or other convincing piece of tissue). Likewise, a true scientist expects the UFO advocate to "show me the body" of the alien or "show me the spacecraft" before taking these claims seriously and considering them to be valid scientific evidence.

Expanding into Universe
Cynthia Stokes Brown

Chapter 1 in *Big History: From the Big Bang to the Present*. New York: The New Press, 2012, rev. ed., pp. 3-15.

Cynthia Stokes Brown (1938-2017) was an American historian and educator. She earned a BA in history from Duke and the M.A.T. and Ph.D. from Johns Hopkins University in the history of education. Brown was a pioneer in field of "big history," an academic discipline that examines the history of the universe from the Big Bang to the present and integrates traditional history with the findings of astronomy, geology, biology, paleontology, psychology and other fields. Human history is placed in the context of a much longer story.

Why we are reading this: This chapter from Brown's book Big History *describes our current scientific understanding of the early universe from its origins about 13.7 billion years ago down to the formation of Planet Earth (4.6 billion years ago). In several passages Brown explains how scientists have come to know things about the early universe and shows us some of the evidence on which they rely. Towards the end, she discusses unanswered questions about the origins of universe as well as some of the proposed solutions. Science is an open-ended process of discovery and there will always be new questions.*

We are all whirling about in space on a small planet, bathed for part of each day in the light and warmth of a nearby star we call the sun. We are traveling 12 million miles a day around the center of the Milky Way galaxy, which is whirling in a universe of more than 100 billion galaxies, each home to 100 billion stars (Fig.1.1).

This universe in which we whirl began as a single point 13.7 billion years ago; it has been expanding ever since, with its temperature steadily decreasing. Our universe has at least four dimensions, three of space and one of time, meaning that time and space are interconnected. Just now the size of our observable universe is roughly 13.7 billion light-years on each of three dimensions by 13.7 billion years on the dimension of time, increasing as I write and you read.

Ever since human being developed, they have been looking at points of light in the nighttime sky with awe and respect, learning what they could from direct observations and using this knowledge to make predictions, to travel on land, and to navigate by sea. Without specialized instruments, however, people could not detect much about the origin of our immense universe and the nature of matter, because the scale of the universe and of matter is so different from that of everyday life. By the late twentieth century, scientists had invented instruments that could begin to view the macroscopic heavens and the microscopic domain. Knowledge about these worlds has recently expanded exponentially. Now everyone can understand the amazing universe that is our home – if we use our imaginations and absorb the photographic images and diagrams that are currently available.[1]

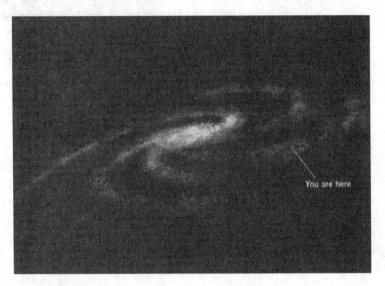

1.1 The Milky Way Galaxy
This drawing shows that our solar system orbits about halfway out to the edge of our galaxy.

Fog and Transparency

It all began with an inconceivable event: the big bang. (This name was given by the British astrophysicist Fred Hoyle on a BBC radio broadcast in 1952.)[2] The universe erupted from a single point, perhaps the size of an

---

[1] For this chapter I relied most heavily on Terence Dickinson, 1992, *The Universe and Beyond*, revised and expanded, Buffalo, NY: Camden; Timothy Ferris, 1997, *The Whole Shebang: A State-of-the-Universe Report*, New York: Simon and Schuster; Brian Greene, 1999, *The Elegant Universe*, New York: Vintage; and Robert T. Kirshner, 2003, *The Extravagant Universe: Exploding Stars, Dark Energy and the Accelerating Cosmos*, Princeton, NJ: Princeton University Press.
[2] Bill Bryson, 2003, *A Short History of Nearly Everything*, New York: Broadway Books, 37.

atom, in which all known matter and energy and space and time were squeezed together in unimaginable density. Compressed space unfurled like a tidal wave, expanding in all directions and cooling, carrying along matter and energy to this very day. The power in this initial expansion was sufficient to fling a hundred billion galaxies for 13.7 billion years and counting. The billowing universe was under way.

Where did this eruption take place? Everywhere, including where each of us is right now. In the beginning all the locations that we see as separate were the same location.

Initially the universe was composed of "cosmic plasma," a homogeneous substance so hot that it had no known structure at all. Matter and energy are interchangeable at temperatures of many trillion degrees; no one knows what energy is, but matter is energy at rest. As the universe cooled, the smallest constituents of matter that we know about, called quarks, began to clump together in groups of three, forming both protons and neutrons (Fig. 1.2). This took place at about one hundred thousandths of a second after the big bang, when the temperature had cooled to about a million times hotter than the sun's interior. A hundredth of a second later, these proton and neutrons began hanging together to form what would later become the nuclei of the two lightest elements, hydrogen and helium.

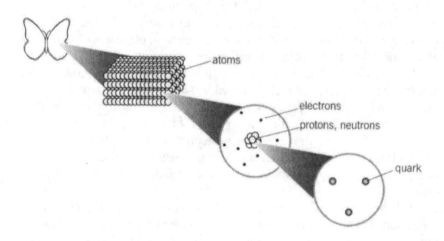

1.2 The Constituents of Matter
Matter is composed of atoms, each of which is composed of electrons circling a nucleus containing protons and neutrons, both of which are made of quarks. Whether quarks are composed of something smaller is currently unknown.

Before one second had elapsed the four fundamental forces that govern matter had come into being: gravitational force, electromagnetic force, the strong nuclear force, and the weak nuclear force. Gravitational force, or gravity, is the weakest of the four forces. It was described by Newton's theory of gravity and by Einstein's general theory of relativity, but it still cannot be defined. Electromagnetic force is a union of the electric and the magnetic forces. The strong nuclear force, the strongest of the four, is responsible for keeping quarks locked inside of protons and neutrons and for keeping protons and neutrons crammed inside of atomic nuclei. The weak nuclear force mediates the decay (or disintegration of the atomic nuclei) of radioactive elements. Scientists believe that all four forces must be aspects of on force, but they have not yet been able to create a unifying theory.

These four forces work in perfect balance to allow the universe to exist and expand at a sustainable rate. If the gravitational force were a tiny bit stronger, all matter would likely implode in on itself. If gravity were slightly weaker, stars could not form. If the temperature of the universe had dropped more slowly, the protons and neutrons might not have stopped at helium and lithium but continued to bond until they formed iron, too heavy to form galaxies and stars. The exquisite balance provided by the four forces seems to be the only way in which the universe can maintain itself. Scientists wonder if perhaps many other universes came into existence but vanished before this one survived. The newborn universe evolved with phenomenal speed, setting in place in a tiny fraction of a second the fundamental properties that have remained stable since.

During about 300,000 years of expanding and cooling, the wildly streaming electrons, negatively charged, slowed down. The atomic nuclei, protons and neutrons, were positively charged. When the electrons had slowed down sufficiently, the nuclei could attract them by their electric charge and form the first electrically neutral atoms: hydrogen (H) and helium (He), the lightest elements, the first matter. Hydrogen consists of one proton and one electron; helium consists of two protons and two electrons.

This became a pivotal moment in the story of the universe. Before the formation of stable atoms, the universe was filled with so many zigzagging particles, some negative, some positive, that light (consisting of subatomic particles called photons) could not move through the bath of charged particles. This was so because photons interact with electrically charged particles and are either deflected or absorbed. If anyone had been there to see it, the universe would have appeared as a dense fog or a blinding snowstorm.

As soon as atoms formed, binding the negative electrons and positive protons together, the photons of light could travel freely. The dense fog of radiation lifted. Matter had formed, and the universe became transparent. Its full expanse came into view – if anyone had been there to see it – consisting mostly of vast empty space filled with huge clouds of hydrogen and helium with immense amounts of energy pouring through them.

Today we can see some of the photons left from the big bang – as "snow" on our television screens. To do so we must disconnect the cable feed and tune to a channel the set does not receive. About 1 percent of the "snow" we see is residual light/heat left from the big bang that forms a cosmic sea of background microwave radiation.[3] If our eyes were sensitive to microwaves, which they are not, we would see a diffuse glow in the world around us.

By using radio equipment, scientists have documented the background microwave radiation. By the 1950s and 1960s physicists realized, from what they already knew about the universe, that the present universe should be filled with primordial photons, cooled over 13.5 billion years to a few degrees above absolute zero. In the spring of 1965 two radio astronomers, Arno A. Penzias and Robert W. Wilson, working for Bell Laboratories in New Jersey, accidentally detected this afterglow as a background hissing noise while they were testing a new microwave antenna to be used with communication satellites. In 1989 NASA sent up the Cosmic Background Explorer (COBE) satellite, which collected information that confirmed with high precision that there are about 400 million photons in every cubic meter of the universe – an invisible cosmic sea of microwave radiation, at 3 degrees above absolute, just as predicted by the theory of the big bang.

In 2002 NASA sent a sixteen-foot probe called the Wilkinson Microwave Anisotropy Probe, or WMAP, a million miles out from Earth. For a year WMAP took time exposures of the entire sky, showing in high resolution the map of the cosmic background radiation (CBR) from 380,000 years after the big bang and confirming again the big bang account of the universe.

Fortunately for astronomers, on the scale of the universe, distance is a time machine. The farther away something is, the younger we see it; this is because the more distant something is, the longer its radiation takes to reach us. We can never see the universe as it is today, only as it once was, because it takes millions and billions of years for the light of distant galaxies and stars, traveling at nearly 6 trillion miles a year, to reach us. Hence, we can see far back into the past. By picking up microwave

---

[3] Ibid., 12.

radiation, we can "see" back nearly to the beginning of the universe (Fig.1.3).

Think of it this way. The light from our nearest star, the sun, takes eight minutes and twenty seconds to reach us. Light from Jupiter takes about thirty-five minutes when it is closest to us, about an hour when it is farthest away in its orbit. The light of the brightest star in the night sky, Sirius, takes 8.6 years to reach us. (The distance the light travels is 8.6 light-years, or 50.5 trillion miles). The light from stars we can see without optical aid takes from four years to 4,000 years to reach us. If we should see a star exploding 3,000 light-years away, then that explosion occurred 3,000 years ago – the time it takes for the light to reach us.

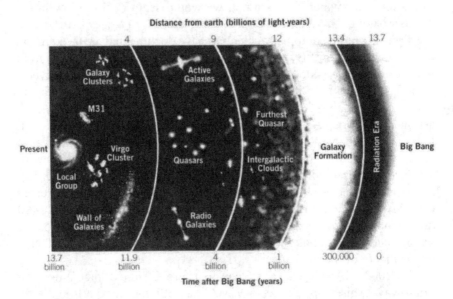

Distance from earth (billions of light-years)

Time after Big Bang (years)

1.3 Our View of the Universe
From our position in the Milky Way galaxy – one of the galaxies in the Local group – we see the universe in the distant past, because the light from remote galaxies takes billions of years to reach us. In this distant past the universe was smaller, and galaxies collided more often. Quasars are very distant objects thought to be the nuclei of younger galaxies, possibly in collision.

Twinkling Galaxies

As described earlier, the universe became transparent some 300,000 years after the big bang. Immense clouds of hydrogen and helium drifted until these clouds broke into about a trillion separate clouds, each with its own dynamics, each escaping from the universe's expansion in that the

148

diameter of each cloud remained the same while the space between the clouds increased.

As the universe cooled and calmed down, each separate cloud of hydrogen and helium became a separate galaxy of stars joined by gravity. This happened as the atoms of hydrogen and helium collided with each other. As they collided, the friction created temperatures so high that the atoms were stripped of their electrons. The hydrogen nuclei started to fuse, forming helium ions. These fusion reactions released a huge amount of heat/energy, according to Einstein's equation $E = mc^2$, in which the loss of a tiny bit of mass results in energy multiplied by the speed of light squared. As the hydrogen begins to burn, millions of tons of matter are transformed into energy each second, and a star is born. The earliest stars formed only about 200,000 years after the big bang.

The universe is filled with an enormous range of objects as measured by their mass. The largest objects are stars, which produce their own energy. The largest stars are up to twenty times more massive than the star that is our sun. The smallest objects in the universe are dust particles visible only under a microscope and which rain down into the Earth's atmosphere at the rate of a hundred tons a day. The silt in the eaves of any house probably contains a minute amount of interstellar material. Planets are middle-range objects; their mass is not sufficient to produce their own energy through hydrogen-fusion reactions.

Stars come in a vast range of sizes and densities, and they evolve over time from one type to another. Most of the stars nearest us are red stars, but the one we know best, the sun, is a stable yellow star burning hydrogen, called hydrogen fusion as described earlier. When its hydrogen is used up, in about 5 billion years, our sun will switch to burning helium, called helium fusion. Since helium fusion is a hotter process with a greater energy output, the pressure from the extra energy will expand the sun until it becomes what is called a red giant. When the helium fuel is used up, the red giant will collapse to a white dwarf. Then it will slowly cool until it becomes a cinder called a black dwarf, about the size of Earth and 200,000 times its mass. No black dwarf has yet been found because the universe is not old enough for any to have completed the slow process of cooling down.

Some yellow stars, the ones that are larger than our sun at their inception, become larger red giants than our sun will. When their red-giant stage is over, they do not shrink into white dwarfs. In them heavier elements are created and burned: carbon, nitrogen, oxygen, magnesium, and finally iron. But iron cannot be used as a stellar fuel. Energy production stops and gravity takes over. The star's core implodes and triggers an immense explosion of the outer layers that blasts most of the star to smithereens. Only the core survives as a white dwarf, a neutron star (tiny and incredibly dense), or a black hole, which is an object so dense that light cannot escape its gravitational field. This explosive self-annihilation of a star is called a supernova; only stars at least six times more massive than our sun can become supernovas.

These supernovas play an immense role in the creativity of the universe. They are the cosmic furnaces out of which new elements are formed and, as we have seen, they initiate the formation of black holes. When a star of more than ten times the mass of our sun explodes, the imploding core that is left may be larger than four times the mass of the sun. If it is, then gravity is so immense that all the matter disappears and a black hole remains, leaving only a gravitational field so strong that it prevents light from escaping. No one knows where the matter goes. The center of a black hole is called a singularity; a black hole created by a star of ten solar masses has a diameter of only forty miles. Around the singularity is a field of gravitational force so powerful that anything that enters the field disappears into the hole.

Astronomers suspect that massive black holes exist at the core of most galaxies, as one seems to at the center of our Milky Way galaxy. Our black hole, a few million solar masses, is called SgA because it appears to lie in the southern hemisphere constellation Sagittarius. Scientists, working for over ten years at the Very Large Telescope in Chile's Atacama Desert, confirmed in 2002 the presence of SgA.

Enormous supernovas become black holes. Smaller ones, those between three and six solar masses, explode outward rather than implode inward. In their burning cores hydrogen is burned into helium, then helium to carbon; nuclei are fused into ever larger nuclei, like oxygen, calcium. And on through the periodic table of elements. At some point an explosion occurs, spewing most of the star back into space as gas, but now containing complex, life-supporting atoms, not merely hydrogen and helium.

Only supernovas can create elements higher than iron. Gradually, over roughly 9 billion years, all the elements of the periodic table were built up in this way. Every scrap of gold on our planet originated in giant stars that exploded before the sun was born. The gold in the ring on your finger has to be more than 4.5 billion years old. Thus explosions of stars created the elements that make life on Earth possible. We quite literally are made of stardust.

Coming back to our story, several hundred thousand years after the big bang, galaxies consolidated as density waves moved through space, shocking the clouds of hydrogen and helium into star formation. Space began to twinkle, with billions of stars flowing in spidery filaments of whirling spirals. Most galaxies took the shape of spirals, but in the early

150

universe matter was crowded, and galaxies often bumped into one another. When they did, the large one absorbed the smaller, but the large one could never recover its spiral shape. Instead, it became a sphere or an ellipse (oval), called an elliptical galaxy. Elliptical galaxies do not produce new stars, since density waves do not move through them to shock the clouds of gases into forming new stars. Our Milky Way galaxy is a perfect spiral, the lucky accident of being in a noncongested area of the early universe about 12 billion years ago.

For some 9 billion years, the first two-thirds of its lifetime thus far, the universe consisted of unimaginable celestial fireworks. Galaxies wheeled and collided. Density waves surged through galaxies, causing new stars to form. Supernovas exploded, scattering new gaseous elements ready to be shocked into new stars by other supernovas or imploding into black holes, losing their matter to who knows where. All the while, space was expanding and the temperature cooling. The universe was a sparkling dance of death and resurrection, ruin and elegance, overwhelming violence and destruction cycled with dazzling beauty and creativity.

The Sun / El Sol / Helios / Die Sonne

About 4.6 billion years ago, in the Milky Way galaxy, a supernova exploded, and a new star – our sun – emerged from the debris. We know this because moon rocks and meteorites, all originating in that supernova, consistently date about 4.56 billion years ago.

This sun was an average-sized star, distinguished by not having a companion star (about two-thirds of the stars in our section of the Milky Way are multiple-star systems). The sun is located two-fifths of the way out on one of the spiral arms, about 30,000 light years from the center of the Milky Way. It takes about 225 to 250 million years to circle around the center of the galaxy in an elliptical, or oval, orbit, traveling about 200,000 miles a day. Accompanied by its system of planets and other bodies, the sun has orbited the center of the Milky Way about twenty times since its origin. Its size indicates it will burn about 10 billion years; it has now burned for about 4.6 billion of those years.

Around our early sun spun a disk of leftover materials – nebulous dust and gases of many elements created by our exploding supernova. As all these gaseous elements collided, they formed small grains whose instabilities shaped the disk into bands. As centers of concentration developed in these bands, the planets emerged, with the sun's gravity making the inner four (Mercury, Venus, Earth, and Mars) heavier and rockier, while the outer ones (Jupiter, Saturn, Uranus, and Neptune) are lighter and more gaseous. Pluto, smaller than our moon, has been declared not large enough to be considered a planet. Jupiter, about 300 times the mass of Earth, is almost, but not quite, large enough to become a star.

(There is no practical way to draw the solar system to scale without using distances the size of city blocks. If Earth were reduced to the size of a pea, Jupiter would be over 1,000 feet away and Neptune would be over a mile away.)[4]

The planets in their earliest state were molten or gaseous. Each planet arranged itself by gravitational interaction; the heaviest elements, such as iron and nickel, sank into the core, while the lighter elements, such as hydrogen and helium, formed the outer layers. The static, gravitational order was broken by the unstable, radioactive elements. When these elements broke apart, their energy kept the planets in a boil, bringing materials up from the deep inside to the surface.

On the three smallest planets – Mercury, Venus, and Mars – all activity came to a halt within a billion years with the formation of rocks. On the four largest planets – Jupiter, Saturn, Uranus, and Neptune – the boiling gaseous activity continues today, similar to what it was at the beginning of the solar system. Only Earth has a size that produces a gravitational and electromagnetic balance, which allows a solid rock crust to form around a burning core. Only Earth has a position in respect to the sun, a mean distance of 93 million miles, that establishes a temperature range in which complex molecules can form. Within our solar system, only here on Earth does chemical activity continue in constant change.

We measure time by the amount of it that Earth takes to circle the sun, called one year. Earth spins on an axis while it circles the sun. This axis is tilted somewhat, about 23.5 degrees, so that Earth's electromagnetic poles are not perpendicular to the sun. Our tilted axis means that while Earth is on one side of the sun, one hemisphere leans toward the sun and receives more sunlight, and while Earth is on the other side of the sun, the other hemisphere does. This tilt of our axis as we spin creates the seasons here on Earth, for if we spun on a vertical axis both hemispheres would receive the same amount of sunlight all year round. (All other planets revolve on a vertical axis except Uranus, which revolves on a nearly horizontal axis.)

During its first half billion years the early Earth suffered the shock of collisions with meteors, asteroids, and planetoids. We need only look at the surface of our moon to see a rockscape with the imprints of these early collisions; the moon is so small that it quickly lost its internal heat and preserved its original surface. Earth was sufficiently large – with a core hot enough that the heat of those early impacts kept it boiling day and night – that no imprints of the collisions could form.

---

[4] Ibid., 24.

When Earth had cooled down enough for rocks to form on its surface, plumes of molten lava rose up from within, bringing chemicals forged in the interior to the surface, changing continually the Earth's atmosphere, composed mostly of methane, hydrogen, ammonia, and carbon. Gigantic electrical storms, with immense bolts of lightning and thunder, stirred the chemical pot. After some half billion years of gestation, Mother Earth lay poised to bring forth living molecules.

Unanswered Questions

My story thus far has been based on what scientists know about our universe, called the Standard Model, developed in the 1960s and 1970s. I have not knowingly strayed into speculation. Yet everything that we think we know needs to be viewed in the context of what we do not know. Many significant questions remain unanswered.

Even the origin of our moon is uncertain. Some say it is a piece broken off from Earth, but most believe that the moon arose when a planetoid crashed against Earth, could not escape its gravity, and went into orbit, knocking Earth off its vertical axis to the slightly tilted one that creates our seasons.

More difficult questions come to mind, such as: "Why do mathematical equations work to account for things like the trajectory of the moon and of the Andromeda galaxy?" and "What came before the big bang?" To the first question, mathematicians just shrug and joke, "God is a mathematician." It is simply amazing that we are able to understand anything about the universe, that our minds can create equations that correlate with reality. As for the second and other questions:

1. What came before the big bang?

No one knows what the initial conditions of the universe were. Some physicists believe the answers to this question lie forever beyond the grasp of the human mind and any of its theories. But theories abound. One, posed by Lee Smolin of Pennsylvania State University,[5] proposes that the initial condition of our universe may have been a black hole in some other universe. The description of a black hole seems similar to the story of the beginning of the universe, except in reverse – matter, energy, space, and time becoming more compacted until they disappear. Physicists who are considering Smolin's idea are theorizing that matter, energy, space, and time may disappear out of the fabric of our universe to reappear somewhere else as a new universe. Perhaps we live in a "multiverse" of

---

[5] Lee Smolin, 1998, *The Life of the Cosmos*, London: Phoenix.

many universes popping out of each other. This is just one of several current theoretical scenarios based on many universes.

2. How did the universe start expanding in the first place?

One likely hypothesis says that in its first instant of existence the universe inflated – that is, it expanded exponentially, at a rate far exceeding the velocity of light, repeatedly doubling its radius over equal intervals of time. This spasm was over in less than a second, and thereafter the universe settled into a steady linear expansion rate, until about 5 billion years ago when its expansion rate began to accelerate. This inflationary hypothesis helps explain several problems in big bang theory, but it has not been conclusively established.

3. How can theories dealing with vast, astronomical scales, called general relativity, and theories dealing with the microscopic properties of the universe, called quantum mechanics, be reconciled?

These two groups of theories contain contradictions, which cannot yet be resolved into one grand unifying theory of everything. Yet, when considering black holes or the universe at the moment of the big bang, physicists need to use both general relativity and quantum mechanics together. When they do, the answers to their equations often equal infinity. This indicates a problem, which can be stated simply in the following way: Quantum mechanics tells us that the universe on the microscopic scale is a chaotic, frenzied arena with everything appearing and disappearing unpredictably. In contrast, general relativity is based on the principle of a smooth spatial geometry. In practice, avoiding extremes of scale, the theories of quantum mechanics and general relativity work perfectly to predict perceivable outcomes; the random, violent undulations of the microscopic world cancel each other out to behave like smooth fabric.

Physicists feel that their knowledge must be considered incomplete until there are no contradictions and inconsistencies in their theories. In 1984 two physicists, Michael Green and John Schwarz, provided the first piece of evidence for a new unifying theory, called superstring or string theory, for short. This idea posits that the most elementary ingredients of the universe are not point particles but wriggling strands, or strings, of energy whose properties depend on their mode of vibration. These miniscule strings are so small – about 10^{-35} centimeters long – that they appear as points, even to the most powerful available equipment. This theory also posits that the universe has more than three dimensions plus time – maybe ten (or more) dimensions plus time. Theoretically, string theory provides a truly unifying theory, positing that all matter and all forces arise from one ingredient: oscillating strings of energy. Since 1984 additional pieces of evidence have fallen in place to reinforce the idea of strings, but experimental evidence to validate the theory has not yet been found.

4. Ever since scientists began, in the 1960s and 1970s, to feel certain that the universe had a specific beginning, they have been wondering: "How will our universe end?"

There seem to be three possibilities. The universe could expand forever until all the light is gone from all the galaxies and every star is a cinder; the expansion of the universe could come to a halt and reverse itself, with all the matter of the universe imploding in on itself in a horrific implosion; or somehow the expansion of the universe could reach a delicate balance at which it slows down but never quite reverses.

In the last few decades physicists have learned that the expansion of the universe is not slowing down but rather is accelerating. Something unknown is pushing the universe farther apart. Scientists are calling this unknown antigravitational force "dark energy," or the energy of nothingness. They also believe there is something called "dark matter," unlike anything on Earth. No one knows yet what dark matter and energy are; scientists currently think that they may constitute more than 90 percent of the universe. The search has only just begun.

The Learning Curve
Atul Gawande

In *The New Yorker*. January 28, 2002.

Atul Gawande (b. 1965) is a winner of the MacArthur "Genius" Fellowship and many other accolades for his work on modern surgical practices and medical ethics. A practicing surgeon, he is professor in both the Department of Health Policy and Management at the Harvard School of Public Health and the Department of Surgery at Harvard Medical School. His four books have all been New York Times *bestsellers; his fourth,* Being Mortal: Medicine and What Matters in the End, *was released October 2014.*

Why we are reading this: This essay reminds us that there are forms of knowledge other than the discursive knowledge typically associated with higher education. Focusing on how surgeons learn their craft, Gawande highlights a form of what philosophers call knowing how *that can be contrasted with* knowing that. *There is a difference between* knowing that *something is a fact and* knowing how *something is done. The essay also considers the ethical implications that arise when important tasks can only be learned by doing them. If every surgery were performed by the most experienced surgeon in the room, no one would could gain the experience needed to become the great surgeons of the future.*

The patient needed a central line. "Here's your chance," S., the chief resident, said. I had never done one before. "Get set up and then page me when you're ready to start."

It was my fourth week in surgical training. The pockets of my short white coat bulged with patient printouts, laminated cards with instructions for doing CPR and reading EKGs and using the dictation system, two surgical handbooks, a stethoscope, wound-dressing supplies, meal tickets, a penlight, scissors, and about a dollar in loose change. As I headed up the stairs to the patient's floor, I rattled.

This will be good, I tried to tell myself: my first real procedure. The patient – fiftyish, stout, taciturn – was recovering from abdominal surgery he'd had about a week earlier. His bowel function hadn't yet returned, and he was unable to eat. I explained to him that he needed intravenous nutrition and that this required a "special line" that would go into his chest. I said that I would put the line in him while he was in his bed, and that it would involve my numbing a spot on his chest with a local anesthetic, and then threading the line in. I did not say that the line was eight inches long and would go into his vena cava, the main blood vessel to his heart. Nor did I say how tricky the procedure could be. There were "slight risks" involved, I said, such as bleeding and lung collapse; in experienced hands, complications of this sort occur in fewer than one case in a hundred.

But, of course, mine were not experienced hands. And the disasters I knew about weighed on my mind: the woman who had died within minutes from massive bleeding when a resident lacerated her vena cava; the man whose chest had to be opened because a resident lost hold of a wire inside the line, which then floated down to the patient's heart; the man who had a cardiac arrest when the procedure put him into ventricular fibrillation. I said nothing of such things, naturally, when I asked the patient's permission to do his line. He said, "O.K."

I had seen S. do two central lines; one was the day before, and I'd attended to every step. I watched how she set out her instruments and laid her patient down and put a rolled towel between his shoulder blades to make his chest arch out. I watched how she swabbed his chest with antiseptic, injected lidocaine, which is a local anesthetic, and then, in full sterile garb, punctured his chest near his clavicle with a fat three-inch needle on a syringe. The patient hadn't even flinched. She told me how to avoid hitting the lung ("Go in at a steep angle," she'd said. "Stay right under the clavicle"), and how to find the subclavian vein, a branch to the vena cava lying atop the lung near its apex ("Go in at a steep angle. Stay right under the clavicle"). She pushed the needle in almost all the way. She drew back on the syringe. And she was in. You knew because the syringe filled with maroon blood. ("If it's bright red, you've hit an artery," she said. "That's not good.") Once you have the tip of this needle poking in the vein, you somehow have to widen the hole in the vein wall, fit the catheter in, and snake it in the right direction – down to the heart, rather than up to the brain – all without tearing through vessels, lung, or anything else.

To do this, S. explained, you start by getting a guide wire in place. She pulled the syringe off, leaving the needle in. Blood flowed out. She picked up a two-foot-long twenty-gauge wire that looked like the steel D string of an electric guitar, and passed nearly its full length through the needle's bore, into the vein, and onward toward the vena cava. "Never force it in," she warned, "and never, ever let go of it." A string of rapid heartbeats fired off on the cardiac monitor, and she quickly pulled the wire back an inch. It had poked into the heart, causing momentary fibrillation. "Guess we're in the right place," she said to me quietly. Then to the patient: "You're doing great. Only a few minutes now." She pulled the needle out over the wire and replaced it with a bullet of thick, stiff plastic, which she pushed in tight to widen the vein opening. She then removed this dilator and threaded the central line – a spaghetti-thick, flexible yellow plastic tube – over the wire until it was all the way in. Now she could remove the wire. She flushed the line with a heparin solution and sutured it to the patient's chest. And that was it.

Today, it was my turn to try. First, I had to gather supplies – a central-line kit, gloves, gown, cap, mask, lidocaine – which took me forever. When I finally had the stuff together, I stopped for a minute outside the patient's door, trying to recall the steps. They remained frustratingly hazy. But I couldn't put it off any longer. I had a page-long list of other things to get done: Mrs. A needed to be discharged; Mr. B needed an abdominal ultrasound arranged; Mrs. C needed her skin staples removed. And every fifteen minutes or so I was getting paged with more tasks: Mr. X was nauseated and needed to be seen; Miss Y's family was here and needed "someone" to talk to them; Mr. Z needed a laxative. I took a deep breath, put on my best don't-worry-I-know-what-I'm-doing look, and went in.

I placed the supplies on a bedside table, untied the patient's gown, and laid him down flat on the mattress, with his chest bare and his arms at his sides. I flipped on a fluorescent overhead light and raised his bed to my height. I paged S. I put on my gown and gloves and, on a sterile tray, laid out the central line, the guide wire, and other materials from the kit. I drew up five cc's of lidocaine in a syringe, soaked two sponge sticks in the yellow-brown Betadine, and opened up the suture packaging.

S. arrived. "What's his platelet count?"

My stomach knotted. I hadn't checked. That was bad: too low and he could have a serious bleed from the procedure. She went to check a computer. The count was acceptable.

Chastened, I started swabbing his chest with the sponge sticks. "Got the shoulder roll underneath him?" S. asked. Well, no, I had forgotten that, too. The patient gave me a look. S., saying nothing, got a towel, rolled it up, and slipped it under his back for me. I finished applying the antiseptic and then draped him so that only his right upper chest was exposed. He squirmed a bit beneath the drapes. S. now inspected my tray. I girded myself.

"Where's the extra syringe for flushing the line when it's in?" Damn. She went out and got it.

I felt for my landmarks. Here? I asked with my eyes, not wanting to undermine the patient's confidence any further. She nodded. I numbed the spot with lidocaine. ("You'll feel a stick and a burn now, sir.") Next, I took the three-inch needle in hand and poked it through the skin. I advanced it slowly and uncertainly, a few millimetres at a time. This is a big goddam needle, I kept thinking. I couldn't believe I was sticking it into someone's

158

chest. I concentrated on maintaining a steep angle of entry, but kept spearing his clavicle instead of slipping beneath it.

"Ow!" he shouted.

"Sorry," I said. S. signaled with a kind of surfing hand gesture to go underneath the clavicle. This time, it went in. I drew back on the syringe. Nothing. She pointed deeper. I went in deeper. Nothing. I withdrew the needle, flushed out some bits of tissue clogging it, and tried again.

"Ow!"

Too steep again. I found my way underneath the clavicle once more. I drew the syringe back. Still nothing. He's too obese, I thought. S. slipped on gloves and a gown. "How about I have a look?" she said. I handed her the needle and stepped aside. She plunged the needle in, drew back on the syringe, and, just like that, she was in. "We'll be done shortly," she told the patient.

She let me continue with the next steps, which I bumbled through. I didn't realize how long and floppy the guide wire was until I pulled the coil out of its plastic sleeve, and, putting one end of it into the patient, I very nearly contaminated the other. I forgot about the dilating step until she reminded me. Then, when I put in the dilator, I didn't push quite hard enough, and it was really S. who pushed it all the way in. Finally, we got the line in, flushed it, and sutured it in place.

Outside the room, S. said that I could be less tentative the next time, but that I shouldn't worry too much about how things had gone. "You'll get it," she said. "It just takes practice." I wasn't so sure. The procedure remained wholly mysterious to me. And I could not get over the idea of jabbing a needle into someone's chest so deeply and so blindly. I awaited the X-ray afterward with trepidation. But it came back fine: I had not injured the lung and the line was in the right place.

Not everyone appreciates the attractions of surgery. When you are a medical student in the operating room for the first time, and you see the surgeon press the scalpel to someone's body and open it like a piece of fruit, you either shudder in horror or gape in awe. I gaped. It was not just the blood and guts that enthralled me. It was also the idea that a person, a mere mortal, would have the confidence to wield that scalpel in the first place.

There is a saying about surgeons: "Sometimes wrong; never in doubt." This is meant as a reproof, but to me it seemed their strength. Every day, surgeons are faced with uncertainties. Information is inadequate; the science is ambiguous; one's knowledge and abilities are never perfect. Even with the simplest operation, it cannot be taken for granted that a patient will come through better off – or even alive. Standing at the operating table, I wondered how the surgeon knew that all the steps would go as planned, that bleeding would be controlled and infection would not set in and organs would not be injured. He didn't, of course. But he cut anyway.

Later, while still a student, I was allowed to make an incision myself. The surgeon drew a six-inch dotted line with a marking pen across an anesthetized patient's abdomen and then, to my surprise, had the nurse hand me the knife. It was still warm from the autoclave. The surgeon had me stretch the skin taut with the thumb and forefinger of my free hand. He told me to make one smooth slice down to the fat. I put the belly of the blade to the skin and cut. The experience was odd and addictive, mixing exhilaration from the calculated violence of the act, anxiety about getting it right, and a righteous faith that it was somehow for the person's good. There was also the slightly nauseating feeling of finding that it took more force than I'd realized. (Skin is thick and springy, and on my first pass I did not go nearly deep enough; I had to cut twice to get through.) The moment made me want to be a surgeon – not an amateur handed the knife for a brief moment but someone with the confidence and ability to proceed as if it were routine.

A resident begins, however, with none of this air of mastery – only an overpowering instinct against doing anything like pressing a knife against flesh or jabbing a needle into someone's chest. On my first day as a surgical resident, I was assigned to the emergency room. Among my first patients was a skinny, dark-haired woman in her late twenties who hobbled in, teeth gritted, with a two-foot-long wooden chair leg somehow nailed to the bottom of her foot. She explained that a kitchen chair had collapsed under her and, as she leaped up to keep from falling, her bare foot had stomped down on a three-inch screw sticking out of one of the chair legs. I tried very hard to look like someone who had not got his medical diploma just the week before. Instead, I was determined to be nonchalant, the kind of guy who had seen this sort of thing a hundred times before. I inspected her foot, and could see that the screw was embedded in the bone at the base of her big toe. There was no bleeding and, as far as I could feel, no fracture.

"Wow, that must hurt," I blurted out, idiotically.

The obvious thing to do was give her a tetanus shot and pull out the screw. I ordered the tetanus shot, but I began to have doubts about pulling out the screw. Suppose she bled? Or suppose I fractured her foot? Or something worse? I excused myself and tracked down Dr. W., the senior surgeon on duty. I found him tending to a car-crash victim. The patient was a mess, and the floor was covered with blood. People were shouting. It was not a good time to ask questions.

I ordered an X-ray. I figured it would buy time and let me check my amateur impression that she didn't have a fracture. Sure enough, getting the X-ray took about an hour, and it showed no fracture – just a common screw embedded, the radiologist said, "in the head of the first metatarsal." I showed the patient the X-ray. "You see, the screw's embedded in the head of the first metatarsal," I said. And the plan? she wanted to know. Ah, yes, the plan.

I went to find Dr. W. He was still busy with the crash victim, but I was able to interrupt to show him the X-ray. He chuckled at the sight of it and asked me what I wanted to do. "Pull the screw out?" I ventured. "Yes," he said, by which he meant "Duh." He made sure I'd given the patient a tetanus shot and then shooed me away.

Back in the examining room, I told her that I would pull the screw out, prepared for her to say something like "You?" Instead she said, "O.K., Doctor." At first, I had her sitting on the exam table, dangling her leg off the side. But that didn't look as if it would work. Eventually, I had her lie with her foot jutting off the table end, the board poking out into the air. With every move, her pain increased. I injected a local anesthetic where the screw had gone in and that helped a little. Now I grabbed her foot in one hand, the board in the other, and for a moment I froze. Could I really do this? Who was I to presume?

Finally, I gave her a one-two-three and pulled, gingerly at first and then hard. She groaned. The screw wasn't budging. I twisted, and abruptly it came free. There was no bleeding. I washed the wound out, and she found she could walk. I warned her of the risks of infection and the signs to look for. Her gratitude was immense and flattering, like the lion's for the mouse – and that night I went home elated.

In surgery, as in anything else, skill, judgment, and confidence are learned through experience, haltingly and humiliatingly. Like the tennis player and the oboist and the guy who fixes hard drives, we need practice to get good at what we do. There is one difference in medicine, though: we practice on people.

My second try at placing a central line went no better than the first. The patient was in intensive care, mortally ill, on a ventilator, and needed the line so that powerful cardiac drugs could be delivered directly to her heart. She was also heavily sedated, and for this I was grateful. She'd be oblivious of my fumbling.

My preparation was better this time. I got the towel roll in place and the syringes of heparin on the tray. I checked her lab results, which were fine. I also made a point of draping more widely, so that if I flopped the guide wire around by mistake again, it wouldn't hit anything unsterile.

For all that, the procedure was a bust. I stabbed the needle in too shallow and then too deep. Frustration overcame tentativeness and I tried one angle after another. Nothing worked. Then, for one brief moment, I got a flash of blood in the syringe, indicating that I was in the vein. I anchored the needle with one hand and went to pull the syringe off with the other. But the syringe was jammed on too tightly, so that when I pulled it free I dislodged the needle from the vein. The patient began bleeding into her chest wall. I held pressure the best I could for a solid five minutes, but still her chest turned black and blue around the site. The hematoma made it impossible to put a line through there anymore. I wanted to give up. But she needed a line and the resident supervising me – a second-year this time – was determined that I succeed. After an X-ray showed that I had not injured her lung, he had me try on the other side, with a whole new kit. I missed again, and he took over. It took him several minutes and two or three sticks to find the vein himself and that made me feel better. Maybe she was an unusually tough case.

When I failed with a third patient a few days later, though, the doubts really set in. Again, it was stick, stick, stick, and nothing. I stepped aside. The resident watching me got it on the next try.

Surgeons, as a group, adhere to a curious egalitarianism. They believe in practice, not talent. People often assume that you have to have great hands to become a surgeon, but it's not true. When I interviewed to get into surgery programs, no one made me sew or take a dexterity test or checked to see if my hands were steady. You do not even need all ten fingers to be accepted. To be sure, talent helps. Professors say that every two or three years they'll see someone truly gifted come through a program – someone who picks up complex manual skills unusually quickly, sees tissue planes before others do, anticipates trouble before it happens. Nonetheless, attending surgeons say that what's most important to them is finding people who are conscientious, industrious, and boneheaded enough to keep at practicing this one difficult thing day and night for years on end. As a former residency director put it to me, given a choice between a Ph.D. who had cloned a gene and a sculptor, he'd pick the Ph.D. every time. Sure, he said, he'd bet on the sculptor's being more physically talented; but he'd bet on the Ph.D.'s being less "flaky." And in the end that matters more. Skill, surgeons believe, can be taught; tenacity cannot. It's an odd approach to recruitment, but it continues all the way up the ranks, even in top surgery departments. They start with minions with no experience in surgery, spend years training them, and then take most of their faculty from these same homegrown ranks.

And it works. There have now been many studies of elite performers – concert violinists, chess grand masters, professional ice-skaters, mathematicians, and so forth – and the biggest difference researchers find between them and lesser performers is the amount of deliberate practice they've accumulated. Indeed, the most important talent may be the talent for practice itself. K. Anders Ericsson, a cognitive psychologist and an expert on performance, notes that the most important role that innate factors play may be in a person's willingness to engage in sustained training. He has found, for example, that top performers dislike practicing just as much as others do. (That's why, for example, athletes and musicians usually quit practicing when they retire.) But, more than others, they have the will to keep at it anyway.

I wasn't sure I did. What good was it, I wondered, to keep doing central lines when I wasn't coming close to hitting them? If I had a clear idea of what I was doing wrong, then maybe I'd have something to focus on. But I didn't. Everyone, of course, had suggestions. Go in with the bevel of the needle up. No, go in with the bevel down. Put a bend in the middle of the needle. No, curve the needle. For a while, I tried to avoid doing another line. Soon enough, however, a new case arose.

The circumstances were miserable. It was late in the day, and I'd had to work through the previous night. The patient weighed more than three hundred pounds. He couldn't tolerate lying flat because the weight of his chest and abdomen made it hard for him to breathe. Yet he had a badly infected wound, needed intravenous antibiotics, and no one could find veins in his arms for a peripheral I.V. I had little hope of succeeding. But a resident does what he is told, and I was told to try the line.

I went to his room. He looked scared and said he didn't think he'd last more than a minute on his back. But he said he understood the situation and was willing to make his best effort. He and I decided that he'd be left sitting propped up in bed until the last possible minute. We'd see how far we got after that.

I went through my preparations: checking his blood counts from the lab, putting out the kit, placing the towel roll, and so on. I swabbed and draped his chest while he was still sitting up. S., the chief resident, was watching me this time, and when everything was ready I had her tip him back, an oxygen mask on his face. His flesh rolled up his chest like a wave. I couldn't find his clavicle with my fingertips to line up the right point of entry. And already he was looking short of breath, his face red. I gave S. a "Do you want to take over?" look. Keep going, she signalled. I made a rough guess about where the right spot was, numbed it with lidocaine, and pushed the big needle in. For a second, I thought it wouldn't be long enough to reach through, but then I felt the tip slip underneath his clavicle. I pushed a little deeper and drew back on the syringe. Unbelievably, it filled with blood. I was in. I concentrated on anchoring the needle firmly

163

in place, not moving it a millimetre as I pulled the syringe off and threaded the guide wire in. The wire fed in smoothly. The patient was struggling hard for air now. We sat him up and let him catch his breath. And then, laying him down one more time, I got the entry dilated and slid the central line in. "Nice job" was all S. said, and then she left.

I still have no idea what I did differently that day. But from then on my lines went in. That's the funny thing about practice. For days and days, you make out only the fragments of what to do. And then one day you've got the thing whole. Conscious learning becomes unconscious knowledge, and you cannot say precisely how.

I have now put in more than a hundred central lines. I am by no means infallible. Certainly, I have had my fair share of complications. I punctured a patient's lung, for example – the right lung of a chief of surgery from another hospital, no less – and, given the odds, I'm sure such things will happen again. I still have the occasional case that should go easily but doesn't, no matter what I do. (We have a term for this. "How'd it go?" a colleague asks. "It was a total flog," I reply. I don't have to say anything more.)

But other times everything unfolds effortlessly. You take the needle. You stick the chest. You feel the needle travel – a distinct glide through the fat, a slight catch in the dense muscle, then the subtle pop through the vein wall – and you're in. At such moments, it is more than easy; it is beautiful.

Surgical training is the recapitulation of this process – floundering followed by fragments followed by knowledge and, occasionally, a moment of elegance – over and over again, for ever harder tasks with ever greater risks. At first, you work on the basics: how to glove and gown, how to drape patients, how to hold the knife, how to tie a square knot in a length of silk suture (not to mention how to dictate, work the computers, order drugs). But then the tasks become more daunting: how to cut through skin, handle the electrocautery, open the breast, tie off a bleeder, excise a tumor, close up a wound. At the end of six months, I had done lines, lumpectomies, appendectomies, skin grafts, hernia repairs, and mastectomies. At the end of a year, I was doing limb amputations, hemorrhoidectomies, and laparoscopic gallbladder operations. At the end of two years, I was beginning to do tracheotomies, small-bowel operations, and leg-artery bypasses.

I am in my seventh year of training, of which three years have been spent doing research. Only now has a simple slice through skin begun to seem like the mere start of a case. These days, I'm trying to learn how to fix an abdominal aortic aneurysm, remove a pancreatic cancer, open blocked carotid arteries. I am, I have found, neither gifted nor maladroit. With practice and more practice, I get the hang of it.

Doctors find it hard to talk about this with patients. The moral burden of practicing on people is always with us, but for the most part it is unspoken. Before each operation, I go over to the holding area in my scrubs and introduce myself to the patient. I do it the same way every time. "Hello, I'm Dr. Gawande. I'm one of the surgical residents, and I'll be assisting your surgeon." That is pretty much all I say on the subject. I extend my hand and smile. I ask the patient if everything is going O.K. so far. We chat. I answer questions. Very occasionally, patients are taken aback. "No resident is doing my surgery," they say. I try to be reassuring. "Not to worry – I just assist," I say. "The attending surgeon is always in charge."

None of this is exactly a lie. The attending is in charge, and a resident knows better than to forget that. Consider the operation I did recently to remove a seventy-five-year-old woman's colon cancer. The attending stood across from me from the start. And it was he, not I, who decided where to cut, how to position the opened abdomen, how to isolate the cancer, and how much colon to take.

Yet I'm the one who held the knife. I'm the one who stood on the operator's side of the table, and it was raised to my six-foot-plus height. I was there to help, yes, but I was there to practice, too. This was clear when it came time to reconnect the colon. There are two ways of putting the ends together – handsewing and stapling. Stapling is swifter and easier, but the attending suggested I handsew the ends – not because it was better for the patient but because I had had much less experience doing it. When it's performed correctly, the results are similar, but he needed to watch me like a hawk. My stitching was slow and imprecise. At one point, he caught me putting the stitches too far apart and made me go back and put extras in between so the connection would not leak. At another point, he found I wasn't taking deep enough bites of tissue with the needle to insure a strong closure. "Turn your wrist more," he told me. "Like this?" I asked. "Uh, sort of," he said.

In medicine, there has long been a conflict between the imperative to give patients the best possible care and the need to provide novices with experience. Residencies attempt to mitigate potential harm through supervision and graduated responsibility. And there is reason to think that patients actually benefit from teaching. Studies commonly find that teaching hospitals have better outcomes than non-teaching hospitals. Residents may be amateurs, but having them around checking on patients, asking questions, and keeping faculty on their toes seems to help. But there is still no avoiding those first few unsteady times a young physician tries

165

to put in a central line, remove a breast cancer, or sew together two segments of colon. No matter how many protections are in place, on average these cases go less well with the novice than with someone experienced.

Doctors have no illusions about this. When an attending physician brings a sick family member in for surgery, people at the hospital think twice about letting trainees participate. Even when the attending insists that they participate as usual, the residents scrubbing in know that it will be far from a teaching case. And if a central line must be put in, a first-timer is certainly not going to do it. Conversely, the ward services and clinics where residents have the most responsibility are populated by the poor, the uninsured, the drunk, and the demented. Residents have few opportunities nowadays to operate independently, without the attending docs scrubbed in, but when we do – as we must before graduating and going out to operate on our own – it is generally with these, the humblest of patients.

And this is the uncomfortable truth about teaching. By traditional ethics and public insistence (not to mention court rulings), a patient's right to the best care possible must trump the objective of training novices. We want perfection without practice. Yet everyone is harmed if no one is trained for the future. So learning is hidden, behind drapes and anesthesia and the elisions of language. And the dilemma doesn't apply just to residents, physicians in training. The process of learning goes on longer than most people know.

I grew up in the small Appalachian town of Athens, Ohio, where my parents are both doctors. My mother is a pediatrician and my father is a urologist. Long ago, my mother chose to practice part time, which she could afford to do because my father's practice became so busy and successful. He has now been at it for more than twenty-five years, and his office is cluttered with the evidence of this. There is an overflowing wall of medical files, gifts from patients displayed everywhere (books, paintings, ceramics with Biblical sayings, hand-painted paperweights, blown glass, carved boxes, a figurine of a boy who, when you pull down his pants, pees on you), and, in an acrylic case behind his oak desk, a few dozen of the thousands of kidney stones he has removed.

Only now, as I get glimpses of the end of my training, have I begun to think hard about my father's success. For most of my residency, I thought of surgery as a more or less fixed body of knowledge and skill which is acquired in training and perfected in practice. There was, I thought, a smooth, upward-sloping arc of proficiency at some rarefied set of tasks (for me, taking out gallbladders, colon cancers, bullets, and appendixes; for him, taking out kidney stones, testicular cancers, and swollen prostates). The arc would peak at, say, ten or fifteen years, plateau for a long time, and perhaps tail off a little in the final five years before retirement. The reality, however, turns out to be far messier. You do get good at certain things, my father tells me, but no sooner do you master something than you find that what you know is outmoded. New technologies and operations emerge to supplant the old, and the learning curve starts all over again. "Three-quarters of what I do today I never learned in residency," he says. On his own, fifty miles from his nearest colleague – let alone a doctor who could tell him anything like "You need to turn your wrist more" – he has had to learn to put in penile prostheses, to perform microsurgery, to reverse vasectomies, to do nerve-sparing prostatectomies, to implant artificial urinary sphincters. He's had to learn to use shock-wave lithotripters, electrohydraulic lithotripters, and laser lithotripters (all instruments for breaking up kidney stones); to deploy Double J ureteral stents and Silicone Figure Four Coil stents and Retro-Inject Multi-Length stents (don't even ask); and to maneuver fibre-optic ureteroscopes. All these technologies and techniques were introduced after he finished training. Some of the procedures built on skills he already had. Many did not.

This is the experience that all surgeons have. The pace of medical innovation has been unceasing, and surgeons have no choice but to give the new thing a try. To fail to adopt new techniques would mean denying patients meaningful medical advances. Yet the perils of the learning curve are inescapable – no less in practice than in residency.

For the established surgeon, inevitably, the opportunities for learning are far less structured than for a resident. When an important new device or procedure comes along, as happens every year, surgeons start by taking a course about it – typically a day or two of lectures by some surgical grandees with a few film clips and step-by-step handouts. You take home a video to watch. Perhaps you pay a visit to observe a colleague perform the operation – my father often goes up to the Cleveland Clinic for this. But there's not much by way of hands-on training. Unlike a resident, a visitor cannot scrub in on cases, and opportunities to practice on animals or cadavers are few and far between. (Britain, being Britain, actually bans surgeons from practicing on animals.) When the pulse-dye laser came out, the manufacturer set up a lab in Columbus where urologists from the area could gain experience. But when my father went there the main experience provided was destroying kidney stones in test tubes filled with a urinelike liquid and trying to penetrate the shell of an egg without hitting the membrane underneath. My surgery department recently bought a robotic surgery device – a staggeringly sophisticated nine-hundred-and-eighty-thousand-dollar robot, with three arms, two wrists, and a camera, all millimetres in diameter, which, controlled from a console, allows a surgeon to do almost any operation with no hand tremor and with only tiny incisions. A team of two surgeons and two nurses flew out to the manufacturer's headquarters, in Mountain View, California, for a full day of training on the machine. And they did get to practice on a pig and on a human cadaver. (The company apparently buys the cadavers from the city of San Francisco.) But even this was hardly thorough training. They learned enough to grasp the principles of using the robot, to start getting a feel for using it, and to understand how to plan an operation. That was about it. Sooner or later, you just have to go home and give the thing a try on someone.

Patients do eventually benefit – often enormously – but the first few patients may not, and may even be harmed. Consider the experience reported by the pediatric cardiac-surgery unit of the renowned Great Ormond Street Hospital, in London, as detailed in the British Medical Journal last April. The doctors described their results from three hundred and twenty-five consecutive operations between 1978 and 1998 on babies with a severe heart defect known as transposition of the great arteries. Such children are born with their heart's outflow vessels transposed: the aorta emerges from the right side of the heart instead of the left and the artery to the lungs emerges from the left instead of the right. As a result, blood coming in is pumped right back out to the body instead of first to the lungs, where it can be oxygenated. The babies died blue, fatigued, never knowing what it was to get enough breath. For years, it wasn't technically feasible to switch the vessels to their proper positions. Instead, surgeons did something known as the Senning procedure: they created a passage inside the heart to let blood from the lungs cross backward to the right heart. The Senning procedure allowed children to live into adulthood. The weaker right heart, however, cannot sustain the body's entire blood flow as long as the left. Eventually, these patients' hearts failed, and although most survived to adulthood, few lived to old age.

By the nineteen-eighties, a series of technological advances made it possible to do a switch operation safely, and this became the favored procedure. In 1986, the Great Ormond Street surgeons made the changeover themselves, and their report shows that it was unquestionably an improvement. The annual death rate after a successful switch procedure was less than a quarter that of the Senning, resulting in a life expectancy of sixty-three years instead of forty-seven. But the price of learning to do it was appalling. In their first seventy switch operations, the doctors had a twenty-five-per-cent surgical death rate, compared with just six per cent with the Senning procedure. Eighteen babies died, more than twice the number during the entire Senning era. Only with time did they master it: in their next hundred switch operations, five babies died.

As patients, we want both expertise and progress; we don't want to acknowledge that these are contradictory desires. In the words of one British public report, "There should be no learning curve as far as patient safety is concerned." But this is entirely wishful thinking.

Recently, a group of Harvard Business School researchers who have made a specialty of studying learning curves in industry decided to examine learning curves among surgeons instead of in semiconductor manufacture or airplane construction, or any of the usual fields their colleagues examine. They followed eighteen cardiac surgeons and their teams as they took on the new technique of minimally invasive cardiac surgery. This study, I was surprised to discover, is the first of its kind. Learning is ubiquitous in medicine, and yet no one had ever compared how well different teams actually do it.

The new heart operation – in which new technologies allow a surgeon to operate through a small incision between ribs instead of splitting the chest open down the middle – proved substantially more difficult than the conventional one. Because the incision is too small to admit the usual tubes and clamps for rerouting blood to the heart-bypass machine, surgeons had to learn a trickier method, which involved balloons and catheters placed through groin vessels. And the nurses, anesthesiologists, and perfusionists all had new roles to master. As you'd expect, everyone experienced a substantial learning curve. Whereas a fully proficient team takes three to six hours for such an operation, these teams took on average three times as long for their early cases. The researchers could not track complication rates in detail, but it would be foolish to imagine that they were not affected.

What's more, the researchers found striking disparities in the speed with which different teams learned. All teams came from highly respected institutions with experience in adopting innovations and received the same three-day training session. Yet, in the course of fifty cases, some teams managed to halve their operating time while others improved hardly at all. Practice, it turned out, did not necessarily make perfect. The crucial variable was how the surgeons and their teams practiced.

Richard Bohmer, the only physician among the Harvard researchers, made several visits to observe one of the quickest-learning teams and one of the slowest, and he was startled by the contrast. The surgeon on the fast-learning team was actually quite inexperienced compared with the one on the slow-learning team. But he made sure to pick team members with whom he had worked well before and to keep them together through the first fifteen cases before allowing any new members. He had the team go

169

through a dry run before the first case, then deliberately scheduled six operations in the first week, so little would be forgotten in between. He convened the team before each case to discuss it in detail and afterward to debrief. He made sure results were tracked carefully. And Bohmer noticed that the surgeon was not the stereotypical Napoleon with a knife. Unbidden, he told Bohmer, "The surgeon needs to be willing to allow himself to become a partner [with the rest of the team] so he can accept input." At the other hospital, by contrast, the surgeon chose his operating team almost randomly and did not keep it together. In the first seven cases, the team had different members every time, which is to say that it was no team at all. And the surgeon had no pre-briefings, no debriefings, no tracking of ongoing results.

The Harvard Business School study offered some hopeful news. We can do things that have a dramatic effect on our rate of improvement – like being more deliberate about how we train, and about tracking progress, whether with students and residents or with senior surgeons and nurses. But the study's other implications are less reassuring. No matter how accomplished, surgeons trying something new got worse before they got better, and the learning curve proved longer, and was affected by a far more complicated range of factors, than anyone had realized.

This, I suspect, is the reason for the physician's dodge: the "I just assist" rap; the "We have a new procedure for this that you are perfect for" speech; the "You need a central line" without the "I am still learning how to do this." Sometimes we do feel obliged to admit when we're doing something for the first time, but even then we tend to quote the published complication rates of experienced surgeons. Do we ever tell patients that, because we are still new at something, their risks will inevitably be higher, and that they'd likely do better with doctors who are more experienced? Do we ever say that we need them to agree to it anyway? I've never seen it. Given the stakes, who in his right mind would agree to be practiced upon?

Many dispute this presumption. "Look, most people understand what it is to be a doctor," a health policy expert insisted, when I visited him in his office not long ago. "We have to stop lying to our patients. Can people take on choices for societal benefit?" He paused and then answered his question. "Yes," he said firmly.

It would certainly be a graceful and happy solution. We'd ask patients – honestly, openly – and they'd say yes. Hard to imagine, though. I noticed on the expert's desk a picture of his child, born just a few months before, and a completely unfair question popped into my mind. "So did you let the resident deliver?" I asked.

There was silence for a moment. "No," he admitted. "We didn't even allow residents in the room."

One reason I doubt whether we could sustain a system of medical training that depended on people saying "Yes, you can practice on me" is that I myself have said no. When my eldest child, Walker, was eleven days old, he suddenly went into congestive heart failure from what proved to be a severe cardiac defect. His aorta was not transposed, but a long segment of it had failed to grow at all. My wife and I were beside ourselves with fear – his kidneys and liver began failing, too – but he made it to surgery, the repair was a success, and although his recovery was erratic, after two and a half weeks he was ready to come home.

We were by no means in the clear, however. He was born a healthy six pounds plus but now, a month old, he weighed only five, and would need strict monitoring to insure that he gained weight. He was on two cardiac medications from which he would have to be weaned. And in the longer term, the doctors warned us, his repair would prove inadequate. As Walker grew, his aorta would require either dilation with a balloon or replacement by surgery. They could not say precisely when and how many such procedures would be necessary over the years. A pediatric cardiologist would have to follow him closely and decide.

Walker was about to be discharged, and we had not indicated who that cardiologist would be. In the hospital, he had been cared for by a full team of cardiologists, ranging from fellows in specialty training to attendings who had practiced for decades. The day before we took Walker home, one of the young fellows approached me, offering his card and suggesting a time to bring Walker to see him. Of those on the team, he had put in the most time caring for Walker. He saw Walker when we brought him in inexplicably short of breath, made the diagnosis, got Walker the drugs that stabilized him, coordinated with the surgeons, and came to see us twice a day to answer our questions. Moreover, I knew, this was how fellows always got their patients. Most families don't know the subtle gradations among players, and after a team has saved their child's life they take whatever appointment they're handed.

But I knew the differences. "I'm afraid we're thinking of seeing Dr. Newburger," I said. She was the hospital's associate cardiologist-in-chief, and a published expert on conditions like Walker's. The young physician looked crestfallen. It was nothing against him, I said. She just had more experience, that was all.

"You know, there is always an attending backing me up," he said. I shook my head.

I know this was not fair. My son had an unusual problem. The fellow needed the experience. As a resident, I of all people should have

171

understood this. But I was not torn about the decision. This was my child. Given a choice, I will always choose the best care I can for him. How can anybody be expected to do otherwise? Certainly, the future of medicine should not rely on it.

In a sense, then, the physician's dodge is inevitable. Learning must be stolen, taken as a kind of bodily eminent domain. And it was, during Walker's stay – on many occasions, now that I think back on it. A resident intubated him. A surgical trainee scrubbed in for his operation. The cardiology fellow put in one of his central lines. If I had the option to have someone more experienced, I would have taken it. But this was simply how the system worked – no such choices were offered – and so I went along.

The advantage of this coldhearted machinery is not merely that it gets the learning done. If learning is necessary but causes harm, then above all it ought to apply to everyone alike. Given a choice, people wriggle out, and such choices are not offered equally. They belong to the connected and the knowledgeable, to insiders over outsiders, to the doctor's child but not the truck driver's. If everyone cannot have a choice, maybe it is better if no one can.

It is 2 P.M. I am in the intensive-care unit. A nurse tells me Mr. G.'s central line has clotted off. Mr. G. has been in the hospital for more than a month now. He is in his late sixties, from South Boston, emaciated, exhausted, holding on by a thread – or a line, to be precise. He has several holes in his small bowel, and the bilious contents leak out onto his skin through two small reddened openings in the concavity of his abdomen. His only chance is to be fed by vein and wait for these fistulae to heal. He needs a new central line.

I could do it, I suppose. I am the experienced one now. But experience brings a new role: I am expected to teach the procedure instead. "See one, do one, teach one," the saying goes, and it is only half in jest.

There is a junior resident on the service. She has done only one or two lines before. I tell her about Mr. G. I ask her if she is free to do a new line. She misinterprets this as a question. She says she still has patients to see and a case coming up later. Could I do the line? I tell her no. She is unable to hide a grimace. She is burdened, as I was burdened, and perhaps frightened, as I was frightened.

She begins to focus when I make her talk through the steps – a kind of dry run, I figure. She hits nearly all the steps, but forgets about checking the labs and about Mr. G.'s nasty allergy to heparin, which is in the flush for the line. I make sure she registers this, then tell her to get set up and page me.

172

I am still adjusting to this role. It is painful enough taking responsibility for one's own failures. Being handmaiden to another's is something else entirely. It occurs to me that I could have broken open a kit and had her do an actual dry run. Then again maybe I can't. The kits must cost a couple of hundred dollars each. I'll have to find out for next time.

Half an hour later, I get the page. The patient is draped. The resident is in her gown and gloves. She tells me that she has saline to flush the line with and that his labs are fine.

"Have you got the towel roll?" I ask.

She forgot the towel roll. I roll up a towel and slip it beneath Mr. G.'s back. I ask him if he's all right. He nods. After all he's been through, there is only resignation in his eyes.

The junior resident picks out a spot for the stick. The patient is hauntingly thin. I see every rib and fear that the resident will puncture his lung. She injects the numbing medication. Then she puts the big needle in, and the angle looks all wrong. I motion for her to reposition. This only makes her more uncertain. She pushes in deeper and I know she does not have it. She draws back on the syringe: no blood. She takes out the needle and tries again. And again the angle looks wrong. This time, Mr. G. feels the jab and jerks up in pain. I hold his arm. She gives him more numbing medication. It is all I can do not to take over. But she cannot learn without doing, I tell myself. I decide to let her have one more try.

How We Listen
Aaron Copland

Chapter 2 of *What to Listen for in Music*. 1939; rpt. New York: McGraw-Hill, 1988.

Aaron Copland (1900-1990), was an American composer and conductor. He had formal musical education in Paris and Rome, but also sought to create music in a distinctively American idiom that would reach out to the ordinary person and not just the upper classes. His ballets Appalachian Spring *and* Rodeo *are among his most well-known works, but Copland also wrote chamber music, operas and film scores.*

Why we are reading this: We all think we "know" how to listen to music. In this essay, Copland suggests that we can listen to music on many different levels – he talks about three, but there may be more. His work reminds us that as our experience and knowledge grow, we can learn to understand music more deeply.

We all listen to music according to our separate capacities. But, for the sake of analysis, the whole listening process may become clearer if we break it up into its component parts, so to speak. In a certain sense we all listen to music on three separate planes. For lack of a better terminology, one might name these: (1) the sensuous plane, (2) the expressive plane, (3) the sheerly musical plane. The only advantage to be gained from mechanically splitting up the listening process into these hypothetical planes is the clearer view to be had of the way in which we listen.

The simplest way of listening to music is to listen for the sheer pleasure of the musical sound itself. That is the sensuous plane. It is the plane on which we hear music without thinking, without considering it in any way. One turns on the radio while doing something else and absent-mindedly bathes in the sound. A kind of brainless but attractive state of mind is engendered by the mere sound appeal of the music. You may be sitting in a room reading this book. Imagine one note struck on the piano. Immediately that one note is enough to change the atmosphere of the room – providing that the sound element in music is a powerful and mysterious agent, which it would be foolish to deride or belittle.

The surprising thing is that many people who consider themselves qualified music lovers abuse that plane in listening. They go to concerts in order to lose themselves. They use music as a consolation or an escape. They enter an ideal world where one doesn't have to think of the realities

174

of everyday life. Of course they aren't thinking about the music either. Music allows them to leave it, and they go off to a place to dream, dreaming because of and apropos of the music yet never quite listening to it.

Yes, the sound appeal of music is a potent and primitive force, but you must not allow it to usurp a disproportionate share of your interest. The sensuous plane is an important one in music, a very important one, but it does not constitute the whole story.

There is no need to digress further on the sensuous plane. Its appeal to every normal human being is self-evident. There is, however, such a thing as becoming more sensitive to the different kinds of sound stuff as used by various composers. For all composers do not use that sound stuff in the same way. Don't get the idea that the value of music is commensurate with its sensuous appeal or that the loveliest sounding music is made by the greatest composer. If that were so, Ravel would be a greater creator than Beethoven. The point is that the sound element varies with each composer, that his usage of sound forms an integral part of his style and must be taken into account when listening. The reader can see, therefore, that a more conscious approach is valuable even on this primary plane of music listening.

The second plane on which music exists is what I have called the expressive one. Here, immediately, we tread on controversial ground. Composers have a way of shying away from any discussion of music's expressive side. Did not Stravinsky himself proclaim that his music was an "object," a "thing," with a life of its own, and with no other meaning than its own purely musical existence? This intransigent attitude of Stravinsky's may be due to the fact that so many people have tried to read different meanings into so many pieces. Heaven knows it is difficult enough to say precisely what it is that a piece of music means, to say it definitely, to say it finally so that everyone is satisfied with your explanation. But that should not lead one to the other extreme of denying to music the right to be "expressive."

My own belief is that all music has an expressive power, some more and some less, but that all music has a certain meaning behind the notes and that the meaning behind the notes constitutes, after all, what the piece is saying, what the piece is about. The whole problem can be stated quite simply by asking, "Is there a meaning to music?" My answer to that would be, "Yes." And "Can you state in so many words what the meaning is?" My answer to that would be, "No." Therein lies the difficulty.

Simple-minded souls will never be satisfied with the answer to the second of these questions. They always want music to have a meaning, and the more concrete it is the better they like it. The more the music reminds them of a train, a storm, a funeral, or any other familiar conception the more expressive it appears to be to them. This popular idea of music's meaning – stimulated and abetted by the usual run of musical commentator – should be discouraged wherever and whenever it is met. One timid lady once confessed to me that she suspected something seriously lacking in her appreciation of music because of her inability to connect it with anything definite. That is getting the whole thing backward, of course.

Still, the question remains, How close should the intelligent music lover wish to come to pinning a definite meaning to any particular work? No closer than a general concept, I should say. Music expresses, at different moments, serenity or exuberance, regrets or triumph, fury or delight. It expresses each of these moods, and many others, in a numberless variety of subtle shadings and differences. It may even express a state of meaning for which there exists no adequate word in any language. In that case, musicians often like to say that it has only a purely musical meaning. They sometimes go further and say that *all* music has only a purely musical meaning. What they really mean is that no appropriate word can be found to express the music's meaning and that, even if it could, they do not feel the need of finding it.

But whatever the professional musician may hold, most musical novices still search for specific words with which to pin down their musical reactions. That is why they always find Tschaikovsky easier to "understand" than Beethoven. In the first place, it is easier to pin a meaning-word on a Tschaikovsky piece than on a Beethoven one. Much easier. Moreover, with the Russian composer, every time you come back to a piece of his it almost always says the same thing to you, whereas with Beethoven it is often quite difficult to put your finger right on what he is saying. And any musician will tell you that that is why Beethoven is the greater composer. Because music which always says the same thing to you will necessarily soon become dull music, but music whose meaning is slightly different with each hearing has a greater chance of remaining alive.

Listen, if you can, to the forty-eight fugue themes of Bach's *Well Tempered Clavichord*. Listen to each theme, one after another. You will soon realize that each theme mirrors a different world of feeling. You will also soon realize that the more beautiful a theme seems to you the harder it is to find any word that will describe it to your complete satisfaction. Yes, you will certainly know whether it is a gay theme or a sad one. You will be able, in other words, in your own mind, to draw a frame of emotional feeling around your theme. Now study the sad one a little closer. Try to pin down the exact quality of its sadness. Is it pessimistically sad or resignedly sad; is it fatefully sad or smilingly sad?

Let us suppose that you are fortunate and can describe to your own satisfaction in so many words the exact meaning of your chosen theme. There is still no guarantee that anyone else will be satisfied. Nor need they be. The important thing is that each one feel for himself the specific expressive quality of a theme or, similarly, an entire piece of music. And if it is a great work of art, don't expect it to mean exactly the same thing to you each time you return to it.

Themes or pieces need not express only one emotion, of course. Take such a theme as the first main one of the *Ninth Symphony,* for example. It is clearly made up of different elements. It does not say only one thing. Yet anyone hearing it immediately gets a feeling of strength, a feeling of power. It isn't a power that comes simply because the theme is played loudly. It is a power inherent in the theme itself. The extraordinary strength and vigor of the theme results in the listener's receiving an impression that a forceful statement has been made. But one should never try to boil it down to "the fateful hammer of life," etc. That is where the trouble begins. The musician, in his exasperation, says it means nothing but the notes themselves, whereas the nonprofessional is only too anxious to hang on to any explanation that gives him the illusion of getting closer to the music's meaning. Now, perhaps, the reader will know better what I mean when I say that music does have an expressive meaning but that we cannot say in so many words what that meaning is.

The third plane on which music exists is the sheerly musical plane. Besides the pleasurable sound of music and the expressive feeling that it gives off, music does exist in terms of the notes themselves and of their manipulation. Most listeners are not sufficiently conscious of this third plane....

Professional musicians, on the other hand, are, if anything, too conscious of the mere notes themselves. They often fall into the error of becoming so engrossed with their arpeggios and staccatos that they forget the deeper aspects of the music they are performing. But from the layman's standpoint, it is not so much a matter of getting over bad habits on the sheerly musical plane as of increasing one's awareness of what is going on, in so far as the notes are concerned.

When the man in the street listens to the "notes themselves" with any degree of concentration, he is most likely to make some mention of the melody. Either he hears a pretty melody or he does not, and he generally lets it go at that. Rhythm is likely to gain his attention next, particularly if it seems exciting. But harmony and tone color are generally taken for granted, if they are thought of consciously at all. As for music's having a definite form of some kind, that idea seems never to have occurred to him.

177

It is very important for all of us to become more alive to music on its sheerly musical plane. After all, an actual musical material is being used. The intelligent listener must be prepared to increase his awareness of the musical material and what happens to it. He must hear the melodies, the rhythms, the harmonies, the tone colors in a more conscious fashion. But above all he must, in order to follow the line of the composer's thought, know something of the principles of musical form. Listening to all of these elements is listening on the sheerly musical plane.

Let me repeat that I have split up mechanically the three separate planes on which we listen merely for the sake of greater clarity. Actually, we never listen on one or the other of these planes. What we do is to correlate them – listening in all three ways at the same time. It takes no mental effort, for we do it instinctively. Perhaps an analogy with what happens to us when we visit the theater will make this instinctive correlation clearer. In the theater, you are aware of the actors and actresses, costumes and sets, sounds and movements. All these give one the sense that the theater is a pleasant place to be in. They constitute the sensuous plane in our theatrical reactions.

The expressive plane in the theater would be derived from the feeling that you get from what is happening on the stage. You are moved to pity, excitement, or gayety. It is this general feeling, generated aside from the particular words being spoken, a certain emotional something which exists on the stage, that is analogous to the expressive quality in music.

The plot and plot development is equivalent to our sheerly musical plane. The playwright creates and develops a character in just the same way that a composer creates and develops a theme. According to the degree of your awareness of the way in which the artist in either field handles his material you will become a more intelligent listener. It is easy enough to see that the theatergoer never is conscious of any of these elements separately. He is aware of them all at the same time. The same is true of music listening. We simultaneously and without thinking listen on all three planes.

In a sense, the ideal listener is both inside and outside the music at the same moment, judging it and enjoying it, wishing it would go one way and watching it go another – almost like the composer at the moment he composes it; because in order to write his music, the composer must also be inside and outside his music, carried away by it and yet coldly critical of it. A subjective and objective attitude is implied in both creating and listening to music.

What the reader should strive for, then, is a more *active* kind of listening. Whether you listen to Mozart or Duke Ellington, you can deepen your understanding of music only by being a more conscious and aware listener – not someone who is just listening, but someone who is listening *for* something.

O Me! O Life!
Walt Whitman

In *Leaves of Grass*, 1855.

Walt Whitman *(1819-1892), was a famous poet, journalist, and essay writer. He was born in Long Island, New York, and finished his formal schooling at age 11, at which time he became an apprentice for a printer. He worked as a journalist for a number of years, and eventually became more interested in poetry. His collection of poems titled* Leaves of Grass *is still considered to include some of the best American poetry, even though it was considered quite risqué during his lifetime. His affinity with deism and transcendentalism can be seen in his poems.*

Why we are reading this: *We often learn important things about the world when we look through someone else's eyes. Most of the remaining readings in the anthology are meant to introduce students to points of view or alternate world views that they might not have considered before. We'll start by considering poetry, which can provide insight into the experience of others and startling new ways of looking at the world. Whitman's poem opens with a person in anguish over eternal existential questions. Like Rene Descartes, he finds his bedrock in the assertion of his own existence. His "answer" to life's questions revolves around a metaphor wherein each of us is somehow an actor or playwright in a massive ongoing theatrical play.*

Oh me! Oh life! of the questions of these recurring,
Of the endless trains of the faithless, of cities fill'd with the foolish,
Of myself forever reproaching myself, (for who more foolish than I, and
      who more faithless?)
Of eyes that vainly crave the light, of the objects mean, of the struggle
      ever renew'd,
Of the poor results of all, of the plodding and sordid crowds I see around
      me,
Of the empty and useless years of the rest, with the rest me intertwined,
The question, O me! so sad, recurring – What good amid these, O me, O
      life?

          Answer.
That you are here – that life exists and identity,
That the powerful play goes on, and you may contribute a verse.

The Solitude of Self: Speech to the House Judiciary Committee

Elizabeth Cady Stanton

In *Hearing of the Woman Suffrage Association Before the Committee on Judiciary*, January 18, 1892, pp. 1-5 (Elizabeth Cady Stanton Papers, Library of Congress).

Elizabeth Cady Stanton (1815-1902) was an American suffragist, abolitionist, and writer who devoted her life to the idea that men and women should have equal rights. She campaigned ceaselessly for a constitutional amendment granting women the right to vote in all elections – an achievement that she sadly did not live long enough to see, as the long-sought Nineteenth Amendment was adopted only in 1920.

Why we are reading this: Men and women may live in the same country, town, or family, share the same language and culture, and generally inhabit the same space – and yet have experiences and viewpoints that differ in systematic ways. One essential way to learn about those differences and to begin pondering their causes and effects is to listen to voices from across gender boundaries. Elizabeth Cady Stanton was attempting such communication in this speech delivered in early 1892. Moving beyond her campaign to gain the vote for women, she seeks to help an all-male Congressional committee understand things from a woman's point of view. She argues that the facts of women's lives – their intellectual and spiritual independence, their self-sovereignty, and their ability to know the world just as well as any man – require rights and freedoms equal to those of men, including property rights, access to a liberal education, and entrance into all occupations and realms of social life. This speech is sometimes considered the birth of modern feminism.

Mr. Chairman and gentlemen of the committee: We have been speaking before Committees of the Judiciary for the last twenty years and we have gone over all the arguments in favor of a sixteenth amendment which are familiar to all you gentlemen; therefore, it will not be necessary that I should repeat them again. [1]

---

[1] Complete women's suffrage had been proposed to the Senate as a sixteenth amendment in 1878, but it sat in committee for years before being rejected in 1887. At the time of this speech there was no suffrage amendment before the

The point I wish plainly to bring before you on this occasion is the individuality of each human soul; our Protestant idea, the right of individual conscience and judgment; our republican idea, individual citizenship. In discussing the rights of woman, we are to consider, first, what belongs to her as an individual, in a world of her own, the arbiter of her own destiny, an imaginary Robinson Crusoe, with her woman Friday on a solitary island. Her rights under such circumstances are to use all her faculties for her own safety and happiness.

Secondly, if we consider her as a citizen, as a member of a great nation, she must have the same rights as all other members, according to the fundamental principles of our Government.

Thirdly, viewed as a woman, an equal factor in civilization, her rights and duties are still the same – individual happiness and development.

Fourthly, it is only the incidental relations of life, such as mother, wife, sister, daughter, which may involve some special duties and training. In the usual discussion in regard to woman's sphere, such men as Herbert Spencer, Frederic Harrison, and Grant Allen uniformly subordinate her rights and duties as an individual, as a citizen, as a woman, to the necessities of these incidental relations, some of which a large class of women may never assume. In discussing the sphere of man we do not decide his rights as an individual, as a citizen, as a man by his duties as a father, a husband, a brother, or a son, relations some of which he may never fill. Moreover he would be better fitted for these very relations and whatever special work he might choose to do to earn his bread by the complete development of all his faculties as an individual.

Just so with woman. The education that will fit her to discharge the duties in the largest sphere of human usefulness will best fit her for whatever special work she may be compelled to do.

The isolation of every human soul and the necessity of self-dependence must give each individual the right to choose his own surroundings.

The strongest reason for giving woman all the opportunities for higher education, for the full development of her faculties, her forces of mind and body; for giving her the most enlarged freedom of thought and action; a complete emancipation from all forms of bondage, of custom, dependence, superstition; from all the crippling influences of fear, is the solitude and personal responsibility of her own individual life. The strongest reason why we ask for woman a voice in the government under which she lives; in the religion she is asked to believe; equality in social life, where she is

Senate. Women's suffrage was finally passed as the Nineteenth Amendment in 1920.

the chief factor; a place in the trades and professions, where she may earn her bread, is because of her birthright to self-sovereignty; because, as an individual, she must rely on herself. No matter how much women prefer to lean, to be protected and supported, nor how much men desire to have them do so, they must make the voyage of life alone, and for safety in an emergency, they must know something of the laws of navigation. To guide our own craft, we must be captain, pilot, engineer; with chart and compass to stand at the wheel; to watch the winds and waves, and know when to take in the sail, and to read the signs in the firmament over all. It matters not whether the solitary voyager is man or woman. Nature having endowed them equally, leaves them to their own skill and judgment in the hour of danger, and, if not equal to the occasion, alike they perish.

To appreciate the importance of fitting every human soul for independent action, think for a moment of the immeasurable solitude of self. We come into the world alone, unlike all who have gone before us, we leave it alone under circumstances peculiar to ourselves. No mortal ever has been, no mortal ever will be like the soul just launched on the sea of life. There can never again be just such a combination of prenatal influences; never again just such environments as make up the infancy, youth and manhood of this one. Nature never repeats herself, and the possibilities of one human soul will never be found in another. No one has ever found two blades of ribbon grass alike, and no one will ever find two human beings alike. Seeing, then, what must be the infinite diversity in human character, we can in a measure appreciate the loss to a nation when any class of the people is uneducated and unrepresented in the government. We ask for the complete development of every individual, first, for his own benefit and happiness. In fitting out an army, we give each soldier his own knapsack, arms, powder, his blanket, cup, knife, fork and spoon. We provide alike for all their individual necessities, then each man bears his own burden.

Again, we ask complete individual development for the general good; for the consensus of the competent on the whole round of human interests; on all questions of national life, and here each man must bear his share of the general burden. It is sad to see how soon friendless children are left to bear their own burdens, before they can analyze their feelings; before they can even tell their joys and sorrows, they are thrown on their own resources. The great lesson that nature seems to teach us at all ages in self-dependence, self-protection, self-support. What a touching instance of a child's solitude; of that hunger of the heart for love and recognition, in the case of the little girl who helped to dress a Christmas tree for the children of the family in which she served. On finding there was no present for herself she slipped away in the darkness and spent the night in an open field sitting on a stone, and when found in the morning was weeping as if her heart would break. No mortal will ever know the thoughts that passed through the mind of that friendless child in the long hours of that cold night, with only the silent stars to keep her company. The mention of her case in the daily papers moved many generous hearts to send her presents, but in the hours of her keenest suffering she was thrown wholly on herself for consolation.

In youth our most bitter disappointments, our brightest hopes and ambitions are known only to ourselves; even our friendship and love we never fully share with another; there is something of every passion, in every situation, we conceal. Even so in our triumphs and our defeats. The successful candidate for the Presidency and his opponent each have a solitude peculiarly his own, and good form forbids either to speak of his pleasure or regret. The solitude of the king on his throne and the prisoner in his cell differs in character and degree, but it is solitude nevertheless.

We ask no sympathy from others in the anxiety and agony of a broken friendship or shattered love. When death sunders our nearest ties, alone we sit in the shadow of our affliction. Alike amid the greatest triumphs and darkest tragedies of life, we walk alone. On the divine heights of human attainment, eulogized and worshiped as a hero or saint, we stand alone. In ignorance, poverty and vice, as a pauper or criminal, alone we starve or steal; alone we suffer the sneers and rebuffs of our fellows; alone we are hunted and hounded through dark courts and alleys, in by-ways and highways; alone we stand in the judgment seat; alone in the prison cell we lament our crimes and misfortunes; alone we expiate them on the gallows. In hours like these we realize the awful solitude of individual life, its pains, its penalties, its responsibilities, hours in which the youngest and most helpless are thrown on their own resources for guidance and consolation. Seeing, then, that life must ever be a march and a battle that each soldier must be equipped for his own protection, it is the height of cruelty to rob the individual of a single natural right.

To throw obstacles in the way of a complete education is like putting out the eyes; to deny the rights of property, like cutting off the hands. To refuse political equality is to rob the ostracized of all self-respect; of credit in the market place; of recompense in the world of work, of a voice in choosing those who make and administer the law, a choice in the jury before whom they are tried, and in the judge who decides their punishment. Shakespeare's play of Titus and Andronicus contains a terrible satire on woman's position in the nineteenth century – "Rude men" (the play tells us) "seized the king's daughter, cut out her tongue, cut off her hands, and then bade her go call for water and wash her hands." What a picture of woman's position. Robbed of her natural rights, handicapped by law and custom at every turn, yet compelled to fight her own battles, and in the emergencies of life to fall back on herself for protection.

The girl of sixteen, thrown on the world to support herself, to make her own place in society, to resist the temptations that surround her and maintain a spotless integrity, must do all this by native force or superior education. She does not acquire this power by being trained to trust others and distrust herself. If she wearies of the struggle, finding it hard work to swim upstream, and allows herself to drift with the current, she will find plenty of company, but not one to share her misery in the hour of her deepest humiliation. If she tries to retrieve her position, to conceal the past, her life is hedged about with fears lest willing hands should tear the veil from what she fain would hide. Young and friendless, *she* knows the bitter solitude of self.

The young wife and mother, at the head of some establishment, with a kind husband to shield her from the adverse winds of life, with wealth, fortune and position, has a certain harbor of safety, secure against the ordinary ills of life. But to manage a household, have a desirable influence in society, keep her friends and the affections of her husband, train her children and servants well, she must have rare common sense, wisdom, diplomacy, and a knowledge of human nature. To do all this, she needs the cardinal virtues and the strong points of character that the most successful statesman possesses.

An uneducated woman trained to dependence, with no resources in herself, must make a failure of any position in life. But society says women do not need a knowledge of the world, the liberal training that experience in public life must give, all the advantages of collegiate education; but when for the lack of all this, the woman's happiness is wrecked, alone she bears her humiliation; and the solitude of the weak and the ignorant is indeed pitiable. In the wild chase for the prizes of life, they are ground to powder.

In age, when the pleasures of youth are passed, children grown up, married and gone, the hurry and bustle of life in a measure over, when the hands are weary of active service, when the old armchair and the fireside are the chosen resorts, then men and women alike must fall back on their own resources. If they cannot find companionship in books, if they have no interest in the vital questions of the hour, no interest in watching the consummation of reforms with which they might have been identified, they soon pass into their dotage. The more fully the faculties of the mind are developed and kept in use, the longer the period of vigor and active interest in all around us continues. If from a lifelong participation in public affairs, a woman feels responsible for the laws regulating our system of education, the discipline of our jails and prisons, the sanitary condition of our private homes, public buildings and thoroughfares, an interest in commerce, finance, our foreign relations, in any or all these questions, her solitude will at least be respectable, and she will not be driven to gossip or scandal for entertainment.

The chief reason for opening to every soul the doors to the whole round of human duties and pleasures is the individual development thus attained, the resources thus provided under all circumstances to mitigate the solitude that at times must come to everyone. I once asked Prince Krapotkin, a Russian nihilist, how he endured his long years in prison, deprived of books, pen, ink, and paper. "Ah," he said, "I thought out many questions in which I had a deep interest. In the pursuit of an idea I took no note of time. When tired of solving knotty problems I recited all the beautiful passages in prose or verse I had ever learned. I became acquainted with myself and my own resources. I had a world of my own, a vast empire, that no Russian jailor or Czar could invade." Such is the value of liberal thought and broad culture when shut off from all human companionship, bringing comfort and sunshine within even the four walls of a prison cell.

As women ofttimes share a similar fate, should they not have all the consolation that the most liberal education can give? Their suffering in the prisons of St. Petersburg; in the long, weary marches to Siberia, and in the mines, working side by side with men, surely call for all the self-support that the most exalted sentiments of heroism can give. When suddenly roused at midnight, with the startling cry of "fire! fire!" to find the house over their heads in flames, do women wait for men to point the way to safety? And are the men, equally bewildered and half suffocated with smoke, in a position to do more than try to save themselves?

At such times the most timid women have shown a courage and heroism in saving their husbands and children that has surprised everybody. Inasmuch, then, as woman shares equally the joys and sorrows of time and eternity, is it not the height of presumption in man to propose to represent her at the ballot box and the throne of grace, to do her voting in the state, her praying in the church, and to assume the position of high priest at the family altar?

Nothing strengthens the judgment and quickens the conscience like individual responsibility. Nothing adds such dignity to character as the recognition of one's self-sovereignty; the right to an equal place, everywhere conceded; a place earned by personal merit, not an artificial attainment by inheritance, wealth, family and position. Seeing, then, that the responsibilities of life rest equally on man and woman, that their destiny is the same, they need the same preparation for time and eternity. The talk of sheltering woman from the fierce storms of life is the sheerest

186

mockery, for they beat on her from every point of the compass, just as they do on man, and with more fatal results, for he has been trained to protect himself, to resist, and to conquer. Such are the facts in human experience, the responsibilities of individual sovereignty. Rich and poor, intelligent and ignorant, wise and foolish, virtuous and vicious, man and woman, it is ever the same, each soul must depend wholly on itself.

Whatever the theories may be of woman's dependence on man, in the supreme moments of her life he cannot bear her burdens. Alone she goes to the gates of death to give life to every man that is born into the world. No one can share her fears, no one can mitigate her pangs; and if her sorrow is greater than she can bear, alone she passes beyond the gates into the vast unknown.

From the mountain tops of Judea long ago, a heavenly voice bade his disciples, "Bear ye one another's burden," but humanity has not yet risen to that point of self-sacrifice and if ever so willing, how few the burdens are that one soul can bear for another. In the highways of Palestine; in prayer and fasting on the solitary mountain top; in the Garden of Gethsemane; before the judgment seat of Pilate; betrayed by one of His trusted disciples at His last supper; in His agonies on the cross, even Jesus of Nazareth, in those last sad days on earth, felt the awful solitude of self. Deserted by man, in agony he cries, "My God! My God! why hast Thou forsaken me?" And so it ever must be in the conflicting scenes of life, in the long, weary march, each one walks alone. We may have many friends, love, kindness, sympathy and charity to smooth our pathway in everyday life, but in the tragedies and triumphs of human experience, each mortal stands alone.

But when all artificial trammels are removed, and women are recognized as individuals, responsible for their own environments, thoroughly educated for all positions in life they may be called to fill; with all the resources in themselves that liberal thought and broad culture can give; guided by their own conscience and judgment; trained to self-protection by a healthy development of the muscular system, and skill in the use of weapons of defense, and stimulated to self-support by a knowledge of the business world and the pleasure that pecuniary independence must ever give; when women are trained in this way they will, in a measure, be fitted for those hours of solitude that come alike to all, whether prepared or otherwise. As in our extremity we must depend on ourselves, the dictates of wisdom point to complete individual development.

In talking of education, how shallow the argument that each class must be educated for the special work it proposes to do, and that all those faculties not needed in this special work must lie dormant and utterly

187

wither for want of use, when, perhaps, these will be the very faculties needed in life's greatest emergencies. Some say, "Where is the use of drilling girls in the languages, the sciences, in law, medicine, theology? As wives, mothers, housekeepers, cooks, they need a different curriculum from boys who are to fill all positions. The chief cooks in our great hotels and ocean steamers are men. In our large cities, men run the bakeries; they make our bread, cake and pies. They manage the laundries; they are now considered our best milliners and dressmakers. Because some men fill these departments of usefulness, shall we regulate the curriculum in Harvard and Yale to their present necessities? If not, why this talk in our best colleges of a curriculum for girls who are crowding into the trades and professions, teachers in all our public schools, rapidly filling many lucrative and honorable positions in life? They are showing, too, their calmness and courage in the most trying hours of human experience."

You have probably all read in the daily papers of the terrible storm in the Bay of Biscay when a tidal wave made such havoc on the shore, wrecking vessels, unroofing houses, and carrying destruction every-where. Among other buildings the woman's prison was demolished. Those who escaped saw men struggling to reach the shore. They promptly by clasping hands made a chain of themselves and pushed out into the sea, again and again, at the risk of their lives, until they had brought six men to shore, carried them to a shelter, and did all in their power for their comfort and protection.

What special school training could have prepared these women for this sublime moment in their lives? In times like this humanity rises above all college curriculums and recognizes Nature as the greatest of all teachers in the hour of danger and death. Women are already the equals of men in the whole realm of thought, in art, science, literature and government. With telescopic vision they explore the starry firmament and bring back the history of the planetary world. With chart and compass they pilot ships across the mighty deep, and with skillful finger send electric messages around the globe. In galleries of art the beauties of nature and the virtues of humanity are immortalized by them on canvas and by their inspired touch dull blocks of marble are transformed into angels of light.

In music they speak again the language of Mendelssohn, Beethoven, Chopin, Schumann, and are worthy interpreters of their great thoughts. The poetry and novels of the century are theirs, and they have touched the keynote of reform, in religion, politics and social life. They fill the editor's and professor's chair, plead at the bar of justice, walk the wards of the hospital, speak from the pulpit and the platform. Such is the type of womanhood that an enlightened public sentiment welcomes today, and such the triumph of the facts of life over the false theories of the past.

Is it, then, consistent to hold the developed woman of this day within the same narrow political limits as the dame with the spinning wheel and knitting needle occupied in the past? No, no! Machinery has taken the labors of woman as well as man on its tireless shoulders; the loom and the spinning wheel are but dreams of the past; the pen, the brush, the easel, the chisel, have taken their places, while the hopes and ambitions of women are essentially changed.

We see reason sufficient in the outer conditions of human beings for individual liberty and development, but when we consider the self dependence of every human soul, we see the need of courage, judgment and the exercise of every faculty of mind and body, strengthened and developed by use, in woman as well as man.

Whatever may be said of man's protecting power in ordinary conditions, amid all the terrible disasters by land and sea, in the supreme moments of danger, alone woman must ever meet the horrors of the situation; the Angel of Death even makes no royal pathway for her. Man's love and sympathy enter only into the sunshine of our lives. In that solemn solitude of self, that links us with the immeasurable and the eternal, each soul lives alone forever. A recent writer says: "I remember once, in crossing the Atlantic, to have gone upon the deck of the ship at midnight, when a dense black cloud enveloped the sky, and the great deep was roaring madly under the lashes of demoniac winds. My feeling was not of danger or fear (which is a base surrender of the immortal soul) but of utter desolation and loneliness; a little speck of life shut in by a tremendous darkness. Again I remember to have climbed the slopes of the Swiss Alps, up beyond the point where vegetation ceases, and the stunted conifers no longer struggle against the unfeeling blasts. Around me lay a huge confusion of rocks, out of which the gigantic ice peaks shot into the measureless blue of the heavens, and again my only feeling was the awful solitude."

And yet, there is a solitude which each and every one of us has always carried with him, more inaccessible than the ice-cold mountains, more profound than the midnight sea; the solitude of self. Our inner being, which we call ourself, no eye nor touch of man or angel has ever pierced. It is more hidden than the caves of the gnome; the sacred adytum of the oracle; the hidden chamber of Eleusinian mystery, for to it only omniscience is permitted to enter.

Such is individual life. Who, I ask you, can take, dare take, on himself the rights, the duties, the responsibilities of another human soul?

We Are All Bound Up Together
Frances Ellen Watkins Harper

In Philip Sheldon Foner and Robert J. Branham, eds., *Lift Every Voice: African American Oratory, 1787-1900*. Tuscaloosa, Ala: University of Alabama Press, 1998, pp. 456-460. Spelling modernized.

Frances Ellen Watkins Harper (1825-1911) was an African-American poet, writer, and lecturer. Born free in Baltimore in 1825, she published her first book of poetry at age 20. In 1860 she married Fenton Harper and lived with him on a farm in Ohio until his death in 1864. By the time of the Civil War (1861-1865), she was a well-known anti-slavery activist; after the war she campaigned for women's suffrage, equal rights for African-Americans, and the prohibition of alcohol. In these movements, the alliance between white and black activists was sometimes strained. Harper attended major women's rights conventions alongside leading white suffragists like Elizabeth Cady Stanton and Susan B. Anthony, but was often the only African American present or permitted to speak. In 1869, when Congress proposed the Fifteenth Amendment, which guaranteed the vote to all men regardless of race but did not address women's suffrage, the women's movement fragmented. Harper and most African-American suffragists, as well as black male activists like Frederick Douglass, supported the amendment as a step forward for racial equality. However, some white suffragists, including Stanton and Anthony, chose to oppose it because it failed to enfranchise women, both black and white. Political alliances that span gender, race, and class lines have often proved fragile at critical moments like this.

Why we are reading this: Black and white women have shared the experience of discrimination and disenfranchisement, yet black women have also faced discrimination and hostility on the basis of race, often from the white women with whom they seemingly shared so much. This is the essence of what some modern writers call intersectionality – the intersection of different forms of identity and oppression based on gender, class, race, and other characteristics. When Frances Harper spoke to the Eleventh National Women's Rights Convention in New York in May 1866, she sought to communicate this situation to her largely white and female audience. Harper frankly describes the dual oppression of sexism and racism that afflicted black women, emphasizing mutual interests with white women, yet challenging them to recognize their own complicity in systems of racial oppression.

I feel I am something of a novice upon this platform. Born of a race whose inheritance has been outrage and wrong, most of my life had been spent in battling against those wrongs. But I did not feel as keenly as others, that I had these rights, in common with other women, which are now demanded. About two years ago, I stood within the shadows of my home. A great sorrow had fallen upon my life. My husband had died suddenly, leaving me a widow, with four children, one my own, and the others stepchildren. I tried to keep my children together. But my husband died in debt; and before he had been in his grave three months, the administrator had swept the very milk-crocks and wash tubs from my hands. I was a farmer's wife and made butter for the Columbus market; but what could I do, when they had swept all away? They left me one thing – and that was a looking glass! Had I died instead of my husband, how different would have been the result! By this time he would have had another wife, it is likely; and no administrator would have gone into his house, broken up his home, and sold his bed, and taken away his means of support.

I took my children in my arms, and went out to seek my living. While I was gone; a neighbor to whom I had once lent five dollars, went before a magistrate and swore that he believed I was a non-resident, and laid an attachment on my very bed. And I went back to Ohio with my orphan children in my arms, without a single feather bed in this wide world, that was not in the custody of the law. I say, then, that justice is not fulfilled so long as woman is unequal before the law.

We are all bound up together in one great bundle of humanity, and society cannot trample on the weakest and feeblest of its members without receiving the curse in its own soul. You tried that in the case of the negro. You pressed him down for two centuries; and in so doing you crippled the moral strength and paralyzed the spiritual energies of the white men of the country. When the hands of the black were fettered, white men were deprived of the liberty of speech and the freedom of the press. Society cannot afford to neglect the enlightenment of any class of its members. At the South, the legislation of the country was in behalf of the rich slaveholders, while the poor white man was neglected. What is the consequence today? From that very class of neglected poor white men, comes the man who stands today, with his hand upon the helm of the nation. He fails to catch the watchword of the hour, and throws himself, the incarnation of meanness, across the pathway of the nation. My objection to Andrew Johnson is not that he has been a poor white man; my objection is that he keeps "poor whits" all the way through. (Applause.) That is the trouble with him.[1]

This grand and glorious revolution which has commenced, will fail to reach its climax of success, until throughout the length and breadth of the American Republic, the nation shall be so color-blind, as to know no man by the color of his skin or the curl of his hair. It will then have no privileged class, trampling upon and outraging the unprivileged classes, but will be then one great privileged nation, whose privilege will be to produce the loftiest manhood and womanhood that humanity can attain.

I do not believe that giving the woman the ballot is immediately going to cure all the ills of life. I do not believe that white women are dew-drops just exhaled from the skies. I think that like men they may be divided into three classes, the good, the bad, and the indifferent. The good would vote according to their convictions and principles; the bad, as dictated by prejudice or malice; and the indifferent will vote on the strongest side of the question, with the winning party.

You white women speak here of rights. I speak of wrongs. I, as a colored woman, have had in this country an education which has made me feel as if I were in the situation of Ishmael, my hand against every man, and every man's hand against me. Let me go tomorrow morning and take my seat in one of your street cars – I do not know that they will do it in New York, but they will in Philadelphia – and the conductor will put up his hand and stop the car rather than let me ride.

A Lady – They will not do that here.

Mrs. Harper – They do in Philadelphia. Going from Washington to Baltimore this Spring, they put me in the smoking car. (Loud Voices – "Shame.") Aye, in the capital of the nation, where the black man consecrated himself to the nation's defense, faithful when the white man was faithless, they put me in the smoking car! They did it once; but the next time they tried it, they failed; for I would not go in. I felt the fight in me; but I don't want to have to fight all the time. Today I am puzzled where to make my home. I would like to make it in Philadelphia, near my own friends and relations. But if I want to ride in the streets of Philadelphia, they send me to ride on the platform with the driver. (Cries of "Shame.") Have women nothing to do with this? Not long since, a colored woman took her seat in an Eleventh Street car in Philadelphia, and the conductor stopped the car, and told the rest of the passengers to get out, and left the

---

[1] Andrew Johnson succeeded Abraham Lincoln as president after the latter's assassination in April 1865. Pres. Johnson sought to undermine the Freedmen's Bureau, which provided material assistance for former slaves, and opposed congressional legislation to extend full civil rights to African Americans.

car with her in it alone, when they took it back to the station. One day I took my seat in a car, and the conductor came to me and told me to take another seat. I just screamed "murder." The man said if I was black I ought to behave myself. I knew that if he was white he was not behaving himself. Are there not wrongs to be righted?

In advocating the cause of the colored man, since the Dred Scott decision, I have sometimes said I thought the nation had touched bottom. But let me tell you there is a depth of infamy lower than that. It is when the nation, standing upon the threshold of a great peril, reached out its hands to a feebler race, and asked that race to help it, and when the peril was over, said, You are good enough for soldiers, but not good enough for citizens. When Judge Taney said that the men of my race had no rights which the white man was bound to respect, he had not seen the bones of the black man bleaching outside of Richmond. He had not seen the thinned ranks and the thickened graves of the Louisiana Second, a regiment which went into battle nine hundred strong, and came out with three hundred. He had not stood at Olustee and seen defeat and disaster crushing down the pride of our banner, until word was brought to Col. Hallowell, "The day is lost; go in and save it;" and black men stood in the gap, beat back the enemy, and saved your army.[2] (Applause.)

We have a woman in our country who has received the name of "Moses,"[3] not by lying about it, but by acting it out (applause) – a woman who has gone down into the Egypt of slavery and brought out hundreds of our people into liberty. The last time I saw that woman, her hands were swollen. That woman who had led one of Montgomery's most successful expeditions, who was brave enough and secretive enough to act as a scout for the American army, had her hands all swollen from a conflict with a brutal conductor, who undertook to eject her from her place. That woman, whose courage and bravery won a recognition from our army and from every black man in the land, is excluded from every thoroughfare of travel. Talk of giving women the ballot box? Go on. It is a normal school, and the white women of this country need it. While there exists this brutal element in society which tramples upon the feeble and treads down the weak, I tell you that if there is any class of people who need to be lifted out of their airy nothings and selfishness, it is the white women of America. (Applause.)

---

[2] At the Battle of Olustee (or Battle of Ocean Pond) in Florida on February 20, 1864, the (African-American) 54th Massachusetts Regiment halted the Confederate rout of Union forces.

[3] Harriett Tubman (1822-1913), abolitionist and conductor on the Underground Railway.

Decolonizing "Truth": Restoring More than Justice
Edward C. Valandra

In *Justice as Healing: Indigenous Ways: Writings on Community Peacemaking and Restorative Justice from the Native Law Centre*, edited by Wanda D. McCaslin. St. Paul, MN: Living Justice Press, 2005, pp. 29-53.

Edward C. Valandra (b. 1955) is a Native American author, educator, and activist. He was born and raised on the Rosebud Sioux Reservation in South Dakota and holds a Ph.D. in American Studies from SUNY-Buffalo. He has taught at several universities, including the University of Manitoba and the University of South Dakota. His teaching and writing focus on the experience of Native Peoples, the effects of conquest and colonization by white settlers, and the national revitalization of the Oceti Sakowin Oyate (People of the Seven Fires, commonly called the Sioux, or the Dakota, Lakota, and Nakota people). He is active in the development of Native Studies as an academic field and has served as president of the American Indian Studies Association.

Why we are reading this: What happened when white settlers of European descent met Native American peoples? How do people in these two groups view each other, and how do they characterize their centuries-long encounter? This article is based on Professor Valandra's presentation on the genocide of Native Peoples at a conference of the National Association of Ethnic Studies in Chicago in March 2005. Valandra argues that the whites were not just "settlers" but colonizers and imperialists who committed genocide against Native People and stole their land – and that this is not just native perception but an objective reality based on historical evidence. For Valandra, telling the truth about this history is an essential prerequisite for any genuine reconciliation. How do you evaluate his arguments? Are you persuaded? (Note that some terms are defined in a glossary at the end of this piece.)

Colonial Oppression as Trauma

Trauma. The word carries immense weight in reconciliation and in reparative and restorative justice circles. Trauma conjures up horrific images and feelings of deep, unresolved pain for both those on the receiving end of harm and those who inflict it. In both cases, guilt, shame, misdirected anger, and outright rage, though hidden from the public eye, find outlets in destructive behaviors. These behaviors range from the individual struggling with an addiction to unhealthy patterns of relationships to a society that, through its basic institutions, inculcates violence as a way of life, most blatantly as the killing of civilians in the name of "national interest."

For Native Peoples, being dispossessed of our homelands through imperialism constitutes the greatest form of trauma, from which we have not recovered. Furthermore, colonialism – as a project of this imperialism perpetrated initially by Europeans and now Americans – remains a major cause of trauma for Native Peoples. Indeed, an honest view of the Native experience with colonialism can only be described in one word: holocaust. To argue otherwise maintains an important feature of the colonial project: outright denial. As recently as January 2003, many Americans, despite clear historical evidence to the contrary, thought that terms such as *imperialism* or *imperialists*, *colonialism* or *colonialists*, and *occupation* or *occupiers* did not apply to them. But the unprovoked attack against the Iraqi people and the subsequent occupation of Iraq by the Americans changed that, piercing the bubble of denial.

It may seem as if I digress from discussing trauma to Native Peoples when I speak of the invasion of Iraq. However, the American conduct toward the Iraqi people feels unnervingly familiar to Natives. When asked by *The Circle*, a Native newspaper serving Minneapolis–St. Paul, Minnesota, about my thoughts on the one-month-old war against Iraq, I remarked, "Native people understand what the Iraqi people are going through. Native Americans know about pre-emptive strikes, regime change, assets in trust, American occupation…. [M]y advice to the Iraqi people is 'hold on to your wallet.' … When they [the white leadership] talk about genocide or repression by a brutal regime [like Saddam Hussein's] … that's our history [too, but with the Americans]." This view, popular or not, contains hard-to-dispute truths that are basic to discussing the traumas Native Peoples have experienced. These truths are also central to healing among Natives and to a possible reconciliation with our *wasicu* colonizers, the American people.

Genocide Is THE Trauma

When I drive from the Rosebud Reservation to Mni Luzahan, I sometimes travel through the Pine Ridge Reservation. Having my share of relatives and friends living there, I stop for a chat, catch up on the latest happenings, and share what is going on within my tiospaye (see the *Glossary* at the end of this article). But then there is another visit that I sometimes make, namely, to Wounded Knee, where at least 300 unarmed Lakota women, children, and men were ruthlessly butchered by American soldiers in December 1890. Even after 110 years, it is a painful place. We still mourn at the mass grave. We still leave prayer offerings. My nation's grief over this massacre is immeasurable, and so is our anger and rage at this senseless murder of people, especially defenseless Elders, women, and children.

But Wounded Knee is not the only time when my people have cruelly suffered and died at American hands. When driving between St. Paul, Minnesota, and the Rosebud Reservation, I stop at Mankato, Minnesota, to honor the thirty-eight Dakota patriots who were hanged in December 1862. This public execution is the largest revenge killing of its kind carried out in the United States. Moreover, the hanging is part of a larger story. At Fort Snelling, Minnesota, approximately 1,700 Dakota, primarily women and children, were interned. This mass internment is arguably the forerunner of both the concentration camps and the detention centers of modern times. In November 1862 prior to their internment, these 1,700 Dakota were forcibly marched along a route that is part of my drive. Our oral tradition describes this horrific 150-mile march: "An unknown number of men, women, and children died along the way from beatings and other assaults perpetrated by both [American] soldiery and [white] citizens. Dakota people of today still do not know what became of their bodies."

Our colonizers have perpetrated many other horrific acts (both historic and contemporary) against us, the Oceti Sakowin Oyate. It is these acts that inform our understanding of what a white leader like George W. Bush really means when he brags to his fellow colonizers about bringing "American justice" to those who resist imperialism. A candid assessment of the wasicu attitude toward Native Peoples readily shows that they always believed Native Peoples to be expendable in order to preserve their Master Narrative as Occupier.[1]

Not surprisingly, this Native holocaust receives very little attention from colonial-based institutions. An education, public or private, in the United States grudgingly concedes that Columbus did not "discover" America but avoids talking about genocide. For example, using qualified terminology, such as "Indian Removal," textbooks minimize the ethnic-cleansing of thousands of Native Peoples east of the Mississippi River. By contrast, the

---

[1] See Richard Drinnon, *Facing West: The Metaphysics of Indian-Hating and Empire-Building* (New York: New American Library, 1980). He establishes racism as the critical link between Euramericans' "settlement" in Native North America and their expansionism on a global scale.

Cherokee People who were on the receiving end of this policy – and who to this day still suffer from it – have a more appropriate and descriptive term: "The Trail of Tears."

The horrific truth of this ethnic cleansing of the Cherokee people – the truth that textbooks avoid telling – staggers the imagination and closely parallels the Germans' twentieth-century policy toward the Jews:[2]

> This history of this removal… may well exceed in weight of the grief and pathos any other passage in American history. Even the much-sung exile of the Acadians falls far behind it in its sum of death and misery. Under [General Winfield] Scott's orders, the troops were disposed at various points throughout the Cherokee country, where stockade forts were erected for gathering in and holding the Indians preparatory to removal. From these, squads of troops were sent to search out with rifle and bayonet every small cabin hidden away in the coves or by the sides of the mountain streams, to seize and bring in as prisoners all the occupants, however or wherever they might be found.
>
> Families at dinner were startled by the sudden gleams of bayonets in the doorway and rose up to be driven with blows and oaths along the weary miles of trail that led to the stockade. Men were seized in their field or going along the road, women were taken from their wheels and children from their play. In many cases… they saw their homes in flames, fired by the lawless rabble that followed on the heels of the soldiers to loot and pillage. So keen were these outlaws on the scent that in some instances they were driving off the cattle and other stock of the Indians almost before the soldiers had fairly started their owners in the other direction…. To prevent escape [of the Cherokee] the soldiers had been ordered to approach and surround each house, so far as possible, to come upon the occupants without warning.[3]

---

[2] See Daniel Johan Goldhagen, *Hitler's Willing Executioners: Ordinary Germans and the Holocaust* (New York: Random House, 1996) and Ward Churchill, *A Little Matter of Genocide: Holocaust and Denial in the Americas 1492 to Present* (San Francisco: City Lights Books, 1997). These are parallel works, showing normal, everyday people as participants in holocausts. Goldhagen shows ordinary Germans as perpetrators against the Jews, while Churchill shows ordinary Americans as perpetrators against Natives. Also, see Elizabeth Cook-Lynn, *Anti-Indianism in Modern America: A Voice from Tatekeya's Earth* (Urbana, IL: University of Illinois Press, 2001). She equates anti-Indianism in North America with Germany's anti-Semitism under Hitler.

[3] James Mooney, *Myths of the Cherokee*, Part I, 19th Annual Report (Washington: Bureau of American Ethnology, 1900), 130.

These and countless other actions by the colonizers to exterminate Native Peoples go untold and unquestioned. In fact, when these acts are recounted, they are viewed as a given – something unfortunate but nonetheless accepted – under the rubric of manifest destiny or Darwin's "survival of the fittest."

Like the Cherokee, my people have experienced their share of lethal Native-hating from the wasicu. Successful armed resistance to the annexation of our land from around 1850 to 1877 provided white imperialists with an excuse to commit genocide as the final solution to their vexing "Sioux Problem." In his governor's address to Minnesota's state legislators, white leader Alexander Ramsey declared in September 1862 that, "The Sioux Indians [Dakota] of Minnesota must be exterminated or driven forever beyond the borders of the state." Following Ramsey's ethnic-cleansing call, ordinary Americans in Minnesota, like the ordinary Germans who answered Hitler's call to exterminate Jews seventy years later, saw to it that any Dakota found in the state became prime candidates for white bloodlust.

Not long after Ramsey declared his ethnic-cleansing policy, white military leaders believed a display of deadly force would intimidate the Oceti Sakowin Oyate. Hence, white general Patrick Connor issued a directive to the 3,100 American soldiers in the 1865 Powder River expedition: "You will not receive overtures of peace or submission from Indians [Lakota, Cheyenne, and Arapaho] but will attack and kill every male Indian over twelve years of age." Successful resistance by the Oceti Sakowin Oyate ended this expedition, but it furthered a campaign to subjugate us. In December 1866, after the Oceti Sakowin Oyate led a stunning defeat of the Americans, another white military leader, William Sherman, wrote to his white superior, President Grant: "We [the white colonizers] must act with vindictive earnestness against the Sioux, even to their extermination, men, women, and children."

In the wasicu version of these events, the Oceti Sakowin Oyate are portrayed as the ruthless perpetrators who deserve to be killed for having committed terrible harms against the poor, innocent white "pioneers and settlers." This version disregards the factual record, which shows that ordinary whites were *regularly* violating all norms of human decency – breaking treaties, trespassing, stealing property, committing murder, and carrying out other depredations – and that we (along with other Native Peoples) were simply defending ourselves against extermination.

When wasicu are confronted with this horrific record, their standard reply is to dismiss this period as an aberration or simply as an unenlightened episode in the colonizer's otherwise glorious history. At other times, like the notorious Abu Ghraib prison scandal in Iraq, far too many wasicu use the "few bad apples" line to explain away atrocities and to absolve themselves of any responsibility. The use of the "bad apple" line is not unknown to the Oceti Sakowin Oyate. We have many stories of the torture and death that occurred in white-run boarding schools, white-run insane asylums, white-run hospitals, white-run prisons, and white border towns. By invoking the "few bad apples" dodge, our colonizers somehow fail to admit or acknowledge their role in these institutions. In other words, white society and its imperial system turns a blind eye to the homicide or torture of colonized people.

Reality, of course, bites deep into the occupier's sanitized story of their "pioneering and settling" of Native North America. Because Oceti Sakowin Oyate patriots continue to challenge the Americans' presence in our land, the cultural programming of a latter-day Ramsey, Connor, and Sherman to kill Indians can reemerge, as it did in 1973. Once again, our colonizers' response to our acts of self-determination at Wounded Knee was to militarily prepare for invasion. In addition to the "17 APCs, 130,000 rounds of M-16 ammunition, 41,000 rounds of M-1 ammunition, 24,000 flares, 12 M-79 grenade launchers, 600 cases of C-S gas, 100 rounds of M-40 high explosives, as well as helicopters, Phantom jets, and personnel" made available to its surrogates,[4] the military also "had billeted a fully uniformed and armed assault unit on twenty-four hour alert."[5]

The authorization to use this much lethal force against the comparatively defenseless Native Peoples at Wounded Knee reaffirmed the American aphorism that "the only good Indian is a dead Indian." It also reminded a dismayed world that, for Native Peoples, physical extermination is our constant companion.[6] In the post-termination era (1968-present), rather than subjugating us, this invasion served as a political watershed and rekindled our national desire to end our colonization.

Despite the overwhelming record documenting the Oceti Sakowin Oyate's claim that a holocaust transpired – and is transpiring – here in Native North America, another typical reaction by our colonizers is to victimize those subjected to the holocaust with misrepresentations. For example, the official line characterizes the 1890 Wounded Knee Massacre as a "battle."

---

[4] Rex Weyler, *Blood of the Land: The Government and Corporate War against the American Indian Movement* (New York: Everest House Publishers, 1982), 81.
[5] Ibid.
[6] White military leader Sheridan is credited with the statement: "The only good Indians I ever saw were dead."

As evidence, colonizers cite the twenty-nine Congressional Medals of Honor bestowed upon the "brave" American soldiers who waged that "fight," perhaps making this so-called battle the most highly awarded in U.S. military history. With so many medal-of-honor recipients, how could Wounded Knee be anything but a battle, right?

Not so. Many of our ancestors survived the soldiers' butchery and lived to tell about it. Based on the survivors' accounts, the Oceti Sakowin Oyate's oral tradition of what happened at Wounded Knee differs remarkably from the official record of our colonizers. The scant candid testimony that does exist about Wounded Knee among those colonizers who were at the scene and who were willing to speak corroborates our claim that Wounded Knee was not merely an "unfortunate incident." Their voices support the larger claim that a policy of genocide was directed against the Oceti Sakowin Oyate. First Lieutenant James D. Mann, for instance, admitted on his deathbed that by yelling "Fire men! Fire!" he gave the order to shoot indiscriminately into the Lakota who were encircled by the soldiers.[7]

The night before the massacre, the soldiers who would participate in the next day's slaughter purchased whiskey from Edward Assay, a white Indian trader.[8] Another man, a freighter, confessed to Reverend James Garvey that he never forgave himself for delivering the whiskey to the soldiers.[9] Several years later, the bodies of the dead soldiers were exhumed from their initial graves at Wounded Knee to be reburied elsewhere. These corpses told their own gruesome story: "The attending physician expected to find only the bones but was shocked to find bodies intact after so many years. His only explanation for this... [was] that the soldiers had consumed large quantities of alcohol and the alcohol preserved the bodies."[10]

Naturally, the Oceti Sakowin Oyate assume that apologists will name alcohol as the culprit and thus once again deflect responsibility away from the American empire. Yet a competing story – our story – to the occupier's narrative remains. A mass murder of women, children, and men at Wounded Knee occurred and constitutes, at the very least, a revenge killing for a real battle in which nearly 300 wasicu soldiers died at the hands of the Lakota, Cheyenne, and Arapaho fourteen years earlier.

In light of the statements by Ramsey, Connor, and Sherman, however, the 1890 massacre at Wounded Knee constitutes far more. It represents a

---

[7] Renee Sansom Flood's 14 April 1990 letter to Legia Spicer, director of South Dakota Peace and Justice Center.
[8] Ibid.
[9] Ibid.
[10] Ibid.

calculated, strategic action on our colonizers' part to commit genocide. With the exception of the United States and a handful of other countries, the world has come to understand genocide or the extermination of a people in a precise way. This internationally agreed-upon understanding forms a basis for talking about a Native holocaust and explains why our colonizers refuse to accept that a holocaust ever occurred.

Shortly after World War II ended, the "civilized" world learned, much to its "morbid fascination,"[11] how the Germans had committed atrocities that, over a span of a few years, caused the physical extermination of about 6,000,000 Jews. Responding to the outcry against this massive premeditated killing, the American, British, French, and Russian governments had, as victors, established the Nuremberg Tribunal. The main purpose of this tribunal was to prosecute the Germans responsible for these atrocities, and subsequently several Germans were held to account for the Jewish Holocaust. The tribunal convicted and sentenced them for committing the greatest of all crimes against humanity: genocide. Not long after the tribunal ended its work, the United Nations took up the question of genocide. A genocide treaty was eventually adopted by the UN Assembly in 1948. For the Oceti Sakowin Oyate, however, the UN's adoption began a real nightmare: the Americans' unwillingness to comply with the genocide treaty. We *know* why.

It is the definition of genocide that most worries the occupiers of our land. Article II of the treaty defines genocide "as resulting from the following categories or acts committed with the intent to destroy, in whole or in part, a national, ethnical [sic], racial, or religious group":

1. killing members of a group;
2. causing serious bodily or mental harm to members of the group;
3. deliberately inflicting on the group conditions of life calculated to bring about its physical destruction in whole or in part;
4. imposing measures intended to prevent births within the group; and
5. forcibly transferring children of the group to another group.

The Oceti Sakowin Oyate can easily produce a list of grievances perpetrated by ordinary whites and their leaders that fall within each of the five categories or that represent combinations thereof. Of the first recognized act, the 1854 Blue Water and the 1890 Wounded Knee massacres are but two of the more well-known killings. Critics, of course, dismiss these massacres as beyond the treaty's scope. Because they happened a long time ago, the colonizers' descendants presumably cannot

---

[11] This characterization is Vine Deloria's.

be held accountable. Well, this attempt to flee responsibility collapses, because acts of genocide have no statute of limitation, especially when these acts have intergenerational consequences.

Moreover, the Oceti Sakowin Oyates' independence movement in the early 1970s broke through the colonial facade of respecting human rights. Our colonizers called in the proverbial "cavalry," reminding us that the time is not past when "Indian killing" can be a national pastime. Much to our discomfort, the Oceti Sakowin Oyate are now watching our colonizers refit the "hostile Indian" image to the "Arab or Muslim terrorists" of today. Here again, "killing members of a group" remains entirely acceptable to Americans in promoting their "national" interests.

As for the other genocide categories, our oral tradition reveals that our colonizers have waged and continue to wage a campaign of terror throughout our homeland. During the 1970s, this terrorism did not preclude killing our traditional Lakota people who viewed the American occupation of our homeland as illegal or those who wanted our colonizers to honor the 1868 Treaty of Fort Laramie. Traditional people who moved away from the Indian Reorganization Act (IRA) governments politically and toward self-determination were silenced through intimidation.[12] Indeed, the colonial administration (the FBI, U.S. Marshals, the BIA, the military, South Dakota, and the courts) refused to fully investigate, apprehend, indict, or prosecute those who threatened our families with physical harm, death, or some other form of reprisal (e.g., incarceration). Such conduct by our colonizers contributed to the atmosphere of terror.

Understandably, the five acts that constitute the crime of genocide make a colonizer like the United States, given its horrific behavior toward Native Peoples, feel – as it should – more than a bit uncomfortable. However, two of the treaty's articles, Articles III and IX, are without question unbearable for our colonizers. Article III makes genocidal acts punishable crimes. These acts include

1. genocide itself;
2. the conspiracy to commit genocide;
3. the direct and public incitement to commit genocide;
4. the attempt to commit genocide; and

---

[12] These "governments" came about in 1934 when Congress, the legislative body of our colonizers, enacted the Indian Reorganization Act. Section 16 of the act provides that Native communities can organize governments under a constitution. However, these governments require the "Manner of Review" in which any actions (e.g., ordinances) are subject to review and approval by our colonizers. Our colonizers applied this exact governmental blueprint to the Iraqi people.

5. complicity in genocide.

Together, Articles II and III frame our understanding of how the international community judges a state and its nationals for engaging in genocide. However, it is Article IX that our colonizers most fear. This article provides that questions or disputes surrounding the treaty's interpretation, application (which includes a state's responsibility for genocide), and fulfillment can be submitted to the International Court of Justice (ICJ). For many Natives and others who have studied the genocide treaty, this article is key.

Not surprisingly, our colonizers "ratified" the treaty on one blanket condition; namely, that they reserve unto themselves the right of exemption from any of the treaty's provisions. In particular, our colonizers have exempted themselves from Article IX. Vine Deloria Jr. wryly commented that this acrobatic political move would have allowed even Germany to go scot-free for the atrocities it had committed against the Jews.[13] In effect, by "ratifying" the genocide treaty so conditionally, our colonizers proclaimed to a stunned world their right to engage in genocidal conduct against the Oceti Sakowin Oyate as well as every other Native nation. This stance by the Americans is indeed a Native Peoples' nightmare and must be rebuked. Given that our colonizers have now manipulated the ratification of a document so fundamental as the right to exist as peoples, how do we proceed? Before tackling this question, we must ponder a more basic question: Are our colonizers so spiritually and morally bankrupt that they lack a "making-itright" sensibility whenever it involves Native Peoples? With few exceptions, the Oceti Sakowin Oyate will emphatically answer "yes." Such brutal honesty comes at a price, though. It exposes our colonizers' epic settlement story – their reason for being here – to be nothing more than a self-serving fable. How can such a fable justify the cost our colonizers have extracted from us? This truth-telling invariably makes them defensive, which they express as either extreme anger or denial or both.

Truth and Reconciliation: The Antidote for Colonizers

From time to time, though, a colonizer or two (so far, never enough to reach a critical mass for change in dealing with Native Peoples) has struggled with this basic question of moral bankruptcy. For instance, during the heyday of the termination era, hundreds of thousands of Natives

---

[13] Vine Deloria, Jr., *Behind the Trail of Broken Treaties: An Indian Declaration of Independence* (Dell Publishing Co., 1974), 242.

were forced into mainstream society so that our colonizers could carry out a massive land grab. Harold Fey, a white writer and an editor for The Christian Century, was disturbed at what he saw happening to Native Peoples. In March 1955, Fey, with sarcasm, posed some unsettling questions to his fellow settlers:

> Why don't the Indians trust us? We mean well toward them. We want them to succeed. Indeed, we would be glad if the Indians were just like ourselves, and what more could they desire than that? We are not like some nations we could mention – deceivers, slave-drivers, treaty-breakers. We are upright people, and it irritates us a little to have to say so. Some of us are in the habit of referring to the United States as a Christian nation. So if the Indian does not trust us, it must be because he has some unfortunate defect in his own character, such as innate suspicion. If so, that is something we should help him overcome.... These things we say to ourselves to calm the uneasiness which clings to the fact that we are not trusted by the original Americans, who have known us longer than anybody else.[14]

Nearly fifty years have passed since Fey posed these questions, and yet his challenge remains unmet. What are our colonizers willing to do in order to start building a much-needed trust? We still await an *authentic* dialogue with our colonizers, one that would even begin to address the numerous harms, past and present, perpetrated against the Oceti Sakowin Oyate.

To be sure, others since Fey have wrestled with the Colonial Question with respect to Native Peoples. In February 1990, white leader George Mickelson (South Dakota governor) proclaimed a year of reconciliation:

> WHEREAS, As the State of South Dakota celebrates the beginning of its second century, we must also remember that statehood was a very sad time for the Native American; and,
>
> WHEREAS, Two tragic events, the killing of Sitting Bull, on December 15, 1890, and the Wounded Knee massacre on December 29, 1890, occurred just 13 months after South Dakota became a state; and,
>
> WHEREAS, The anniversary of these tragic conflicts, as well as the celebration of 100 years of statehood, offer an opportunity for South Dakotans to learn more about the life and culture of the Dakota-Lakota people; and,

---

[14] "Our National Indian Policy," *The Christian Century*, 30 March 1955, 72 (13): 395.

WHEREAS, Strife between the cultures in South Dakota has, for 100 years, been of grave concern and continues to be of great concern; and, WHEREAS, Any improvement in cultural understanding in the past can be attributed to the work of the Indian and non-Indian people of South Dakota who have striven to understand our differences and to educate those of us who have grown up together but who have never made the effort to bridge the cultural gap; and, WHEREAS, A statewide effort to develop trust and respect between Indians and non-Indians can, and must, include participation from the private and public sector, from churches and church associations, from tribal and state governments, and from individuals and community organizations; and, WHEREAS, That mutuality of interest provides a sound basis for constructive change, given a shared commitment to achieving our goals of equal opportunity, social justice and economic prosperity; and, WHEREAS, By celebrating our cultural differences and drawing on those differences for the betterment of all, we can create a new respect among our citizens: NOW, THEREFORE, I, GEORGE S. MICKELSON, Governor of the State of South Dakota, do hereby proclaim, with the advice and consent of the state's tribal leaders, 1990 as a YEAR OF RECONCILIATION in South Dakota, and call on our citizens, both Indian and non-Indian, to look for every opportunity to lay aside fears and mistrust, to build friendships, to join together and take part in shared cultural activities, to learn about one another, to have fun with one another, and to begin a process of mutual respect and understanding that will continue to grow into South Dakota's second hundred years.

Without flinching, the governor noted that the resident colonizers had just finished "celebrating" *their* 100 years of statehood, and I suppose statehood was, to put it mildly, "a very sad time" for my people. After all, prior to South Dakota's establishment as a state on 2 November 1889, the colonizers' ancestors had cleared a path to present-day statehood by imposing two illegal partitions of our 26,000,000-acre homeland, shown on older maps as the Great Sioux Reservation. These two partitions resulted in the dubious "annexation" of our homeland by our colonizer(s).

The first partition occurred in February 1877. To this day, the 7,300,000 acres of partitioned land are officially acknowledged as stolen property, and as stolen property the Oceti Sakowin Oyate demand its rightful return.

The colonizers, however, view the land's return as antithetical to their Occupier Narrative, and so instead of returning the 7.3 million acres, they have insulted us by offering money to justify their theft.

Despite this 128-year (and still counting) wrongful taking, despite the commercial development of the land, and despite the restrictions placed on our access to it, the Oceti Sakowin Oyate maintain their relationship to He Sapa. Unlike our colonizers, we are intimately familiar with He Sapa's many ancient places, calling them either Wamaka Ognaka Onakizin or Tatanka Tacante.[15] Indeed, He Sapa is fondly known as "the heart of our home, and the home of our heart."[16] Because of our love for He Sapa – and to underscore the unhealed wound between us and our colonizers – we continually refuse to accept any of the monetary compensation that our colonizers have offered for their admitted theft of our land. As the center of our spiritual universe, He Sapa is not for sale, and we remain committed to its rightful return.

The second partition, called the Great Sioux Agreement Act, happened in March 1889, eight months before Dakota Territory became the two states of South and North Dakota. With 18,700,000 acres remaining of the Great Sioux Reservation, our colonizers wanted between 9,000,000 to 11,000,000 acres of the reservation "opened." One colonizer admitted why a second partition was desired just twelve years after the first one: "One of the obstacles to achieving [South Dakota] Statehood was the huge reservation separating the Black Hills and the settlements easts [sic] of the Missouri River. With the news that the Dakota Indians had agreed to sell eleven million acres of land for $1.25 an acre, South Dakota became a state on November 2, 1889."[17] Depicting the Oceti Sakowin Oyate (the "Dakota Indians") as an "obstacle," the colonizer's story is obviously skewed against my people, and our response to this lie is our usual refrain: "So what else is new?"

The one story purposely omitted from the lie concerns the "land sale" and how it came about. Not surprisingly, the Occupier Narrative fails to explain what made us "agree to sell" so much land in the first place. Fortunately, Deloria fills in the crucial information:

---

[15] See S. Bradley Bill, 705, section 11. These two designations are generic names for specific ceremonial or sacred sites.

[16] David Blue Thunder's statement, see Ronald Goodman, *Lakota Star Knowledge* (Rosebud Sioux Reservation: Sinte Gleska University, 1992), 14.

[17] Don C. Clowser, *Dakota Indian Treaties: From Nomad To Reservation* (Deadwood, SD: Don C. Clowser, 1974), 245.

Some years after the great plains wars, pressure grew to allot the Great Sioux reservation which extended over almost all of western South Dakota. Thousands of [land] hungry whites demanded that the vast reservation be allotted and the surplus lands be opened to white settlement. Thus it was that General Crook, "Three Stars[,]" was sent out to negotiate the Great Sioux Agreement of 1889. With Crook sitting at the table[,] the Sioux were reminded that if they didn't agree to cede their lands[,] the Army would come in and exterminate them. In spite of such pressure by the United States government[,] less than 10 per cent of the adult males signed the paper agreeing to the cession.

Claiming total accord [with Article 12 of the 1868 Ft. Laramie Treaty], the negotiators rushed to Washington and pushed the agreement through Congress as a statute.[18]

In other words, the critical and contested point about these two land partitions – "ceded land" in colonial-speak – concerns their legal status. Article 12 of the 1868 Fort Laramie Treaty is clear about what the Oceti Sakowin Oyate require before any land cession could be considered valid:

No treaty for the cession of any portion or part of the [Great Sioux] reservation herein described which may be held in common shall be of any validity or force as against the said Indians ["Sioux Nation" in colonial-speak], unless executed and signed by at least three-fourths of all the adult male Indians.

In the case of both partitionings, our colonizers utterly failed to obtain our consent, and any claim of legality is pure fiction. Without our approval, then, the Oceti Sakowin Oyate position is that the resident colonizers are illegal aliens and that their state, carved from the Great Sioux Reservation, is illegitimate.

The greatest difficulty of reconciliation, therefore, is that our colonizers – with whom we have sometimes developed close relationships – fail to see themselves as perpetuators or agents of the status quo. In an 11 March 1990 editorial, four weeks after the governor proposed reconciliation, the *Rapid City Journal* informed its readership that Mickelson "opposed negotiations to give land back to the Sioux." Here, again, we are not surprised by how our colonizers frame the land return debate, missing the bigger picture necessary for reconciliation. "To give land back" assumes

---

[18] Vine Deloria, Jr., *Of Utmost Good Faith* (San Francisco: Straight Arrow Books, 1971), 52.

that the land rightfully belonged to our colonizers, but the record shows otherwise. Because the land in question is stolen property, *the only thing our colonizers are in a position to do is to return – not to give back – the stolen property.*

No doubt, what I have just written will offend many people, including my own to some degree.[19] Yet an inescapable component of reconciliation is a commitment to truth-telling. On 6 April 1990, not long after the February 1990 proclamation, Ada Deer, chair of the Native American Rights Fund (NARF), responded to a *New York Times* article on South Dakota's attempt at reconciliation. Addressing Jack Rosenthal, the page editor for the newspaper, Ada Deer commended Mickelson for issuing the proclamation, but she admonished both peoples with a reminder that more is needed than recognizing the existence of a problem: "If this is to be a sincere effort toward genuine reconciliation, the historic and compelling injustices involving broken treaties and broken promises must be addressed. Let us remember that actions speak louder than words."[20]

Moreover, Deer eloquently elaborated what sincerity and genuineness might, on the part of our colonizers, really entail:

> The first step that must be taken by the State to begin this healing process is to honor the terms of the treaties which guaranteed that the Black Hills would remain part of the land of the Great Sioux Nation. Federal legislation to return federally held land in the Black Hills must be supported to close this open wound bleeding the bodies, minds and spirits of the Sioux people. Second, the State must recognize the sovereignty of each tribal government in South Dakota. This means respecting their authority and right to govern their land and peoples without State encroachment.
>
> These and other issues underlying the historic tensions between Indians and non-Indians in South Dakota must be seriously addressed. We must not permit South Dakota to proclaim the desire for *harmony* in theory while doing nothing in *practice*…. Will South Dakota and its people demonstrate their humanity by showing their compassion and making a commitment to resolving these longstanding injustices?[21]

---

[19] Being brainwashed by colonization, we excuse the shortcomings of our colonial masters and become uncomfortable when confronted with the truth about them. As colonial subjects, we are often employed by our colonizers to dismiss or marginalize those who support an anti-colonial agenda, such as reconciliation. But this is another story.

[20] Deer's 6 April 1990 letter to Rosenthal.

[21] Ibid.

The wording of Mickelson's proclamation, however, reveals why his efforts would fall short of such genuine reconciliation. Most likely, he was taking his cue from his fellow colonizers who desired something less than the decolonized truth.

By May 1990, the much-heralded "Year of Reconciliation" showed clear signs of failure, precisely because our colonizers failed to heed Deer's warning that reconciliation must "go beyond organizing pow-wows and feel-good feasts."[22] The state's Reconciliation Commission set up by Mickelson dodged contentious issues, such as land return or the political reform of colonization, and instead promoted warm-fuzzy projects, such as public education campaigns on various topics of interest. By contrast, the South Dakota Peace and Justice Center (SDPJC) planned a series of authentic dialogues between the colonizers and the Oceti Sakowin Oyate.[23] These initial dialogues produced the not-too-surprising litmus test that the Oceti Sakowin Oyate use to gauge the sincerity of reconciliation: land return as the core issue between our two peoples.

Wasiglaki Istamni Yanpi

From this discussion about the historic relationship between the Oceti Sakowin Oyate and our colonizers and the ongoing impact of this history on contemporary relations, the ill-fated 1990 proclamation and the subsequent activities revealed how far our colonizers are from any meaningful reconciliation. Desmond Tutu, chair of South Africa's Truth and Reconciliation Commission, believes reconciliation is, at its best, a two-way street. The apology, the contrition, the confession, and the reparations are all to be borne by the perpetrator(s), and only then can the victim(s) move toward forgiveness.

While I believe this to be true – that reconciliation must begin with the colonizers – it does not mean we are hostages to their moral awakening, if indeed this should ever occur. We do not have to wait patiently and hope for a time when the colonizers-as-perpetrators will finally come to their senses. No, not even the most venerable Tutu believed in doing that. Such passivity would invite more abuse by not holding the perpetrators accountable.

---

[22] Ibid.

[23] Founded in 1979, the South Dakota Peace and Justice Center is a statewide organization whose members support work on social issues from a spiritual foundation.

So, in spite of our colonizers' unwillingness to engage in true reconciliation, we initiated our own healing from within the center of our nation's heart. The most well-known healing-from-within for the Oceti Sakowin Oyate happened in December 1990, exactly 100 years after the soldiers murdered our people at Wounded Knee. The Si Tanka Wokiksuye Ride retraced a route that the Si Tanka Oyate took after Tatanka Iyotaka, a beloved leader, was killed by wasicu surrogates on 15 December 1890 for resisting colonization. The purpose of this ride was "to bring the survivors of Chief Big Foot [Big Foot's people] out of mourning in 1990."[24] Standing among the hundreds of people at the massive burial site on that bitterly cold December day in 1990, I watched and prayed as the procession of riders rode their horses toward the mass grave. As the riders gathered at the grave, the emotions of immense grief, pain, and rage that we collectively experienced that day over the senseless slaughter of defenseless women, children, and men was as real and unbearable for us as it was for our ancestors on that same date a century before.

It was difficult to be there, to acknowledge what had happened to us as a people, and to honor those who have suffered since. The ride accomplished far more than it intended, however. Once all the riders and waiting crowd were gathered together, a Wiping of the Tears took place. Normally, this ceremony is conducted by community members for individuals or families who are in mourning over the loss of a loved one. The ceremony encourages the individual or family to participate once again in the community's life. It is our way of saying compassionately to a person in profound grief that she or he is deeply missed by the community and that without her or his participation in community activities, the community is, in some intangible way, less whole. In other words, the long-term grieving of one community member affects the whole community, and the Wiping of the Tears heals that grief.

Yet because we had experienced not only an individual and family loss but also a national loss as a result of trauma-by-colonization, we had no precedent for conducting a Wiping of the Tears ceremony of such magnitude. Who, we wondered, could wipe the tears of a nation? The Si Tatanka Wokiksuye Ride provided the answer to this difficult question. For the first time in our nation's memory, this ceremony was conducted by the traumatized for the traumatized. From that day onward, knowing that we survived the greatest of all holocausts in human history – namely, the 500-year unrelenting genocide of Native Peoples in North America – the Oceti Sakowin had returned. The holocaust is by no means over. It is

---

[24] Debra White Plume, "Voices from Bridger," *Si Tanka Wokiksuye Wowapi*, 30 March 1990 (1)(3): 1.

still being waged, but we no longer suffer within the silence of our pain and anger. Indeed, our colonizers are increasingly unsettled by our national resilience and national revitalization. Our very existence and survival are testaments that stand to haunt and confound them.

For example, as the quincentennial of Columbus's invasion was approaching and our colonizers were busily preparing to celebrate, the Oceti Sakowin Oyate's voice rose above the hoopla, reminding them that they were celebrating 500 years of genocide and that true reconciliation remained an unfinished task. When asked by the SDPJC what we had to say to our colonizers in 1992, Cheryl Crazy Bull explained how truth-telling can undo oppression:

> Conciliation. That is the word for whose image I search in 1992. We Indigenous people are presenting the truth about the genocide which occurs in Indian country. We must disclose the truth about the historic genocide in which millions of us have been killed by white people. We must relate how tribally specific cultural knowledge is lost or distorted due to white oppression…. We must reveal to white people how we experience poverty and poor living conditions void of beauty and connection to the Earth as one of the many masks which genocide wears…. These forms of genocide which we experience are not our own creation. They come to us from the Europeans who have been seeking to conquer and control us during the hundreds of years since the arrival of Columbus on our lands…. The process of conciliation – acceptance – is one of healing and learning. It is opening your eyes and ears to see us and hear the voices of Native peoples. It is stopping the individuals and institutions who oppress Native peoples…. Conciliation is not achieved without anger, sorrow, and pain. We who come from Unci Maka, our Grandmother Earth, have everything to gain by living in balance and harmony with all creation. The only thing we have to lose is our lives.[25]

This quincentennial statement represents an example of how the Oceti Sakowin Oyate's truth-telling has continued since December 1990. My people have conducted other truth-telling events, such as the Makato Wokiksuye Iyanka Pi and the Manipi Hena Owasin Wicunkiksuye Pi. The former is a 90-mile relay that is run annually in December from Fort Snelling to Mankato. The latter is a 150-mile walk that approximates the

---

[25] "Reconciliation" (Watertown, SD: South Dakota Peace and Justice Center, n.d.), 4.

route of the 1,700 Dakota women, children, and men who were force-marched from the Lower Sioux Reservation to Mankato to Fort Snelling. This walk is held in November, and its 150th year is currently being planned. The purpose for these events is the internal healing they provide for the Oceti Sakowin Oyate, since an important aspect of our healing includes telling the truth about the shameful ethnic-cleansing behavior of our colonizers.

When other opportunities arise, my people are quick to respond, since we take the responsibility to heal through truth-telling seriously. For instance, a "Call to the Oceti Sakowin" flyer was sent out in September 2004 to enlist our people and others in constructively engaging our colonizers around their bicentennial reenactment of their so-called Lewis and Clark Expedition. This reenactment celebrates American colonial occupation. The call powerfully challenged the wasicu narrative around the expedition – a narrative that has never allowed our voice to emerge:

> In the 1800's the Lakota encountered the Wasicu... Lewis & Clark Expedition. Now, America is holding a re-enactment of Lewis & Clark.... The U.S. has never addressed the stolen land, disease, genocide, & our sacred He Sapa (Black Hills).
>
> If the re-enactment continues on without the consent of the Lakota, just as our ancestors stood against the Lewis & Clark Expedition entry into Lakota territory, we, the descendants of the Free Lakota, will make a stand to tell the world about the 1851 & 1868 Ft. Laramie Treaties & how America fails to abide by its own laws.
>
> When we encounter the Lewis & Clark re-enactment of the original trespass, we call to all freedom thinking people of the Oceti Sakowin & all of our allies to stand in a sacred manner with a sovereign heart & send our message to the world: Honor the U.S. treaties with indigenous people on Turtle Island.

Such calls for direct action upset our colonizers, especially since their most recent imperialist expedition, the military occupation of Iraq, still begs for a resolution. One can imagine that Americans, as Fey noted, do in fact get more than a little irritated at having to say to the world that they really are an upright people and that they are not like "those others" who deceive the world. I guess, too, it is even more irritating to our wasicu colonizers when we point out that, "Well, yes, Saddam Hussein may have violated several UN resolutions as white leader George W. Bush alleged, but what about the nearly 400 treaties that the *American people* have unilaterally and arbitrarily broken with the hundreds of Native nations?" In other words, the existence and testimony of Native Peoples lay bare the hypocrisy and disingenuousness of our colonizers. Though our colonizers label others as "evil-doers," "thugs," or "killers," these labels fit them perfectly.

Restorative Worthiness and Decolonization

On 11 September the wasicu watched the destruction of the World Trade Center's twin towers by a handful of men with utter disbelief. In the days that followed, our colonizers invoked Pearl Harbor to emotionally frame what had just happened to them, but one would have to go back further than 7 December 1941 to find an event that had a comparable emotional impact. On 25 June 1876, the news of nearly 300 American soldiers dying within ninety minutes, the first-ever capture of the U.S. colors in battle, and the death of Custer – a hero of "legendary" fame among whites – stunned the colonizers in much the same way as the collapse of the Twin Towers did. After all, our colonizers were in the cant of celebrating – albeit at a time when post-civil war politics were threatening to undo the Union – their 100 years of "independence." Thousands of spectators had flocked to the Centennial Exhibition in Philadelphia that opened on 10 May and were treated to the imperial themes of "manifest destiny" and the "progress" of white civilization. The colonizers were also engulfed in a presidential contest that, for the first time ever, would award the office to a candidate who lost the popular vote but won the electoral college.

In this intense glow of white hubris, the startling news that a preemptive American strike against anti-colonial forces had ended in disaster was met with complete dismay. There was an automatic, 11-September-like call for vengeance and an all-out retaliation against the Oceti Sakowin Oyate. This "righteous call" overlooked the fact that my people, like other nonwestern or colonized peoples since, had had the temerity to resist subjugation.

What is the relevance of this story to the larger discussion of trauma, reconciliation, and reparative or restorative justice? As the colonizers helplessly witnessed the destruction of their World Trade Center and the damage to their Pentagon as well as learned that either their White House or their Capitol had been targeted, they experienced a little of what it means to be traumatized. After all, the colonizers' primary economic, military, and political icons were being assaulted. Because their emotional and psychological well-being have been intimately tied to these icons, the colonizers felt – much as their ancestors believed as they reacted to the Oceti Sakowin Oyates' defeat of Custer in the summer of 1876 – that their "way of life" was being fundamentally called into question.

Indeed, almost all the white students in one of my classes that September morning were frightened and expressed a well-known "this isn't really happening" trauma response. They wanted to talk about "their" feelings. As I have said, we of the Oceti Sakowin Oyate do not miss opportunities for truth-telling, and 11 September provided one of my more memorable moments of teaching. As the white students were expressing their fears, I purposely redirected the discussion, stating that, as a Native, I understood something about the experience of trauma. I mentioned the destruction of our cultural and spiritual icons and social institutions – our way of life – through unprovoked attacks against my people by the Americans. Feeling empowered, Black students spoke eloquently of their ongoing emotional struggles over slavery, Jim Crow, racial profiling, and now incarceration at the hands of whites. Other nonwhite students expressed similar feelings about how they felt in a society that condones racist behaviors.

Before long, the white students' emotions shifted from anxiety to anger precisely because we did not privilege their trauma. Their trauma on that day did not receive any more attention than anyone else's, neither was their trauma treated as somehow special simply because they were white. No, much to the colonizers' angst, their trauma was not viewed as different, and that is evidently what upset them the most. The lesson learned through the shared truth-telling that day showed many people of color just how long a journey the colonizers would have to travel before reconciliation, reparations, or restorative justice would have any real chance of success.

Sadly, in the years following this lesson, it seems our colonizers have learned little about anyone's trauma but their own. In the aftermath of 11 September, the so-called public rallied to support the victims' families through various relief measures. From an Oceti Sakowin Oyate perspective, Angela Cavender Wilson addressed what one measure – the September 11th Victims' Compensation Fund – means to non-Natives on one hand and to Native Peoples on the other:

> By the time the deadline for filing passed, 95% of the victims [individuals or relatives of deceased individuals who were killed or physically injured as a result of the... aircraft crashes of September 1, 2001] applied for their piece of the government compensation program. Save the voices who rejected the government offer and are pursuing lawsuits seeking accountability for their suffering, there has been no public outcry regarding the use of federal funds to compensate these families. Indeed, the victims of 9-11 have been deemed worthy,

their suffering understandable, and their need for compensation justified.[26]

State compensation satisfies the public's sense of duty and justice to aid those – the worthy victims – who directly suffered from the events of 11 September. Yet U.S. history discloses many millions of victims of white terrorist acts. Wilson uses this history to examine the law's corollary messages about who is worthy of compensation and who is not:

> If American compensation to victims of suffering is a measure of worthiness, then the Indigenous Peoples in the United States who have suffered acts of terrorism on our lands, persons, and resources too numerous to count are apparently considered unworthy.... [T]he pain suffered by Indigenous Peoples in the United States has been forgotten, considered a thing of the past, and become normalized. Rather than acknowledging that there has been a terrible wrong, colonization has imposed on us responsibility for our own pain. We have been taught that our current predicament is a consequence of our own shortcomings, that we are to blame. While policies of genocide, ethnic cleansing, and ethnocide have been perpetuated against us, and our lands and resources have been threatened decade after decade, century after century, we are taught that we are to blame or that we should just get over it. There has been no adequate formal body to address our suffering or acknowledgment that we have been wronged by the policies of the United States.[27]

Other compensatory measures taken by white leaders on behalf of their "people," like the preemptive military attack against innocent Iraqi people, demonstrate our colonizers' firm belief that their pain and suffering are second to none and therefore that the pain and suffering that they have experienced must be paid for not only with money but also with the resources and blood of others. At their core, these 11-September-inspired measures are straightforward acts of vengeance against those who dare to resist American hegemony and hubris in their homelands. The Oceti Sakowin Oyate recognize the pattern. We know of what we speak, for after more than a century, we are still resisting American colonization.

Moreover, while we firmly believe in reconciliation and reparative or restorative justice, we have yet to receive any genuine or sincere

---

[26] "Reviewing Our Suffering: Indigenous Decolonization and a United States Truth Commission" (Unpublished manuscript, 2004), 1–2.
[27] Ibid., 2.

acknowledgment from our perpetrators – the wasicu – for the egregious harms they have committed and continue to commit against us Native Peoples. Even so, like the freighter who genuinely and sincerely confessed to having never forgiven himself for delivering the whiskey to the soldiers, our colonizers may one day find it within themselves to do the same. I suspect at some future time when this happens – when our former colonizers (yes, former) come to their senses and want to confess, apologize, ask for forgiveness, and be reconciled with us – it will be because the world they inhabit has drastically changed.

Herein lies the tragedy for our colonizers. The Oceti Sakowin Oyate will not have waited for that day but will long since have gone forward in our revitalization. As time passes, what our former colonizers do or fail to do will have virtually no impact on us either way. The paths of healing and decolonization could be shared, but we will not allow either path to be slowed by our colonizers' failure to acknowledge our worthiness as human beings. The window for engaging in genuinely reconciliatory process is open but closing. The permanent loss of this opportunity is the greatest risk our present day colonizers take by failing to act now.

Glossary

He Sapa: Black Hills.
Makato Wokiksuye Iyanka Pi: Blue Earth Run To Remember.
Manipi Hena Owasin Wicunkiksuye Pi: Remember Those Who Walked.
Mni Luzahan Wakpa: Swift Water. A traditional gathering place of the Oceti Sakowin Oyate in the He Sapa, now occupied by wasicu and called Rapid City.
Oceti Sakowin Oyate: People of Seven Council Fires. These terms describe our socio-political organization. We comprise the Sisitunwan, Wahpekute, Wahpetunwan, Mdewakantunwan, Ihanktunwan, Ihanktunwani, and Titunwan. The first four Fires reside in the eastern part of our traditional homeland and speak Dakota. The next two Fires reside in the central portion of our homeland and speak Nakota. The last Fire resides in the western part of our homeland and speaks Lakota.
Si Tanka Oyate Wokiksuye: Remembering Big Foot's People.
Tatanka Iyotaka: Sitting Buffalo. A Hunkpapa Lakota who helped lead the Oceti Sakowin Oyate at the Battle of the Little Big Horn and who was later assassinated on 15 December 1890 by U.S. surrogates. Erroneously translated as Sitting Bull.

216

Tatanka TaCante: The Heart of the Buffalo. A term denoting traditional or ceremonial sites located within the He Sapa.

Tiospaye: Related Community. The Oceti Sakowin kinship system's basic unit of community and local governance. Sometimes translated as extended family.

Wamaka Ognaka Onakizin: The Sanctuary of Everything That Is. A term denoting a space for living things who have a sacred relationship with the Oceti Sakowin Oyate.

Wasicu: Fat Takers. A term describing the behavior of whites or Americans. In Oceti Sakowin Oyate thought and philosophy, "taking the fat" connotes hoarding beyond what is necessary, being stingy. It also connotes a glib tongue, dishonesty, and mercenary habits.

Wasigla Ki Istamni Yanpi: Wiping of the Tears. A ceremony conducted for persons grieving from the trauma experienced by the loss of a loved one.

"Authenticity," or the Lesson of Little Tree
Henry Louis Gates, Jr.

Originally published in *The New York Times Book Review*, 1991.
Reprinted in *The Henry Louis Gates, Jr. Reader*. Ed. Abby Wolf. New
York: Basic Civitas Books, 2012, pp. 515-22.

*Henry Louis Gates, Jr. (b. 1950), is the Director of the Hutchins Center
for African and African American Research at Harvard University, where
he is also a professor. Gates grew up in Keyser, West Virginia, and
completed his undergraduate degree in history at Yale in 1973. He earned
his Ph.D. from the University of Cambridge in 1979. He is a prolific writer
and cultural critic, and he is also known for his Emmy-Award winning
documentary films and series, including* Finding Your Roots *and* Africa's
Great Civilizations.

*Why we are reading this: Do women writers represent an authentic
"women's voice"? Do African-American novelists write in a particular
"African-American" style? In 1991 it was learned that a classic Native
American autobiography (*The Education of Little Tree, *published in
1976) was actually written by a white supremacist and racist. In the piece
below, written soon after the Little Tree revelation, Gates reminds us that
gifted writers can learn to represent the points of view of people very
different from themselves – people of a different gender, race, class,
religion, sexual orientation, or nationality. We learn that some of the most
popular "first-person" accounts of slave life published before the civil war
were written by white abolitionists and historians, or by blacks who had
never been slaves. What makes an account "authentic"? Its accuracy? Its
correspondence with reality? The identity of its author?*

It's a perennial question: Can you really tell? The great black trumpeter
Roy Eldridge once made a wager with the critic Leonard Feather that he
could distinguish white musicians from black ones – blindfolded. Mr.
Feather duly dropped the needle onto a variety of record albums whose
titles and soloists were concealed from the trumpeter. More than half the
time, Eldridge guessed wrong.

Mr. Feather's blindfold test is one that literary critics would do well
to ponder, for the belief that we can "read" a person's racial or ethnic
identity from his or her writing runs surprisingly deep. There is an
assumption that we could fill a room with the world's great literature, train
a Martian to analyze these books, and then expect that Martian to

categorize each by the citizenship or ethnicity or gender of its author. "Passing" and "impersonation" may sound like quaint terms of a bygone era, but they continue to inform the way we read. Our literary judgments, in short, remain hostage to the ideology of authenticity.

And while black Americans have long boasted of their ability to spot "one of our own," no matter how fair the skin, straight the hair, or aquiline the nose – and while the nineteenth-century legal system in this county went to absurd lengths to demarcate even octoroons and demioctoroons from their white sisters and brothers – authentic racial and ethnic differences have always been difficult to define. It's not just a black thing, either.

The very idea of a literary tradition is itself bound up in suppositions – dating back at least to an eighteenth-century theorist of nationalism, Johann Gottfried Herder – that ethnic or national identity finds unique expression in literary forms. Such assumptions hold sway even after we have discarded them. After the much ballyhooed "death of the author" pronounced by two decades of literary theory, the author is very much back in the saddle. As the literary historian John Guillory observes, today's "battle of the books" is really not so much about books as it is about authors, authors who can be categorized according to race, gender, ethnicity, and so on, standing in as delegates of a social constituency.

And the assumption that the works they create transparently convey the authentic, unmediated experience of their social identities – though officially renounced – has crept quietly in through the back door. Like any dispensation, it raises some works and buries others. Thus Zora Neale Hurston's *Their Eyes Were Watching God* has prospered, while her *Seraph on the Suwanee,* a novel whose main characters are white, remains in limbo. *Our Nig,* recently identified as the work of a black woman, almost immediately went from obscurity to required reading in black and women's literature courses.

The case of Forrest Carter, the author of the best-selling *The Education of Little Tree,* provided yet another occasion to reflect on the troublesome role of authenticity. Billed as a true story, Carter's book was written as the autobiography of Little Tree, orphaned at the age of ten, who learns the ways of Indians from his Cherokee grandparents in Tennessee. *The Education of Little Tree,* which has sold more than 600,000 copies, received an award from the American Booksellers Association as the title booksellers most enjoyed selling. It was sold on the gift tables of Indian reservations and assigned as supplementary reading for courses on Native American literature. Major studios vied for movie rights.

And the critics loved it. *Booklist* praised its "natural approach to life." A reviewer for the *Chattanooga Times* pronounced it "deeply felt" One poet and storyteller of Abenaki descent hailed it as a masterpiece – "one of the finest American autobiographies ever written" – that captured the unique vision of Native American culture. It was, he wrote blissfully, "like a Cherokee basket, woven out of the materials given by nature, simple and strong in its design, capable of carrying a great deal." A critic in *The (Santa Fe) New Mexican* told his readers: "I have come on something that is good, so good I want to shout 'Read this! It's beautiful. It's real.'"

Or was it?

To the embarrassment of the book's admirers, Dan T. Carter, a history professor at Emory University, unmasked "Forrest Carter" as a pseudonym for the late Asa Earl Carter, whom he described as "a Ku Klux Klan terrorist, right wing radio announcer, home grown American fascist and anti- Semite, rabble-rousing demagogue and secret author of the famous 1963 speech by Gov. George Wallace of Alabama: 'Segregation now... Segregation tomorrow... Segregation forever.'" Forget Pee-wee Herman – try explaining this one to the kids.

This is only the latest embarrassment to beset the literary ideologues of authenticity, and its political stakes are relatively trivial. It was not always such. The authorship of slave narratives published between 1760 and 1865 was also fraught with controversy. To give credence to their claims about the horrors of slavery, American abolitionists urgently needed a cadre of ex-slaves who could compellingly indict their masters with first-person accounts of their bondage. For this tactic to succeed, the ex-slaves had to be authentic, their narratives full of convincing, painstaking verisimilitude.

So popular did these become, however, that two forms of imitators soon arose: white writers, adopting a first-person black narrative persona, gave birth to the pseudoslave narrative; and black authors, some of whom had never even seen the South, a plantation or a whipping post, became literary lions virtually overnight.

Generic confusion was rife in those days. The 1836 slave narrative of Archy Moore turned out to have been a novel written by a white historian, Richard Hildreth; and the gripping *Autobiography of a Female Slave* (1857) was also a novel, written by a white woman, Mattie Griffith. Perhaps the most embarrassing of these publishing events, however, involved one James Williams, an American slave – the subtitle of his narrative asserts – "who was for several years a driver on a cotton plantation in Alabama." Having escaped to the North (or so he claimed), Williams sought out members of the Anti-Slavery Society, and told a remarkably well-structured story about the brutal treatment of the slaves in the South and of his own miraculous escape, using the literacy he had secretly acquired to forge the necessary documents.

So compelling, so gripping, so *useful* was his tale that the abolitionists decided to publish it immediately. Williams arrived in New York on New Year's Day, 1838. By January 24, he had dictated his complete narrative to John Greenleaf Whittier. By February 15, it was in print, and was also being serialized in the abolitionist newspaper *The Anti-Slavery Examiner*. Even before Williams's book was published, rumors spread in New York that slave catchers were on his heels, and so his new friends shipped him off to Liverpool – where, it seems, he was never heard from again. Once the book was published, the abolitionists distributed it widely, sending copies to every state and to every Congressman.

Alas, Williams's stirring narrative was not authentic at all, as outraged Southern slaveholders were quick to charge and as his abolitionist friends reluctantly had to concede. It was a work of fiction, the production, one commentator put it, "purely of the Negro imagination" – as, no doubt, were the slave catchers who were in hot pursuit, and whose purported existence earned Williams a free trip to England and a new life.

Ersatz slave narratives had an even rougher time of it a century later, and one has to wonder how William Styron's *The Confessions of Nat Turner* – a novel that aroused the strenuous ire of much of the black intelligentsia when it was published in 1976 – might have been received had it been published by James Baldwin. "Hands off our history," we roared at Mr. Styron, the white Southern interloper, as we shopped around our list of literary demands. It was the real thing we wanted, and we wouldn't be taken in by imitators.

The real black writer, accordingly, could claim the full authority of experience denied Mr. Styron. Indeed, the late 1960s and early '70s were a time in which the notion of ethnic literature began to be consolidated and, in some measure, institutionalized. That meant policing the boundaries, telling true from false. But it was hard to play this game without a cheat sheet. When Dan McCall published *The Man Says Yes* in 1969, a novel about a young black teacher who comes up against the eccentric president of a black college, many critics assumed the author was black, too. The reviewer for *The Amsterdam News,* for example, referred to him throughout as "Brother McCall." Similar assumptions were occasionally made about Shane Stevens when he published the gritty bildungsroman *Way Uptown in Another World* in 1971, which detailed the brutal misadventures of its hero from Harlem, Marcus Garvey Black. In this case, the new voice from the ghetto belonged to a white graduate student at Columbia.

But the ethnic claim to its own experience cut two ways. For if many of their readers imagined a black face behind the prose, many avid readers of Frank Yerby's historical romances or Samuel R. Delany's science fiction novels are taken aback when they learn that these authors are black. And James Baldwin's *Giovanni's Room,* arguably his most accomplished novel, is seldom taught in black literature courses because its characters are white *and* gay.

Cultural commentators have talked about the "cult of ethnicity" in post-war America. You could dismiss it as a version of what Freud called "the narcissism of small differences." But you also see it as a salutary reaction to a regional Anglo-American culture that has declared itself as universal. For too long, "race" was something that blacks had, "ethnicity" was what "ethnics" had. In mid-century America, Norman Podhoretz reflected in *Making It,* his literary memoirs, "to write fiction out of the experience of big-city immigrant Jewish life was to feel oneself, and to be felt by others, to be writing exotica at best; nor did there exist a respectably certified narrative style in English which was anything but facsimile-WASP. Writing was hard enough but to have to write with *only* that part of one's being which had been formed by the acculturation-minded public schools and by the blindly ethnicizing English departments of the colleges was like being asked to compete in a race with a leg cut off at the thigh."

All this changed with the novelistic triumphs of Saul Bellow and Philip Roth – and yet a correlative disability was entered in the ledger, too. In the same year that Mr. Styron published *The Confessions of Nat Turner,* Philip Roth published *When She Was Good,* a novel set in the rural heartland of gentile middle America and infused with the chilly humorlessness of its small-town inhabitants. This was, to say the least, a departure. Would critics who admired Mr. Roth as the author of *Goodbye, Columbus* accept him as a chronicler of the Protestant Corn Belt?

Richard Gilman, in *The New Republic,* compared Mr. Roth to a "naturalist on safari to a region unfamiliar to him" and declared himself unable to "account for the novel's existence, so lacking is it in any true literary interest." Maureen Howard in *Partisan Review* said she felt "the presence of a persona rather than a personal voice." To Jonathan Baumbach, writing in *Commonweal,* the book suggested "Zero Mostel doing an extended imitation of Jimmy Stewart." "He captures the rhythms of his characters' speech," Mr. Baumbach says of Mr. Roth, "but not, I feel, what makes them human." If the book was written partly in defiance of the strictures of ethnic literature, those very strictures were undoubtedly what made the book anathema to so many reviewers.

And what if *When She Was Good* had been published under the name Philip McGrath? Would the same reviewers still have denounced it as an artistic imposture? Does anyone imagine that Zero Mostel would have come to mind? Yet there is a twist in the tale. Even a counterfeit can be praised for its craft. For some, the novel's worth was enhanced precisely because of its "inauthenticity" – because it was seen as an act of imagination unassisted by memory.

Under any name, Kazuo Ishiguro's *Remains of the Day* – *a* novel narrated by an aging and veddy English butler – would be a tour de force; but wasn't the acclaim that greeted it heightened by a kind of critical double take at the youthful Japanese face on the dust jacket? To take another example, no one is surprised that admirers of Norman Rush's novel *Mating* would commend the author on the voice of its female narrator. Subtract from the reality column, add to the art column. Thus Doris Grumbach, who commended Mr. Roth's novel for its careful observation, concludes her own review with an assessment of technique: "To bring off this verisimilitude is, to my mind, an enormous accomplishment." Would she have been so impressed with the virtuosity of a Philip McGrath?

Sometimes, however, a writer's identity is in fact integral to a work's artifice. Such is the case with John Updike's *Bech: A Book,* the first of two collections of short stories featuring Mr. Updike's Jewish novelist, Henry Bech. The 1970 book opens with a letter from the protagonist, Henry, to his creator, John, fussing about the literary components from which he was apparently jury-rigged. At first blush (Bech muses), he sounds like "some gentlemanly Norman Mailer; then that London glimpse of *silver* hair glints more of gallant, glamorous Bellow... My childhood seems out of Alex Portnoy and my ancestral past out of I. B. Singer. I get a whiff of Malamud in your city breezes, and am I paranoid to feel my 'block' an ignoble version of the more or less noble renunciations of H. Roth, D. Fuchs and J. Salinger? Withal, something Waspish, theological, scared and insultingly ironical that derives, my wild surmise is, from you."

What is clear is that part of the point of John Updike's Bech is that he is *John Updike's* Bech: an act Cynthia Ozick has described as "cultural impersonation." The contrast between Bech and Updike, then, far from being irrelevant, is itself staged within the fictional edifice. You could publish *Bech* under a pseudonym, but, I maintain, it would be a different book.

Conversely – but for similar reasons – one might argue that exposing the true author of *Famous All Over Town,* a colorful picaresque novel set in a Los Angeles barrio, was a form of violence against the book itself. Published in 1983 under the nom de plume Danny Santiago, the book was hailed by Latino critics for its vibrancy and authenticity, and received the Richard and Hinda Rosenthal Foundation Award from the American Academy of Arts and Letters for an outstanding work of fiction. But

Santiago, assumed to be a young Chicano talent, turned out to be Daniel L. James, a septuagenarian WASP educated at Andover and Yale, a playwright, screenwriter and, in his later years, a social worker. And yet Danny Santiago was much more than a literary conceit to his creator, who had for twenty years lost faith in his own ability to write; Danny was the only voice available to him. Judging from the testimony of his confidant, John Gregory Dunne, Mr. James may well have felt that the attribution was the only just one; that *Famous All Over Town* belonged to Danny Santiago before it quite belonged to Daniel James.

Death-of-the-author types cannot come to grips with the fact that a book is a cultural event; authorial identity, mystified or not, can be part of that event. What the ideologues of authenticity cannot quite come to grips with is that fact and fiction have always exerted a reciprocal effect on each other. However truthful you set out to be, your autobiography is never unmediated by literary structures of expression. Many authentic slave narratives were influenced by Harriet Beecher Stowe; on the other hand, authentic slave narratives were among Stowe's primary sources for her own imaginative work, *Uncle Tom's Cabin.* By the same token, to recognize the slave narrative as a genre is to recognize that, for example, Frederick Douglass's mode of expression was informed by the conventions of antecedent narratives, some of which were (like James Williams's) whole-cloth inventions.

So it is not just a matter of the outsider boning up while the genuine article just writes what he or she knows. If Shane Stevens was deeply influenced by Richard Wright, so too were black protest novelists like John O. Killens and John A. Williams. And if John Updike can manipulate the tonalities of writers like Saul Bellow, Bernard Malamud, and Philip Roth, must we assume that a Bruce Jay Friedman, say, is wholly unaffected by such models?

The distasteful truth is that like it or not, all writers are "cultural impersonators."

Even real people, moreover, are never quite real. My own favorite (fictional) commentary on the incursion of fiction upon a so-called real life is provided by Nabokov's Humbert Humbert as he reflects upon the bothersome task of swapping life stories with a new and unwanted wife. Her confessions were marked by "sincerity and artlessness," his were "glib compositions"; and yet, he muses, "technically the two sets were congeneric since both were affected by the same stuff (soap operas, psychoanalysis, and cheap novelettes) upon which I drew for my characters and she for her mode of expression."

Start interrogating the notion of cultural authenticity and our most trusted critical categories come into question. Maybe Danny Santiago's

Famous All Over Town can usefully be considered a work of Chicano literature; maybe Shane Stevens's *Way Uptown in Another World* can usefully be considered within the genre of black protest novels. In his own version of the blindfold test, the mathematician Alan Turing famously proposed that we credit a computer with intelligence if we can conduct a dialogue with it and not know whether a person or machine has been composing the responses. Should we allow ethnic literatures a similar procedure for claiming this title?

At this point, it is important to go slow. Consider the interviewer's chestnut: are you a woman writer or a writer who happens to be a woman? A black writer or a writer who happens to be a black? Alas, these are deadly disjunctions. After struggling to gain the recognition that a woman or a black (or, exemplarily, a black woman) writer is, in the first instance, a writer, many authors yet find themselves uneasy with the supposedly universalizing description. How can ethnic or sexual identity be reduced to a mere contingency when it is so profoundly a part of who a writer is?

And yet if, for example, black critics claim special authority as interpreters of black literature, and black writers claim special authority as interpreters of black reality, are we not obliged to cede an equivalent dollop of authority to our white counterparts?

We easily become entrapped by what the feminist critic Nancy K. Miller has called "as a" criticism: where we always speak "as a" white middle- class woman, a person of color, a gay man, and so on. And that, too, is a confinement – in the republic of letters as in the larger policy. "Segregation today… Segregation tomorrow… Segregation forever": that line, which Asa Earl Carter wrote for George Wallace's inauguration speech as Governor, may still prove his true passport to immortality. And yet segregation – as Carter himself would demonstrate – is as difficult to maintain in the literary realm as it is in the civic one.

The lesson of the literary blindfold test is not that our social identities don't matter. They do matter. And our histories, individual and collective, do affect what we wish to write and what we are able to write. But that relation is never one of fixed determinism. No human culture is inaccessible to someone who makes the effort to understand, to learn, to inhabit another world.

Yes, Virginia, there is a Danny Santiago. And – if you like that sort of thing – there is a Little Tree, too, just as treacly now as he ever was. And as long as there are writers who combine some measure of imagination and curiosity, there will continue to be such interlopers of the literary imagination. What, then, of the vexed concept of authenticity? To borrow from Samuel Goldwyn's theory of sincerity, authenticity remains essential: once you can fake that, you've got it made.

Of Cannibals
Michel de Montaigne

In *The Complete Essays of Montaigne*. Trans. Donald M. Frame. Stanford: Stanford University Press, 1958.

French statesman and philosopher **Michel de Montaigne** *(1533-1592) is credited with the invention of the modern essay, in which an author explores a topic by blending historical details and philosophical insights with elements of the author's own experience. His three volumes of essays display a perceptive mind, a remarkably modern and humanistic temperament, and a robust skepticism of received wisdom (his famous motto was "what do I know?"). A Roman Catholic himself, Montaigne was disgusted by the violence and inhumanities perpetrated by both Catholics and Protestants during the "Wars of Religion" of his day.*

Why we are reading this: *While in the town of Rouen in 1562, Montaigne met a cannibal who had been brought to France from Brazil. Some years later he employed a man who had lived in Brazil in the 1550s-1560s and had observed the customs of the Tupinambá people. In this essay, written around 1577, Montaigne writes about these "barbarians" of the New World, and does something radically new for his time and place: he tries to understand the lives of these cannibals on their own terms and from within their own cultural framework, making this essay a landmark work in the development of cultural relativism. As Montaigne famously notes in this piece: "each man calls barbarism whatever is not his own practice."*

When King Pyrrhus passed over into Italy, after he had reconnoitered the formation of the army that the Romans were sending to meeting him, he said: "I do not know what barbarians these are" (for so the Greeks called all foreign nations), "but the formation of this army that I see is not at all barbarous" (Plutarch, *Life of Pyrrhus*). The Greeks said as much of the army that Flaminius brought into their country, and so did Philip, seeing from a knoll the order and distribution of the Roman camp, in his kingdom, under Publius Sulpicius Galba. Thus we should beware of clinging to vulgar opinions, and judge things by reason's way, not by popular say.

I had with me for a long time a man who had lived for ten or twelve years in that other world which has been discovered in our century, in the place where Villegagnon landed, and which he called Antarctic France.[1] This discovery of a boundless country seems worthy of consideration. I don't know if I can guarantee that some other such discovery will not be made in the future, so many personages greater than ourselves having been mistaken about this one. I am afraid we have eyes bigger than our stomachs, and more curiosity than capacity. We embrace everything, but we clasp only wind.

Plato brings in Solon, telling how he had learned from the priests of the city of Sas in Egypt that in days of old, before the Flood, there was a great island named Atlantis, right at the mouth of the Strait of Gibraltar, which contained more land than Africa and Asia put together, and that the kings of that country, who not only possessed that island but had stretched out so far on the mainland that they held the breadth of Africa as far as Egypt, and the length of Europe as far as Tuscany, undertook to step over into Asia and subjugate all the nations that border on the Mediterranean, as far as the Black Sea; and for this purpose crossed the Spains, Gaul, Italy, as far as Greece, where the Athenians checked them; but that some time after, both the Athenians and themselves and their island were swallowed up by the Flood.

It is quite likely that that extreme devastation of waters made amazing changes in the habitations of the earth, as people maintain that the sea cut off Sicily from Italy –

> Tis said an earthquake once asunder tore
> These lands with dreadful havoc, which before
> Formed but one land, one coast
> (Virgil, *Aeneid*)

– Cyprus from Syria, the island of Euboea from the mainland of Boeotia; and elsewhere joined lands that were divided, filling the channels between them with sand and mud:

> A sterile marsh, long fit for rowing, now
> Feeds neighbor towns, and feels the heavy plow
> (Horace, *Ars Poetica*)

---

[1] In Montaigne's time, Antarctica had not yet been discovered. This refers instead to a French colony in Brazil founded by Nicolas Durand de Villegagnon at present-day Rio de Janeiro. The colony lasted a mere twelve years, from 1555 to 1567.

But there is no great likelihood that that island was the new world which we have just discovered; for it almost touched Spain, and it would be an incredible result of a flood to have forced it away as far as it is, more than twelve hundred leagues; besides, the travels of the moderns have already almost revealed that it is not an island, but a mainland connected with the East Indies on one side, and elsewhere with the lands under the two poles; or, if it is separated from them, it is by so narrow a strait and interval that it does not deserve to be called an island on that account.

It seems that there are movements, some natural, others feverish, in these great bodies, just as in our own. When I consider the inroads that my river, the Dordogne, is making in my lifetime into the right bank in its descent, and that in twenty years it has gained so much ground and stolen away the foundations of several buildings, I clearly see that this is an extraordinary disturbance; for if it had always gone at this rate, or was to do so in the future, the face of the world would be turned topsy-turvy. But rivers are subject to changes: now they overflow in one direction, now in another, now they keep to their course. I am not speaking of the sudden inundations whose causes are manifest. In Medoc, along the seashore, my brother, the Sieur d'Arsac, can see an estate of his buried under the sands that the sea spews forth; the tops of some buildings are still visible; his farms and domains have changed into very thin pasturage. The inhabitants say that for some time the sea has been pushing toward them so hard that they have lost four leagues of land. These sands are its harbingers; and we see great dunes of moving sand that march half a league ahead of it and keep conquering land.

The other testimony of antiquity with which some would connect this discovery is in Aristotle, at least if that little book Of Unheard-of Wonders is by him. He there relates that certain Carthaginians, after setting out upon the Atlantic Ocean from the Strait of Gibraltar and sailing a long time, at last discovered a great fertile island, all clothed in woods and watered by great deep rivers, far remote from any mainland; and that they, and others since, attracted by the goodness and fertility of the soil, went there with their wives and children, and began to settle there. The lords of Carthage, seeing that their country was gradually becoming depopulated, expressly forbade anyone to go there any more, on pain of death, and drove out these new inhabitants, fearing, it is said, that in course of time they might come to multiply so greatly as to supplant their former masters and ruin their state. This story of Aristotle does not fit our new lands any better than the other.

This man I had was a simple, crude fellow – a character fit to bear true witness; for clever people observe more things and more curiously, but they interpret them; and to lend weight and conviction to their interpretation, they cannot help altering history a little. They never show you things as they are, but bend and disguise them according to the way they have seen them; and to give credence to their judgment and attract you to it, they are prone to add something to their matter, to stretch it out and amplify it. We need a man either very honest, or so simple that he has not the stuff to build up false inventions and give them plausibility; and wedded to no theory. Such was my man; and besides this, he at various times brought sailors and merchants, whom he had known on that trip, to see me. So I content myself with his information, without inquiring what the cosmographers say about it.

We ought to have topographers who would give us an exact account of the places where they have been. But because they have over us the advantage of having seen Palestine, they want to enjoy the privilege of telling us news about all the rest of the world. I would like everyone to write what he knows, not only in this, but in all other subjects; for a man may have some special knowledge and experience of the nature of a river or a fountain, who in other matters knows only what everybody knows. However, to circulate this little scrap of knowledge, he will undertake to write the whole of physics. From this vice spring many great abuses.

Now, to return to my subject, I think there is nothing barbarous and savage in that nation, from what I have been told, except that each man calls barbarism whatever is not his own practice; for indeed it seems we have no other test of truth and reason than the example and pattern of the opinion and customs of the country we live in. There is always the perfect religion, the perfect government, the perfect and accomplished manners in all things. Those people are wild, just as we call wild the fruits that Nature has produced by herself and in her normal course; where really it is those that we have changed artificially and led astray from the common order, that we should rather call wild. The former retain alive and vigorous their genuine, their most useful and natural, virtues and properties, which we have debased in the latter in adapting them to gratify our corrupted taste. And yet for all that, the savor and delicacy of some uncultivated fruits of those countries is quite as excellent, even to our taste, as that of our own. It is not reasonable that art should win the place of honor over our great and powerful mother Nature. We have so overloaded the beauty and richness of her works by our inventions that we have quite smothered her. Yet wherever her purity shines forth, she wonderfully puts to shame our vain and frivolous attempts: "Ivy comes readier without our care;/In lonely caves the arbutus grows more fair;/No art with artless bird song can compare" (Propertius). All our efforts cannot even succeed in reproducing the nest of the tiniest little bird, its contexture, its beauty and convenience; or even the web of the puny spider. All things, says Plato (*Laws*), are produced by nature, by fortune, or by art; the greatest and most beautiful by one or the other of the first two, the least and most imperfect by the last.

These nations, then, seem to me barbarous in this sense, that they have been fashioned very little by the human mind, and are still very close to their original naturalness. The laws of nature still rule them, very little corrupted by ours; and they are in such a state of purity that I am sometimes vexed that they were unknown earlier, in the days when there were men able to judge them better than we. I am sorry that Lycurgus and Plato did not know of them; for it seems to me that what we actually see in these nations surpasses not only all the pictures in which poets have idealized the golden age and all their inventions in imagining a happy state of man, but also the conceptions and the very desire of philosophy. They could not imagine a naturalness so pure and simple as we see by experience; nor could they believe that our society could be maintained with so little artifice and human solder. This is a nation, I should say to Plato, in which there is no sort of traffic, no knowledge of letters, no science of numbers, no name for a magistrate of for political superiority, no custom of servitude, no riches or poverty, no contacts, no successions, no partitions, no occupations but leisure ones, no care for any but common kinship, no clothes, no agriculture, no metal, no use of wine or wheat. The very words that signify lying, treachery, dissimulation, avarice, envy, belittling, pardon – unheard of. How far from this perfection would he find the republic that he imagines: Men fresh sprung from the gods (Seneca, *Epistle*). "These manners nature first ordained" (Virgil, *Georgics*).

For the rest, they live in a country with a very pleasant and temperate climate, so that according to my witnesses it is rare to see a sick man there; and they have assured me that they never saw one palsied, bleary-eyed, toothless, or bent with age. They are settled along the sea and shut in on the land side by great high mountains, with a stretch about a hundred leagues wide in between. They have a great abundance of fish and flesh which bear no resemblance to ours, and they eat them with no other artifice than cooking. The first man who rode a horse there, though he had had dealings with them on several other trips, so horrified them in this posture that they shot him dead with arrows before they could recognize him. Their buildings are very long, with a capacity of two or three hundred souls; they are covered with the bark of great trees, the strips reaching to the ground at one end and supporting and leaning on one another at the top, in the manner of some of our barns, whose covering hangs down to the ground and acts as a side. They have wood so hard that they cut with it and make of it their swords and grills to cook their food. Their beds are of a cotton weave, hung from the roof like those in our ships, each man having his own; for the wives sleep apart from their husbands.

They get up with the sun, and eat immediately upon rising, to last them through the day; for they take no other meal than that one. Like some other Eastern peoples, of whom Suidas[2] tells us, who drank apart from meals, they do not drink then; but they drink several times a day, and to capacity. Their drink is made of some root, and is of the color of our claret wines. They drink it only lukewarm. This beverage keeps only two or three days; it has a slightly sharp taste, is not at all heady, is good for the stomach, and has a laxative effect upon those who are not used to it; it is a very pleasant drink for anyone who is accustomed to it. In place of bread they use a certain white substance like preserved coriander. I have tried it; it tastes sweet and a little flat.

The whole day is spent in dancing. The younger men go to hunt animals with bows. Some of the women busy themselves meanwhile with warming their drink, which is their chief duty. Some one of the old men, in the morning before they begin to eat, preaches to the whole barnful in common, walking from one end to the other, and repeating one single sentence several times until he has completed the circuit (for the buildings are fully a hundred paces long). He recommends to them only two things: valor against the enemy and love for their wives. And they never fail to point out this obligation, as their refrain, that it is their wives who keep their drink warm and seasoned.

There may be seen in several places, including my own house, specimens of their beds, of their ropes, of their wooden swords and the bracelets with which they cover their wrists in combats, and of the big canes, open at one end, by whose sound they keep time in their dances. They are close shaven all over, and shave themselves much more cleanly than we, with nothing but a wooden or stone razor. They believe that souls are immortal and that those who have deserved well of the gods are lodged in that part of heaven where the sun rises, and the damned in the west.

They have some sort of priests and prophets, but they rarely appear before the people, having their home in the mountains. On their arrival there is a great feast and solemn assembly of several villages – each barn, as I have described it, makes up a village, and they are about one French league from each other. The prophet speaks to them in public, exhorting them to virtue and their duty; but their whole ethical science contains only these two articles; resoluteness in war and affection for their wives. He prophesies to them things to come and the results they are to expect from their undertakings, and urges them to war or holds them back from it; but this is on the condition that when he fails to prophesy correctly, and if things turn out otherwise than he has predicted, he is cut into a thousand

---

[2] A Greek lexicon-encyclopedia, compiled in the 900s CE. [Ed.]

pieces if they catch him, and condemned as a false prophet. For this reason, the prophet who has once been mistaken is never seen again.

Divination is a gift of God; that is why its abuse should be punished as imposture. Among the Scythians, when the soothsayers failed to hit the mark, they were laid, chained hand and foot, on carts full of heather and drawn by oxen, on which they were burned. Those who handle matters subject to the control of human capacity are excusable if they do the best they can. But these others, who come and trick us with assurances of an extraordinary faculty that is beyond our ken, should they not be punished for making good their promise, and for the temerity of their imposture?

They have their wars with the nations beyond the mountains, further inland, to which they go quite naked, with no other arms than bows or wooden swords ending in a sharp point, in the manner of the tongues of our boar spears. It is astonishing what firmness they show in their combats, which never end but in slaughter and bloodshed; for as to routs and terror, they know nothing of either.

Each man brings back as his trophy the head of the enemy he has killed, and sets it up at the entrance to his dwelling. After they have treated their prisoners well for a long time with all the hospitality they can think of, each man who has a prisoner calls a great assembly of his acquaintances. He ties a rope to one of the prisoner's arms, by the end of which he holds him, a few steps away, for fear of being hurt, and gives his dearest friend the other arm to hold in the same way; and these two, in the presence of the whole assembly, kill him with their swords. This done, they roast him and eat him in common and send some pieces to their absent friends. This is not, as people think, for nourishment, as of old the Scythians used to do; it is to betoken an extreme revenge. And the proof of this came when they saw the Portuguese, who had joined forces with their adversaries, inflict a different kind of death on them when they took them prisoner, which was to bury them up to the waist, shoot the rest of their body full of arrows, and afterward hang them. They thought that these people from the other world, being men who had sown the knowledge of many vices among their neighbors and were much greater masters than themselves in every sort of wickedness, did not adopt this sort of vengeance without some reason, and that it must be more painful than their own; so they began to give up their old method and to follow this one.

I am not sorry that we notice the barbarous horror of such acts, but I am heartily sorry that, judging their faults rightly, we should be so blind to our own. I think there is more barbarity in eating a man alive than in eating him dead; and in tearing by tortures and the rack a body still full of feeling, in roasting a man bit by bit, in having him bitten and mangled by dogs and swine (as we have not only read but seen within fresh memory, not among ancient enemies, but among neighbors and fellow citizens, and what is worse, on the pretext of piety and religion), than in roasting and eating him after he is dead.

Indeed, Chrysippus and Zeno, heads of the Stoic sect, thought there was nothing wrong in using our carcasses for any purpose in case of need, and getting nourishment from them; just as our ancestors, when besieged by Caesar in the city of Alsia, resolved to relieve their famine by eating old men, women, and other people useless for fighting.

> The Gascons once, 'tis said, their life renewed
> By eating of such food
>> Juvenal, *Satires*

And physicians do not fear to use human flesh in all sorts of ways for our health, applying it either inwardly or outwardly. But there never was any opinion so disordered as to excuse treachery, disloyalty, tyranny, and cruelty, which are our ordinary vices.

So we may well call these people barbarians, in respect to the rules of reason, but not in respect to ourselves, who surpass them in every kind of barbarity

Their warfare is wholly noble and generous, and as excusable and beautiful as this human disease can be; its only basis among them is their rivalry in valor. They are not fighting for the conquest of new lands, for they still enjoy that natural abundance that provides them without toil and trouble with all necessary things in such profusion that they have no wish to enlarge their boundaries. They are still in that happy state of desiring only as much as their natural needs demand; anything beyond that is superfluous to them.

They generally call those of the same age, brothers; those who are younger, children; and the old men are fathers to all the others. These leave to their heirs in common the full possession of their property, without division or any other title at all than just the one that Nature gives to her creatures in bringing them into the world.

If their neighbors cross the mountains to attack them and win a victory, the gain of the victor is glory, and the advantage of having proved the master in valor and virtue; for apart from this they have no use for the goods of the vanquished, and they return to their own country, where they lack neither anything necessary nor that great thing, the knowledge of how to enjoy their condition happily and be content with it. These men of ours do the same in their turn. They demand of their prisoners no other ransom than that they confess and acknowledge their defeat. But there is not one in a whole century who does not choose to die rather than to relax a single bit, by word or look, from the grandeur of an invincible courage; not one who would not rather be killed and eaten than so much as ask not to be. They treat them very freely, so that life may be all the dearer to them, and usually entertain them with threats of their coming death, of the torments they will have to suffer, the preparations that are being made for that purpose, the cutting up of their limbs, and the feast that will be made at their expense. All this is done for the purpose of extorting from their lips some weak or base word, or making them want to flee, so as to gain the advantage of having terrified them and broken down their firmness. For indeed, if you take it the right way, it is in this point alone that true victory lies:

> It is no victory
> Unless the vanquished foe admits your mastery
>   Claudian

The Hungarians, very bellicose fighters, did not in olden times pursue their advantage beyond putting the enemy at their mercy. For having wrung a confession from him to this effect, they let him go unharmed and unransomed, except, at most, for exacting his promise never again to take up arms against them.

We win enough advantages over our enemies that are borrowed advantages, not really our own. It is the quality of a porter, not of valor, to have sturdier arms and legs; agility is a dead and corporeal quality; it is a stroke of luck to make our enemy stumble, or dazzle his eyes by the sunlight; it is a trick of art and technique, which may be found in a worthless coward, to be an able fencer. The worth and value of a man is in his heart and his will; there lies his real honor. Valor is the strength, not of legs and arms, but of heart and soul; it consists not in the worth of our horse or our weapons, but in our own. He who falls obstinate in his courage, if he has fallen, he fights on his knees (Seneca). He who releases none of his assurance, no matter how great the danger of imminent death; who, giving up his soul, still looks firmly and scornfully at his enemy – he is beaten not by us, but by fortune; he is killed, not conquered.

The most valiant are sometimes the most unfortunate. Thus there are triumphant defeats that rival victories. Nor did those four sister victories, the fairest that the sun ever set eyes on – Salamis, Plataea, Mycale, and Sicily – ever date match all their combined glory against the glory of the annihilation of King Leonidas and his men at the pass of Thermopylae.

Who ever hastened with more glorious and ambitious desire to win a battle than Captain Ischolas to lose one (Diodorus Siculus)? Who ever secured his safety more ingeniously and painstakingly than he did his destruction? He was charged to defend a certain pass in the Peloponnesus against the Arcadians. Finding himself wholly incapable of doing this, in view of the nature of the place and the inequality of the forces, he made up his mind that all who confronted the enemy would necessarily have to remain on the field. On the other hand, deeming it unworthy both of his own virtue and magnanimity and of the Lacedaemonian name to fail in his charge, he took a middle course between these two extremes, in this way. The youngest and fittest of his band he preserved for the defense and service of their country, and sent them home; and with those whose loss was less important, he determined to hold this pass, and by their death to make the enemy buy their entry as dearly as he could. And so it turned out. For he was presently surrounded on all sides by the Arcadians, and after slaughtering a large number of them, he and his men were all put to the sword. Is there a trophy dedicated to victors that would not be more due to these vanquished? The role of true victory is in fighting, not in coming off safely; and the honor of valor consists in combating, not in beating.

To return to our story. These prisoners are so far from giving in, in spite of all that is done to them, that on the contrary, during the two or three months that they are kept, they wear a gay expression; they urge their captors to hurry and put them to the test; they defy them, insult them, reproach them with their own cowardice and the number of battles they have lost to the prisoners' own people.

I have a song composed by a prisoner which contains this challenge, that they should all come boldly and gather to dine off him, for they will be eating at the same time their own fathers and grandfathers, who have served to feed and nourish his body. "These muscles," he says, "this flesh and these veins are your own, poor fools that you are. You do not recognize that the substance of your ancestors' limbs is still contained in them. Savor them well; you will find in them the taste of your own flesh." An idea that certainly does not smack of barbarity. Those that paint these people dying, and who show the execution, portray the prisoner spitting in the face of his slayers and scowling at them. Indeed, to the last gasp they never stop braving and defying their enemies by word and look. Truly here are real savages by our standards; for either they must be thoroughly so, or we must be; there is an amazing distance between their character and ours.

The men there have several wives, and the higher their reputation for valor the more wives they have. It is a remarkably beautiful thing about their marriages that the same jealousy our wives have to keep us from the affection and kindness of other women, theirs have to win this for them. Being more concerned for their husbands' honor than for anything else, they strive and scheme to have as many companions as they can, since that is a sign of their husbands' valor.

Our wives will cry "Miracle!" but it is no miracle. It is a properly matrimonial virtue, but one of the highest order. In the Bible, Leah, Rachel, Sarah, and Jacob's wives gave their beautiful handmaids to their husbands; and Livia seconded the appetites of Augustus, to her own disadvantage; and Stratonice, the wife of King Deiotarus, not only lent her husband for his use a very beautiful young chambermaid in her service, but carefully brought up her children, and backed them up to succeed to their father's estates.

And lest it be thought that all this is done through a simple and servile bondage to usage and through the pressure of the authority of their ancient customs, without reasoning or judgement, and because their minds are so stupid that they cannot take any other course, I must cite some examples of their capacity. Besides the warlike song I have just quoted, I have another, a love song, which begins in this vein: "Adder, stay; stay, adder, that from the pattern of your coloring my sister may draw the fashion and the workmanship of a rich girdle that I may give to my love; so may your beauty and your pattern be forever preferred to all other serpents." This first couplet is the refrain of the song. Now I am familiar enough with poetry to be a judge of this: not only is there nothing barbarous in this fancy, but it is altogether Anacreontic.[3] Their language, moreover, is a soft language, with an agreeable sound, somewhat like Greek in its ending.

Three of these men, ignorant of the price they will pay some day, in loss of repose and happiness, for gaining knowledge of the corruptions of this side of the ocean; ignorant also of the fact that of this intercourse will come their ruin (which I suppose is already well advanced: poor wretches, to let themselves be tricked by the desire for new things, and to have left the serenity of their own sky to come and see ours!) – three of these men were at Rouen, at the time the late King Charles IX was there.[4] The king talked to them for a long time; they were shown our ways, our splendor, the aspect of a fine city. After that, someone asked their opinion, and wanted to know what they had found most amazing. They mentioned three things, of which I have forgotten the third, and I am very sorry for it; but I still remember two of them. They said that in the first place they thought it very strange that so many grown men, bearded, strong, and armed, who were around the king (it is likely that they were talking about the Swiss of his guard) should submit to obey a child, and that one of them was not chosen to command instead. Second (they have a way in their language of speaking of men as halves of one another, they had noticed that there were

---

[3] This refers to the Greek lyric poet Anacreon (c. 582 BCE-c. 485 BCE). [Ed.]
[4] King Charles IX of France took the throne in 1562 at age ten and reigned until his early death from tuberculosis in 1574 at age 23.

among us men full and gorged with all sorts of good things, and that their other halves were beggars at their doors, emaciated with hunger and poverty; and they thought it strange that these needy halves could endure such an injustice, and did not take the others by the throat, or set fire to their houses.

I had a very long talk with one of them; but I had an interpreter who followed my meaning so badly, and who was so hindered by his stupidity in taking in my ideas, that I could get hardly any satisfaction from the man. When I asked him what profit he gained from his superior position among his people (for he was a captain, and our sailors called him king), he told me that it was to march foremost in war. How many men followed him? He pointed to a piece of ground, to signify as many as such a space could hold; it might have been four or five thousand men. Did all his authority expire with the war? He said that this much remained, that when he visited the villages dependent on him, they made paths for him through the underbrush by which he might pass quite comfortably.

All this is not bad – but what's the use? They don't wear breeches.

Consider the Lobster
David Foster Wallace

In *Gourmet*, August 2004. Reprinted in David Foster Wallace, *Consider the Lobster and Other Essays*. New York: Little, Brown and Company, 2005.

David Foster Wallace (1962-2008) was a US American novelist, short story author, essayist and journalist, generally considered one of the most significant writers of the latter part of the 20ᵗʰ Century. Known especially for a dry approach to humor, as well as a fascination with footnotes, Wallace was particularly fond of taking often mundane or by-the-way events and facts of life (cruises, mid-level tennis players, state fairs) and with subtlety placing them in front of the audience for consideration. His most well-known novel is Infinite Jest *(1996).*

Why we are reading this: Commissioned by Gourmet *magazine in 2004 to write a light account of the annual Maine Lobster Festival, Wallace unexpectedly embarks upon a deep scientific, philosophical, and sometimes whimsical investigation into whether one could consider it ethical to boil lobsters alive. His quest involves a detailed exploration of the world of the lobster. Do lobsters feel pain when we boil them? How might we answer this question? Can we see the world from a lobster's point of view?*

For 56 years, the Maine Lobster Festival has been drawing crowds with the promise of sun, fun, and fine food. One visitor would argue that the celebration involves a whole lot more.

The enormous, pungent, and extremely well marketed Maine Lobster Festival is held every late July in the state's midcoast region, meaning the western side of Penobscot Bay, the nerve stem of Maine's lobster industry. What's called the midcoast runs from Owl's Head and Thomaston in the south to Belfast in the north. (Actually, it might extend all the way up to Bucksport, but we were never able to get farther north than Belfast on Route 1, whose summer traffic is, as you can imagine, unimaginable.) The region's two main communities are Camden, with its very old money and yachty harbor and five-star restaurants and phenomenal B&Bs, and

Rockland, a serious old fishing town that hosts the Festival every summer in historic Harbor Park, right along the water.[1]

Tourism and lobster are the midcoast region's two main industries, and they're both warm-weather enterprises, and the Maine Lobster Festival represents less an intersection of the industries than a deliberate collision, joyful and lucrative and loud. The assigned subject of this article is the 56th Annual MLF, July 30 to August 3, 2003, whose official theme was "Lighthouses, Laughter, and Lobster." Total paid attendance was over 80,000, due partly to a national CNN spot in June during which a Senior Editor of a certain other epicurean magazine hailed the MLF as one of the best food-themed festivals in the world. 2003 Festival highlights: concerts by Lee Ann Womack and Orleans, annual Maine Sea Goddess beauty pageant, Saturday's big parade, Sunday's William G. Atwood Memorial Crate Race, annual Amateur Cooking Competition, carnival rides and midway attractions and food booths, and the MLF's Main Eating Tent, where something over 25,000 pounds of fresh-caught Maine lobster is consumed after preparation in the World's Largest Lobster Cooker near the grounds' north entrance. Also available are lobster rolls, lobster turnovers, lobster sauté, Down East lobster salad, lobster bisque, lobster ravioli, and deep-fried lobster dumplings. Lobster Thermidor is obtainable at a sit-down restaurant called The Black Pearl on Harbor Park's northwest wharf. A large all-pine booth sponsored by the Maine Lobster Promotion Council has free pamphlets with recipes, eating tips, and Lobster Fun Facts. The winner of Friday's Amateur Cooking Competition prepares Saffron Lobster Ramekins, the recipe for which is available for public downloading at www.mainelobsterfestival.com. There are lobster T-shirts and lobster bobblehead dolls and inflatable lobster pool toys and clamp-on lobster hats with big scarlet claws that wobble on springs. Your assigned correspondent saw it all, accompanied by one girlfriend and both his own parents – one of which parents was actually born and raised in Maine, albeit in the extreme northern inland part, which is potato country and a world away from the touristic midcoast.[2]

For practical purposes, everyone knows what a lobster is. As usual, though, there's much more to know than most of us care about – it's all a matter of what your interests are. Taxonomically speaking, a lobster is a marine crustacean of the family Homaridae, characterized by five pairs of jointed legs, the first pair terminating in large pincerish claws used for

---

[1] There's a comprehensive native apothegm: "Camden by the sea, Rockland by the smell."

[2] N.B. All personally connected parties have made it clear from the start that they do not want to be talked about in this article.

subduing prey. Like many other species of benthic carnivore, lobsters are both hunters and scavengers. They have stalked eyes, gills on their legs, and antennae. There are dozens of different kinds worldwide, of which the relevant species here is the Maine lobster, *Homarus americanus*. The name "lobster" comes from the Old English *loppestre*, which is thought to be a corrupt form of the Latin word for locust combined with the Old English *loppe*, which meant spider.

Moreover, a crustacean is an aquatic arthropod of the class Crustacea, which comprises crabs, shrimp, barnacles, lobsters, and freshwater crayfish. All this is right there in the encyclopedia. And an arthropod is an invertebrate member of the phylum Arthropoda, which phylum covers insects, spiders, crustaceans, and centipedes/millipedes, all of whose main commonality, besides the absence of a centralized brain-spine assembly, is a chitinous exoskeleton composed of segments, to which appendages are articulated in pairs.

The point is that lobsters are basically giant sea-insects.[3] Like most arthropods, they date from the Jurassic period, biologically so much older than mammalia that they might as well be from another planet. And they are – particularly in their natural brown-green state, brandishing their claws like weapons and with thick antennae awhip – not nice to look at. And it's true that they are garbagemen of the sea, eaters of dead stuff,[4] although they'll also eat some live shellfish, certain kinds of injured fish, and sometimes each other.

But they are themselves good eating. Or so we think now. Up until sometime in the 1800s, though, lobster was literally low-class food, eaten only by the poor and institutionalized. Even in the harsh penal environment of early America, some colonies had laws against feeding lobsters to inmates more than once a week because it was thought to be cruel and unusual, like making people eat rats. One reason for their low status was how plentiful lobsters were in old New England. "Unbelievable abundance" is how one source describes the situation, including accounts of Plymouth pilgrims wading out and capturing all they wanted by hand, and of early Boston's seashore being littered with lobsters after hard storms – these latter were treated as a smelly nuisance and ground up for fertilizer. There is also the fact that premodern lobster was often cooked dead and then preserved, usually packed in salt or crude hermetic containers. Maine's earliest lobster industry was based around a dozen such seaside canneries in the 1840s, from which lobster was shipped as far

---

[3] Midcoasters' native term for a lobster is, in fact, "bug," as in "Come around on Sunday and we'll cook up some bugs."

[4] Factoid: Lobster traps are usually baited with dead herring.

away as California, in demand only because it was cheap and high in protein, basically chewable fuel.

Now, of course, lobster is posh, a delicacy, only a step or two down from caviar. The meat is richer and more substantial than most fish, its taste subtle compared to the marine-gaminess of mussels and clams. In the U.S. pop-food imagination, lobster is now the seafood analog to steak, with which it's so often twinned as Surf 'n' Turf on the really expensive part of the chain steak house menu.

In fact, one obvious project of the MLF, and of its omnipresently sponsorial Maine Lobster Promotion Council, is to counter the idea that lobster is unusually luxe or rich or unhealthy or expensive, suitable only for effete palates or the occasional blow-the-diet treat. It is emphasized over and over in presentations and pamphlets at the Festival that Maine lobster meat has fewer calories, less cholesterol, and less saturated fat than chicken.[5] And in the Main Eating Tent, you can get a "quarter" (industry shorthand for a 1 ¼ -pound lobster), a 4-ounce cup of melted butter, a bag of chips, and a soft roll w/ butter-pat for around $12.00, which is only slightly more expensive than supper at McDonald's.

Be apprised, though, that the Main Eating Tent's suppers come in Styrofoam trays, and the soft drinks are iceless and flat, and the coffee is convenience-store coffee in yet more Styrofoam, and the utensils are plastic (there are none of the special long skinny forks for pushing out the tail meat, though a few savvy diners bring their own). Nor do they give you near enough napkins, considering how messy lobster is to eat, especially when you're squeezed onto benches alongside children of various ages and vastly different levels of fine-motor development – not to mention the people who've somehow smuggled in their own beer in enormous aisle-blocking coolers, or who all of a sudden produce their own plastic tablecloths and try to spread them over large portions of tables to try to reserve them (the tables) for their little groups. And so on. Any one example is no more than a petty inconvenience, of course, but the MLF turns out to be full of irksome little downers like this – see for instance the Main Stage's headliner shows, where it turns out that you have to pay $20 extra for a folding chair if you want to sit down; or the North Tent's mad scramble for the NyQuil-cup-size samples of finalists' entries handed out after the Cooking Competition; or the much-touted Maine Sea Goddess pageant finals, which turn out to be excruciatingly long and to consist

---

[5] Of course, the common practice of dipping the lobster meat in melted butter torpedoes all these happy fat-specs, which none of the Council's promotional stuff ever mentions, any more than potato-industry PR talks about sour cream and bacon bits.

mainly of endless thanks and tributes to local sponsors. What the Maine Lobster Festival really is is a midlevel county fair with a culinary hook, and in this respect it's not unlike Tidewater crab festivals, Midwest corn festivals, Texas chili festivals, etc., and shares with these venues the core paradox of all teeming commercial demotic events: It's not for everyone.[6] Nothing against the aforementioned euphoric Senior Editor, but I'd be surprised if she'd spent much time here in Harbor Park, watching people slap canal-zone mosquitoes as they eat deep-fried Twinkies and watch Professor Paddywhack, on six-foot stilts in a raincoat with plastic lobsters protruding from all directions on springs, terrify their children.

---

[6] In truth, there's a great deal to be said about the differences between working-class Rockland and the heavily populist flavor of its Festival versus comfortable and elitist Camden with its expensive view and shops given entirely over to $200 sweaters and great rows of Victorian homes converted to upscale B&Bs. And about these differences as two sides of the great coin that is U.S. tourism. Very little of which will be said here, except to amplify the above-mentioned paradox and to reveal your assigned correspondent's own preferences. I confess that I have never understood why so many people's idea of a fun vacation is to don flip-flops and sunglasses and crawl through maddening traffic to loud hot crowded tourist venues in order to sample a "local flavor" that is by definition ruined by the presence of tourists. This may (as my Festival companions keep pointing out) all be a matter of personality and hardwired taste: The fact that I just do not like tourist venues means that I'll never understand their appeal and so am probably not the one to talk about it (the supposed appeal). But, since this note will almost surely not survive magazine-editing anyway, here goes:

As I see it, it probably really is good for the soul to be a tourist, even if it's only once in a while. Not good for the soul in a refreshing or enlivening way, though, but rather in a grim, steely-eyed, let's-look-honestly-at-the-facts-and-find-some-way-to-deal-with-them way. My personal experience has not been that traveling around the country is broadening or relaxing, or that radical changes in place and context have a salutary effect, but rather that intranational tourism is radically constricting, and humbling in the hardest way – hostile to my fantasy of being a real individual, of living somehow outside and above it all. (Coming up is the part that my companions find especially unhappy and repellent, a sure way to spoil the fun of vacation travel.) To be a mass tourist, for me, is to become a pure late-date American: alien, ignorant, greedy for something you cannot ever have, disappointed in a way you can never admit. It is to spoil, by way of sheer ontology, the very unspoiledness you are there to experience. It is to impose yourself on places that in all noneconomic ways would be better, realer, without you. It is, in lines and gridlock and transaction after transaction, to confront a dimension of yourself that is as inescapable as it is painful: As a tourist, you become economically significant but existentially loathsome, an insect on a dead thing.

Lobster is essentially a summer food. This is because we now prefer our lobsters fresh, which means they have to be recently caught, which for both tactical and economic reasons takes place at depths of less than 25 fathoms. Lobsters tend to be hungriest and most active (i.e., most trappable) at summer water temperatures of 45–50°F. In the autumn, some Maine lobsters migrate out into deeper water, either for warmth or to avoid the heavy waves that pound New England's coast all winter. Some burrow into the bottom. They might hibernate; nobody's sure. Summer is also lobsters' molting season – specifically early- to mid-July. Chitinous arthropods grow by molting, rather the way people have to buy bigger clothes as they age and gain weight. Since lobsters can live to be over 100, they can also get to be quite large, as in 20 pounds or more – though truly senior lobsters are rare now, because New England's waters are so heavily trapped.[7] Anyway, hence the culinary distinction between hard- and soft-shell lobsters, the latter sometimes a.k.a. shedders. A soft-shell lobster is one that has recently molted. In midcoast restaurants, the summer menu often offers both kinds, with shedders being slightly cheaper even though they're easier to dismantle and the meat is allegedly sweeter. The reason for the discount is that a molting lobster uses a layer of seawater for insulation while its new shell is hardening, so there's slightly less actual meat when you crack open a shedder, plus a redolent gout of water that gets all over everything and can sometimes jet out lemonlike and catch a tablemate right in the eye. If it's winter or you're buying lobster someplace far from New England, on the other hand, you can almost bet that the lobster is a hard-shell, which for obvious reasons travel better.

As an à la carte entrée, lobster can be baked, broiled, steamed, grilled, sautéed, stir-fried, or microwaved. The most common method, though, is boiling. If you're someone who enjoys having lobster at home, this is probably the way you do it, since boiling is so easy. You need a large kettle w/ cover, which you fill about half full with water (the standard advice is that you want 2.5 quarts of water per lobster). Seawater is optimal, or you can add two tbsp salt per quart from the tap. It also helps to know how much your lobsters weigh. You get the water boiling, put in the lobsters one at a time, cover the kettle, and bring it back up to a boil. Then you bank the heat and let the kettle simmer – ten minutes for the first pound of lobster, then three minutes for each pound after that. (This is assuming you've got hard-shell lobsters, which, again, if you don't live between Boston and Halifax, is probably what you've got. For shedders, you're supposed to subtract three minutes from the total.) The reason the kettle's

---

[7] Datum: In a good year, the U.S. industry produces around 80 million pounds of lobster, and Maine accounts for more than half that total.

lobsters turn scarlet is that boiling somehow suppresses every pigment in their chitin but one. If you want an easy test of whether the lobsters are done, you try pulling on one of their antennae – if it comes out of the head with minimal effort, you're ready to eat.

A detail so obvious that most recipes don't even bother to mention it is that each lobster is supposed to be alive when you put it in the kettle. This is part of lobster's modern appeal: It's the freshest food there is. There's no decomposition between harvesting and eating. And not only do lobsters require no cleaning or dressing or plucking (though the mechanics of actually eating them are a different matter), but they're relatively easy for vendors to keep alive. They come up alive in the traps, are placed in containers of seawater, and can, so long as the water's aerated and the animals' claws are pegged or banded to keep them from tearing one another up under the stresses of captivity,[8] survive right up until they're boiled. Most of us have been in supermarkets or restaurants that feature tanks of live lobster, from which you can pick out your supper while it watches you point. And part of the overall spectacle of the Maine Lobster Festival is that you can see actual lobstermen's vessels docking at the wharves along the northeast grounds and unloading freshly caught product, which is transferred by hand or cart 100 yards to the great clear tanks stacked up around the Festival's cooker – which is, as mentioned, billed as the World's Largest Lobster Cooker and can process over 100 lobsters at a time for the Main Eating Tent.

So then here is a question that's all but unavoidable at the World's Largest Lobster Cooker, and may arise in kitchens across the U.S.: Is it all right to boil a sentient creature alive just for our gustatory pleasure? A related set of concerns: Is the previous question irksomely PC or sentimental? What does "all right" even mean in this context? Is it all just a matter of individual choice?

As you may or may not know, a certain well-known group called People for the Ethical Treatment of Animals thinks that the morality of

---

[8] N.B. Similar reasoning underlies the practice of what's termed "debeaking" broiler chickens and brood hens in modern factory farms. Maximum commercial efficiency requires that enormous poultry populations be confined in unnaturally close quarters, under which conditions many birds go crazy and peck one another to death. As a purely observational side-note, be apprised that debeaking is usually an automated process and that the chickens receive no anesthetic. It's not clear to me whether most gourmet readers know about debeaking, or about related practices like dehorning cattle in commercial feedlots, cropping swine's tails in factory hog farms to keep psychotically bored neighbors from chewing them off, and so forth. It so happens that your assigned correspondent knew almost nothing about standard meat-industry operations before starting work on this article.

lobster-boiling is not just a matter of individual conscience. In fact, one of the very first things we hear about the MLF ...well, to set the scene: We're coming in by cab from the almost indescribably odd and rustic Knox County Airport[9] very late on the night before the Festival opens, sharing the cab with a wealthy political consultant who lives on Vinalhaven Island in the bay half the year (he's headed for the island ferry in Rockland). The consultant and cabdriver are responding to informal journalistic probes about how people who live in the midcoast region actually view the MLF, as in is the Festival just a big-dollar tourist thing or is it something local residents look forward to attending, take genuine civic pride in, etc. The cabdriver – who's in his seventies, one of apparently a whole platoon of retirees the cab company puts on to help with the summer rush, and wears a U.S.-flag lapel pin, and drives in what can only be called a very deliberate way – assures us that locals do endorse and enjoy the MLF, although he himself hasn't gone in years, and now come to think of it no one he and his wife know has, either. However, the demilocal consultant's been to recent Festivals a couple times (one gets the impression it was at his wife's behest), of which his most vivid impression was that "you have to line up for an ungodly long time to get your lobsters, and meanwhile there are all these ex–flower children coming up and down along the line handing out pamphlets that say the lobsters die in terrible pain and you shouldn't eat them."

And it turns out that the post-hippies of the consultant's recollection were activists from PETA. There were no PETA people in obvious view at the 2003 MLF,[10] but they've been conspicuous at many of the recent

---

[9] The terminal used to be somebody's house, for example, and the lost-luggage-reporting room was clearly once a pantry.

[10] It turned out that one Mr. William R. Rivas-Rivas, a high-ranking PETA official out of the group's Virginia headquarters, was indeed there this year, albeit solo, working the Festival's main and side entrances on Saturday, August 2, handing out pamphlets and adhesive stickers emblazoned with "Being Boiled Hurts," which is the tagline in most of PETA's published material about lobster. I learned that he'd been there only later, when speaking with Mr. Rivas-Rivas on the phone. I'm not sure how we missed seeing him *in situ* at the Festival, and I can't see much to do except apologize for the oversight – although it's also true that Saturday was the day of the big MLF parade through Rockland, which basic journalistic responsibility seemed to require going to (and which, with all due respect, meant that Saturday was maybe not the best day for PETA to work the Harbor Park grounds, especially if it was going to be just one person for one day, since a lot of diehard MLF partisans were off-site watching the parade (which, again with no offense intended, was in truth kind of cheesy and boring, consisting mostly of slow homemade floats and various midcoast people waving at one another, and with an extremely annoying man dressed as Blackbeard ranging up

245

Festivals. Since at least the mid-1990s, articles in everything from *The Camden Herald* to *The New York Time*s have described PETA urging boycotts of the MLF, often deploying celebrity spokespeople like Mary Tyler Moore for open letters and ads saying stuff like "Lobsters are extraordinarily sensitive" and "To me, eating a lobster is out of the question." More concrete is the oral testimony of Dick, our florid and extremely gregarious rental-car guy, to the effect that PETA's been around so much in recent years that a kind of brittlely tolerant homeostasis now obtains between the activists and the Festival's locals, e.g.: "We had some incidents a couple years ago. One lady took most of her clothes off and painted herself like a lobster, almost got herself arrested. But for the most part they're let alone. [Rapid series of small ambiguous laughs, which with Dick happens a lot.] They do their thing and we do our thing."

This whole interchange takes place on Route 1, 30 July, during a four-mile, 50-minute ride from the airport[11] to the dealership to sign car-rental papers. Several irreproducible segues down the road from the PETA anecdotes, Dick – whose son-in-law happens to be a professional lobsterman and one of the Main Eating Tent's regular suppliers – articulates what he and his family feel is the crucial mitigating factor in the whole morality-of-boiling-lobsters-alive issue: "There's a part of the brain in people and animals that lets us feel pain, and lobsters' brains don't have this part."

Besides the fact that it's incorrect in about 11 different ways, the main reason Dick's statement is interesting is that its thesis is more or less echoed by the Festival's own pronouncement on lobsters and pain, which is part of a Test Your Lobster IQ quiz that appears in the 2003 MLF program courtesy of the Maine Lobster Promotion Council: "The nervous system of a lobster is very simple, and is in fact most similar to the nervous system of the grasshopper. It is decentralized with no brain. There is no cerebral cortex, which in humans is the area of the brain that gives the experience of pain."

Though it sounds more sophisticated, a lot of the neurology in this latter claim is still either false or fuzzy. The human cerebral cortex is the

---

and down the length of the crowd saying "Arrr" over and over and brandishing a plastic sword at people, etc.; plus it rained)).

[11] The short version regarding why we were back at the airport after already arriving the previous night involves lost luggage and a miscommunication about where and what the local National Car Rental franchise was – Dick came out personally to the airport and got us, out of no evident motive but kindness. (He also talked nonstop the entire way, with a very distinctive speaking style that can be described only as manically laconic; the truth is that I now know more about this man than I do about some members of my own family.)

brain-part that deals with higher faculties like reason, metaphysical self-awareness, language, etc. Pain reception is known to be part of a much older and more primitive system of nociceptors and prostaglandins that are managed by the brain stem and thalamus.[12] On the other hand, it is true that the cerebral cortex is involved in what's variously called suffering, distress, or the emotional experience of pain – i.e., experiencing painful stimuli as unpleasant, very unpleasant, unbearable, and so on.

Before we go any further, let's acknowledge that the questions of whether and how different kinds of animals feel pain, and of whether and why it might be justifiable to inflict pain on them in order to eat them, turn out to be extremely complex and difficult. And comparative neuroanatomy is only part of the problem. Since pain is a totally subjective mental experience, we do not have direct access to anyone or anything's pain but our own; and even just the principles by which we can infer that others experience pain and have a legitimate interest in not feeling pain involve hard-core philosophy – metaphysics, epistemology, value theory, ethics. The fact that even the most highly evolved nonhuman mammals can't use language to communicate with us about their subjective mental experience is only the first layer of additional complication in trying to extend our reasoning about pain and morality to animals. And everything gets progressively more abstract and convoluted as we move farther and farther out from the higher-type mammals into cattle and swine and dogs and cats and rodents, and then birds and fish, and finally invertebrates like lobsters.

The more important point here, though, is that the whole animal-cruelty-and-eating issue is not just complex, it's also uncomfortable. It is, at any rate, uncomfortable for me, and for just about everyone I know who enjoys a variety of foods and yet does not want to see herself as cruel or unfeeling. As far as I can tell, my own main way of dealing with this conflict has been to avoid thinking about the whole unpleasant thing. I should add that it appears to me unlikely that many readers of *Gourmet* wish to think hard about it, either, or to be queried about the morality of their eating habits in the pages of a culinary monthly. Since, however, the assigned subject of this article is what it was like to attend the 2003 MLF, and thus to spend several days in the midst of a great mass of Americans all eating lobster, and thus to be more or less impelled to think hard about

---

[12] To elaborate by way of example: The common experience of accidentally touching a hot stove and yanking your hand back before you're even aware that anything's going on is explained by the fact that many of the processes by which we detect and avoid painful stimuli do not involve the cortex. In the case of the hand and stove, the brain is bypassed altogether; all the important neurochemical action takes place in the spine.

lobster and the experience of buying and eating lobster, it turns out that there is no honest way to avoid certain moral questions.

There are several reasons for this. For one thing, it's not just that lobsters get boiled alive, it's that you do it yourself – or at least it's done specifically for you, on-site.[13] As mentioned, the World's Largest Lobster Cooker, which is highlighted as an attraction in the Festival's program, is right out there on the MLF's north grounds for everyone to see. Try to imagine a Nebraska Beef Festival[14] at which part of the festivities is watching trucks pull up and the live cattle get driven down the ramp and slaughtered right there on the World's Largest Killing Floor or something – there's no way.

The intimacy of the whole thing is maximized at home, which of course is where most lobster gets prepared and eaten (although note already the semiconscious euphemism "prepared," which in the case of lobsters really means killing them right there in our kitchens). The basic scenario is that we come in from the store and make our little preparations like getting the kettle filled and boiling, and then we lift the lobsters out of the bag or whatever retail container they came home in ...whereupon some uncomfortable things start to happen. However stuporous the lobster is from the trip home, for instance, it tends to come alarmingly to life when placed in boiling water. If you're tilting it from a container into the steaming kettle, the lobster will sometimes try to cling to the container's sides or even to hook its claws over the kettle's rim like a person trying to

---

[13] Morality-wise, let's concede that this cuts both ways. Lobster-eating is at least not abetted by the system of corporate factory farms that produces most beef, pork, and chicken. Because, if nothing else, of the way they're marketed and packaged for sale, we eat these latter meats without having to consider that they were once conscious, sentient creatures to whom horrible things were done. (N.B. PETA distributes a certain video – the title of which is being omitted as part of the elaborate editorial compromise by which this note appears at all – in which you can see just about everything meat-related you don't want to see or think about. (N.B. Not that PETA's any sort of font of unspun truth. Like many partisans in complex moral disputes, the PETA people are fanatics, and a lot of their rhetoric seems simplistic and self-righteous. Personally, though, I have to say that I found this unnamed video both credible and deeply upsetting.))

[14] Is it significant that "lobster," "fish," and "chicken" are our culture's words for both the animal and the meat, whereas most mammals seem to require euphemisms like "beef" and "pork" that help us separate the meat we eat from the living creature the meat once was? Is this evidence that some kind of deep unease about eating higher animals is endemic enough to show up in English usage, but that the unease diminishes as we move out of the mammalian order? (And is "lamb"/"lamb" the counterexample that sinks the whole theory, or are there special, biblico-historical reasons for that equivalence?)

248

keep from going over the edge of a roof. And worse is when the lobster's fully immersed. Even if you cover the kettle and turn away, you can usually hear the cover rattling and clanking as the lobster tries to push it off. Or the creature's claws scraping the sides of the kettle as it thrashes around. The lobster, in other words, behaves very much as you or I would behave if we were plunged into boiling water (with the obvious exception of screaming).[15] A blunter way to say this is that the lobster acts as if it's in terrible pain, causing some cooks to leave the kitchen altogether and to take one of those little lightweight plastic oven timers with them into another room and wait until the whole process is over.

There happen to be two main criteria that most ethicists agree on for determining whether a living creature has the capacity to suffer and so has genuine interests that it may or may not be our moral duty to consider.[16] One is how much of the neurological hardware required for pain-experience the animal comes equipped with – nociceptors, prostaglandins, neuronal opioid receptors, etc. The other criterion is whether the animal demonstrates behavior associated with pain. And it takes a lot of intellectual gymnastics and behaviorist hairsplitting not to see struggling, thrashing, and lid-clattering as just such pain-behavior. According to marine zoologists, it usually takes lobsters between 35 and 45 seconds to die in boiling water. (No source I could find talked about how long it takes them to die in superheated steam; one rather hopes it's faster.)

There are, of course, other fairly common ways to kill your lobster on-site and so achieve maximum freshness. Some cooks' practice is to drive a sharp heavy knife point-first into a spot just above the midpoint between

---

[15] There's a relevant populist myth about the high-pitched whistling sound that sometimes issues from a pot of boiling lobster. The sound is really vented steam from the layer of seawater between the lobster's flesh and its carapace (this is why shedders whistle more than hard-shells), but the pop version has it that the sound is the lobster's rabbitlike death scream. Lobsters communicate via pheromones in their urine and don't have anything close to the vocal equipment for screaming, but the myth's very persistent – which might, once again, point to a low-level cultural unease about the boiling thing.

[16] "Interests" basically means strong and legitimate preferences, which obviously require some degree of consciousness, responsiveness to stimuli, etc. See, for instance, the utilitarian philosopher Peter Singer, whose 1974 *Animal Liberation* is more or less the bible of the modern animal-rights movement: "It would be nonsense to say that it was not in the interests of a stone to be kicked along the road by a schoolboy. A stone does not have interests because it cannot suffer. Nothing that we can do to it could possibly make any difference to its welfare. A mouse, on the other hand, does have an interest in not being kicked along the road, because it will suffer if it is."

249

the lobster's eyestalks (more or less where the Third Eye is in human foreheads). This is alleged either to kill the lobster instantly or to render it insensate – and is said at least to eliminate the cowardice involved in throwing a creature into boiling water and then fleeing the room. As far as I can tell from talking to proponents of the knife-in-the-head method, the idea is that it's more violent but ultimately more merciful, plus that a willingness to exert personal agency and accept responsibility for stabbing the lobster's head honors the lobster somehow and entitles one to eat it. (There's often a vague sort of Native American spirituality-of-the-hunt flavor to pro-knife arguments.) But the problem with the knife method is basic biology: Lobsters' nervous systems operate off not one but several ganglia, a.k.a. nerve bundles, which are sort of wired in series and distributed all along the lobster's underside, from stem to stern. And disabling only the frontal ganglion does not normally result in quick death or unconsciousness. Another alternative is to put the lobster in cold salt water and then very slowly bring it up to a full boil. Cooks who advocate this method are going mostly on the analogy to a frog, which can supposedly be kept from jumping out of a boiling pot by heating the water incrementally. In order to save a lot of research-summarizing, I'll simply assure you that the analogy between frogs and lobsters turns out not to hold.

Ultimately, the only certain virtues of the home-lobotomy and slow-heating methods are comparative, because there are even worse/crueler ways people prepare lobster. Time-thrifty cooks sometimes microwave them alive (usually after poking several extra vent holes in the carapace, which is a precaution most shellfish-microwavers learn about the hard way). Live dismemberment, on the other hand, is big in Europe: Some chefs cut the lobster in half before cooking; others like to tear off the claws and tail and toss only these parts in the pot.

And there's more unhappy news respecting suffering-criterion number one. Lobsters don't have much in the way of eyesight or hearing, but they do have an exquisite tactile sense, one facilitated by hundreds of thousands of tiny hairs that protrude through their carapace. "Thus," in the words of T.M. Prudden's industry classic *About Lobster*, "it is that although encased in what seems a solid, impenetrable armor, the lobster can receive stimuli and impressions from without as readily as if it possessed a soft and delicate skin." And lobsters do have nociceptors,[17] as well as

---

[17] This is the neurological term for special pain receptors that are (according to Jane A. Smith and Kenneth M. Boyd's *Lives in the Balance*) "sensitive to potentially damaging extremes of temperature, to mechanical forces, and to chemical substances which are released when body tissues are damaged."

invertebrate versions of the prostaglandins and major neurotransmitters via which our own brains register pain.

Lobsters do not, on the other hand, appear to have the equipment for making or absorbing natural opioids like endorphins and enkephalins, which are what more advanced nervous systems use to try to handle intense pain. From this fact, though, one could conclude either that lobsters are maybe even *more* vulnerable to pain, since they lack mammalian nervous systems' built-in analgesia, or, instead, that the absence of natural opioids implies an absence of the really intense pain-sensations that natural opioids are designed to mitigate. I for one can detect a marked upswing in mood as I contemplate this latter possibility: It could be that their lack of endorphin/enkephalin hardware means that lobsters' raw subjective experience of pain is so radically different from mammals' that it may not even deserve the term *pain*. Perhaps lobsters are more like those frontal-lobotomy patients one reads about who report experiencing pain in a totally different way than you and I. These patients evidently do feel physical pain, neurologically speaking, but don't dislike it – though neither do they like it; it's more that they feel it but don't feel anything *about* it – the point being that the pain is not distressing to them or something they want to get away from. Maybe lobsters, who are also without frontal lobes, are detached from the neurological-registration-of-injury-or-hazard we call pain in just the same way. There is, after all, a difference between (1) pain as a purely neurological event, and (2) actual suffering, which seems crucially to involve an emotional component, an awareness of pain as unpleasant, as something to fear/dislike/want to avoid.

Still, after all the abstract intellection, there remain the facts of the frantically clanking lid, the pathetic clinging to the edge of the pot. Standing at the stove, it is hard to deny in any meaningful way that this is a living creature experiencing pain and wishing to avoid/escape the painful experience. To my lay mind, the lobster's behavior in the kettle appears to be the expression of a *preference*; and it may well be that an ability to form preferences is the decisive criterion for real suffering.[18] The logic of this (preference → suffering) relation may be easiest to see in the negative case. If you cut certain kinds of worms in half, the halves will often keep crawling around and going about their vermiform business as if nothing had happened. When we assert, based on their post-op behavior, that these worms appear not to be suffering, what we're really saying is that there's

---

[18] "Preference" is maybe roughly synonymous with "interest," but it is a better term for our purposes because it's less abstractly philosophical – "preference" seems more personal, and it's the whole idea of a living creature's personal experience that's at issue.

no sign that the worms know anything bad has happened or would *prefer* not to have gotten cut in half.

Lobsters, however, are known to exhibit preferences. Experiments have shown that they can detect changes of only a degree or two in water temperature; one reason for their complex migratory cycles (which can often cover 100-plus miles a year) is to pursue the temperatures they like best.[19] And, as mentioned, they're bottom-dwellers and do not like bright light: If a tank of food lobsters is out in the sunlight or a store's fluorescence, the lobsters will always congregate in whatever part is darkest. Fairly solitary in the ocean, they also clearly dislike the crowding that's part of their captivity in tanks, since (as also mentioned) one reason why lobsters' claws are banded on capture is to keep them from attacking one another under the stress of close-quarter storage.

In any event, at the Festival, standing by the bubbling tanks outside the World's Largest Lobster Cooker, watching the fresh-caught lobsters pile over one another, wave their hobbled claws impotently, huddle in the rear corners, or scrabble frantically back from the glass as you approach, it is difficult not to sense that they're unhappy, or frightened, even if it's some rudimentary version of these feelings …and, again, why does rudimentariness even enter into it? Why is a primitive, inarticulate form of suffering less urgent or uncomfortable for the person who's helping to

---

[19] Of course, the most common sort of counterargument here would begin by objecting that "like best" is really just a metaphor, and a misleadingly anthropomorphic one at that. The counterarguer would posit that the lobster seeks to maintain a certain optimal ambient temperature out of nothing but unconscious instinct (with a similar explanation for the low-light affinities about to be mentioned in the main text). The thrust of such a counterargument will be that the lobster's thrashings and clankings in the kettle express not unpreferred pain but involuntary reflexes, like your leg shooting out when the doctor hits your knee. Be advised that there are professional scientists, including many researchers who use animals in experiments, who hold to the view that nonhuman creatures have no real feelings at all, only "behaviors." Be further advised that this view has a long history that goes all the way back to Descartes, although its modern support comes mostly from behaviorist psychology.

To these what-look-like-pain-are-really-only-reflexes counterarguments, however, there happen to be all sorts of scientific and pro-animal-rights countercounterarguments. And then further attempted rebuttals and redirects, and so on. Suffice to say that both the scientific and the philosophical arguments on either side of the animal-suffering issue are involved, abstruse, technical, often informed by self-interest or ideology, and in the end so totally inconclusive that as a practical matter, in the kitchen or restaurant, it all still seems to come down to individual conscience, going with (no pun) your gut.

inflict it by paying for the food it results in? I'm not trying to give you a PETA-like screed here – at least I don't think so. I'm trying, rather, to work out and articulate some of the troubling questions that arise amid all the laughter and saltation and community pride of the Maine Lobster Festival. The truth is that if you, the Festival attendee, permit yourself to think that lobsters can suffer and would rather not, the MLF can begin to take on aspects of something like a Roman circus or medieval torture-fest.

Does that comparison seem a bit much? If so, exactly why? Or what about this one: Is it not possible that future generations will regard our own present agribusiness and eating practices in much the same way we now view Nero's entertainments or Aztec sacrifices? My own immediate reaction is that such a comparison is hysterical, extreme – and yet the reason it seems extreme to me appears to be that I believe animals are less morally important than human beings;[20] and when it comes to defending such a belief, even to myself, I have to acknowledge that (a) I have an obvious selfish interest in this belief, since I like to eat certain kinds of animals and want to be able to keep doing it, and (b) I have not succeeded in working out any sort of personal ethical system in which the belief is truly defensible instead of just selfishly convenient.

Given this article's venue and my own lack of culinary sophistication, I'm curious about whether the reader can identify with any of these reactions and acknowledgments and discomforts. I am also concerned not to come off as shrill or preachy when what I really am is confused. Given the (possible) moral status and (very possible) physical suffering of the animals involved, what ethical convictions do gourmets evolve that allow them not just to eat but to savor and enjoy flesh-based viands (since of course refined *enjoyment*, rather than just ingestion, is the whole point of gastronomy)? And for those gourmets who'll have no truck with convictions or rationales and who regard stuff like the previous paragraph as just so much pointless navel-gazing, what makes it feel okay, inside, to dismiss the whole issue out of hand? That is, is their refusal to think about any of this the product of actual thought, or is it just that they don't want to think about it? Do they ever think about their reluctance to think about it? After all, isn't being extra aware and attentive and thoughtful about one's food and its overall context part of what distinguishes a real

---

[20] Meaning a *lot* less important, apparently, since the moral comparison here is not the value of one human's life vs. the value of one animal's life, but rather the value of one animal's life vs. the value of one human's taste for a particular kind of protein. Even the most diehard carniphile will acknowledge that it's possible to live and eat well without consuming animals.

gourmet? Or is all the gourmet's extra attention and sensibility just supposed to be aesthetic, gustatory?

These last couple queries, though, while sincere, obviously involve much larger and more abstract questions about the connections (if any) between aesthetics and morality, and these questions lead straightaway into such deep and treacherous waters that it's probably best to stop the public discussion right here. There are limits to what even interested persons can ask of each other.

The Evolution of Human Science
Ted Chiang

First published as "Catching Crumbs from the Table" in *Nature* 405 (1 June 2000):517. Reprinted as "The Evolution of Human Science" in *Stories of Your Life and Others*, New York: Vintage Books, 2002, pp. 201-203.

Ted Chiang (Chinese name Chiang Feng-nan, b. 1967) is an American science fiction writer, whose short stories and novellas have garnered multiple Nebula, Hugo, and Locus awards. In 2016 his novella "Story of Your Life" was adapted into the major motion picture Arrival, *starring Amy Adams and Jeremy Renner.*

Why we are reading this: *What if there were genetically advanced humans who could do scientific research so advanced that ordinary humans could not understand it? This is the kind of future that Chiang explores in this story, written in the form of a magazine article at some unspecified time in the future. As he said in a 2010 interview, "Science fiction is very well suited to asking philosophical questions; questions about the nature of reality, what it means to be human, how do we know the things that we think we know. When philosophers propose thought experiments as a way of analyzing certain questions, their thought experiments often sound a lot like science fiction. I think that there's a very good fit between the two" (https://medium.com/learning-for-life/stories-of-ted-chiangs-life-and-others-694cb3c80d13).*

It has been twenty-five years since a report of original research was last submitted to our editors for publication, making this an appropriate time to revisit the question that was so widely debated then: what is the role of human scientists in an age when the frontiers of scientific inquiry have moved beyond the comprehension of humans?

No doubt many of our subscribers remember reading papers whose authors were the first individuals ever to obtain the results they described. But as metahumans began to dominate experimental research, they increasingly made their findings available only via DNT (digital neural transfer), leaving journals to publish secondhand accounts translated into human language. Without DNT humans could not fully grasp prior developments nor effectively utilize the new tools needed to conduct research, while metahumans continued to improve DNT and rely on it even more. Journals for human audiences were reduced to vehicles of popularization, and poor ones at that, as even the most brilliant humans found themselves puzzled by translations of the latest findings.

No one denies the many benefits of metahuman science, but one of its costs to human researchers was the realization that they would likely never make an original contribution to science again. Some left the field altogether, but those who stayed shifted their attention away from original research and toward hermeneutics: interpreting the scientific work of metahumans.

Textual hermeneutics became popular first, since there were already terabytes of metahuman publications whose translations, while cryptic, were presumably not entirely inaccurate. Deciphering these texts bears little resemblance to the task performed by traditional paleographers, but progress continues: recent experiments have validated the Humphries decipherment of decade-old publications on histocompatibility genetics.

The availability of devices based on metahuman science gave rise to artifact hermeneutics. Scientists began attempting to "reverse engineer" these artifacts, their goal being not to manufacture competing products, but simply to understand the physical principles underlying their operation. The most common technique is the crystallographic analysis of nanoware appliances, which frequently provides us with new insights into mechanosynthesis.

The newest and by far the most speculative mode of inquiry is remote sensing of metahuman research facilities. A recent target of investigation is the ExaCollider recently installed beneath the Gobi Desert, whose puzzling neutrino signature has been the subject of much controversy. (The portable neutrino detector is, of course, another metahuman artifact whose operating principles remain elusive.)

The question is, are these worthwhile undertakings for scientists? Some call them a waste of time, likening them to a Native American research effort into bronze smelting when steel tools of European manufacture are readily available. This comparison might be more apt if humans were in competition with metahumans, but in today's economy of abundance there is no evidence of such competition. In fact, it is important to recognize that – unlike most previous low-technology cultures confronted with a high-technology one – humans are in no danger of assimilation or extinction.

There is still no way to augment a human brain into a meta human one; the Sugimoto gene therapy must be performed before the embryo begins neurogenesis in order for a brain to be compatible with DNT. This lack of an assimilation mechanism means that human parents of a metahuman child face a difficult choice: to allow their child DNT interaction with metahuman culture, and watch their child grow incomprehensible to them;

or else restrict access to DNT during the child's formative years, which to a metahuman is deprivation like that suffered by Kaspar Hauser. It is not surprising that the percentage of human parents choosing the Sugimoto gene therapy for their children has dropped almost to zero in recent years. As a result, human culture is likely to survive well into the future, and. the scientific tradition is a vital part of that culture. Hermeneutics is a legitimate method of scientific inquiry and increases the body of human knowledge just as original research did. Moreover, human researchers may discern applications overlooked by metahumans whose advantages tend to make them unaware of our concerns. For example, imagine if research offered hope of a different intelligence-enhancing therapy, one that would allow individuals to gradually "upgrade" their minds to a metahuman-equivalent level. Such a therapy would offer a bridge across what has become the greatest cultural divide in our species' history, yet it might not even occur to metahumans to explore it; that possibility alone justifies the continuation of human research.

We need not be intimidated by the accomplishments of metahuman science. We should always remember that the technologies that made metahumans possible were originally invented by humans, and they were no smarter than we.

The Weight of Glory
C. S. Lewis

Published in *Theology*, November 1941, and as part of the book *The Weight of Glory and Other Addresses*, MacMillan, 1949, and HarperCollins, 2001.

*C. S. Lewis (1898-1963) was a British writer, lay theologian, and professor of English literature at both Oxford University (1925-54) and Cambridge University (1954-63). He is best known for his works of fiction (*Chronicles of Narnia, The Space Trilogy, *and* The Screwtape Letters) *and his Christian apologetics (*Mere Christianity, The Problem of Pain, *and* Miracles).*

Why we are reading this: What follows is a sermon delivered by C. S. Lewis on June 8, 1941, in the Church of St Mary the Virgin at Oxford University. It remains one of his most popular public addresses on Christian belief. He explores his vision of heaven and reflects on the sort of life and approach that would help one arrive in heaven in the afterlife. This essay affords us an opportunity to reflect on some of the "ways of knowing" questions raised by Noel Boyle in the introduction to this volume: Is intuition or a gut feeling a way of knowing? Is faith? Can scripture provide us with knowledge? If so, what kind?

If you asked twenty good men to-day what they thought the highest of the virtues, nineteen of them would reply, Unselfishness. But if you asked almost any of the great Christians of old he would have replied, Love. You see what has happened? A negative term has been substituted for a positive, and this is of more than philological importance. The negative ideal of Unselfishness carries with it the suggestion not primarily of securing good things for others, but of going without them ourselves, as if our abstinence and not their happiness was the important point. I do not think this is the Christian virtue of Love. The New Testament has lots to say about self-denial, but not about self-denial as an end in itself. We are told to deny ourselves and to take up our crosses in order that we may follow Christ; and nearly every description of what we shall ultimately find if we do so contains an appeal to desire. If there lurks in most modern minds the notion that to desire our own good and earnestly to hope for the enjoyment of it is a bad thing, I submit that this notion has crept in from Kant and the Stoics and is no part of the Christian faith. Indeed, if we consider the unblushing promises of reward and the staggering nature of the rewards promised in the Gospels, it would seem that Our Lord finds our desires, not too strong, but too weak. We are half-hearted creatures, fooling about with drink and sex and ambition when infinite joy is offered us, like an ignorant child who wants to go on making mud pies in a slum because he cannot imagine what is meant by the offer of a holiday at the sea. We are far too easily pleased.

We must not be troubled by unbelievers when they say that this promise of reward makes the Christian life a mercenary affair. There are different kinds of reward. There is the reward which has no natural connexion with the things you do to earn it, and is quite foreign to the desires that ought to accompany those things. Money is not the natural reward of love; that is why we call a man mercenary if he marries a woman for the sake of her money. But marriage is the proper reward for a real lover, and he is not mercenary for desiring it. A general who fights well in order to get a peerage is mercenary; a general who fights for victory is not, victory being the proper reward of battle as marriage is the proper reward of love. The proper rewards are not simply tacked on to the activity for which they are given, but are the activity itself in consummation. There is also a third case, which is more complicated. An enjoyment of Greek poetry is certainly a proper, and not a mercenary, reward for learning Greek; but only those who have reached the stage of enjoying Greek poetry can tell from their own experience that this is so. The schoolboy beginning Greek grammar cannot look forward to his adult enjoyment of Sophocles as a lover looks forward to marriage or a general to victory. He has to begin by working for marks, or to escape punishment, or to please his parents, or, at best, in the hope of a future good which he cannot at present imagine or desire. His position, therefore, bears a certain resemblance to that of the mercenary; the reward he is going to get will, in actual fact, be a natural or proper reward, but he will not know that till he has got it. Of course, he gets it gradually; enjoyment creeps in upon the mere drudgery, and nobody could point to a day or an hour when the one ceased and the other began. But it is just in so far as he approaches the reward that be becomes able to desire it for its own sake; indeed, the power of so desiring it is itself a preliminary reward.

The Christian, in relation to heaven, is in much the same position as this schoolboy. Those who have attained everlasting life in the vision of God doubtless know very well that it is no mere bribe, but the very consummation of their earthly discipleship; but we who have not yet attained it cannot know this in the same way, and cannot even begin to know it at all except by continuing to obey and finding the first reward of our obedience in our increasing power to desire the ultimate reward. Just in proportion as the desire grows, our fear lest it should be a mercenary desire will die away and finally be recognized as an absurdity. But probably this will not, for most of us, happen in a day; poetry replaces grammar, gospel replaces law, longing transforms obedience, as gradually as the tide lifts a grounded ship.

But there is one other important similarity between the schoolboy and ourselves. If he is an imaginative boy he will, quite probably, be revelling in the English poets and romancers suitable to his age some time before he begins to suspect that Greek grammar is going to lead him to more and more enjoyments of this same sort. He may even be neglecting his Greek to read Shelley and Swinburne in secret. In other words, the desire which Greek is really going to gratify already exists in him and is attached to objects which seem to him quite unconnected with Xenophon and the verbs in μι. Now, if we are made for heaven, the desire for our proper place will be already in us, but not yet attached to the true object, and will even appear as the rival of that object. And this, I think, is just what we find. No doubt there is one point in which my analogy of the schoolboy breaks down. The English poetry which he reads when he ought to be doing Greek exercises may be just as good as the Greek poetry to which the exercises are leading him, so that in fixing on Milton instead of journeying on to Aeschylus his desire is not embracing a false object. But our case is very different. If a transtemporal, transfinite good is our real destiny, then any other good on which our desire fixes must be in some degree fallacious, must bear at best only a symbolical relation to what will truly satisfy.

In speaking of this desire for our own far off country, which we find in ourselves even now, I feel a certain shyness. I am almost committing an indecency. I am trying to rip open the inconsolable secret in each one of you – the secret which hurts so much that you take your revenge on it by calling it names like Nostalgia and Romanticism and Adolescence; the secret also which pierces with such sweetness that when, in very intimate conversation, the mention of it becomes imminent, we grow awkward and affect to laugh at ourselves; the secret we cannot hide and cannot tell, though we desire to do both. We cannot tell it because it is a desire for something that has never actually appeared in our experience. We cannot hide it because our experience is constantly suggesting it, and we betray ourselves like lovers at the mention of a name. Our commonest expedient is to call it beauty and behave as if that had settled the matter. Wordsworth's expedient was to identify it with certain moments in his own past. But all this is a cheat. If Wordsworth had gone back to those moments in the past, he would not have found the thing itself, but only the reminder of it; what he remembered would turn out to be itself a remembering. The books or the music in which we thought the beauty was located will betray us if we trust to them; it was not in them, it only came through them, and what came through them was longing. These things –

the beauty, the memory of our own past – are good images of what we really desire; but if they are mistaken for the thing itself they turn into dumb idols, breaking the hearts of their worshippers. For they are not the thing itself; they are only the scent of a flower we have not found, the echo of a tune we have not heard, news from a country we have never yet visited. Do you think I am trying to weave a spell? Perhaps I am; but remember your fairy tales. Spells are used for breaking enchantments as well as for inducing them. And you and I have need of the strongest spell that can be found to wake us from the evil enchantment of worldliness which has been laid upon us for nearly a hundred years. Almost our whole education has been directed to silencing this shy, persistent, inner voice; almost all our modern philosophies have been devised to convince us that the good of man is to be found on this earth. And yet it is a remarkable thing that such philosophies of Progress or Creative Evolution themselves bear reluctant witness to the truth that our real goal is elsewhere. When they want to convince you that earth is your home, notice how they set about it. They begin by trying to persuade you that earth can be made into heaven, thus giving a sop to your sense of exile in earth as it is. Next, they tell you that this fortunate event is still a good way off in the future, thus giving a sop to your knowledge that the fatherland is not here and now. Finally, lest your longing for the transtemporal should awake and spoil the whole affair, they use any rhetoric that comes to hand to keep out of your mind the recollection that even if all the happiness they promised could come to man on earth, yet still each generation would lose it by death, including the last generation of all, and the whole story would be nothing, not even a story, for ever and ever. Hence all the nonsense that Mr. Shaw puts into the final speech of Lilith, and Bergson's remark that the élan vital is capable of surmounting all obstacles, perhaps even death – as if we could believe that any social or biological development on this planet will delay the senility of the sun or reverse the second law of thermodynamics.

Do what they will, then, we remain conscious of a desire which no natural happiness will satisfy. But is there any reason to suppose that reality offers any satisfaction to it? "Nor does the being hungry prove that we have bread." But I think it may be urged that this misses the point. A man's physical hunger does not prove that that man will get any bread; he may die of starvation on a raft in the Atlantic. But surely a man's hunger does prove that he comes of a race which repairs its body by eating and inhabits a world where eatable substances exist. In the same way, though I do not believe (I wish I did) that my desire for Paradise proves that I shall enjoy it, I think it a pretty good indication that such a thing exists and that some men will. A man may love a woman and not win her; but it would be very odd if the phenomenon called "falling in love" occurred in a sexless world.

Here, then, is the desire, still wandering and uncertain of its object and still largely unable to see that object in the direction where it really lies. Our sacred books give us some account of the object. It is, of course, a symbolical account. Heaven is, by definition, outside our experience, but all intelligible descriptions must be of things within our experience. The scriptural picture of heaven is therefore just as symbolical as the picture which our desire, unaided, invents for itself; heaven is not really full of jewelry any more than it is really the beauty of Nature, or a fine piece of music. The difference is that the scriptural imagery has authority. It comes to us from writers who were closer to God than we, and it has stood the test of Christian experience down the centuries. The natural appeal of this authoritative imagery is to me, at first, very small. At first sight it chills, rather than awakes, my desire. And that is just what I ought to expect. If Christianity could tell me no more of the far-off land than my own temperament led me to surmise already, then Christianity would be no higher than myself. If it has more to give me, I must expect it to be less immediately attractive than "my own stuff." Sophocles at first seems dull and cold to the boy who has only reached Shelley. If our religion is something objective, then we must never avert our eyes from those elements in it which seem puzzling or repellent; for it will be precisely the puzzling or the repellent which conceals what we do not yet know and need to know.

The promises of Scripture may very roughly be reduced to five heads. It is promised, firstly, that we shall be with Christ; secondly, that we shall be like Him; thirdly, with an enormous wealth of imagery, that we shall have "glory"; fourthly, that we shall, in some sense, be fed or feasted or entertained; and, finally, that we shall have some sort of official position in the universe – ruling cities, judging angels, being pillars of God's temple. The first question I ask about these promises is: "Why any of them except the first?" Can anything be added to the conception of being with Christ? For it must be true, as an old writer says, that he who has God and everything else has no more than he who has God only. I think the answer turns again on the nature of symbols. For though it may escape our notice at first glance, yet it is true that any conception of being with Christ which most of us can now form will be not very much less symbolical than the other promises; for it will smuggle in ideas of proximity in space and loving conversation as we now understand conversation, and it will probably concentrate on the humanity of Christ to the exclusion of His deity. And, in fact, we find that those Christians who attend solely to this first promise always do fill it up with very earthly imagery indeed – in fact, with hymeneal or erotic imagery. I am not for a moment condemning such imagery. I heartily wish I could enter into it more deeply than I do, and pray that I yet shall. But my point is that this also is only a symbol, like the reality in some respects, but unlike it in others, and therefore needs correction from the different symbols in the other promises. The variation of the promises does not mean that anything other than God will be our ultimate bliss; but because God is more than a Person, and lest we should imagine the joy of His presence too exclusively in terms of our present poor experience of personal love, with all its narrowness and strain and monotony, a dozen changing images, correcting and relieving each other, are supplied.

I turn next to the idea of glory. There is no getting away from the fact that this idea is very prominent in the New Testament and in early Christian writings. Salvation is constantly associated with palms, crowns, white robes, thrones, and splendour like the sun and stars. All this makes no immediate appeal to me at all, and in that respect I fancy I am a typical modern. Glory suggests two ideas to me, of which one seems wicked and the other ridiculous. Either glory means to me fame, or it means luminosity. As for the first, since to be famous means to be better known than other people, the desire for fame appears to me as a competitive passion and therefore of hell rather than heaven. As for the second, who wishes to become a kind of living electric light bulb?

When I began to look into this matter I was shocked to find such different Christians as Milton, Johnson and Thomas Aquinas taking heavenly glory quite frankly in the sense of fame or good report. But not fame conferred by our fellow creatures – fame with God, approval or (I might say) "appreciation" by God. And then, when I had thought it over, I saw that this view was scriptural; nothing can eliminate from the parable the divine accolade, "Well done, thou good and faithful servant." With that, a good deal of what I had been thinking all my life fell down like a house of cards. I suddenly remembered that no one can enter heaven except as a child; and nothing is so obvious in a child – not in a conceited child, but in a good child – as its great and undisguised pleasure in being praised. Not only in a child, either, but even in a dog or a horse. Apparently what I had mistaken for humility had, all these years. prevented me from understanding what is in fact the humblest, the most childlike, the most creaturely of pleasures – nay, the specific pleasure of the inferior: the pleasure a beast before men, a child before its father, a pupil before his teacher, a creature before its Creator. I am not forgetting how horribly this most innocent desire is parodied in our human ambitions, or how very quickly, in my own experience, the lawful pleasure of praise from those whom it was my duty to please turns into the deadly poison of self-admiration. But I thought I could detect a moment – a very, very short moment – before this happened, during which the satisfaction of having pleased those whom I rightly loved and rightly feared was pure. And that is enough to raise our thoughts to what may happen when the redeemed soul, beyond all hope and nearly beyond belief, learns at last that she has pleased Him whom she was created to please. There will be no room for vanity then. She will be free from the miserable illusion that it is her doing. With no taint of what we should now call self-approval she will most innocently rejoice in the thing that God has made her to be, and the moment which heals her old inferiority complex for ever will also drown her pride deeper than Prospero's book. Perfect humility dispenses with modesty. If God is satisfied with the work, the work may be satisfied with itself; "it is not for her to bandy compliments with her Sovereign." I can imagine someone saying that he dislikes my idea of heaven as a place where we are patted on the back. But proud misunderstanding is behind that dislike. In the end that Face which is the delight or the terror of the universe must be turned upon each of us either with one expression or with the other, either conferring glory inexpressible or inflicting shame that can never be cured or disguised. I read in a periodical the other day that the fundamental thing is how we think of God. By God Himself, it is not! How God thinks of us is not only more important, but infinitely more important. Indeed, how we think of Him is of no importance except in so far as it is related to how He thinks of us. It is written that we shall "stand before" Him, shall appear, shall be inspected. The promise of glory is the promise, almost incredible and only possible by the work of Christ, that some of us, that any of us who really chooses, shall actually survive that examination, shall find approval, shall please God. To please God...to be a real ingredient in the divine happiness...to be loved by God, not merely pitied, but delighted in as an artist delights in his work or a father in a son – it seems impossible, a weight or burden of glory which our thoughts can hardly sustain. But so it is.

And now notice what is happening. If I had rejected the authoritative and scriptural image of glory and stuck obstinately to the vague desire which was, at the outset, my only pointer to heaven, I could have seen no connexion at all between that desire and the Christian promise. But now, having followed up what seemed puzzling and repellent in the sacred books, I find, to my great surprise, looking back, that the connexion is perfectly clear. Glory, as Christianity teaches me to hope for it, turns out to satisfy my original desire and indeed to reveal an element in that desire which I had not noticed. By ceasing for a moment to consider my own wants I have begun to learn better what I really wanted. When I attempted, a few minutes ago, to describe our spiritual longings, I was omitting one of their most curious characteristics. We usually notice it just as the moment of vision dies away, as the music ends or as the landscape loses the celestial light. What we feel then has been well described by Keats as "the journey homeward to habitual self." You know what I mean. For a few minutes we have had the illusion of belonging to that world. Now we wake to find that it is no such thing. We have been mere spectators. Beauty has smiled, but not to welcome us; her face was turned in our direction, but not to see us. We have not been accepted, welcomed, or taken into the dance. We may go when we please, we may stay if we can: "Nobody marks us." A scientist may reply that since most of the things we call beautiful are inanimate, it is not very surprising that they take no notice of us. That, of course, is true. It is not the physical objects that I am speaking of, but that indescribable something of which they become for a moment the messengers. And part of the bitterness which mixes with the sweetness of that message is due to the fact that it so seldom seems to be a message intended for us but rather something we have overheard. By bitterness I mean pain, not resentment. We should hardly dare to ask that any notice be taken of ourselves. But we pine. The sense that in this universe we are treated as strangers, the longing to be acknowledged, to meet with some response, to bridge some chasm that yawns between us and reality, is part of our inconsolable secret. And surely, from this point of view, the promise of glory, in the sense described, becomes highly relevant to our deep desire. For glory meant good report with God, acceptance by God, response, acknowledgment, and welcome into the heart of things. The door on which we have been knocking all our lives will open at last.

Perhaps it seems rather crude to describe glory as the fact of being "noticed" by God. But this is almost the language of the New Testament. St. Paul promises to those who love God not, as we should expect, that they will know Him, but that they will be known by Him (I Cor. viii. 3). It is a strange promise. Does not God know all things at all times? But it is dreadfully reechoed in another passage of the New Testament. There we are warned that it may happen to any one of us to appear at last before the face of God and hear only the appalling words: "I never knew you. Depart from Me." In some sense, as dark to the intellect as it is unendurable to the feelings, we can be both banished from the presence of Him who is present everywhere and erased from the knowledge of Him who knows all. We can be left utterly and absolutely outside – repelled, exiled, estranged, finally and unspeakably ignored. On the other hand, we can be called in, welcomed, received, acknowledged. We walk every day on the razor edge between these two incredible possibilities. Apparently, then, our lifelong nostalgia, our longing to be reunited with something in the universe from which we now feel cut off, to be on the inside of some door which we have

265

always seen from the outside, is no mere neurotic fancy, but the truest index of our real situation. And to be at last summoned inside would be both glory and honour beyond all our merits and also the healing of that old ache.

And this brings me to the other sense of glory – glory as brightness, splendour, luminosity. We are to shine as the sun, we are to be given the Morning Star. I think I begin to see what it means. In one way, of course, God has given us the Morning Star already: you can go and enjoy the gift on many fine mornings if you get up early enough. What more, you may ask, do we want? Ah, but we want so much more – something the books on aesthetics take little notice of. But the poets and the mythologies know all about it. We do not want merely to see beauty, though, God knows, even that is bounty enough. We want something else which can hardly be put into words – to be united with the beauty we see, to pass into it, to receive it into ourselves, to bathe in it, to become part of it. That is why we have peopled air and earth and water with gods and goddesses and nymphs and elves – that, though we cannot, yet these projections can, enjoy in themselves that beauty grace, and power of which Nature is the image. That is why the poets tell us such lovely falsehoods. They talk as if the west wind could really sweep into a human soul; but it can't. They tell us that "beauty born of murmuring sound" will pass into a human face; but it won't. Or not yet. For if we take the imagery of Scripture seriously, if we believe that God will one day give us the Morning Star and cause us to put on the splendour of the sun, then we may surmise that both the ancient myths and the modern poetry, so false as history, may be very near the truth as prophecy. At present we are on the outside of the world, the wrong side of the door. We discern the freshness and purity of morning, but they do not make us fresh and pure. We cannot mingle with the splendours we see. But all the leaves of the New Testament are rustling with the rumour that it will not always be so. Some day, God willing, we shall get in. When human souls have become as perfect in voluntary obedience as the inanimate creation is in its lifeless obedience, then they will put on its glory, or rather that greater glory of which Nature is only the first sketch. For you must not think that I am putting forward any heathen fancy of being absorbed into Nature. Nature is mortal; we shall outlive her. When all the suns and nebulae have passed away, each one of you will still be alive. Nature is only the image, the symbol; but it is the symbol Scripture invites me to use. We are summoned to pass in through Nature, beyond her, into that splendour which she fitfully reflects.

And in there, in beyond Nature, we shall eat of the tree of life. At present, if we are reborn in Christ, the spirit in us lives directly on God; but the mind, and still more the body, receives life from Him at a thousand removes – through our ancestors, through our food, through the elements. The faint, far-off results of those energies which God's creative rapture implanted in matter when He made the worlds are what we now call physical pleasures; and even thus filtered, they are too much for our present management. What would it be to taste at the fountain-head that stream of which even these lower reaches prove so intoxicating? Yet that, I believe, is what lies before us. The whole man is to drink joy from the fountain of joy. As St. Augustine said, the rapture of the saved soul will "flow over" into the glorified body. In the light of our present specialized and depraved appetites we cannot imagine this *torrens voluptatis*, and I warn everyone seriously not to try. But it must be mentioned, to drive out thoughts even more misleading – thoughts that what is saved is a mere ghost, or that the risen body lives in numb insensibility. The body was made for the Lord, and these dismal fancies are wide of the mark.

Meanwhile the cross comes before the crown and tomorrow is a Monday morning. A cleft has opened in the pitiless walls of the world, and we are invited to follow our great Captain inside. The following Him is, of course, the essential point. That being so, it may be asked what practical use there is in the speculations which I have been indulging. I can think of at least one such use. It may be possible for each to think too much of his own potential glory hereafter; it is hardly possible for him to think too often or too deeply about that of his neighbour. The load, or weight, or burden of my neighbour's glory should be laid daily on my back, a load so heavy that only humility can carry it, and the backs of the proud will be broken. It is a serious thing to live in a society of possible gods and goddesses, to remember that the dullest and most uninteresting person you talk to may one day be a creature which, if you saw it now, you would be strongly tempted to worship, or else a horror and a corruption such as you now meet, if at all, only in a nightmare. All day long we are, in some degree, helping each other to one or other of these destinations. It is in the light of these overwhelming possibilities, it is with the awe and the circumspection proper to them, that we should conduct all our dealings with one another, all friendships, all loves, all play, all politics. There are no ordinary people. You have never talked to a mere mortal. Nations, cultures, arts, civilization – these are mortal, and their life is to ours as the life of a gnat. But it is immortals whom we joke with, work with, marry, snub, and exploit – immortal horrors or everlasting splendours. This does not mean that we are to be perpetually solemn. We must play. But our merriment must be of that kind (and it is, in fact, the merriest kind) which exists between people who have, from the outset, taken each other seriously – no flippancy, no superiority, no presumption. And our charity must be a real and costly love, with deep feeling for the sins in spite of which we love the sinner – no mere tolerance or indulgence which parodies love as flippancy parodies merriment. Next to the Blessed Sacrament itself, your neighbour is the holiest object presented to your senses. If he is your Christian neighbour he is holy in almost the same way, for in him also Christ *vere latitat* – the glorifier and the glorified, Glory Himself, is truly hidden.

The Land of Sad Oranges

Ghassan Kanafani

In *Men in the Sun and Other Palestinian Stories*. Trans. Hilary Kirkpatrick. Boulder, CO: Lynne Rienner Publishers, 1999, pp. 75-80.

Ghassan Kanafani (1936-1972) was born in the town of Acre, in British-ruled Palestine. When the British withdrew from Palestine in 1948 and the first Arab-Israeli war broke out, Kanafani's family became refugees, as did about 700,000 other Palestinians. Later in life Kanafani became a leading member of the Popular Front for the Liberation of Palestine (a secular Marxist organization) and the author of several novels and short stories about the Arab Palestinian experience. He was assassinated by the Mossad in 1972.

Why we are reading this: *This short story, first published in Arabic in 1958, is a fictional representation of a family in the process of becoming refugees during the same conflict that had turned Kanafani's own life upside down. His depiction of displacement, social disruption, and psychological trauma draws on the specific Palestinian experience. Yet his refusal to explore the larger political context and his close focus on the day-to-day tragedy of a single family, people who are passive victims of events outside their control, gives his story a more universal quality.*

When we set out from Jaffa for Acre, there was nothing tragic about our departure. We were just like anybody who goes to spend the festival season every year in another city. Our time in Acre passed as usual, with nothing untoward. I was young then, and so I probably enjoyed those days because they kept me from going to school. But whatever the fact of the matter, the picture gradually became clearer on the night of the great attack on Acre. That night passed, cruel and bitter, amidst the despondency of the men and the prayers of the women. You and I and the others of our age were too young to understand what the story meant from beginning to end, but that night the threads began to grow clearer. In the morning, when the Jews withdrew, threatening and fuming, a big lorry was standing at the door of our house. A simple collection of bedding was being thrown into it, from here and there, quickly and feverishly. I was standing leaning against the ancient wall of the house when I saw your mother climb into the lorry, followed by your aunt and the children. Your father started tossing you and your brothers and sisters into the lorry, and on top of the belongings, and then he seized me from my corner and lifted me over his head into the iron rack on the roof of the driver's cab, where I found my brother Riyad sitting quietly. The lorry was already moving off before I had settled myself into a comfortable position. Beloved Acre was already disappearing behind the bends in the road going up to Ras Naquora.

It was rather cloudy, and a chilly feeling invaded my body. Riyad was sitting quite quietly, with his legs hanging over the edge of the rack, leaning his back against the luggage, as he stared into the sky. I sat silently, with my chin between my knees and my arms wrapped round them. The groves of orange trees followed each other in succession along the side of the road. We were all eaten up with fear. The lorry panted over the damp earth, and the sound of distant shots rang out like a farewell.

When Ras Naqoura came into sight in the distance, cloudy on the blue horizon, the lorry stopped. The women climbed down over the luggage and made for a peasant sitting cross-legged with a basket of oranges just in front of him. They picked up the oranges, and the sound of their weeping reached our ears. I thought then that oranges were something dear and these big, clean fruits were beloved objects in our eyes. When the women had bought some oranges, they brought them over to the lorry and your father climbed down from the driver's side and stretched out his hand to take one. He began to gaze at it in silence, and then burst into tears like a despairing child.

In Ras Naqoura our lorry stopped beside many others. The men began handing their weapons to the policeman stationed there for the purpose, and as our turn came and I saw the rifles and machine guns lying on the table and looked towards the long line of lorries entering Lebanon, rounding the bends in the roads and putting more and more distance between themselves and the land of the oranges, I too burst into a storm of weeping. Your mother was still looking silently at the orange. And all the orange trees that your father had abandoned to the Jews shone in his eyes, all the well-tended orange trees that he had bought one by one were printed on his face and reflected in the tears that he could not control in front of the officer at the police post.

In the afternoon, when we reached Sidon, we had become refugees.

We were among those swallowed up by the road. Your father looked as though it was a long time since he had slept. He was standing in the street in front of the belongings heaped on the ground, and I quite imagined that if I ran over to say something to him he would explode in my face: "Damn your father! Damn...!" Those two oaths were clearly etched on his face. I myself, a child educated in a strict religious school, at that moment doubted whether this God really wanted to make men happy. I also doubted whether this God could hear and see everything. The colored pictures that were handed out to us in the school chapel showing the Lord having compassion on children and smiling in their faces seemed like another of the lies made up by people who open strict schools in order to get higher fees. I was sure that the God we had known in Palestine had left it too, and was a refugee in some place that I did not know, unable to find a solution to his own problems. And we, human refugees, sitting on the pavement waiting for a new Fate to bring some solution, were responsible for providing a roof under which to spend the night. Pain had begun to undermine the child's simple mind.

Night is a fearful thing. The darkness that gradually came down over us cast terror into my heart. The mere thought that I would spend the night on the pavement aroused all kinds of fears within me. They were cruel and harsh. No one was prepared to have pity on me. I could not find anyone to console me. Your father's silent glance cast fresh terror into my breast. The orange that your mother held in her hand set my head on fire. Everyone was silent, staring at the black road, keen for Fate to appear round the corner and hand out solutions to our difficulties, so that we could follow him to some shelter. Suddenly Fate did come; your uncle had reached the town before us, and he was our fate.

Your uncle never had great faith in ethics, and when he found himself on the pavement like us, he lost it entirely. He made for a house occupied by a Jewish family, opened the door, threw his belongings inside and jerked his round face at them, saying very distinctly: "Go to Palestine!" It is certain that they did not go, but they were frightened by his desperation, and they went into the next room, leaving him to enjoy the roof and tiled floor.

Your uncle led us to that shelter of his and pitched us into it with his belongings and family. During the night we slept on the floor, and it was completely taken up with our small bodies. We used the men's coats for coverings, and when we got up in the morning we found that the men had passed the night sitting up. The tragedy had begun to eat into our very souls.

We did not stay long in Sidon. Your uncle's room was not large enough for half of us, but it held us for three nights. Then your mother asked your father to look for some job, or let us return to the orange trees. Your father shouted in her face, the rancor trembling in his voice, and she fell silent. Our family problems had begun. The happy, united family we had left behind, with the land, the house, and the martyrs killed defending them.

I don't know where your father got the money from. I know that he sold the gold he had bought for your mother when he wanted to make her happy and proud that she was his wife. But the gold did not bring in a sum large enough to solve our problems. There must have been another source.

Did he borrow at all? Did he sell something else he had brought away without our noticing? I don't know. But I do remember that we moved to a village on the outskirts of Sidon, and there your father sat on the high stone balcony, smiling for the first time and waiting for the fifteenth of May in order to return in the wake of the victorious armies.

The fifteenth of May came, after a bitter period of waiting. At exactly midnight your father poked me with his foot as I lay asleep and said in a voice vibrant with hope: "Get up and see for yourself as the Arab armies enter Palestine." I was up like a shot, and we clambered down barefoot over the hills to the main road, which lay a full kilometer from the village. All of us, young and old, panted as we ran like madmen. The lights of the lorries climbing to Ras Naqoura shone in the distance. When we got to the road we felt cold, but your father's shout drove everything else from our minds. He had begun to race after the lorries like a small boy. He was calling out to them. He was giving hoarse shouts and gasping for breath, but still he raced along after the string of lorries like a little boy. We ran along beside him, shouting in unison with him. The friendly soldiers were looking at us from under their helmets, silent and motionless. We were gasping for breath. Meanwhile your father, racing along despite his fifty years, pulled cigarettes out of his pocket to throw to the soldiers and went on shouting to them. We were still running along beside him, like a little flock of goats.

Suddenly the lorries were at an end. We went back to the house exhausted, our breathing coming with a low whistle as we gasped for air. Your father was absolutely silent, and we too were incapable of speech. When the lights of a passing car fell on your father's face, his cheeks were wet with tears.

Things dragged past extremely slowly after that. The communiques deceived us, and then the truth in all its bitterness cheated us. Despondency found its way back to people's faces. Your father began to find enormous difficulty in mentioning Palestine and talking of the happy past spent in his plantations and houses. And we were the ones who formed the massive walls of the tragedy that dominated his new life, as well as being the wretches who discovered, without any difficulty at all, that the idea behind climbing the hills in the early morning, as your father ordered, was to distract us from demanding breakfast.

Complications set in. In some extraordinary way the simplest thing was enough to rouse your father. I remember perfectly the time when someone asked him for something – I neither know nor recall what. He shuddered, and then began trembling as though he had received an electric shock. His eyes glittered as they roamed over our faces. A diabolical thought had implanted itself in his brain, and he jumped up like a man who has found a satisfactory conclusion. Overwhelmed by his awareness that he was able to put an end to his difficulties, and by the dread of someone who is about to undertake a momentous action, he began to mutter to himself as he turned round and round, looking for something we could not see. Then he pounced on a chest that had accompanied us from Acre and started to scatter its contents with terrible nervous movements. Your mother had understood everything in an instant and, caught up in the agitation that mothers feel when their children are exposed to danger, she set about pushing us out of the room and telling us to run away to the mountain. But we stayed by the window. We plastered our little ears to its shutters, and heard your father's voice: "I want to kill them. I want to kill myself. I want to be done with... I want..."

Your father fell silent. When we looked into the room again, through the cracks in the door, we saw him lying on the ground, gasping for breath and grinding his teeth as he wept, while your mother sat at one side watching him anxiously.

We did not understand. But I remember that when I saw the black revolver lying on the floor beside him, I understood everything. Driven by the mortal terror of a child who has suddenly caught sight of an ogre, I ran off towards the mountain, fleeing from the house.

As I left the house behind, I left my childhood behind too. I realized that our life had ceased to be pleasant, and it was no longer easy for us to live in peace. Things had reached the point where the only solution was a bullet in the head of each one of us. So we must take care to behave suitably in all that we did, not asking for something to eat even when we were hungry, keeping silent when your father spoke of his difficulties and nodding and smiling when he said to us: "Go and climb the mountain, and don't come back till midday."

I returned home in the evening, when dusk had fallen. Your father was still ill and your mother was sitting beside him. Your eyes all had a catlike glitter and your lips were sealed as though they had never been opened, as though they were the scars left by an old wound not properly healed.

You were huddled there, as far from your childhood as you were from the land of the oranges – the oranges that, according to a peasant who used to cultivate them until he left, would shrivel up if a change occurred and they were watered by a strange hand.

Your father was still ill in bed. Your mother was choking back the tears of a tragedy that has not left her eyes till now. I slipped into the room like a pariah. When my glance fell on your father's face, which was twitching with impotent fury, I saw at the same moment the black revolver lying on the low table, and beside it an orange.

The orange was dried up and shriveled.

273

Of Our Spiritual Strivings
W.E.B. DuBois

Chapter 1 in *The Souls of Black Folk*. Chicago: A. C. McClurg, 1903.

W.E.B. DuBois (1868-1963) was an American intellectual and activist. A polymath, he published books and articles in, among other things, philosophy, history, sociology, political thought and literature. DuBois was among the founders of the National Association for the Advancement of Colored People (NAACP) and the first editor of its influential magazine, The Crisis. *DuBois spent decades advancing the cause of black people in America, along the way doing important and startlingly perceptive work conceptualizing black identity, politics, and art. A committed internationalist and cosmopolitan, DuBois was also among the founders of Pan-Africanism, a transatlantic political movement among peoples of African descent. In a strange historical coincidence, he died in exile in Ghana in the summer of 1963, a day before the March on Washington, arguably the high point of the American civil rights movement. This essay, "Of Our Spiritual Strivings" is a part of one of the great nonfiction works written by an American in the 20th century,* The Souls of Black Folk *(1903).*

Why we are reading this: Writing in 1903, the author takes stock of the state of race relations forty years after Lincoln's Emancipation Proclamation had freed slaves in the South during the Civil War. He explores the "double consciousness" that had developed among African Americans by that point and argues for the value of education for blacks to achieve the liberation that still seemed to elude them.

O water, voice of my heart, crying in the sand,
All night long crying with a mournful cry,
As I lie and listen, and cannot understand
The voice of my heart in my side or the voice of the sea,
O water, crying for rest, is it I, is it I?
All night long the water is crying to me.

Unresting water, there shall never be rest
Till the last moon droop and the last tide fail,
And the fire of the end begin to burn in the west;
And the heart shall be weary and wonder and cry like the sea,

All life long crying without avail,
As the water all night long is crying to me.

ARTHUR SYMONS[1]

[musical notation from "Nobody Knows the Trouble I've Seen"]

Between me and the other world there is ever an unasked question: unasked by some through feelings of delicacy; by others through the difficulty of rightly framing it. All, nevertheless, flutter round it. They approach me in a half-hesitant sort of way, eye me curiously or compassionately, and then, instead of saying directly, How does it feel to be a problem? they say, I know an excellent colored man in my town; or, I fought at Mechanicsville; or, Do not these Southern outrages make your blood boil? At these I smile, or am interested, or reduce the boiling to a simmer, as the occasion may require. To the real question, How does it feel to be a problem? I answer seldom a word.

And yet, being a problem is a strange experience, – peculiar even for one who has never been anything else, save perhaps in babyhood and in Europe. It is in the early days of rollicking boyhood that the revelation first bursts upon one, all in a day, as it were. I remember well when the shadow swept across me. I was a little thing, away up in the hills of New England, where the dark Housatonic winds between Hoosac and Taghkanic to the sea. In a wee wooden schoolhouse, something put it into the boys' and girls' heads to buy gorgeous visiting-cards – ten cents a package – and exchange. The exchange was merry, till one girl, a tall newcomer, refused my card, – refused it peremptorily, with a glance. Then it dawned upon me with a certain suddenness that I was different from the others; or like, mayhap, in heart and life and longing, but shut out from their world by a vast veil. I had thereafter no desire to tear down that veil, to creep through; I held all beyond it in common contempt, and lived above it in a region of blue sky and great wandering shadows. That sky was bluest when I could beat my mates at examination-time, or beat them at a foot-race, or even beat their stringy heads. Alas, with the years all this fine contempt began to fade; for the words I longed for, and all their dazzling opportunities,

---

[1] Arthur Symons (1865-1945) was a British poet.

275

were theirs, not mine. But they should not keep these prizes, I said; some, all, I would wrest from them. Just how I would do it I could never decide: by reading law, by healing the sick, by telling the wonderful tales that swam in my head, – some way. With other black boys the strife was not so fiercely sunny: their youth shrunk into tasteless sycophancy, or into silent hatred of the pale world about them and mocking distrust of everything white; or wasted itself in a bitter cry, Why did God make me an outcast and a stranger in mine own house? The shades of the prison-house closed round about us all: walls strait and stubborn to the whitest, but relentlessly narrow, tall, and unscalable to sons of night who must plod darkly on in resignation, or beat unavailing palms against the stone, or steadily, half hopelessly, watch the streak of blue above.

After the Egyptian and Indian, the Greek and Roman, the Teuton and Mongolian, the Negro is a sort of seventh son, born with a veil, and gifted with second-sight in this American world, – a world which yields him no true self-consciousness, but only lets him see himself through the revelation of the other world. It is a peculiar sensation, this double-consciousness, this sense of always looking at one's self through the eyes of others, of measuring one's soul by the tape of a world that looks on in amused contempt and pity. One ever feels his twoness, – an American, a Negro; two souls, two thoughts, two unreconciled strivings; two warring ideals in one dark body, whose dogged strength alone keeps it from being torn asunder.

The history of the American Negro is the history of this strife, – this longing to attain self-conscious manhood, to merge his double self into a better and truer self. In this merging he wishes neither of the older selves to be lost. He would not Africanize America, for America has too much to teach the world and Africa. He would not bleach his Negro soul in a flood of white Americanism, for he knows that Negro blood has a message for the world. He simply wishes to make it possible for a man to be both a Negro and an American, without being cursed and spit upon by his fellows, without having the doors of Opportunity closed roughly in his face.

This, then, is the end of his striving: to be a co-worker in the kingdom of culture, to escape both death and isolation, to husband and use his best powers and his latent genius. These powers of body and mind have in the past been strangely wasted, dispersed, or forgotten. The shadow of a mighty Negro past flits through the tale of Ethiopia the Shadowy and of Egypt the Sphinx. Through history, the powers of single black men flash here and there like falling stars, and die sometimes before the world has rightly gauged their brightness. Here in America, in the few days since Emancipation, the black man's turning hither and thither in hesitant and doubtful striving has often made his very strength to lose effectiveness, to seem like absence of power, like weakness. And yet it is not weakness, – it is the contradiction of double aims. The double-aimed struggle of the black artisan – on the one hand to escape white contempt for a nation of mere hewers of wood and drawers of water, and on the other hand to plough and nail and dig for a poverty-stricken horde – could only result in making him a poor craftsman, for he had but half a heart in either cause. By the poverty and ignorance of his people, the Negro minister or doctor was tempted toward quackery and demagogy; and by the criticism of the other world, toward ideals that made him ashamed of his lowly tasks. The would-be black *savant* was confronted by the paradox that the knowledge his people needed was a twice-told tale to his white neighbors, while the knowledge which would teach the white world was Greek to his own flesh and blood. The innate love of harmony and beauty that set the ruder souls of his people a-dancing and a-singing raised but confusion and doubt in the soul of the black artist; for the beauty revealed to him was the soul-beauty of a race which his larger audience despised, and he could not articulate the message of another people. This waste of double aims, this seeking to satisfy two unreconciled ideals, has wrought sad havoc with the courage and faith and deeds of ten thousand thousand people, – has sent them often wooing false gods and invoking false means of salvation, and at times has even seemed about to make them ashamed of themselves.

Away back in the days of bondage they thought to see in one divine event the end of all doubt and disappointment; few men ever worshipped Freedom with half such unquestioning faith as did the American Negro for two centuries. To him, so far as he thought and dreamed, slavery was indeed the sum of all villainies, the cause of all sorrow, the root of all prejudice; Emancipation was the key to a promised land of sweeter beauty than ever stretched before the eyes of wearied Israelites. In song and exhortation swelled one refrain – Liberty; in his tears and curses the God he implored had Freedom in his right hand. At last it came, – suddenly, fearfully, like a dream. With one wild carnival of blood and passion came the message in his own plaintive cadences: –

Shout, O children!
Shout, you're free!
For God has bought your liberty!

Years have passed away since then, – ten, twenty, forty; forty years of national life, forty years of renewal and development, and yet the swarthy spectre sits in its accustomed seat at the Nation's feast. In vain do we cry to this our vastest social problem: –

Take any shape but that, and my firm nerves
Shall never tremble!

The Nation has not yet found peace from its sins; the freedman has not yet found in freedom his promised land. Whatever of good may have come in these years of change, the shadow of a deep disappointment rests upon the Negro people, – a disappointment all the more bitter because the unattained ideal was unbounded save by the simple ignorance of a lowly people.

The first decade was merely a prolongation of the vain search for freedom, the boon that seemed ever barely to elude their grasp, – like a tantalizing will-o'-the-wisp, maddening and misleading the headless host. The holocaust of war, the terrors of the Ku-Klux Klan, the lies of carpet-baggers, the disorganization of industry, and the contradictory advice of friends and foes, left the bewildered serf with no new watchword beyond the old cry for freedom. As the time flew, however, he began to grasp a new idea. The ideal of liberty demanded for its attainment powerful means, and these the Fifteenth Amendment gave him. The ballot, which before he had looked upon as a visible sign of freedom, he now regarded as the chief means of gaining and perfecting the liberty with which war had partially endowed him. And why not? Had not votes made war and emancipated millions? Had not votes enfranchised the freedmen? Was anything impossible to a power that had done all this? A million black men started with renewed zeal to vote themselves into the kingdom. So the decade flew away, the revolution of 1876 came, and left the half-free serf weary, wondering, but still inspired. Slowly but steadily, in the following years, a new vision began gradually to replace the dream of political power, – a powerful movement, the rise of another ideal to guide the unguided, another pillar of fire by night after a clouded day. It was the ideal of "book-learning"; the curiosity, born of compulsory ignorance, to know and test the power of the cabalistic letters of the white man, the longing to know. Here at last seemed to have been discovered the mountain path to Canaan; longer than the highway of Emancipation and law, steep and rugged, but straight, leading to heights high enough to overlook life.

Up the new path the advance guard toiled, slowly, heavily, doggedly; only those who have watched and guided the faltering feet, the misty minds, the dull understandings, of the dark pupils of these schools know how faithfully, how piteously, this people strove to learn. It was weary work. The cold statistician wrote down the inches of progress here and there, noted also where here and there a foot had slipped or some one had fallen. To the tired climbers, the horizon was ever dark, the mists were often cold, the Canaan was always dim and far away. If, however, the vistas disclosed as yet no goal, no resting-place, little but flattery and criticism, the journey at least gave leisure for reflection and self-examination; it changed the child of Emancipation to the youth with dawning self-consciousness, self-realization, self-respect. In those sombre forests of his striving his own soul rose before him, and he saw himself, – darkly as through a veil; and yet he saw in himself some faint revelation of his power, of his mission. He began to have a dim feeling that, to attain his place in the world, he must be himself, and not another. For the first time he sought to analyze the burden he bore upon his back, that dead-weight of social degradation partially masked behind a half-named Negro problem. He felt his poverty; without a cent, without a home, without land, tools, or savings, he had entered into competition with rich, landed, skilled neighbors. To be a poor man is hard, but to be a poor race in a land of dollars is the very bottom of hardships. He felt the weight of his ignorance, – not simply of letters, but of life, of business, of the humanities; the accumulated sloth and shirking and awkwardness of decades and centuries shackled his hands and feet. Nor was his burden all poverty and ignorance. The red stain of bastardy, which two centuries of systematic legal defilement of Negro women had stamped upon his race, meant not only the loss of ancient African chastity, but also the hereditary weight of a mass of corruption from white adulterers, threatening almost the obliteration of the Negro home.

A people thus handicapped ought not to be asked to race with the world, but rather allowed to give all its time and thought to its own social problems. But alas! while sociologists gleefully count his bastards and his prostitutes, the very soul of the toiling, sweating black man is darkened by the shadow of a vast despair. Men call the shadow prejudice, and learnedly explain it as the natural defence of culture against barbarism, learning against ignorance, purity against crime, the "higher" against the "lower" races. To which the Negro cries Amen! and swears that to so much of this strange prejudice as is founded on just homage to civilization, culture, righteousness, and progress, he humbly bows and meekly does obeisance. But before that nameless prejudice that leaps beyond all this he stands helpless, dismayed, and well-nigh speechless; before that personal disrespect and mockery, the ridicule and systematic humiliation, the distortion of fact and wanton license of fancy, the cynical ignoring of the better and the boisterous welcoming of the worse, the all-pervading desire to inculcate disdain for everything black, from Toussaint to the devil, – before this there rises a sickening despair that would disarm and discourage any nation save that black host to whom "discouragement" is an unwritten word.

But the facing of so vast a prejudice could not but bring the inevitable self-questioning, self-disparagement, and lowering of ideals which ever accompany repression and breed in an atmosphere of contempt and hate. Whisperings and portents came home upon the four winds: Lo! we are diseased and dying, cried the dark hosts; we cannot write, our voting is vain; what need of education, since we must always cook and serve? And the Nation echoed and enforced this self-criticism, saying: Be content to be servants, and nothing more; what need of higher culture for half-men? Away with the black man's ballot, by force or fraud, – and behold the suicide of a race! Nevertheless, out of the evil came something of good, – the more careful adjustment of education to real life, the clearer perception of the Negroes' social responsibilities, and the sobering realization of the meaning of progress.

So dawned the time of *Sturm und Drang:* storm and stress to-day rocks our little boat on the mad waters of the world-sea; there is within and without the sound of conflict, the burning of body and rending of soul; inspiration strives with doubt, and faith with vain questionings. The bright ideals of the past, – physical freedom, political power, the training of brains and the training of hands, – all these in turn have waxed and waned, until even the last grows dim and overcast. Are they all wrong, – all false? No, not that, but each alone was over-simple and incomplete, – the dreams of a credulous race-childhood, or the fond imaginings of the other world which does not know and does not want to know our power. To be really true, all these ideals must be melted and welded into one. The training of the schools we need to-day more than ever, – the training of deft hands, quick eyes and ears, and above all the broader, deeper, higher culture of gifted minds and pure hearts. The power of the ballot we need in sheer self-defence, – else what shall save us from a second slavery? Freedom, too, the long-sought, we still seek, – the freedom of life and limb, the freedom to work and think, the freedom to love and aspire. Work, culture, liberty, – all these we need, not singly but together, not successively but together, each growing and aiding each, and all striving toward that vaster ideal that swims before the Negro people, the ideal of human brotherhood, gained through the unifying ideal of Race; the ideal of fostering and developing the traits and talents of the Negro, not in opposition to or contempt for other races, but rather in large conformity to the greater ideals of the American Republic, in order that some day on American soil two world-races may give each to each those characteristics both so sadly lack. We the darker ones come even now not altogether empty-handed: there are to-day no truer exponents of the pure human spirit of the Declaration of Independence than the American Negroes; there is no true American music but the wild sweet melodies of the Negro slave; the American fairy tales and folklore are Indian and African; and, all in all, we black men seem the sole oasis of simple faith and reverence in a dusty desert of dollars and smartness. Will America be poorer if she replace her brutal dyspeptic blundering with light-hearted but determined Negro humility? or her coarse and cruel wit with loving jovial good-humor? or her vulgar music with the soul of the Sorrow Songs?

Merely a concrete test of the underlying principles of the great republic is the Negro Problem, and the spiritual striving of the freedmen's sons is the travail of souls whose burden is almost beyond the measure of their strength, but who bear it in the name of an historic race, in the name of this the land of their fathers' fathers, and in the name of human opportunity.

And now what I have briefly sketched in large outline let me on coming pages tell again in many ways, with loving emphasis and deeper detail, that men may listen to the striving in the souls of black folk.

Afterimages
Audre Lorde

In *Chosen Poems: Old and New*, Norton, 1982.

Audre Lorde (1934-1992) was an African-American poet, writer, feminist, librarian, teacher, and civil rights activist. Born to Caribbean immigrant parents in New York City, Lorde became a masterful poet, often conveying anger and outrage at the social injustice she witnessed. In her prose works, she was an important innovator and theorist of black feminism, lesbianism, personal identity, and intersectionality.

Why we are reading this: *Poetry can give us access to someone else's memories, perspectives, and subjective view of the world. In this poem, written in 1981, the poet reflects on her memories of two traumatic events. The first was the murder of Emmett Till, a fourteen-year-old black boy from Chicago who was visiting relatives in the small town of Money, Mississippi, in the summer of 1955. He apparently flirted or whistled at a white woman working in a small grocery store, violating the color line that was drawn much more strictly than he realized. Four days later, the woman's husband and his half-brother abducted, tortured, and murdered Till, dumping his body in the nearby Tallahatchie river. The two men were acquitted by an all-white jury, though they later admitted to the crime in a magazine interview. Between the 1880s and 1960s, over 3,000 African Americans were lynched in the United States, including more than 500 in Mississippi, but this particular case became notorious. Till's mother insisted that he be given an open-casket funeral in Chicago and allowed news photographs of his mutilated body to be published in newspapers and magazines around the country and abroad. The murder, photographs, and subsequent trial directed attention to the injustices suffered by African Americans in the U.S. South and helped galvanize the Civil Rights movement. The second event referenced in the poem is the devastating flood of the Pearl River in April 1979, which placed most of Jackson, the state capital of Mississippi, under water and forced more than 17,000 people from their homes. Audre Lorde experienced both events from a distance, through the mediation of journalism and television. She imagines a metaphysical connection between these two events and offers insight into the workings of memory and imagination.*

I

However the image enters
its force remains within
my eyes
rockstrewn caves where dragonfish evolve
wild for life, relentless and acquisitive
learning to survive
where there is no food
my eyes are always hungry
and remembering
however the image enters
its force remains.
A white woman stands bereft and empty
a black boy hacked into a murderous lesson
recalled in me forever
like a lurch of earth on the edge of sleep
etched into my visions
food for dragonfish that learn
to live upon whatever they must eat
fused images beneath my pain.

II

The Pearl River floods through the streets of Jackson
A Mississippi summer televised.
Trapped houses kneel like sinners in the rain
a white woman climbs from her roof to a passing boat
her fingers tarry for a moment on the chimney
now awash
tearless and no longer young, she holds
a tattered baby's blanket in her arms.
In a flickering afterimage of the nightmare rain
a microphone
thrust up against her flat bewildered words
        "we jest come from the bank yestiddy
            borrowing money to pay the income tax
            now everything's gone. I never knew
            it could be so hard."
Despair weighs down her voice like Pearl River mud
caked around the edges
her pale eyes scanning the camera for help or explanation

unanswered
she shifts her search across the watered street, dry-eyed
"hard, but not this hard."
Two tow-headed children hurl themselves against her
hanging upon her coat like mirrors
until a man with ham-like hands pulls her aside
snarling "She ain't got nothing more to say!"
and that lie hangs in his mouth
like a shred of rotting meat.

III

I inherited Jackson, Mississippi.
For my majority it gave me Emmett Till
his 15 years puffed out like bruises
on plump boy-cheeks
his only Mississippi summer
whistling a 21 gun salute to Dixie
as a white girl passed him in the street
and he was baptized my son forever
in the midnight waters of the Pearl.

His broken body is the afterimage of my 21st year
when I walked through a northern summer
my eyes averted
from each corner's photographies
newspapers protest posters magazines
Police Story, Confidential, True
the avid insistence of detail
pretending insight or information
the length of gash across the dead boy's loins
his grieving mother's lamentation
the severed lips, how many burns
his gouged out eyes
sewed shut upon the screaming covers
louder than life
all over
the veiled warning, the secret relish
of a black child's mutilated body
fingered by street-corner eyes
bruise upon livid bruise
and wherever I looked that summer

I learned to be at home with children's blood
with savored violence
with pictures of black broken flesh
used, crumpled, and discarded
lying amid the sidewalk refuse
like a raped woman's face.

A black boy from Chicago
whistled on the streets of Jackson, Mississippi
testing what he'd been taught was a manly thing to do
his teachers
ripped his eyes out his sex his tongue
and flung him to the Pearl weighted with stone
in the name of white womanhood
they took their aroused honor
back to Jackson
and celebrated in a whorehouse
the double ritual of white manhood
confirmed.

IV

"If earth and air and water do not judge them who are
we to refuse a crust of bread?"

Emmett Till rides the crest of the Pearl, whistling
24 years his ghost lay like the shade of a raped woman
and a white girl has grown older in costly honor
(what did she pay to never know its price?)
now the Pearl River speaks its muddy judgment
and I can withhold my pity and my bread.

"Hard, but not this hard."
Her face is flat with resignation and despair
with ancient and familiar sorrows
a woman surveying her crumpled future
as the white girl besmirched by Emmett's whistle
never allowed her own tongue
without power or conclusion
unvoiced
she stands adrift in the ruins of her honor
and a man with an executioner's face

285

pulls her away.

Within my eyes
the flickering afterimages of a nightmare rain
a woman wrings her hands
beneath the weight of agonies remembered
I wade through summer ghosts
betrayed by vision
hers and my own
becoming dragonfish to survive
the horrors we are living
with tortured lungs
adapting to breathe blood.

A woman measures her life's damage
my eyes are caves, chunks of etched rock
tied to the ghost of a black boy
whistling
crying and frightened
her tow-headed children cluster
like little mirrors of despair
their father's hands upon them
and soundlessly
a woman begins to weep.

On Being "White" ... and Other Lies
James Baldwin

In *Essence*, April 1984.

James Baldwin (1924-1987) was a prominent American novelist, social critic, essayist and playwright. Born in an African-American family in Harlem, Baldwin's talents as a writer emerged before he finished high school. Frustrated by the racism he experienced in the United States, Baldwin chose to live his entire adult life in France, where he felt he could define himself as a writer without being read as "merely a Negro; or, even, merely a Negro writer." He lived for two decades in Paris before relocating to the south of France. In his writings and numerous trips back to America, Baldwin played an active role in the civil rights movement. He was also an early supporter of LGBT rights, as exemplified by his novel Giovanni's Room *(1956). Deeply engaged in cultural and literary affairs throughout his life, Baldwin was a friend and mentor to many writers, including Maya Angelou, Toni Morrison, and Nikki Giovanni.*

Why we are reading this: In this brief essay, a prominent black writer who often wrote in the voice of white characters (see Gates' essay above) reflects on the nature of white identity. Baldwin points out the socially-constructed nature of white identity (new immigrants were, say, Irish-Americans for a long while before becoming "white") and the historical association of "whiteness" in America with enslavement of Africans and genocide of Native Americans. Baldwin asserts along the way that black identity was constructed as well. Baldwin is speaking for himself and does not represent "the" African-American view of whites, yet it is certainly "an" African-American view. Some students may find this "black" vision of "whites" to be jarring and unexpected, taking issue with certain claims, or they might find some points of agreement. This is what happens when we encounter new points of view. Expect lively discussions.

The crisis of leadership in the white community is remarkable – and terrifying – because there is, in fact, no white community.

This may seem an enormous statement – and it is. I'm willing to be challenged. I'm also willing to attempt to spell it out.

My frame of reference is, of course, America, or that portion of the North American continent that calls itself America. And this means I am speaking, essentially, of the European vision of the world – or more precisely; perhaps, the European vision of the universe. It is a vision as remarkable for what it pretends to include as for what it remorselessly diminishes, demolishes or leaves totally out of account.

There is, for example – at least, in principle – an Irish community: here, there, anywhere, or, more precisely, Belfast, Dublin and Boston. There is a German community: both sides of Berlin, Bavaria and Yorkville. There is an Italian community: Rome, Naples, the Bank of the Holy Ghost and Mulberry Street. And there is a Jewish community, stretching from Jerusalem to California to New York. There are English communities. There are French communities. There are Swiss consortiums. There are Poles: in Warsaw (where they would like us to be friends) and in Chicago (where because they are white we are enemies). There are, for that matter, Indian restaurants and Turkish baths. There is the underworld – the poor (to say nothing of those who intend to become rich) are always with us – but this does not describe a community. It bears terrifying witness to what happened to everyone who got here, and paid the price of the ticket. The price was to become "white." No one was white before he/she came to America. It took generations, and a vast amount of coercion, before this became a white country.

It is probable that it is the Jewish community or more accurately, perhaps, its remnants – that in America has paid the highest and most extraordinary price for becoming white. For the Jews came here from countries where they were not white, and they came here, in part, because they were not white; and incontestably in the eyes of the Black American (and not only in those eyes) American Jews have opted to become white, and this is how they operate. It was ironical to hear, for example, former Israeli prime minister Menachem Begin declare some time ago that "the Jewish people bow only to God" while knowing that the state of Israel is sustained by a blank check from Washington. Without further pursuing the implication of this mutual act of faith, one is nevertheless aware that the Black presence, here, can scarcely hope – at least, not yet – to halt the slaughter in South Africa.

And there is a reason for that.

America became white – the people who, as they claim, "settled" the country became white – because of the necessity of denying the Black presence, and justifying the Black subjugation. No community can be based on such a principle – or, in other words, no community can be established on so genocidal a lie. White men – from Norway, for example, where they were *Norwegians* – became white: by slaughtering the cattle, poisoning the wells, torching the houses, massacring Native Americans, raping Black women.

This moral erosion has made it quite impossible for those who think of themselves as white in this country to have any moral authority at all –

288

privately, or publicly. The multitudinous bulk of them sit, stunned, before their TV sets, swallowing garbage that they know to be garbage, and – in a profound and unconscious effort to justify this torpor that disguises a profound and bitter panic – pay a vast amount of attention to athletics: even though they know that the football player (the Son of the Republic, *their* sons!) is merely another aspect of the money-making scheme. They are either relieved or embittered by the presence of the Black boy on the team. I do not know if they remember how long and hard they fought to keep him off it. I know that they do not dare have any notion of the price Black people (mothers and fathers) paid and pay. They do not want to know the meaning, or face the shame, of what they compelled – out of what they took as the necessity of being white – Joe Louis or Jackie Robinson or Cassius Clay (aka Muhammad Ali) to pay I know that they, themselves, would not have liked to pay it.

There has never been a labor movement in this country, the proof being the absence of a Black presence in the so-called father-to-son unions. There are, perhaps, some niggers in the window; but Blacks have no power in the labor unions.

Just so does the white community, as a means of keeping itself white, elect, as they imagine, their political (!) representatives. No nation in the world, including England, is represented by so stunning a pantheon of the relentlessly mediocre. I will not name names – I will leave that to you.

But this cowardice, this necessity of justifying a totally false identity and of justifying what must be called a genocidal history, has placed everyone now living into the hands of the most ignorant and powerful people the world has ever seen: And how did they get that way?

By deciding that they were white. By opting for safety instead of life. By persuading themselves that a Black child's life meant nothing compared with a white child's life. By abandoning their children to the things white men could buy. By informing their children that Black women, Black men and Black children had no human integrity that those who call themselves white were bound to respect. And in this debasement and definition of Black people, they debased and defamed themselves.

And have brought humanity to the edge of oblivion: because they think they are white. Because they think they are white, they do not dare confront the ravage and the lie of their history. Because they think they are white, they cannot allow themselves to be tormented by the suspicion that all men are brothers. Because they think they are white, they are looking for, or bombing into existence, stable populations, cheerful natives and cheap labor. Because they think they are white, they believe, as even no child believes, in the dream of safety. Because they think they are white, however vociferous they may be and however multitudinous, they are as speechless as Lot's wife – looking backward, changed into a pillar of salt.

However – ! White being, absolutely, a moral choice (for there *are* no white people), the crisis of leadership for those of us whose identity has been forged, or branded, as Black is nothing new. We – who were not Black before we got here either, who were defined as Black by the slave trade – have paid for the crisis of leadership in the white community for a very long time, and have resoundingly, even when we face the worst about ourselves, survived, and triumphed over it. If we had not survived and triumphed, there would not be a Black American alive.

And the fact that we are still here – even in suffering, darkness, danger, endlessly defined by those who do not dare define, or even confront, themselves – is the key to the crisis in white leadership. The past informs us of various kinds of people – criminals, adventurers and saints, to say nothing, of course, of popes – but it is the Black condition, and only that, which informs us concerning white people. It is a terrible paradox, but those who believed that they could control and define Black people divested themselves of the power to control and define themselves.

Prologue to *Hidden Figures*
Margot Lee Shetterly

In *Hidden Figures: The American Dream and the Untold Story of the Black Women Mathematicians Who Helped Win the Space Race.* New York: William Morrow (HarperCollins), 2016, pp. xi-xviii

Margot Lee Shetterly (b. 1969) grew up in Hampton, Virginia, attended the University of Virginia, and worked in investment banking and the media industry before deciding to write a book about the black women "computers" (mathematicians) who worked for the National Aeronautics and Space Administration (NASA) – the U.S. government agency in charge of space exploration. Her book was adapted as the 2016 film Hidden Figures. *She continues to collect information about women mathematicians in the space program.*

Why we are reading this: Until recently, most people were unaware that from the 1950s onward NASA employed black women as mathematicians and scientists, as well as many white women and black men, in an age when the fields of science and engineering were disproportionately white and male. But Margot Lee Shetterly knew something about this, since she grew up in an African-American family in a town where most of the black folk she knew, including her father, worked for the space agency. It was only as an adult that she truly came to appreciate what these "hidden figures" had accomplished and decided to learn more about their stories. How many other stories and histories remain unknown, awaiting an intrepid researcher and storyteller to recover them?

"Mrs. Land worked as a computer out at Langley," my father said, taking a right turn out of the parking lot of First Baptist Church in Hampton, Virginia.

My husband and I visited my parents just after Christmas in 2010, enjoying a few days away from our full-time life and work in Mexico. They squired us around town in their twenty-year-old green minivan, my father driving, my mother in the front passenger seat, Aran and I buckled in behind like siblings. My father, gregarious as always, offered a stream of commentary that shifted fluidly from updates on the friends and neighbors we'd bumped into around town to the weather forecast to elaborate discourses on the physics underlying his latest research as a sixty-six-year-old doctoral student at Hampton University. He enjoyed touring my Maine-born-and-raised husband through our neck of the woods and refreshing my connection with local life and history in the process.

During our time home, I spent afternoons with my mother catching matinees at the local cinema, while Aran tagged along with my father and his friends to Norfolk State University football games. We gorged on fried-fish sandwiches at hole-in-the-wall joints near Buckroe Beach, visited the Hampton University Museum's Native American art collection, and haunted local antiques shops.

As a callow eighteen-year-old leaving for college, I'd seen my hometown as a mere launching pad for a life in worldlier locales, a place to be from rather than a place to be. But years and miles away from home could never attenuate the city's hold on my identity, and the more I explored places and people far from Hampton, the more my status as one of its daughters came to mean to me.

That day after church, we spent a long while catching up with the formidable Mrs. Land, who had been one of my favorite Sunday school teachers. Kathaleen Land, a retired NASA mathematician, still lived on her own well into her nineties and never missed a Sunday at church. We said our good-byes to her and clambered into the minivan, off to a family brunch. "A lot of the women around here, black and white, worked as computers;" my father said, glancing at Aran in the rearview mirror but addressing us both. "Kathryn Peddrew, Ophelia Taylor, Sue Wilder;" he said, ticking off a few more names. "And Katherine Johnson, who calculated the launch windows for the first astronauts."

The narrative triggered memories decades old, of spending a much-treasured day off from school at my father's office at the National Aeronautics and Space Administration's Langley Research Center. I rode shotgun in our 1970s Pontiac, my brother, Ben, and sister Lauren in the back as our father drove the twenty minutes from our house, straight over the Virgil I. Grissom Bridge, down Mercury Boulevard, to the road that led to the NASA gate. Daddy flashed his badge, and we sailed through to a campus of perfectly straight parallel streets lined from one end to the other by unremarkable two-story redbrick buildings. Only the giant hypersonic wind tunnel complex – a one-hundred-foot ridged silver sphere presiding over four sixty-foot smooth silver globes – offered visual evidence of the remarkable work occurring on an otherwise ordinary-looking campus.

Building 1236, my father's daily destination, contained a byzantine complex of government-gray cubicles, perfumed with the grown-up smells of coffee and stale cigarette smoke. His engineering colleagues with their rumpled style and distracted manner seemed like exotic birds in a sanctuary. They gave us kids stacks of discarded 11x14 continuous-form computer paper, printed on one side with cryptic arrays of numbers, the blank side a canvas for crayon masterpieces. Women occupied many of the cubicles; they answered phones and sat in front of typewriters, but they also made hieroglyphic marks on transparent slides and conferred with my father and other men in the office on the stacks of documents that littered their desks. That so many of them were African American, many of them my grandmother's age, struck me as simply a part of the natural order of things: growing up in Hampton, the face of science was brown like mine.

My dad joined Langley in 1964 as a coop student and retired in 2004 an internationally respected climate scientist. Five of my father's seven siblings made their bones as engineers or technologists, and some of his best buddies – David Woods, Elijah Kent, Weldon Staton – carved out successful engineering careers at Langley. Our next-door neighbor taught physics at Hampton University. Our church abounded with mathematicians. Supersonics experts held leadership positions in my mother's sorority, and electrical engineers sat on the board of my parents' college alumni associations. My aunt Julia's husband, Charles Foxx, was the son of Ruth Bates Harris, a career civil servant and fierce advocate for the advancement of women and minorities; in 1974, NASA appointed her deputy assistant administrator, the highest-ranking woman at the agency. The community certainly included black English professors, like my mother, as well as black doctors and dentists, black mechanics, janitors, and contractors, black cobblers, wedding planners, real estate agents, and undertakers, several black lawyers, and a handful of black Mary Kay salespeople. As a child, however, I knew so many African Americans working in science, math, and engineering that I thought that's just what black folks did.

My father, growing up during segregation, experienced a different reality. "Become a physical education teacher;" my grandfather said in 1962 to his eighteen-year-old son, who was hell-bent on studying electrical engineering at historically black Norfolk State College.

In those days, college-educated African Americans with book smarts and common sense put their chips on teaching jobs or sought work at the post office. But my father, who built his first rocket in junior high metal shop class following the Sputnik launch in 1957, defied my grandfather and plunged full steam ahead into engineering. Of course, my grandfather's fears that it would be difficult for a black man to break into engineering weren't unfounded. As late as 1970, just 1 percent of all American engineers were black – a number that doubled to a whopping 2 percent by 1984. Still, the federal government was the most reliable employer of African Americans in the sciences and technology: in 1984, 8.4 percent of NASA's engineers were black.

NASA's African American employees learned to navigate their way through the space agency's engineering culture, and their successes in turn afforded their children previously unimaginable access to American society. Growing up with white friends and attending integrated schools, I took much of the groundwork they'd laid for granted.

Every day I watched my father put on a suit and back out of the driveway to make the twenty-minute drive to Building 1236, demanding the best from himself in order to give his best to the space program and to his family. Working at Langley, my father secured my family's place in the comfortable middle class, and Langley became one of the anchors of our social life. Every summer, my siblings and I saved our allowances to buy tickets to ride ponies at the annual NASA carnival. Year after year, I confided my Christmas wish list to the NASA Santa at the Langley children's Christmas party. For years, Ben, Lauren, and my youngest sister, Jocelyn, still a toddler, sat in the bleachers of the Langley Activities Building on Thursday nights, rooting for my dad and his "NBA" (NASA Basketball Association) team, the Stars. I was as much a product of NASA as the Moon landing.

The spark of curiosity soon became an all-consuming fire. I peppered my father with questions about his early days at Langley during the mid-1960s, questions I'd never asked before. The following Sunday I interviewed Mrs. Land about the early days of Langley's computing pool, when part of her job responsibility was knowing which bathroom was marked for "colored" employees. And less than a week later I was sitting on the couch in Katherine Johnson's living room, under a framed American flag that had been to the Moon, listening to a ninety-three-year-old with a memory sharper than mine recall segregated buses, years of teaching and raising a family, and working out the trajectory for John Glenn's spaceflight. I listened to Christine Darden's stories of long years spent as a data analyst, waiting for the chance to prove herself as an engineer.

Even as a professional in an integrated world, I had been the only black woman in enough drawing rooms and boardrooms to have an inkling of the chutzpah it took for an African American woman in a segregated southern workplace to tell her bosses she was sure her calculations would put a man on the Moon. These women's paths set the stage for mine; immersing myself in their stories helped me understand my own.

Even if the tale had begun and ended with the first five black women who went to work at Langley's segregated west side in May 1943 – the women later known as the "West Computers" – I still would have committed myself to recording the facts and circumstances of their lives. Just as islands – isolated places with unique, rich biodiversity – have relevance for the ecosystems everywhere, so does studying seemingly isolated or overlooked people and events from the past turn up unexpected connections and insights to modern life. The idea that black women had been recruited to work as mathematicians at the NASA installation in the South during the days of segregation defies our expectations and challenges much of what we think we know about American history. It's a great story, and that alone makes it worth telling.

In the early stages of researching this book, I shared details of what I had found with experts on the history of the space agency. To a person they encouraged what they viewed as a valuable addition to the body of knowledge, though some questioned the magnitude of the story.

"How many women are we talking about? Five or six?"

I had known more than that number just growing up in Hampton, but even I was surprised at how the numbers kept adding up. These women showed up in photos and phone books, in sources both expected and unusual. A mention of a Langley job in an engagement announcement in the *Norfolk Journal and Guide*. A handful of names from the daughter of one of the first West Computers. A 1951 memo from the Langley personnel officer reporting on the numbers and status of its black employees, which unexpectedly made reference to one black woman who was a "GS-9 Research Scientist." I discovered one 1945 personnel document describing a beehive of mathematical activity in an office in a new building on Langley's west side, staffed by twenty-five black women coaxing numbers out of calculators on a twenty-four-hour schedule, overseen by three black shift supervisors who reported to two white head computers. Even as I write the final words of this book, I'm still doing the numbers. I can put names to almost fifty black women who worked as computers, mathematicians, engineers, or scientists at the Langley Memorial Aeronautical Laboratory from 1943 through 1980, and my intuition is that twenty more names can be shaken loose from the archives with more research.

And while the black women are the most hidden of the mathematicians who worked at the NACA, the National Advisory Committee for Aeronautics, and later at NASA, they were not sitting alone in the shadows: the white women who made up the majority of Langley's computing workforce over the years have hardly been recognized for their contributions to the agency's long-term success. Virginia Biggins worked the Langley beat for the *Daily Press* newspaper, covering the space program starting in 1958. "Everyone said, 'This is a scientist, this is an engineer,' and it was always a man," she said in a 1990 panel on Langley's human computers. She never got to meet any of the women. "I just assumed they were all secretaries," she said. Five white women joined Langley's first computing pool in 1935, and by 1946, four hundred "girls" had already been trained as aeronautical foot soldiers. Historian Beverly Golemba, in a 1994 study, estimated that Langley had employed "several hundred" women as human computers. On the tail end of the research for *Hidden Figures,* I can now see how that number might top one thousand.

To a first-time author with no background as a historian, the stakes involved in writing about a topic that was virtually absent from the history books felt high. I'm sensitive to the cognitive dissonance conjured by the phrase "black female mathematicians at NASA." From the beginning, I knew that I would have to apply the same kind of analytical reasoning to my research that these women applied to theirs. Because as exciting as it was to discover name after name, finding out who they were was just the first step. The real challenge was to document their work. Even more than the surprisingly large numbers of black and white women who had been hiding in a profession seen as universally white and male, the body of work they left behind was a revelation.

There was Dorothy Hoover, working for Robert T. Jones in 1946 and publishing theoretical research on his famed triangle-shaped delta wings in 1951. There was Dorothy Vaughan, working with the white "East Computers" to write a textbook on algebraic methods for the mechanical calculating machines that were their constant companions. There was Mary Jackson, defending her analysis against John Becker, one of the world's top aerodynamicists. There was Katherine Coleman Goble Johnson, describing the orbital trajectory of John Glenn's flight, the math in her trailblazing 1959 report as elegant and precise and grand as a symphony. There was Marge Hannah, the white computer who served as the black women's first boss, coauthoring a report with Sam Katzoff, who became the laboratory's chief scientist. There was Doris Cohen, setting the bar for them all with her first research report – the NACA's first female author – back in 1941.

My investigation became more like an obsession; I would walk any trail if it meant finding a trace of one of the computers at its end. I was determined to prove their existence and their talent in a way that meant they would never again be lost to history. As the photos and memos and equations and family stories became real people, as the women became my companions and returned to youth or returned to life, I started to want something more for them than just putting them on the record. What I wanted was for them to have the grand, sweeping narrative that they

296

deserved, the kind of American history that belongs to the Wright Brothers and the astronauts, to Alexander Hamilton and Martin Luther King Jr. Not told as a separate history, but as a part of the story we all know. Not at the margins, but at the very center, the protagonists of the drama. And not just because they are black, or because they are women, but because they are part of the American epic.

Today, my hometown – the hamlet that in 1962 dubbed itself "Spacetown USA" – looks like any suburban city in a modern and hyperconnected America. People of all races and nationalities mingle on Hampton's beaches and in its bus stations, the WHITES ONLY signs of the past now relegated to the local history museum and the memories of survivors of the civil rights revolution. Mercury Boulevard no longer conjures images of the eponymous mission that shot the first Americans beyond the atmosphere, and each day the memory of Virgil Grissom fades away from the bridge that bears his name. A downsized space program and decades of government cutbacks have hit the region hard; today, an ambitious college grad with a knack for numbers might set her sights on a gig at a Silicon Valley startup or make for one of the many technology firms that are conquering the NASDAQ from the Virginia suburbs outside of Washington, DC.

But before a computer became an inanimate object, and before Mission Control landed in Houston; before Sputnik changed the course of history, and before the NACA became NASA; before the Supreme Court case *Brown v. Board of Education of Topeka* established that separate was in fact not equal, and before the poetry of Martin Luther King Jr.'s "I Have a Dream" speech rang out over the steps of the Lincoln Memorial, Langley's West Computers were helping America dominate aeronautics, space research, and computer technology, carving out a place for themselves as female mathematicians who were also black, black mathematicians who were also female. For a group of bright and ambitious African American women, diligently prepared for a mathematical career and eager for a crack at the big leagues, Hampton, Virginia, must have felt like the center of the universe.